How to Build an Aircraft Carrier

Chris Terrill is an anthropologist and one of the UK's leading adventure documentary makers. In 2007 he participated in and passed the rigorous 32-week training undertaken by Royal Marine Commandos before deploying with them to Afghanistan (*Commando on the Front Line* – ITV). Becoming the first civilian and oldest person to win the coveted green beret, he documented his experience in the film *The 55-Year-Old Commando* (ITV) and book *Commando*. His other previous books, *HMS Brilliant* and *Shipmates*, are also documentary tie-ins about the physical and emotional demands of being a member of the Royal Navy at sea and on active service. In 2015 Terrill became a Fellow of The Maritime Foundation and was presented with a Lifetime Achievement Award. In 2017 he was conferred Doctor of Science by the University of Durham for 'pioneering work in anthropology and film-making' Throughout 2016–2018, he was embedded in the ship's company of HMS *Queen Elizabeth* to make two major documentary series for the BBC (*Britain's Biggest Warship* and *Britain's Biggest Warship Goes to Sea*). In 2021 he deployed with the aircraft carrier once again on her first operational deployment to the South China Seas.

How to Build an Aircraft Carrier

The Incredible Story of the Men and Women Who Brought Britain's Biggest Warship to Life

CHRIS TERRILL

MICHAEL JOSEPH

MICHAEL JOSEPH

UK | USA | Canada | Ireland | Australia
India | New Zealand | South Africa

Michael Joseph is part of the Penguin Random House group of companies
whose addresses can be found at global.penguinrandomhouse.com

First published 2022
001

Copyright © Chris Terrill, 2022

The moral right of the author has been asserted

The names of three minor characters have been changed for security reasons

Insets – Crown Copyright ©: p.1, LB03 under Forth Rail Bridge; p.2 Pod City; p.3, Nelsonian cannon;
German bomb; *Illustrious* beside *QE*; p.5, Squeezing out of the inner harbour; First Aircraft on deck;
Beauty and Beast combined; p.8, Portsmouth; A day to remember; p.9, Procedure Alpha; The first landing;
Gray and Edgell approach *QE*; p.10, Nathan launches; p.12–13, Crest; p.14, New York beckons.
Aircraft Carrier Alliance ©: p.2, Goliath astride the *QE*. Courtesy of Maria Vaughn: p.7, Jak London.
Main text – Royal Navy, care of PA Graphics/Press Association Images: p.446, cutaway diagram

Every effort has been made to contact copyright holders. The publishers will be glad to
correct any errors or omissions in future editions

Set in 13.5/16pt Garamond MT Std
Typeset by Jouve (UK), Milton Keynes
Printed and bound in Great Britain by Clays Ltd, Elcograf S.p.A.

The authorized representative in the EEA is Penguin Random House Ireland,
Morrison Chambers, 32 Nassau Street, Dublin D02 YH68

A CIP catalogue record for this book is available from the British Library

ISBN: 978–0–241–40010–4

www.greenpenguin.co.uk

Penguin Random House is committed to a
sustainable future for our business, our readers
and our planet. This book is made from Forest
Stewardship Council® certified paper.

To Chris and Molly
and in memory of my parents

'When a crew and a captain understand each other to the core, it takes a gale, and more than a gale, to put their ship ashore.'

Rudyard Kipling

'HMS *Queen Elizabeth* is just a metal box full of wires and gadgetry. It is only when you add the flesh, blood and emotion of the men and women who will sail her that she becomes a warship.'

Captain Jerry Kyd, RN

Contents

CONTENTS

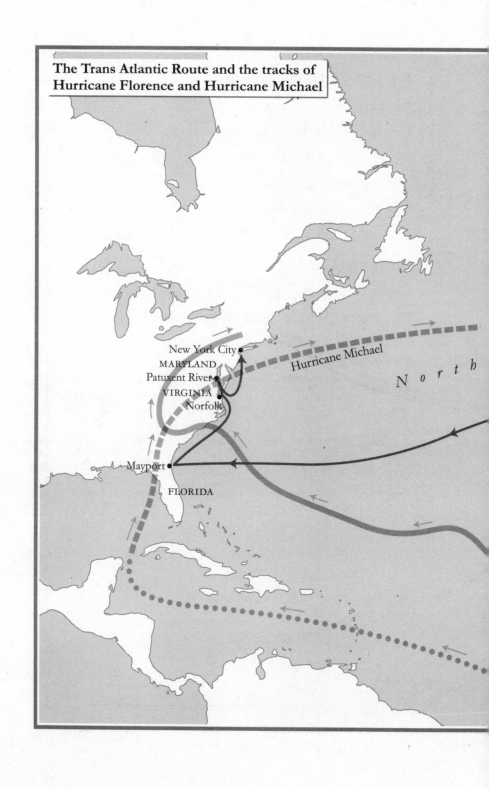

The Trans Atlantic Route and the tracks of
Hurricane Florence and Hurricane Michael

Hurricane Michael

New York City
MARYLAND
Patuxent River
VIRGINIA
Norfolk

Mayport

FLORIDA

North

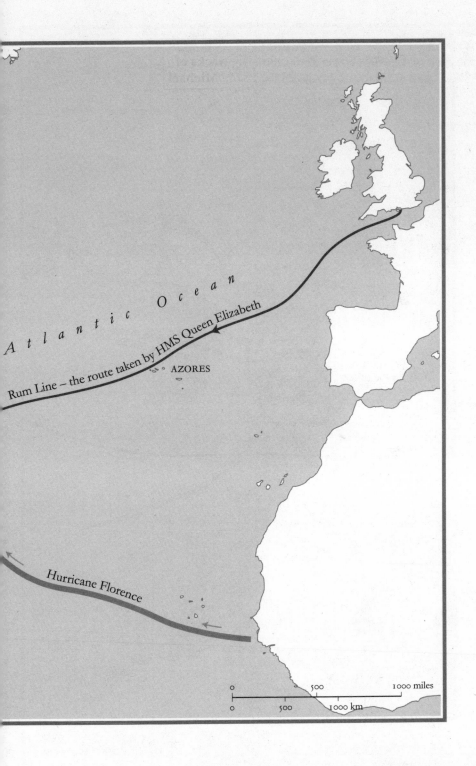

Atlantic Ocean

Rum Line – the route taken by HMS Queen Elizabeth

AZORES

Hurricane Florence

| 0 | | 500 | | 1000 miles |

| 0 | | 500 | 1000 km |

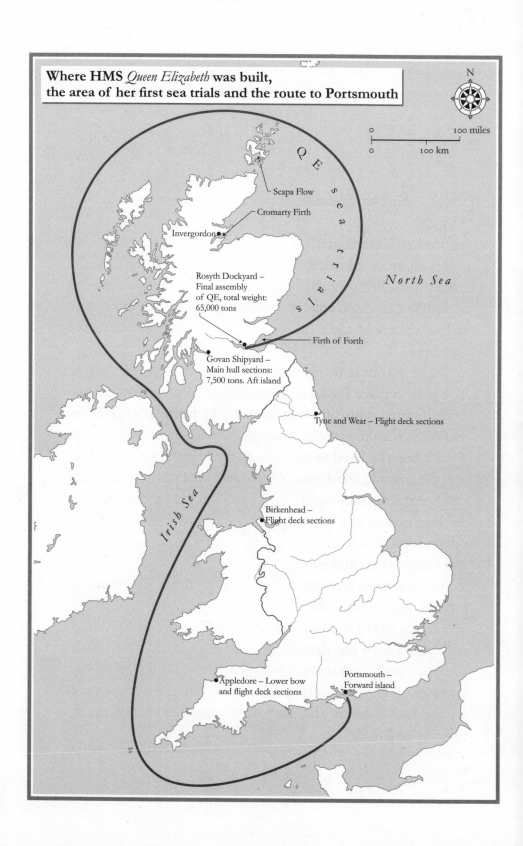

Where HMS *Queen Elizabeth* was built, the area of her first sea trials and the route to Portsmouth

N

100 miles

100 km

Q E s e a t r i a l s

Scapa Flow

Cromarty Firth

Invergordon

North Sea

Rosyth Dockyard –
Final assembly
of QE, total weight:
65,000 tons

Firth of Forth

Govan Shipyard –
Main hull sections:
7,500 tons. Aft island

Tyne and Wear – Flight deck sections

Irish Sea

Birkenhead –
Flight deck sections

Appledore – Lower bow
and flight deck sections

Portsmouth –
Forward island

Prologue

Kajaki, Helmand Province, 1 January 2007

'Incoming! Take cover!'

An ominous whistle overlaid the automatic gunfire, and a rocket-propelled grenade exploded fifty feet away, showering us with hot sand and engulfing us with acrid smoke. I crouched as low as I could while the marines to my left and right fixed bayonets.

There was next to no cover for us on that rocky hillside. The perfect place for an ambush. It was New Year's Day, and I was filming with fifty members of M Company, 42 Commando, in Kajaki, a precipitous region of southern Afghanistan. They'd been ordered to advance to the high ground and flush out the enemy. We'd started under cover of darkness and climbed through the night but were silhouetted at dawn against the brightening sky. That was when over a hundred militants opened up – first with a barrage from semi-automatic AK-47s, and then rockets and mortars.

Incoming fire was intermittent but accurate. The marines' job was to neutralize the enemy. My job was to film the front-line action for ITV and report on it for the *Telegraph*. I'd been embedded with the Royal Navy's elite shock troops for the last year, both in training and in combat, to understand the mindset of Britain's only specialist commando force – crack amphibious soldiers able to switch from sea to land operations as required.

'Withdraw!' yelled the young officer in command. 'Move towards the wadi at the bottom of the slope. Go!'

Ten marines, crouching low, risked their lives to return fire and cover us as we made a run for it. One by one we made the dash to safety across 100 yards of rough ground, well within the range of enemy firepower.

Now it was my turn.

'Chris – run, run, run!' shouted the marine behind me. 'And don't look back.'

I didn't need much encouragement. I sprinted down the slope as fast as I could, doing my best to film whilst maintaining a hunched, defensive upper-body position in the full expectation that hot lead was about to rip into my back.

The friable desert surface gave way underfoot, but I somehow made it to the dry river bed, in the middle of which a gaping bomb crater offered a modicum of cover. I dived into it, pushing my body as deep as it would go into the scorched sand.

I was not alone. Two other marines, Tom and Rich, were firing back at the enemy muzzle flashes from the rocky horizon. We were relatively safe here, but well and truly pinned down. We could hear the Commanding Officer through our headsets, from further along the wadi, calling in mortar cover from HQ and air support from the main British bases at Camp Bastion and Kandahar.

'Keep your fuckin' head down, Chris.' Tom placed his right boot helpfully on my helmet and pushed my face unceremoniously into the ground.

'Cheers, Tom!' I replied through a mouthful of sand and grit.

'No worries, shipmate!' He grinned as he continued to blast away with his SA 80 assault rifle.

Even when caught in a deadly firefight in the middle of a

landlocked wilderness, I had the Royal Navy all around me. The marines are trained primarily to fight on or via the sea, but are specialists in Arctic, desert and jungle warfare. The aerial back-up we were waiting for, if not an Army Apache gunship, was likely to be a Sea King helicopter to evacuate us, or a Fleet Air Arm Harrier jet fighter to lay waste to the enemy.

Enemy rounds continued to zip over our heads. They made a sinister buzzing noise as they came closer. For obvious reasons, my companions nicknamed such near misses 'lead wasps' or 'Afghan bees', and swarms of the damn things kept descending on our position.

Staying low, we reached into our back-sacks for combat rations – beef biltong, nuts and a block of edible granite optimistically labelled 'chocolate'. Tom crawled back up to the rim of the crater to keep watch while Rich and I settled back and waited.

'Look on the bright side,' Tom said. 'At least we're not on a fuckin' warship. You can't get off those things when people start shooting at you. Nowhere to hide, no convenient bomb craters. Bleedin' death traps. If you're not blown up or burned to a flamin' frazzle, you drown.'

He scanned the horizon with his telescopic sight and then slid down to rejoin us. 'That new super aircraft carrier they're planning? Waste of money, if you ask me.'

'Bog off, Tom!' Rich snapped back. 'She'll be hoofing, Chris. The size of a small country. Gonna be an absolute world-beater.'

Tom sniffed and shook his head. 'You won't catch me on that mother. Biggest bleeding target of 'em all –'

The scream of a low-flying Harrier GR7 cut him short. The pilot's voice crackled through our secure comms headsets as it swept over our heads. *'Recoil checking in.'*

The callsign confirmed he was from the supporting Fleet Air Arm (FAA) squadron. Our FAC (forward air controller), Marty Stapleton, still up on the high ground, responded immediately: '*Recoil, TIC* [troops in contact], *danger close, request rockets and immediate attack, my initials MS, marking position with smoke.*'

Any hope of the FAA pilot de-escalating the fight by flying fast and low over the enemy position hadn't worked. The lead wasps were buzzing around us with renewed ferocity.

'*MS copied, my initials NG,*' came the response from the circling jet. By exchanging initials, both ground and air callsigns acknowledged that the imminent threat to our lives necessitated an immediate attack, despite our close proximity to enemy forces running the risk of casualties from friendly fire.

'*OK Royal,*' NG said. '*Get your head down and take cover. Tally target, visual friendlies, in hot, rockets.*'

'*Cleared hot,*' the FAC confirmed.

Within seconds a series of well-aimed CRV7 rockets rippled from the aircraft towards the encroaching enemy, who instantly fell silent. From the high ground the FAC transmitted: '*Recoil stand by for BDA* [battle damage assessment], *smoke obscuring target.*'

The words we all wanted to hear came moments later. '*Recoil, that's a Delta Hotel* [direct hit], *friendlies safe, stand by for retasking, new TIC, Sangin. You're cleared to switch, Nath. Thanks, mate.*' The FAC had recognized the pilot, Nathan Gray. I was told later that he had his own coveted green beret, so was considered one of the brotherhood.

'*Copied. At your service, mate,*' Gray responded. '*Shout if you need me again, switching.*' He dipped his wings in salute and headed into the Helmand valley.

I was destined to meet the faceless aviator with a crackly

voice who'd saved our bacon some years later, under very different, though no less challenging, circumstances – on the flight deck of HMS *Queen Elizabeth*. And those chance remarks by two marines under fire in an Afghan bomb crater not only alerted me to the prospect of the first British super-carrier but gave me a hint of the passion and controversy that would surround her.

Untouchable game-changer or floating bull's eye?

Two and a half years later, I would embark on an epic journey in search of answers to that question – one that would afford me a deep and very personal insight into the role of maritime aviation in the twenty-first century. Which is why our story really begins over one hundred years ago, towards the end of the First World War.

On the morning of 2 August 1917, over the chill waters of Scapa Flow in the Orkneys, twenty-five-year-old Squadron Commander Edwin Dunning of the Royal Naval Air Service was poised to change the course of modern warfare. Climbing into the open cockpit of his single-seater Sopwith Pup, he was bidding to become the first man to land an aircraft on a moving vessel – the gigantic battlecruiser HMS *Furious*.

The central positioning of funnels, bridge and general superstructure left no room for any sort of strip, so aircraft had to be launched by catapult, and, if land was out of range, ditch in the sea before being winched back on board – hazardous in the extreme, especially during conflict – or abandoned. The Americans had already succeeded in land-ing an aircraft on a stationary vessel, but the big prize would go to whoever managed to land one on a moving vessel.

A huge amount rested, therefore, on Dunning's shoulders. According to modern flight test protocols, his objective would be considered so far outside the safety envelope as to be suicidal. But those were different times, and what the pilots lacked in technical sophistication they made up for with sheer audacity.

Dunning's plan was to fly his biplane alongside HMS *Furious*, underway and heading into wind, until he came abreast of the bridge, and then, matching her speed, sideslip over an improvised flight deck specially constructed for the occasion. The manoeuvre required the most delicate touch on the controls as well as supreme hand-eye coordination and spatial awareness if the down-wing was not to hit the superstructure before the plane levelled for landing. Even now, it's hard enough to achieve on land without a crosswind, but perilous in the extreme on a swell, buffeted by the unpredictable gusts that can swirl around a vessel in motion.

Descending from height and rolling out of his final turn, Dunning would have been struck by how diminutive HMS *Furious* appeared from his cockpit and how small the makeshift runway on top of her now seemed. As he got closer to the ship he would have selected precisely the right percentage of flap to reduce his approach speed to around 35 knots, allowing him to draw level with the platform, nose down to see as clearly as possible in front of him.

What followed was the finest balancing act: to control his line-up whilst adjusting the angle of his glide path and regulating his air speed with the throttle. Wings level and the aircraft trimmed, he had to make sure his rate of descent was neither too fast nor too slow, then sideslip and stall just before his wheels hit the deck.

Stalling speed, by definition, is the point at which airflow over the wings breaks free and no longer provides enough lift to maintain flight. A stalled aircraft at height will simply fall out of the sky; even regulated and close to the ground, it is still fraught with danger. Dunning's margin of error would have been virtually nil. He knew that the slightest gust, with no cushion of altitude and no time to recover, could prove catastrophic. The only help at hand was the sailors ready to grab the plane out of the air.

No matter how talented and courageous the pilots in Dunning's day, their simple handmade machines were no match for nature if she decided to turn nasty. And at sea, nature is nearly always nasty. But against all the odds, his first landing went almost completely to plan.

He may have known that he'd won a race against the Americans, but he couldn't have appreciated the immensity of his contribution to the future of maritime warfare.

After a second successful landing the day after, he insisted on making one more. Only then would he be prepared to let others try. It was a measure of the man that he always put his comrades' safety before his own.

On Tuesday, 7 August 1917, flying as always into the wind, he approached HMS *Furious* for the third time. Once again, his glide path was perfect, his speed spot on. Then, caught at the last moment by a sudden crosswind, Dunning tried to open the throttle, to overshoot and reposition for another attempt. But the Sopwith's engine spluttered and died. It fell on to the make-do flight deck and burst its starboard tyre, causing it to slew to the right. A courageous attempt by those on deck to grab the Pup's wheel axle before impact also failed; his would-be rescuers could not prevent the young squadron commander from plunging into the sea.

On impact with the water, Dunning hit his head on the instrument panel and was knocked unconscious. Still strapped in his seat, he drowned before anyone could reach him.

1. Some Assembly Required

Govan, Scotland

It is 9 o'clock on the morning of 7 July 2009. In less than an hour, the very first cut will be made in the steel for the biggest warship ever to be built in Great Britain. Glasgow's Govan shipyard is a hive of activity. There's a lot to do – not least the laying of a long red carpet in one of their main heavy construction sheds.

Govan used to be at the centre of Clyde shipbuilding but steadily declined during the 1930s to become an overspill for the Gorbals slums and then a byword for poverty and destitution. Even now, the main street, running parallel to the dockyard, is lined with empty stores and failed businesses, leaving only off-licences, pawnbrokers and betting shops. But all that could be about to change.

BAE Systems has secured a massive new order for substantial sections of two new supercarriers at its Surface Ship Operations. HMS *Queen Elizabeth* and HMS *Prince of Wales* will create thousands of jobs over many years for Govan. It could be a fairytale turnaround.

And all the best fairytales start with a princess.

At 9.20, police motorbike outriders with blue lights flashing lead a retinue of vehicles through the main dockyard gates. At the rear is a highly polished black Daimler with a small

9

multi-coloured flag attached to its bonnet. The Royal Crest ripples in the strong breeze from the Firth. The limousine stops in front of the vast British Aerospace fabricating plant. A young rating steps forward, opens the rear door and snaps a smart salute. Her Royal Highness Princess Anne, the Princess Royal, is ushered inside by her equerry and bodyguards, followed by an entourage of high-ranking naval officers, grey-suited industrialists and Scottish political notables.

The red carpet now stretches from the huge sliding doors at the north end of the cavernous space to a raised dais at its southern end. On either side, variously attired in blue, orange or white overalls, is a small army of marine engineers, steelworkers, block-makers, welders, fabricators, scaffolders, electricians, riggers, plumbers, rope-makers and carpenters.

They cheer as the royal entourage walks past.

Accompanied by her husband, Vice Admiral Tim Laurence in full dress uniform, the princess is herself bedecked in the livery of a rear admiral, her honorary rank. Smiling brightly, she pauses to chat with anyone who catches her eye.

'And what do you do?' she asks a tall, nervous-looking man in freshly ironed orange overalls.

He hesitates for a second, struggling to recall what it said on the main board about addressing the princess, and takes the belt-and-braces option. 'Your Royal Highness ... er, ma'am. I'm a welder ...'

'Looking forward to building this ship?'

'Aye, ma'am.' He hits his stride. 'It's going to be a grand job. And great for Govan. Great for Scotland.'

The princess moves on to a young woman in bright white overalls and gleaming hard hat.

'And what's your job?'

'I'm an apprentice engineer, ma'am.'

'How old are you?'

'Eighteen, ma'am.'

'So how old will you be when the ship is finished?'

'Um, twenty-six.'

'Do you think you'll still be here then?'

'I don't know, ma'am. Hope so.'

The Princess Royal proceeds to the dais, where she's greeted by Admiral Sir Jonathon Band, the redoubtable First Sea Lord. Coming to the end of his term in office, he's been a long-time champion of the QE class of carrier, despite escalating costs and delays to the start of construction, and sees today as a big tick in the box. 'This ship represents the future of the Royal Navy,' he told the press posse earlier. 'We're not punching above our weight – the simple truth is that if Britain wants to remain a major power these ships are essential.'

Typically forthright in response to probing questions about delivery schedule and budget, he was adamant that the nation would be getting a big bang for its buck.

'At 65,000 tons, HMS *Queen Elizabeth* and HMS *Prince of Wales* will not only be the biggest warships ever built for the Royal Navy but also the most powerful and advanced in terms of military technology and stealth capabilities – especially when married to the F-35B Lightning stealth fighter.'

Military hardware is an emotive subject, especially in the context of huge capital expenditure that might otherwise be spent on housing, welfare or the NHS. But the eventual bill of £6 billion for the two vessels, though nearly double the original estimate, is still modest compared to the eye-watering $15 billion price tag (not including the nuclear power plant) of USS *George H. W. Bush*, an American supercarrier of similar proportions.

'It's a long, long road ahead,' Band warned. 'And I wouldn't be surprised if there were some twists and turns before we know if the in-service dates and costs can be met. But we aim to meet targets and deliver on time.'

The First Sea Lord introduces the Princess Royal to Scott Ballingall, a young engineer, who leads her to a plasma laser steel-cutting machine. Together they mount the platform that allows them to look down on a large grey steel plate, about 30 feet square, submerged in a shallow pool of water no more than 4 inches deep.

'Why is the steel underwater?' she asks.

Scott is ready for this question. He practised likely answers last night with his mum. 'It reduces heat and smoke, ma'am. Makes the cutting time a bit longer, but it's much safer and better for the environment.'

The princess nods, and Scott delivers his pièce de résistance. 'The laser heats up to 50,000 degrees, which is about ten times the surface temperature of the sun.'

'Wow!' the Princess Royal mouths, genuinely impressed.

'Press the green button, ma'am, when you're ready . . .'

A royal finger depresses the starter button. The water glows red, and starts to bubble and then steam as the laser nozzle swings into action. The dignitaries applaud, and the workers cheer all the louder.

The First Sea Lord rises to his feet and, moving to a lectern draped with a White Ensign, addresses the crowd in a deep, resonant voice. 'Your Royal Highness, my lords, ladies and gentlemen. The Queen Elizabeth Class of aircraft carrier, comprising HMS *Queen Elizabeth* with HMS *Prince of Wales* to follow, will provide Britain with the means to deliver air power from the sea, wherever and whenever required, and in a stronger and more decisive form than ever before. In addition, they'll be able to undertake a wide range of tasks including support to peacekeeping operations and delivery of humanitarian aid in time of crisis. They'll undoubtedly prove a tremendous asset both to the Royal Navy and to the UK as a whole . . .'

He pauses to allow a spontaneous burst of applause to run its course.

'Once built, the QE Class carriers will be the centrepiece of Britain's military capability for many years to come.'

The event is concluded with a short, glossily produced CGI film showing the *Queen Elizabeth* sailing majestically on the high seas. Virtual F-35 jets take off from her flight deck as Chinook and Merlin helicopters circle overhead. Alongside is her sister ship. It's a PlayStation vision of the future, though how far into the future no one can guess. The completion date remains a moveable feast. The sailing dates for sea trials are very approximate, and VAD (Vessel Acceptance Day), when the shipbuilders hand her over to be formally commissioned, is too far off to be given even a provisional date.

Early on in the tendering process, British Aerospace and Thales, the French engineering giant, were both invited to come up with a blueprint for the carriers to become operational early in the twenty-first century. They joined forces as the Aircraft Carrier Alliance (ACA) with Babcock, the British shipbuilders, and the MoD.

The sales pitch for the supercarriers came with a staggering array of commendations. They would be so highly automated that they'd require only 'lean-manned' crews – less than 1,000 per vessel, not counting aircrew, or about one-fifth of an American crew on a similar-sized vessel. They would each have a flight deck the size of three and a half football fields, nine decks, 3,300 compartments and

3 miles of passageways. Crew members would be given GPS and special apps on their phones to find their way around.

Each of their propellers would weigh 33 tons, and together exert the same thrust as fifty high-speed trains. This gives the ship a maximum speed of over 27 knots (31 mph).* Her six engines (two mighty gas turbines and four diesels) would produce enough energy to power a city the size of Swindon, and her electrical cabling and wiring would stretch six times round the world. Each ship would weigh the same as 35,000 family cars and carry enough fuel to take those cars to the moon and back a dozen times. The paint needed for the interior and exterior would be enough to cover Hyde Park . . . From today until the warship's completion every British county will contribute something to her construction, whether it be steel-making, heavy engineering, radar communication equipment, gas turbine and diesel engines, soft furnishing, bedding, cutlery, crockery or hand-engraved crystal port decanters. The *Queen Elizabeth* will not only be a weapons platform leviathan but a home-from-home for her future ship's companies.

Govan, Portsmouth, Devon, Tyne and Wear, Birkenhead and Rosyth will manufacture her components, partly because she's too massive to build in a single location, and partly to spread the benefit of her employment opportunities. As each section is completed, it will be towed by barge to Rosyth for assembly.†

---

* The massive propulsion from her propellers is reflected in her fuel economy – approximately 80 metres per gallon.

† Rosyth shipyard was chosen for the final assembly of the QE not only because it boasts the biggest dry dock in the UK but also because her eventual testing grounds will be large stretches of the North Sea immediately to the east. At that critical time it might be important, if things go wrong, for the prototype ship to be within easy reach of a dry dock that could take her.

It's estimated that between now and the moment she departs for her first sea trials – scheduled for 2017 – some 15,000 shipbuilders will have worked in excess of 51 million hours to deliver the ship to the nation. Much will change in their lives during that time. Some will stay with the project throughout, some will move on, get promoted or switch jobs and careers. The nation's fortunes will rise and fall; parliamentary elections, Eurovision Song Contests and FA Cups will be lost and won, the economy will ebb and flow, and celebrities will come and go, but even the vagaries of defence policy are unlikely to prevent the supercarrier from assuming her predetermined shape, whatever else may change around her. But for now, the proto-warship exists only as a single sheet of submerged steel bearing a solitary cut – the mark of a princess seared by the white heat of ten suns.

'Delivering the Nation's Flagships' – the Aircraft Carrier Alliance's strapline – is a painstaking process. It takes two years for Lower Block 03, a 7,500-ton hull section built in Govan, to be completed. Over 65 feet high, 200 feet long and 130 feet wide, it's heavier than a destroyer, yet less than 20 per cent of what is currently known as Ship 1.

On Sunday, 31 July 2011, LB03 is loaded on to one of the two largest semi-submergible barges in the world for a 600-mile journey round the north of Scotland. It takes days to ensure that its centre of gravity is just right for sailing. Finally, fully secured, it sets off, pulled by two tugboats, on Tuesday, 16 August – an astounding sight for those who line the Clyde for its send-off.

To mark the occasion, more than fifty cyclists – comprising many of the workers who helped construct the block – leave Govan yard on a gruelling 500-mile ride through Glencoe and the Great Glen in an attempt to 'beat the block' to its destination.

Six days later, on the evening of Monday, 22 August, LB03 arrives in the Firth of Forth. The next time it goes under the iconic Forth Rail Bridge it will be heading out to sea. But that will not be for at least another five years. The cyclists cross the line in Rosyth dockyard, pipping LB03 by a matter of minutes.

The Govan workforce turns its attention to the 11,300-ton Lower Block 04. Designed to house two main engine rooms, the medical centre and much of the accommodation, it's the largest and by far the most complicated component, but it takes the most circuitous route to its destination. Bad weather forces it south, around Land's End, along the English Channel, up the east coast of England and into the North Sea – an epic 1,200-mile journey.

In the century since Rosyth's establishment in the First World War for the repair of massive Dreadnought battleships (including the first HMS *Queen Elizabeth*, which was suffering a defective turbine), not one vessel has been built in its cavernous dry docks. But over the following three years, Ship 1 arrives here, bit by gigantic bit. The lower bow section from Appledore in Devon. The flight deck sections from Appledore, Tyne and Wear and Birkenhead. The for'ard island from Portsmouth and the aft island from Govan.

By the beginning of 2013, these massive blocks have travelled a combined distance of at least 4,000 miles, to be lifted into position by the biggest and most powerful crane in the world. Brought over from Shanghai, and capable of lifting 1,000 tons at a time, 'Goliath' will remain here until both carriers have been completed.

Ship 1's build has been plagued by overruns and delays and the near doubling in costs which has earned the ACA a 'red' warning from the Major Projects Authority, but she is almost fully assembled in dry dock by the end of that year.

She now comprises 40,000 tons of basic steel, 17 million individual parts, 3.4 million yards of cable, 362,000 miles of pipes and, thus far, 550,000 gallons of grey paint. The two islands give her a unique silhouette. The for'ard island houses the bridge for navigation and the captain's quarters, the aft is the flying control tower (Flyco) from where all flying operations will be directed. Huge floor-to-ceiling windows provide a 290-degree view of the flight deck and the immense 'ski-jump' at her bow which will help her fighter jets leap towards the skies.

In March 2014, Admiral Zambellas, the current First Sea Lord, makes a very significant phone call. He invites Commodore Jerry Kyd, Commander Amphibious Task Group, to be the first seagoing captain of HMS *Queen Elizabeth*, taking command in 2016. Kyd is shocked, but honoured. After talking to his wife Karen, he gratefully accepts, even though it will technically entail taking a temporary demotion.

On 4 July, thousands assemble for more royal pomp and pageantry to witness the official naming of Ship 1 by Her Majesty Queen Elizabeth II. She remains in dry dock, but to mark the occasion the Navy has positioned its current largest warship, HMS *Illustrious*, in the adjacent (flooded) dock. 'Lusty', as she is affectionately known, barely a third of the size of her successor, is due to be decommissioned three weeks from now, so this is her last official engagement. By chance she was also Jerry Kyd's previous command and still holds a very special place in his heart.

Kyd watches Her Majesty, with Prince Philip at her side, address the crowd and the TV cameras. 'HMS *Queen Elizabeth*', she says, 'marks a new phase in our naval history; an exciting new era. In sponsoring this new aircraft carrier, I believe the *Queen Elizabeth* will be a source of inspiration and pride for us all.' She concludes, 'May God bless her, and all who sail in her', and in recognition of the ship's Scottish provenance she triggers the smashing of a bottle of Islay whisky on her hull. It's more than fifteen years since the Queen has performed this ceremony.*

The first HMS *Queen Elizabeth*, a state-of-the-art, heavily armed and highly powered Dreadnought Class battleship, was launched at Portsmouth in October 1913. She became flagship for the ill-fated Dardanelles campaign, and later of the Atlantic Fleet, seeing active service in both world wars. Her successor will take on her name, motto (*Semper Eadem – Ever the Same*), her battle honours, her insignia, the Tudor Rose and her ship's bell,† all of which bestow a ready-made reputation and a sense of continuity and survival – psychologically and emotionally important for sailors in the face of both the enemy and the elements.

Thirteen days later, on the morning of 17 July, the dry dock is flooded, and HMS *Queen Elizabeth* is floated into the adjacent 'build basin' and secured to the eastern sea wall.

---

* The common assumption is that this is because the ship is named after the Queen herself, but that is very definitely not the case. Ship's names are passed on through the generations, so because the first HMS *Queen Elizabeth* was built in 1913, well before the present queen was born let alone crowned, it follows that the ship's namesake is Queen Elizabeth I. Some names adopted by the Royal Navy for its warships are long-standing favourites. There have been, for example, five incarnations of *Ark Royal*, twelve of *Repulse*, fourteen of *London* and thirty-nine of *Swallow*. There have been only two HMS *Queen Elizabeth*s (1913 and 2017), but there have been a further eight warships named HMS *Elizabeth* between 1647 and 1807 (all named after Elizabeth I).
† The QE's ship's bell (used ornamentally) is from the original HMS *Queen Elizabeth* – the Super-Dreadnought battleship built in 1913.

The 'QE', as she is now referred to up here, will be a work in progress for some time to come. Her unusual, angular shape has dramatically transformed the Rosyth skyline, but she does not yet look her best. There's still a great deal to do in the build basin, both externally and internally. Her superstructure requires painting and repainting with every refinement, so she's decorated in at least fifty shades of battleship grey. The rusty red of her unsurfaced flight deck gives her an aged appearance, and her external profile is also camouflaged by the growing mass of scaffolding that now enshrouds her bow, stern and two island sections.

Even if she had propellers, which she won't for at least nine months, the budding warship couldn't move even an inch. She's tethered to the quayside by a hundred ropes and umbilically connected by countless electrical cables, service lines and water pipes, confined to the dockyard's inner basin and separated from the open sea by four substantial walls.

There's still an unimaginable amount of work to be done, but the men and women of the Royal Navy who will breathe life into her are on their way.

2. Sailors Not Included

Rosyth, Scotland, 16 January 2016

The 0630 from Edinburgh to Rosyth is crossing the Forth Rail Bridge.

'Blimey, it's really chucking it down now . . .'

Lieutenant Commander Bob Hawkins peers through the rain-spattered window. Arriving to take up his new job, he's desperate to catch his first glimpse of the massive ship he's heard so much about.

He cups his hands around his eyes and presses them against the glass. The ghostly outline of what he thinks must be the QE comes and goes until he's not sure whether he's actually seeing it or dreaming it.

'They told me I'd get a great view from here,' he complains. 'This is bollocks.'

The driving rain lashes angrily at the train window, and HMS *Queen Elizabeth* remains concealed by the penumbral Scottish gloom.

'Dinna worry, sir. I promise you she's there!'

Hawkins has struck up a conversation with the passenger sitting opposite. Dougie, a young welder from Glasgow, is returning to work after three weeks' paternity leave.

'I'll take your word for it.' He settles back into his seat. 'Boy or girl, Dougie?'

'Wee lassie. That's one of each now.'

The naval officer smiles the smile of a kindred spirit. He

has two kids of his own. Jamie and Cameron are grown up now but were born in Scotland. Their mum was a Scot. And at the age of fifty-four, Hawkins feels like he's coming home. He began his career in the Royal Naval Dockyard, Rosyth, back in 1982.

As First Lieutenant of HMS *Queen Elizabeth*, he'll be one of the most senior officers on board, and part of the command structure responsible for getting her to sea for the first time. In charge of the executive function of the ship, Hawkins will oversee everything from welfare, discipline and morale to the intricacies of rubbish disposal and shore leave. In leadership terms, he'll be seventh in line to the throne, should those above him succumb to illness, injury or death in combat.

As the train draws in, he ponders how far he's travelled in the last forty-eight hours. Until the day before yesterday he'd been in Malaysia as Lead Navy Planner. For most of his two-year posting to Penang he had no idea what his next job would be, or even if there would be one; then, two months ago, his Navy Appointer suggested the QE job. Hawkins didn't need asking twice. *Bugger retirement*, he thought. Although he'd always been a small-ship sailor, serving on frigates, destroyers and minehunters, this was too exciting a prospect to pass up.

Bob Hawkins loves the Royal Navy and is a fine officer. He knows further promotion is unlikely at his age and secretly regrets he never made full commander. He's landed himself in hot water on more than one occasion by being more forthright than he should have been. His friends, of which he has a huge number inside and outside the Navy, hope he's learned his lesson but fear that Robert Henry Hawkins, or 'Bob the Dog' as he's affectionately known to all, remains his own worst enemy.

The train comes to a halt. Hawkins says farewell to Dougie and strides up the puddled platform to the taxi rank.

Twenty minutes later, he arrives at the main gate of HMS *Caledonia*, a shore base directly overlooking Rosyth dockyard. 'Cally' will be home to all the officers until the ship's company is allowed to move on board – which won't be for a year at the very least. In the intervening period it's vital to build the crew to its full strength, and acquaint them with their new ship, even during construction. The newly arriving sailors, although initially shore-based, will be given intermittent access to the QE to allow the engineers, warfare specialists, seamen, aviators, stewards and navigators the opportunity to familiarize themselves with the novel characteristics of the supercarrier well before they have to take her to sea.

Hawkins reports to the guardroom to pick up his newly laminated security pass and heads for his quarters in the main block. On the way he bumps into Steve Prest, a young commander who's been appointed Head of Weapons Engineering on the QE, and ten minutes later the two officers are peering through a metal slatted fence into the dockyard's inner basin. For the first time, Hawkins is able to separate the supercarrier from the murk that surrounds it.

'She's bloody *massive!*'

'Imagine coming up against that on the high seas,' Prest says.

'Damn right!' Hawkins laughs. 'Glad she's one of ours . . .'

The only discernible movement on board is the shifting of seagulls on the scaffolding bars that still surround and obscure the forward and aft islands and radar positions. Suddenly, a shock of electric-blue light floods the flight deck. The stark radiance of the high-powered working lamps is diffused by the mizzle, creating a ghostly aura. Seconds later, the silence is shattered by the blast of a klaxon.

The seagulls scream in reply, launching themselves in untidy waves to circle the inner basin. Prest shouts over the din, 'And so starts the working day!'

Hawkins watches entranced as a line of construction workers streams through the main gate below them. He wonders if Dougie the welder is among them. Hundreds of engineers, craftsmen and steelworkers make their way to the inner basin to start another twelve-hour shift of riveting, painting, grinding, welding and fitting on what looks more like a building site than a front-line aircraft carrier.

So far, about 100 sailors have arrived in Rosyth. Another 600 will report for duty within the next two months, to be billeted in temporary accommodation pods, mostly in the grounds of HMS *Caledonia*. The 200 prefabricated two-man living units, arranged in several neat rows, is already dubbed 'Pod City'.

New batches of sailors, arriving almost every day now, are immediately given an introductory tour of the ship. Today a group of 'baby sailors' straight from training is being shepherded around by Baz Barrett, a jovial thirty-eight-year-old petty officer (PO) AWT (Above Water Tactical – a radar specialist). Their van is waved through the main gate of the dockyard by the security guards. Barrett has become well practised at these guided tours, and likes to lighten the mood.

'On your port-hand side is the main dry dock,' he says. 'Anybody know what that big thing is sticking out of it?'

'Yes, PO,' a young female rating says. 'HMS *Prince of Wales*.'

'Well done, that sailor,' Barrett beams. 'HMS *Prince of Wales* is about eighteen months behind the QE and will be floated as soon as the QE has vacated the basin. That's when you lot will be taking her to sea for the first time – if the big plan comes together.'

'When do you think that'll be, PO?' asks a bespectacled sailor from the back of the van.

'Ah now, there's the 64,000-dollar question,' Barrett says. 'Later on, I'll get out my special general-issue crystal ball and consult it for you!'

Decanted from the van, the fresh-faced young mariners don their high-visibility waistcoats, hard hats and protective glasses and follow Barrett towards the imposing grey hulk.

'You have a treat today, team,' he says. 'Look on top of the for'ard island and you'll see the main radar burning and turning. They're just testing now, but that thing'll be able to see well over the horizon when we go to sea and tell us where everybody is – friend or foe. It'll have the ability to track up to 1,000 aerial targets up to 250 nautical miles away. Useful bit of kit, that. Right, safety goggles on, team. Follow me.'

He leads the nervous-looking newcomers up the access tower to the main hangar. It's a long climb, 267 steps, and, eager to impress, they try not to look too puffed-out at the top, but without total success.

'You all look bollocksed!' Barrett yells over the racket of automatic drills, angle grinders and welding torches. 'OK, ladies and gentlemen, rest up and listen up. This is an active building site. Trip hazards everywhere, so watch your step and don't wander off. If we lose you on a ship this size, we might never find you again. I don't wanna have to tell your folks we've misplaced you on day one. They may not take that too well, and I know I won't – too much blinking paperwork – so stay close.'

Kirsty Rugg, a twenty-four-year-old steward from Burton-on-Trent, is awed by the sheer scale of the vessel. 'Blooming gi-normous. I can't believe they're still building inside!' A former hotel manager, now in the Logistics branch, she's been earmarked as one of the captain's stewards when he arrives in a few months. Rugg's in search of fresh horizons and knows that Rosyth is the first step towards them, but she's already missing her sailor boyfriend Stephen, currently at sea on the frigate HMS *Dragon*.

Baz Barrett gestures to the cavernous hangar that stretches in front of them. 'This is big enough to house 400 double-decker buses,' he bellows. 'Or, to put it another way, it's the same volume as four Olympic-sized swimming pools. Or, more to the point, ladies and gentlemen, it could house up to twenty-two F-35 Lightning stealth fighters. Right, follow me, team . . .'

Bob Hawkins unpacks and carefully hangs up his array of working and ceremonial uniforms. He places a solid gold half-hunter in one of the desk drawers, which he carefully locks. The timepiece, an 1898 Reynoldson, was given to him by his father on his eighteenth birthday. Two months later, in September 1973, when he passed out of Dartmouth, his father also gave him his own ceremonial sword. He places it carefully on the windowsill. Both have gone with him on every ship he's served in.

Now in overalls, hard hat and steel-toe-capped boots, Hawkins heads down to the dockyard for his own introductory tour. It's stopped raining now, so he makes a call to his wife while he walks. It goes to voicemail.

He touches an electronic fob to the turnstile and punches in his own dedicated code. The ship's still about a quarter of a mile away and mostly concealed behind office blocks and building sheds, so he keeps sight of the top of her pole-mast – a powerful radio antenna upon which is perched a triumphant black-headed seagull.

After passing the dry dock and the *Prince of Wales*, he spots a line of decommissioned submarines waiting to have their nuclear power plants extracted before being broken up. Beyond them he can see all the way to Queensferry at the base of the railway bridge he crossed this morning. This miracle of nineteenth-century engineering is now brushed by the few rays of sunlight that have managed to penetrate the cloud cover, while the feet of its massive central pillars remain shrouded by the morning mist.

Nearer, at the water's edge, he spots a collection of dilapidated sheds. The faded lettering on one reads 'Naval Stores' and on another, 'Ropery'. It's an emotional reminder that this is where, more than thirty years ago, his career began before Rosyth dockyard was privatized.

He leans on a capstan to take it all in when his phone rings.

'Hello, love,' he says softly. 'I'm having a bit of a moment . . .'

Trudy, Bob's second wife, fully understands. The rush of memories. The intensity of his devotion to his shipmates, and to his country. And when his voice falters, she knows what he is thinking – Rosyth is the place he met Joan, the mother of his sons, who died of brain cancer eleven years ago.

Ten minutes later, fully composed, Bob reaches the inner security gate, where Jay Early, the ship's Bosun (a warrant or petty officer in charge of rigging, anchors, cables, deck crew and sea boats) is waiting to escort him on board and show him round. Early is a cheerful, square-chinned man in his late thirties whose enormous biceps – of which he is extremely proud – are testament to his position as the QE's arm-wrestling champion.

Hawkins gestures to the pole-mast. 'Taller than Nelson's Column, Bosun?'

'Yes, sir. Or, if you're talking to a Yank, 4 metres higher than Niagara Falls.'

Bypassing the exit to the hangar, they climb the access tower to the flight deck. Hawkins hesitates before walking down the gangway. 'Do we salute as we go on, Bosun?'

'Not yet, sir. She's still a civilian platform.'

Hawkins surveys the endless expanse of flight deck and although much of it's still covered in work tents and scaffolding he tries to imagine it as it will be on operations. He can almost hear the roar of F-35 jet fighters as they come in to land. In his mind's eye he can see Merlin helicopters preparing to launch. And in his nostrils he can smell the aviation fuel, exhaust and diesel that will fill the air as the carrier cuts a swathe through the wide-open ocean.

Jay Early appears to be reading his mind. 'Haven't even had sight of the driver's manual yet, sir.'

Hawkins gives him a wry smile. 'We'll be writing that manual, Bosun.'

Baz Barrett leads his baby sailors towards a huge white tent covering most of the middle section of the flight deck, whose surface an army of workers in white overalls have taken right down to the bare, gleaming metal.

'You're now lookin' at something very special,' proclaims the jovial PO. 'In a few years, F-35 stealth fighters will be landing right where you're standin'. Comin' down vertically, they'll exert huge downward pressure and heat. The flight deck's going to take one hell of a bashin', so the boffins 'ave invented a special spray to harden the metal. Thermal Metal Spray bonds titanium and steel at the molecular level – that's why they're scrapin' the deck right down to its bone and keepin' it ultra clean for the bonding process. This makes it, in technical parlance, "fuckin' 'ard", but until the first F-35 lands we won't really know if it'll be fuckin' 'ard enough!'

The party proceeds to the centre of the flight deck, where an officer, shielding his eyes from the sun, is peering up at the aft island. 'Morning, sir.' Barrett salutes.

'Good morning!' Mark Deller replies brightly.

The former helicopter pilot is the QE's first Commander Air, commonly known as 'Wings'. He is in charge of aviation on board the QE. Or he will be once there are aircraft to be in charge of.

'Morning, everyone!' he says to the newcomers. 'I hope the PO's saying nice things about naval pilots.'

Barrett shakes his head but grins.

'Anybody know why the ship has two islands?' Deller challenges.

'To separate navigation from air traffic control,' says one young sailor.

'Why would you want to do that?'

'To spread the risk, sir? So if one island's hit we've got another?'

'Good answer!' Deller says. 'Yes, if the bridge comes a cropper, Flyco can carry on fighting. In fact, Flyco has a secondary bridge built in so any surviving navigators can continue to drive from the aft island. It works the other way round too. If Flyco gets smashed we can transfer to the for'ard island, where there's a mini Flyco for emergency use.'

Deller is pointing out a fundamental design feature of the

entire ship – inbuilt resilience through extensive fall-back systems. Even the back-up systems have back-up systems. If the steering mechanisms from the bridge and Flyco were compromised or destroyed, the rudders could be manually turned using a huge flywheel in the stern. It would be intensely physical work and require a small army of muscular sailors to spin, but they'd be able to turn the ship.

'The other reason we 'ave two islands,' Barrett says, 'is that they help us separate our two gas turbine engines. These monsters give us 36 MW of power each and are kept apart, so that if one gets clobbered we still 'ave the other one.'

'But what's that got to do with the islands?' one puzzled-looking sailor asks.

'Patience, Lofty!' Barrett barks. 'I was just getting to that.'

'Sorry, PO.'

'Both engines need funnels for the exhaust,' Barrett continues. 'So the islands house those funnels right up their middles. Clever stuff, eh?'

Deller points upwards. 'If you look at the big windows that surround Flyco tower, you'll see they have windscreen wipers to keep them clean at all times. At over 3 metres in length, I'm reliably informed they're the biggest in the world.'

'Reinforced glass, sir?' a sailor ventures.

'I'm also reliably informed they could withstand a strike from a Chinook's rotor blade,' Deller says. 'But for all that I can't help thinking what stonking tomatoes we could grow up there. In fact, I think I will!'

The sailors grin sheepishly, not quite sure if Commander Air is being serious.

'Now, if you'll excuse me, I have an appointment.' Deller turns to go. 'I have to see a man about a sofa.'

*

Bob Hawkins and Jay Early are in the hangar, chatting to Fiona Percival, Commander Logistics, who's organizing the loading of 500 office cabinets.

'I've got three hours to get them on before the crane operators' shift change. After that they'll need the cranes for construction.'

Commander Percival, the most senior female officer on the QE, came over to the UK from her native Zimbabwe when she was eight. Her lilting accent, friendly demeanour and infectious laugh belie a steely determination to get things done. Her crucial role is to supply the empty vessel with everything it'll need before going to sea.

'Ma'am . . .' a junior rating says breathlessly, 'more toilet paper's arrived. Another lorryload.'

'Oh no.' Her brow furrows. 'Direct it to the warehouse.'

Percival turns back to Bob Hawkins and Jay Early. 'We've already had one delivery today. I'll have to keep it all in the warehouse for as long as possible. So difficult to store on board. It has to be kept bone dry.'

When they do go on board, toilet rolls will be stowed in the higher compartments where there's less chance of flooding.

'Good God, yes!' Early says. 'Run out of that mid-ocean and we'll have a mutiny on our hands.'

'Too right!' Hawkins adds. 'Don't ask sailors to go into battle without bog rolls.'

Mark Deller introduces himself.

'How's it being a Wings with negative aircraft?' Hawkins asks mischievously.

Deller laughs. 'I'd certainly prefer to be overseeing active aviation, but all in good time. ACA rules are a bloody bind to be honest. I wanted to bring my favourite leather sofa, but they refused permission. Said it wasn't safety checked.'

'Stymied by Big Brother!' Hawkins says.

'Well . . .' Deller looks around conspiratorially. 'I smuggled it on last night. Got a couple of hefty matelots to help. It's hidden in one of the locked compartments. We'll keep moving it around until we go to sea, then I'll shift it to my cabin.'

3. Lemon Sole for Tea

0730

Efforts to get the QE shipshape and seaworthy are by no means confined to Rosyth. Five hundred miles away, preparations are already underway for her arrival at what will be her home port, even though it's still eighteen months away. Right now, there's no way of getting her into the ancient harbour, let alone manoeuvring her to her berth. Why? She's too damn big.

American observers, used to massive military ports like Norfolk, Santiago or Pearl Harbor, think it madness to bring a ship the size of the QE into Portsmouth. The Royal Navy think otherwise and are confident not only of their inherent seamanship but also their ingenuity. Marine engineers are erecting a series of fourteen steel structures in the seabed to the west of its entrance which will support the maritime version of landing lights.

But there's another problem. If the QE sailed in today she'd run aground well before reaching her berth, in fact long before even reaching the harbour. Boskalis, the Dutch dredging experts, have mounted a two-year operation to remove 4 million tons of sand and gravel from the harbour and the 'shipping approach channel' in the Solent. Currently 2.2 miles long and approximately 250 yards at its widest, it needs to be doubled to around 500 yards at its widest point and deepened throughout. The 120-yard width of the entrance will remain unchanged, but parts of the inner harbour will also have to be dredged to create a deep enough 'berth pocket' (a parking space for the QE) and turning area. She'll come in forwards but will have to spin round before she leaves.

A fleet of specialist vessels – survey boats, crane barges, tugs, dive-boats and suction-hopper dredgers – are now working round the clock. Harry Krishna Bagwandeen, a fifty-one-year-old explosives consultant, is very much at the sharp end of these efforts.

Today, working a twelve-hour shift from 0600 to 1800, Bagwandeen is on the *Shoalway*, a 4,000-ton suction-hopper. It's equipped with a 900-mm suction pipe, capable of dredging to a depth of 30 metres. Every couple of hours the suction head has to be hoisted out of the water for a routine check.

'Bring the arm down!' Bagwandeen says through his radio and advances to explore the dark, gridded interior of the suction pipe when the operator on the bridge lowers the head on to its cradle.

'Going in!' He stoops beneath what looks like the flared head of a gigantic snake. He flicks on his helmet torch and starts prodding and poking with a sharp iron rod.

'Stand back!' he shouts to a deckhand who's got too close. 'Just in case I jab something that wants to go bang.'

Bagwandeen pulls out an old piece of timber and some cabling then reaches further inside for a spherical object wedged in the grating.

The object drops to the deck with a thud. 'Bingo!' he says. 'Another cannonball for the collection.'

He examines the ancient projectile more closely. 'It's not iron,' he tells Henk Bloom, the Dutch captain. 'Solid stone. That makes it pre-1660.'

'How many have we got now?' Bloom asks.

'Well, this makes four stone cannonballs since we started dredging in January. I've also found two solid iron ones – those will be late seventeenth century – and one fused-ball that would have held a charge – probably eighteenth century.'

'Quite a collection, *ja*?'

'Oh yeah! And that's not including shed loads of Napoleonic musket balls, old mortars and masses of Martini–Henry cartridges from the First World War. We're sucking up enough to start a museum of ordnance. The good news is, nothing's exploded. Yet!'

After four hours of dredging the *Shoalway* is full to the brim. Captain Bloom promptly takes her to the dumping grounds south of the Isle of Wight. Once his cargo is offloaded, he'll return – probably managing three or even four 4,000-ton loads before the shift change at 1800.

Rosyth Dockyard

0930

At the other end of the country, Bob Hawkins waits at the base of the access tower at the aft end of the QE. A slim man in a captain's uniform leaps out of a black Mercedes and walks briskly towards him. Hawkins snaps a respectful salute, which is returned with a broad grin then a warm handshake. They are old friends.

'Welcome to HMS *Queen Elizabeth*,' the First Lieutenant says. 'Your ship, Captain Kyd.'

Forty-nine-year-old Jerry Kyd, the former CO of HMS *Ark Royal* and *Illustrious*, is a carrier man through and through,

but knows the QE is going to be a very different propos-
ition. There is no one to tell him how this ship works. They'll
all be starting from scratch. This job is the most challenging
of his high-flying career. Not only does he have to get this
monster to sea and prove her, but his ultimate mission is to
oversee the return of carrier-strike capability and fixed-wing
aviation to the Royal Navy.

Failure is not an option.

1055

There are 456 sailors in their Number One uniforms assembled on the drill square at HMS *Caledonia*. Below them in the
dockyard, Goliath is still lifting massive sections of HMS
Prince of Wales into position. A little further off, the QE
stretches out in the morning sun.

The black Mercedes comes into sight.

'Commanding Officer approaching!' the parade officer
shouts.

A Royal Marines bugler promptly sounds an alert that
echoes across the open space. Stepping out beside a raised
platform, Kyd prompts an order to bring everyone to
attention.

'HMS *Queen Elizabeth* . . . Ho!'

The waiting sailors bring their right boot to their left with
one thunderous crunch on the tarmac.

Commander Darren Houston, the second in command
and known as the Commander, steps forward to greet his
new captain. After an exchange of salutes he escorts him to
the dais from where Kyd will deliver his inaugural address at
his first 'Clear Lower Deck' – the practice of bringing everyone together.

The parade officer bellows a further order. 'Ship's Company . . . stand at . . . ease!'

Kyd pauses a moment to survey his new ship's company. He's encouraged by the number of senior ratings, non-commissioned officers and officers he recognizes. Quite a few have served under him before. But he's also mindful of the array of fresh young faces.

'Good morning, HMS *Queen Elizabeth*!' he says with gusto. 'I cannot tell you how honoured I am to be your first sea-going captain. I don't think there's been a Royal Navy crew with as much responsibility resting on their shoulders for the past two hundred years. Many of you are straight out of training and will be nervous about what lies ahead . . .'

He pauses to let his words sink in.

'I won't lie to you, the challenge is enormous and won't be without its dangers. This is an untried and untested warship. Getting her ready for sea won't be a bed of roses. I can promise you this, though: I'll always do my best to look after you and keep you safe.'

He turns and points to his new command.

'We have to get our ship to sea as soon as we can. She has to be properly tested and readied for duty. The world's a frisky place at the moment – all sorts of dangers lurking, and security risks everywhere. And we have to be ready to respond to threats which I think are coming sooner rather than later. HMS *Queen Elizabeth*, as big and as sophisticated as she might be, is really just a huge metal box, full of pipes, wires, gadgetry and computer terminals. She's missing one vital ingredient.'

Kyd points this time to the men and women in front of him.

'Without the flesh, blood, muscle and hearts of you, my

sailors, that ship is just a robot. It's only as good as those who breathe life into it. You're the most important resource at my disposal.'

Kyd turns once again to the giant warship-in-waiting.

'I see the tabloids already refer to the *Queen Elizabeth* as "Big Lizzie". I like that. It means she already holds the nation's affections. But we'll only get her to sea by working together, guys. Britain needs Big Lizzie. The world needs Big Lizzie . . .'

Portsmouth

1800

The *Shoalway*, finished for the day, is handing over duty to the night dredger. Harry Bagwandeen has had a rewarding shift. His job might involve poking around for bullets and bombs, any one of which could seriously spoil his day, but there are fringe benefits – he's often able to retrieve fresh fish from the main ballast tanks once the dredged load is dropped.

Today, Bagwandeen's personal tally after twelve hours of solid dredging: one seventeenth-century cannonball, five Napoleonic musketballs, three First World War cartridges, part of an old television set, circa 1970 and, best of all, a fresh lemon sole.

'Loverly!' he says to Captain Bloom. 'Fried with a bit of butter. That's my tea sorted.'

4. Hats Off to the F-35

0900

More and more sailors have been arriving in Rosyth. Pod City has grown as the ship's company has expanded to more than 600, but not one sailor is yet working on the QE full time. In fact, apart from Fiona Percival and her team's intermittent attempts to get stores on board, very few members of the Royal Navy are even working on the vessel part time. Ship 1, as the civilian workforce still refer to her, remains the strict preserve of the Aircraft Carrier Alliance and will remain a civilian platform for some time to come.

The sailors are forced to work from the Lowden Building, a nondescript dockyard office block. Long, orange-bricked and unprepossessing, the three-storey complex is located within sight of both carriers. Ship 1, tethered to a sea wall in the build basin, is about 200 yards to the north, and Ship 2, perched in the dry dock and straddled by Goliath, is some 400 yards to the south.

The Lowden Building is what sailors call 'a ship ashore' or 'stone frigate', and they run it, as best they can, as if it were. Each branch has its own dedicated section: Warfare, Seafaring, Logistics, Marine Engineering, Weapons Engineering, Navigation and Aviation.

There's one large canteen on the ground floor, but all the

cooking is done by civilian dockyard staff. The QE's own chefs are perhaps the most frustrated of all. Leading Chef Waseel Mohamad Khan, known to everyone as Wes, is desperate to do what he's trained and paid to do – cook for hungry sailors. He's famous throughout the Navy for his curries, but at the moment has no opportunity to impress.

'I don't know how long I can put up with all this spare time!' he only half jokes to his best friend, a galley storeman from Nepal.

'Relax, Wes,' Ramesh Rai laughs. 'Enjoy the peace whilst it lasts!'

Khan, a devoted Muslim, is originally from Kenya but now lives with his wife Shah in Birmingham. He's been in the Royal Navy for fifteen years and has spent long periods at sea or on deployment. He met Ramesh Rai when posted to Afghanistan in 2011. The Nepalese was a serving Gurkha at the time, but Khan persuaded him to transfer.

'It's just so . . . boring!' the portly Khan complains. 'Us cooks are like finely tuned athletes – we need to keep up our training and galley fitness.'

'Not sure I'd call you a finely tuned athlete,' chuckles the ex-Gurkha.

'Whadya mean?' Khan affects an injured tone whilst rubbing his ample stomach.

Training for life on board the QE has started, to a limited extent. The ACA is allowing the ship's company some restricted and highly controlled access so they can start to acquaint themselves with the ship, on a department-by-department basis, for only a few hours a week. With over 3,000 compartments and 3 miles of passageways it's going to take time for the sailors to find their way around. They are therefore encouraged, in the little time they get, to explore the complicated geography of the massive vessel, not only for damage control parties to be able to fight fires or stem floods, but also for personnel to escape smoke-filled passageways and find their way to the open air without delay.

The Fleet Standard Time to get to a fire on board a warship is thirty seconds, and another sixty to put it out. All training is geared to this, because after ninety seconds a fire will probably be out of control – a very tall order on a vessel this size, and designed through automation to be lean manned. Not including aircrew, the QE will have a basic crew complement of 679 for her first sea trials. A US carrier of roughly the same size will have in excess of 3,500.

The Delivery Director for the ACA has also given special dispensation to some of the ship's specialist marine engineers to help fire up the engines for the first time. The four Wärtsilä 38 marine diesel engines and two Rolls-Royce MT30 gas turbines will generate in excess of 109 megawatts – enough to meet the energy demands of a city the size of Aberdeen. Much of this power will be converted to high-voltage electricity, up to 11,000 volts, which will require a very different approach to health and safety routines. Fire, for instance, will have to be attacked with foam rather than water.

Early familiarity with these monster power plants is essential for the sailors who'll be running them, maintaining them and keeping them safe. At this stage, however, training and preparation of the burgeoning ship's company is as much about building fellowship and sustaining morale as specific technical instruction. Kyd and his officers know they must seize every opportunity to strengthen the bonds of loyalty that will sustain the sailors in the face of their future challenges and hazards.

Team-building is the name of the game, and right now in one of the larger offices in the Lowden Building, the Aviation complement, though devoid of hardware, is pushing on regardless. The QE's chosen jet fighter, the F-35B Lightning, is the most advanced warplane in the world and at £100 million a pop will require careful marshalling around the flight deck.

For now, specialist aircraft handlers practise moving cardboard cut-outs across a tabletop. Everything is strictly to scale, except the Lego men who represent the flight-deck team, borrowed from one of their kids' toy boxes. Mark Deller, to his delight, is represented by Thor, the hammer-wielding god of thunder.

The flight team spends hours every day talking through the complexities of what is potentially one of the most dangerous jobs in the world. Emma Ranson, a sparky twenty-eight-year-old Liverpudlian, will be one of the people in charge of the QE flight deck once they go to sea. Last year, along with other Royal Navy personnel, she spent nine months on USS *Harry S. Truman*, shadowing American aircraft handlers. The supercarrier, on deployment to the Middle East during Operation Enduring Freedom (the fight against global terrorism), was able to give the British sailors vital hands-on experience before joining the QE.

Nearly ten years have passed since the Royal Navy operated its own carriers, and many if not most of the sailors from that era have moved on or left service altogether. Ranson is part of its great reinvention, and there is much to relearn. She, like the rest of her team, cannot wait to start working on the flight deck for real but recognizes that building up to that moment requires baby steps.

Whilst it'll be almost a year before they can get their hands on their own F-35s, they will have their first chance to see them in the flesh tomorrow.

Rosyth, 1 July 2016

1355

Hundreds of ACA workers and Royal Navy personnel have crowded on to an unseasonably cold and windy flight deck and are peering expectantly into a steely-grey sky. In five minutes, at precisely two o'clock, two F-35B Lightnings are due to fly over – a salute by the most advanced warplane in the world to the most advanced aircraft carrier. At least, that's the plan.

In 2001, Britain joined the United States' most ambitious programme yet to build the strike fighter jets of the future. As a Tier 1 partner in the development of Lightning II, it has taken a key role in its design, heralding a new era of 'interoperability' – the new buzzword for collaboration. Developed and built in the US, although significant parts and components have been conceived and manufactured in the UK, the stealth fighters are here for the Royal International Air Tattoo. The QE has been designed to carry the F-35B variant of the single-seat, single-engine, all-weather, multi-role Joint Strike Fighter, so this is a significant event. On paper they are compatible, but before the F-35B can fly off the ship operationally it will have to go through extensive flight trials on America's eastern seaboard in 2017.

Jerry Kyd is standing on the ski-jump with the ACA Delivery Director and Commander Air. Mark Deller glances at his watch. 'One minute to go.' The flight will be split-second accurate – from south to north, wide turn and then back to Culdrose in Cornwall.

Jerry Kyd scans the sky but then glances at the open sea. 'Uh oh! Squall coming in . . .'

An ominous cloud bank is moving rapidly towards the ship – below which a dark, rippling curtain hangs down to the increasingly agitated waves.

Too late to shelter, everyone braces for impact.

Stinging rain lashes the deck, and at least three officers' caps spin like frisbees into the Forth. All heads are lowered as a deafening roar breaks through the sound of the icy wind. The F-35s are dead on time, but remain enshrouded by the murk.

'Bugger it!' Jerry Kyd says, drenched from head to foot. 'Missed 'em.'

'We might see them on their second pass,' Deller says hopefully.

A minute later, the thunder of the Pratt & Whitney engines can be heard again, but the jets are hidden from view once more as they head for home.

'Well, at least we heard them,' Kyd says, knowing that they now won't see an F-35 until the flight trials next year.

'Look . . .' Deller says. 'It's only bloody well clearing!'

The weather gods, at their most mischievous, have parted the clouds to reveal a clear blue sky. Sunshine now glistens on the flight deck.

'Hold on . . .' Deller says. 'Where's my sodding hat?'

5. Gut-Wrenching, Blood-Spattering Annihilation

Royal Forest, Windsor, 19 October 2016

The autumn leaves are falling as the axe slices through the air.

The blade cuts deep into the thick, crocodile skin, then rises and strikes again. White flesh shows in the wedge-shaped wound.

'Ready!'

As the woodsman reaches for his chainsaw, his companions stand back in readiness for the 'drop'. Among them is a man dressed not in Kevlar but a tweed overcoat, woollen scarf and leather gloves. Nick Gutfreund watches intently as the mighty oak starts to list.

'Stand away!'

The tree creaks, cracks and crashes to the forest floor.

Gutfreund squeezes his eyes shut against the explosion of dust and splinters and walks forward to examine its tight growth rings.

'Fine wood,' he says.

'Suit your needs, sir?' the axeman asks.

'Beautifully.'

'What's it for, if you don't mind my asking?'

'The new warship they're building up in Scotland.'

'Didn't know they still used this stuff for warships!'

'Oh, the bit I'm making will be almost entirely oak.' Gutfreund smiles. 'With a few other bits and pieces for good measure. A bit of burr oak, probably, and walnut and maybe some semi-fossilized bog oak, but that's getting increasingly difficult to find.'

Nick Gutfreund is one of the country's most accomplished cabinetmakers. He's been commissioned to make a special table for the QE, which should sit up to twelve people and somehow represent the spirit of the ship. The idea was Jerry Kyd's, and a wealthy but anonymous benefactor will foot the bill.

High-quality oaks are rarely felled, so the cabinetmaker decided to come to Windsor and witness this event for himself. His designs are meticulous, his craft painstaking. He wants to find ways to link the piece with the people, the service and the environment for which it's being created. Kyd has a clear vision of how he wants his flagship to be perceived, and therefore what the table should convey. 'A statement of intent and strength, but also collaboration.'

It needs to be both functional and decorative. Queen Elizabeth I's *Tudor Rose* is Gutfreund's principal inspiration, and he wishes it to evoke both Britain's seafaring heritage and the innate character of the ship herself – unique, stealthy, state-of-the-art. Mystery, exploration, odyssey, discovery, even piracy and hidden treasure are colouring his vision.

The table must fit the space available in Kyd's day cabin, allowing him to hold private meetings with his commanders or visiting notables and VIPs. For that reason he's already decided it should be a round table, in tune with Arthurian legend.

But Gutfreund wants something more. He has an idea to make the table utterly unique. And if it works, he will not reveal it until he delivers what will be called the Rose Table to the QE sometime next year.

HMS Caledonia, *Rosyth, 21 October 2016*

2000

Bob Hawkins adjusts his black silk bowtie in the mirror.

Steve Prest puts his head round the door. 'You coming, shipmate?'

'Just need this and I'm good to go.' Hawkins slips his precious Reynoldson half-hunter into the waistcoat pocket of his best dress uniform and the two head for the wardroom. It's Trafalgar Night – the annual commemoration of Admiral Lord Nelson's famous victory on 21 October 1805.

A Royal Marines bugler opens the proceedings, and everyone moves to take their seats in the dining hall, where long tables have been set for a banquet and adorned with silverware and massive twelve-candle candelabras.

2200

The roast beef feast concludes with the placement of dark-chocolate ships of the line (British and French) on each of the tables, along with heavy brass hammers. 18 inches long, 7 inches wide and 2 feet tall, the ships are stuffed with handmade chocolates. They will be ritually smashed and consumed after Jerry Kyd's keynote speech.

Darren Houston bangs the gavel, the house-lights dim, and Jerry Kyd rises, illuminated only by a candelabra.

'Ladies and gentlemen . . .' He smiles. 'It's an absolute privilege to be here at my first mess dinner as the captain of HMS *Elizabeth*.'

Everybody cheers.

'It is of course a great sadness that we cannot celebrate

this year's Traf' Night on our own ship, but that time will come – The *Queen Elizabeth* has at least fifty Traf' nights ahead of her, more than can be said for those of us here tonight – with the exception, perhaps, of the First Lieutenant, who seems to be immortal. Bob, I am reliably informed, was present at the Battle of Trafalgar himself . . .'

The room reverberates once again.

'He was bald then as well!' Kyd adds with perfect comic timing.

Bob Hawkins raises a fist in triumph.

'OK, guys . . .' The captain holds up his hands. 'Time for a bit of seriousness.'

The room falls silent.

With the candlelight flickering across his face, Kyd asks, 'Why on earth are we here?'

There is no answer from the floor.

'Civilians often think that Trafalgar Night's just some sort of quaint naval tradition. So why do we do this, year after year? Just to remember some far-off naval battle? To wallow in some distant and irrelevant victory at sea? I do sometimes hear young officers asking why we still talk about Nelson, who died over 200 years ago. What possible relevance could he have to a twenty-first-century navy?'

Kyd glances at his handwritten notes.

'So what is it about this diminutive, insecure, one-armed, one-eyed sailor that brings us together in our mess kit year on year? What is it about the man who continues to capture our imagination? And it's not just the Navy. In 2002 Nelson was voted the ninth most famous Briton in history. The reputation of this little man has longevity. Today, after 211 years, I submit he has never been more relevant to me, to you and to our ship's company. Let me tell you why . . .'

Kyd takes a sip of water.

'Nelson was a great *leader*,' he says. 'In fact, he was a *brilliant* leader. His men loved him and would do anything for him. He was also very generous; he often put his hand in his own pocket to buy blankets and food for them. He was incredibly courageous. And let me tell you, guys, courage is our stock-in-trade. Field Marshal Lord Slim, one of our greatest British Army generals, said: "I don't believe there's any man ..."' Kyd breaks off. 'Or woman, these days of course, ". . . who in their heart-of-hearts wouldn't rather be called brave, than any other virtue attributed to him. And this elemental attitude is a sound one. Because courage is not merely a virtue – it is *the* virtue; without it there are no others. Faith, hope, charity and all the rest don't become virtues without courage – for it takes courage to exercise them. Courage is not only the basis of all virtue, it is its very expression."'

Kyd surveys his officers, some senior and experienced, but most still young, with much to learn. None has been tested in combat. Yet.

As a student of naval history, Bob Hawkins doesn't need reminding of Nelson's relevance to today's Navy, but he is moved by the captain's words and the heartfelt sincerity with which he is delivering them. Hawkins was posted to Rosyth at the time of the Falklands War, but he knew many who went to the South Atlantic, and some who never came back. More recently, he's known marines who died in Afghanistan, and others who survived but now carry life-changing injuries. He's in awe of such men and the courage they continue to display.

'We're only as good as the men and women we lead,' Kyd continues. 'And aren't we lucky to have people under us who

I know would put their lives on the line for Queen and country?'

The tables rumble once again.

'But that precious sense of duty and self-sacrifice has to be earned. You have an obligation . . . an obligation of leadership that Nelson fully understood, and I want each one of you here to reflect upon this as I do. Reflect on yourselves and be honest. It can be uncomfortable sometimes, because no man or woman is flawless. Even Nelson. Perhaps especially Nelson. He was the archetypal flawed naval officer. Married, but a serial philanderer. He was a vain man, a shameless self-publicist and indeed no reluctant celebrity. He would've been the first on to Graham Norton's couch, I am sure. But for all that, his men loved him and cried tears of grief when he died. And I am talking about rough men, press-ganged men, brutalized men. They wept like babies when Nelson was killed by a French musketball. But he died in victory by vanquishing the French, who were about to invade our country . . . He ripped up the rule books and did things his way. A maverick, certainly, probably infuriating, but by God he knew and believed in what he was doing.

'He determined not just to beat the French but destroy them completely . . . He broke through their formation and then *unleashed hell*. . . Nelson was not about winning on margin, or by deception or "information exploitation" as we call it today. No. He was all about full-spectrum targeting. Gut-wrenching, blood-spattering annihilation. This was no fun and games, guys. This was no-quarter fighting. And why am I sensationalizing this?'

Kyd's level gaze fixes upon every one of his officers.

'I'll tell you why,' he says. 'Because for the last twenty years we've been engaged in discretionary, counter-insurgency warfare. We've witnessed extraordinarily brave acts in places like Iraq and Afghanistan, but we haven't fought to protect our sovereignty since the Falklands, or endured a proper state-on-state action since the Second World War. And I say this with a certain amount of reflection, because the world is a dangerous place. We have increasing political tensions. Russia is ever-menacing; China, a rising force; North Korea, volatile. Add to this the destabilizing effects of rampant migration, economic inequality and the terrible consequences of global warming.

'The time is coming, I believe, when we will be back in Nelson's shoes. So I want you to remember that as you put on your uniform every day, and especially when we move on board our ship, that we are in this together. Together we train, together we fight, together we lead our ship's company. It is a duty and an obligation. It is not for the faint-hearted; when the going gets tough who knows how we will react?

'Fighting a fire on board, pulling bodies out of the water, stemming a shipmate's blood flow from an artery severed by shrapnel. It's all about teamwork and your love for each other. That is why the band of brothers of Nelson's era is important today. That's why we are here tonight.

'If there is one thing I want you to take away, it is this. For as long as I am your captain, I want your trust, and I want you to ensure you have the trust of those you lead, because as long as we have trust, we have proper leadership, and then we can lead our way out of anything. We have tough times ahead, I can assure you.'

Kyd gestures towards the distant dockyard security lights.

'We're due to leave the wall in March and head out on our first sea trials. That's just five months from now. And we're not even on board yet. We have an enormous mountain to climb. If we don't work as a team, we won't make it to the top. Thank you.'

Kyd's impassioned address prompts loud and continuous applause. The tables tremble with the impact of sixty pounding palms. The blood-red port ripples in the decanters and the sugar-paper sails on the chocolate ships shake, as if filled by a strengthening wind.

'That's the way to make a Trafalgar Night speech,' Bob Hawkins says to Fiona Percival.

'Utterly brilliant!' she agrees.

After the toast, Jerry Kyd's officers crack open the chocolate ships and belt out sea shanties into the wee small hours.

0200

Bob Hawkins returns to his room. Moderately inebriated, he unravels his bow tie, slumps into his armchair and pours himself a small nightcap.

He contemplates all his captain has said, and the enormous task ahead of them. The one-time clearance diver and bomb-disposal expert ponders the unlikely progression of his long and varied career.

What the hell lies ahead, he wonders as he glances up at a portrait of Nelson on his cabin wall. He takes a deep breath and raises his glass once more.

'To your Lordship,' he says quietly.

6. Faux Fighters

The first major mechanism and arguably the most important apparatus on board – the Mass Evacuation System (MES) – is going to be fully tested today. The need to secure the means by which the ship's company would escape if she were sinking is lost on no one.

The ACA has stipulated that the equipment can be deployed but no personnel must use it, for health and safety reasons, and Bob Hawkins is seething. 'They're expecting us to test equipment designed to save human beings without any human involvement,' he complains to Jay Early. 'I've never heard anything so ridiculous!'

'I agree, sir,' says the Bosun. 'But our hands are tied.'

Despite Hawkins' frustration, the trial must take the form of a dry-run, but even without human guinea-pigs it promises high drama.

On the order 'Abandon ship!' a series of explosive charges blows out three steel plates just below the flight deck, leaving three gaping holes about 6 feet square at equal intervals along the port side, through which hydraulic plungers unfurl enormous orange chutes. After hitting the water, they inflate into rigid arms, similar to the emergency slides deployed from airliners in extremis, but many times bigger. It's a spectacular sight. Six hundred people per half hour can be evacuated from every chute without any having to jump the 100 feet into an unforgiving ocean. Theoretically, therefore, it should take less than that time to evacuate the ship's maximum complement using three slides. The starboard MES, currently facing the quay, will be tested another day. If the ship is listing it may be impossible to deploy the chutes on the more elevated side, because their angle of descent would be too steep for safety.

Hawkins and Early watch, mesmerized, as covered landing platforms inflate at the bottom of each chute, where escapees would await rescue. Detachable as rafts, they have a reduced radar signature to help confound the enemy, and each carries its own stock of fresh water, rations and emergency medical supplies.

'You'd pay good money for a ride like that at Alton Towers!' Early chuckles.

'Amazing,' Hawkins says. But he knows the real test will be logistical – especially in the event of combat damage and injuries. 'I want to know how we'd pace the people going down. Too rapid and you'd have them dropping on each other. Potential bloody clusterfuck!'

He's also thinking that this system could be invaluable for humanitarian relief, with the right choreography. 'We could very rapidly deploy them to provide a waterline-platform. Picking up refugees or victims of piracy. I guess it'd be possible to winch people up the chutes. Maybe one day we'll be able to test these damn things properly.'

At the debriefing, the ACA are evidently delighted. Bob Hawkins bites his lip. He knows that whilst health and safety issues are important, there will come a time when greater risks will have to be taken to test equipment than would ever be palatable in the civilian world.

Other tensions have been mounting between the ACA

and the Navy, due to different working practices and the crew's infuriating lack of access to their 'own' ship. Even when they do move on board full-time, they'll still have to co-exist with the construction workers – at least 600 of whom will accompany them throughout the sea trials. It won't be until the QE is commissioned towards the end of next year that ownership will be transferred. Until then, to all intents and purposes, she will remain a civilian platform even though Jerry Kyd's job is to turn it into a working warship. That is for him an enduring problem.

One of the issues is timekeeping. Sailors are trained to be five minutes early for every appointment. Merely being 'on time' isn't enough. The civilian attitude has led to frustration. And the ACA hasn't always given the Navy prior notice when certain passageways or even entire decks have been placed out of bounds for construction work. Naval precision and practicality have gone head to head with cost sheets, profit margins and health and safety regulations.

Alcohol has also become a contentious issue. The Admiralty no longer shares Captain Cook's conviction that their 'top men' benefit from a mug or two of wine before scaling the rigging in high winds but still takes the view that, in the interests of morale, drink should be allowed on board – though not to excess and never at defence or action stations (when the 'fridges are locked'). The traditional daily tot of rum has been replaced by two tins of beer, although every mess will have a bar, and officers will be served wine and port on special occasions. The ACA, on the other hand, operates a strict zero-tolerance policy and say it won't even allow anyone on board if they've been drinking ashore.

Jerry Kyd doesn't need to be told that the rigorous application of such draconian rules will be unworkable and counterproductive. Even if they did manage to apply them in Rosyth, he knows that on sea trials it'll be a different story. A stop has been scheduled at Invergordon after three weeks when it would be impractical, indeed nonsensical, to tell nearly 700 sailors to stick to orange juice on a well-deserved run ashore. He's already concerned by the news that the town has only two pubs and is unlikely to have enough beer to go round.

Whilst the ACA's role is vital in the physical construction of his flagship, as far as Kyd is concerned, the QE needs to be under full naval command – and the sooner he can leave port, the better.

13 November 2016

Despite the standoff with the ACA over the testing of the Mass Evacuation System, at least they know the emergency equipment is in good working order. But moving the QE through the water at speed is now at the forefront of everyone's mind, not the fear of sinking. The ship's company is poised to move on board before Christmas, and a sailing date for sea trials has been set for 10 March 2017.

HMS *Gleaner* is currently surveying the basin in which the QE is tethered. Using multi-beam sonar, they have to ensure there's sufficient clearance to float the supercarrier out into the Firth of Forth when the time comes. Its average depth is barely 39 feet, although shallower in places, so the QE's 36-feet draft means extra dredging will be essential before she can leave safely. At only 50 feet and with a crew of nine, *Gleaner* is one-three-thousandth the weight of the QE. But without the help of the Navy's smallest ship, its biggest would be forever incarcerated in the dockyard.

And it's not only the inner basin the navigators are worried about. It's sixty years since the Forth Estuary was last surveyed, so it's essential the *Gleaner* brings things up to date, not least because the new Forth Road Bridge, due to open around the same time as the carrier sails, will have affected the flow of the river, and the silt accumulating in the shipping channels.

Since she'll have to squeeze under three bridges – two road and one rail – the QE's height is also a critical concern. She's 240 feet from the tip of her pole-mast on the aft island to the bottom of her keel, which means 203 above the waterline – and the two oldest bridges have a clearance of barely 148 feet. Ingeniously, the engineers have hinged the 62-feet pole-mast so it can be lowered until almost horizontal, but there will still only be a few feet to spare, depending on the state of the tide.

Leaving nothing to chance, Jerry Kyd is heading out on a tug today to check the bridges and experience the currents for himself. With him is his Navigator, Jez Brettel, Commander Navigation Giles Palin and First Lieutenant Bob Hawkins. They motor under the two road bridges and then move on to the Rail Bridge.

Kyd scrutinizes the underside of the famous Victorian structure through his binoculars. 'It's going to be a tight squeeze, for sure.'

'We'll have to leave the build basin at high tide,' Palin says. 'To maximize water depth under the hull.'

'Yup,' Brettel chips in. 'And then wait for low tide before negotiating these fellows.'

'How long's the wait?' asks Hawkins.

'At least four hours.'

'That has all sorts of implications for security,' Jerry Kyd says. 'We'll need close guarding by Fleet Protection until we've made it to open water.'

Sitting at anchor so close to shore until the tide's low enough could make them a sitting target. Terrorist attack will always be a threat, though more likely is the prospect of Scottish Independence or Peace activists launching some sort of protest.

'If those bridges aren't policed, I can see pink paint being dropped on our flight deck,' says Hawkins.

The Royal Marines from 43 Commando, the Fleet Protection Unit, are already committed to patrol the Firth of Forth on the day. Deployed on fast-moving, heavily armed RIBs (rigid inflatable boats), they'll be instantly ready to respond.

Kyd continues to scan the underside of the Forth Rail Bridge. 'You know what? No matter how certain we are that we're going to clear that bridge – and all the mathematics tell us that we are – I bet we'll all duck as we go under.'

'Absolutely, sir!' Brettel grins.

'Mind you,' Kyd says, 'given that we're going under a rail bridge, I could be in for a bottle of port if I'm lucky.'

He's referring to an old naval tradition which decrees that anyone bringing a ship under a bridge at the same time as a train is passing over the top, a sign of good luck, wins a bottle of port.

The tug turns back to the build basin. Jerry Kyd wants a look at the gate through which the QE must eventually pass to reach open water.

They edge closer to the black gate, which is currently shut and supports a single-lane road. Hydraulically operated, the sliding mechanism will provide just enough width for the ship to squeeze through – leaving only 14 inches' clearance on each side and a maximum of 20 inches of water under the keel.

'Fine margins!' Kyd says.

'Yes, sir.' Hawkins smiles. 'If we're going to have to duck when we go under the bridges, we'll have to breathe in going through the gate . . .'

Royal Naval Air Station Culdrose, Cornwall, 16 November 2016

While preparations for sea trials continue in Rosyth, the Aviation Department has achieved all it can with cardboard cut-outs of F-35s and little yellow Lego men, so has graduated to outdoor training at the far end of the country. Mark Deller and his team are now at Culdrose on the Lizard Peninsula. They have an intensive week ahead, which will involve firefighting real fire and aircraft-handling real aircraft.

Well, sort of.

They are standing on a dummy deck – a life-size carrier flight deck carved out of the Cornish countryside, tarmacked over and marked-up – watching in awed silence as two F-35B jets are pulled towards them. This is the closest any of the ship's company has been to one since the ill-fated flypast in July. As of 2016, no F-35s are yet permanently based in the UK. Of the 138 on order for the RAF and the Navy, the first won't be delivered for at least two years.

But these ones will soon be close enough to touch. The airfield tractors tow them on to the dummy deck for inspection. Emma Ranson brushes a fingertip across the underside of a wing. 'Amazing!' she breathes.

The birds of prey are savagely beautiful, even without bombs or missiles attached. But these particular aircraft can't fly or even move along the ground under their own power.

'Gather round,' an instructor shouts. 'As you know, F-35s will land on the QE for the first time next year. Your hand signals to the pilots need to be bold and clear at all times. These fibreglass jobbies will help prepare the way.'

Made locally in Newquay, the two supersized 'Airfix' kits have been fitted with water tanks which simulate fuel and weapons loads between 16 and 24 tonnes. Another two will have opening cockpits so the handlers can practise rescuing injured pilots after a crash. While they have no engines, sensors or weapons, the Faux Fighters will provide everybody with serious hands-on experience until they meet the real thing.

7. Berthing Pains

The dredging operation continues round the clock. Hundreds of thousands of tons of sludge, sand and mud have been removed from the seabed. Harry Bagwandeen is still on the *Shoalway* in the outer Solent, while Orlando Ironside, today's duty diver, is minutely inspecting the area beneath the 'berth pocket' immediately adjacent to what will be the Princess Royal Jetty, where the QE will sit when in the harbour. Any Objects of Concern (OOC) – old cables, chains, lumps of concrete and even engine blocks – are being methodically raised by floating cranes. So far over 4,000 have been identified which could either harm the carrier's hull or damage the dredgers' suction arms, and finding them is not always easy.

'Looks pretty murky down there, Orlando.' Andy Archer, a Boskalis sonar operator, peers at his screen, following the diver's every move.

'*Too right,*' comes the disembodied reply. '*Visibility virtually zero.*'

Breathing regularly but heavily, the diver feels rather than sees his way forward. His oxygen and communication lines link him to the surface platform 60 feet above, where the images from his helmet-mounted camera are being monitored. Right now, the CCTV displays the swirling patterns of sand and sediment pierced by the beam of his head-torch.

Beneath the platform there's also an underwater sonar

camera capable of 'seeing' through the gloom, or at least defining blurred shapes by bouncing sound waves off the seabed and converting them to images which Archer can scrutinize and attempt to decipher. He's directing Ironside towards an OOC he spotted yesterday. It appeared to be a solid object on the sonar screen, although it's impossible to tell how much of it is embedded in the sludge without going down to look. It's probably a bit of old harbour stockade, an anchor or an ancient cannon, but because this area is to be deepened by several metres, anything solid and suspect must be cleared before the dredgers move in.

Portsmouth has seen thousands of warships come and go over the centuries, and all manner of detritus has been thrown or dropped overboard. The harbour floor is proving a veritable treasure trove for archaeologists and historians. Eight cannon have been lifted so far, and 96 cannonballs, an aircraft engine, an old British torpedo, 36 anchors and an eighteenth-century human skull, along with a multitude of eighteenth- and nineteenth-century shoes, ceramics, plates and cutlery, and vintage thick-glass wine bottles that could have graced Nelson's table.

'*Tide's on the turn, churning up the silt*,' Ironside says. '*Take me in on sonar, Andy.*'

'Switching to sonar screen,' Archer says. 'Let me find you then I'll guide you in.'

Archer quickly identifies a trail of bubbles, then Ironside's outline. The electronic soundwaves bouncing off him are converted into pixelated shapes in varying shades of blue, but the detail is remarkable. His triangular fins are clearly visible as they propel him gently forward.

'OK, Orlando. You're on screen now,' Archer says. 'Advance. Forty-five degrees to your right. Just about on it.'

Ironside feels around blindly.

'You're right on it now, Orlando. Reach out, mate – an arm's length.'

'*OK . . . Got it!*'

The diver's helmet-camera reveals something barnacle-encrusted protruding from the mud and grime.

'Whadya reckon, Orlando?'

'*Pretty sure it's metal.*'

'Can you get your arms round it?'

The diver hugs the object close to his chest. '*Not all the way.*'

'Describe it by feel, mate.'

The screen shows him stretching his arms the length of the black object.

'*Stuck fast in the mud . . . but I reckon . . . 2 metres long, maybe . . . like a kingsize cigar tube . . .*'

'What shape is the bit sticking out the top?'

Ironside reaches up.

'*Fuck me . . .!*'

'What is it?'

Ironside doesn't answer. His heart is thumping so loud he can hear it inside his helmet. At the same time he can feel his body enveloped by a cold sweat beneath his thick rubber dry suit.

'Orlando. You OK?'

'*Er, Andy . . .*'

'Yes, mate?'

'*It's kind of . . . pointy . . .*'

'Pointy?'

'*Yes mate, very fuckin' pointy.*'

The seabed around Portsmouth is littered with unexploded Second World War ordnance. The city took a terrible battering in the early 1940s, the naval dockyard being a prime target for

Luftwaffe pilots. On the night of 10 January 1941 alone, 25,000 incendiaries and numerous high-explosive bombs rained down upon the city. Thousands of homes and public buildings were destroyed, but not everything hit its target. The wayward projectiles have since been effectively neutralized by submergence and, in many cases, the inundation of sea water, but if disturbed, some could detonate with destructive effect.

Archer shudders. 'Gotta be airdrop. Mark it and get the hell out of there.'

'*I've just been cuddling the bastard . . .*' Ironside says.

'Once marked, surface, mate. Pronto.'

'*Wilco!*'

Ironside fishes a bright-orange plastic ribbon out of the tool-bag suspended from his belt and loops it carefully around the Object of Concern – now an object of very great concern – so that it can be found again and identified. He's still working blind, so the process takes longer than he would like. He reassures himself that if the thing went bang now he wouldn't know much about it. Cold comfort.

'*OK, Andy. All done. Coming up.*'

'Kettle's on, mate.'

Within the hour, a team of Royal Navy Clearance Divers has confirmed it's a 1,500-kilo German bomb. Nobody assumed that constructing HMS *Queen Elizabeth* and preparing her for sea was going to be straightforward, but the possibility that a message from Hitler has been lying in wait for nearly eighty years is still something of a shock.

It will have to be detonated, but not here.

'Blimey . . .' Ironside looks down on them from the surface. 'I wonder how many more of those are loitering with intent.'

'Shedloads,' Andy Archer says. 'Glad we got that one, though. The QE's hull would have been centimetres away.'

'Which end?'

'Stern, I reckon. So it would have taken out her propellers, driveshafts and motors – at the very least. Probably the whole aft end . . .'

'Gone down with all hands. Doesn't bear thinking about.'

'Another cuppa?' Archer asks. 'You've earned it.'

'Wouldn't say no. Biscuits?'

'Now you're really pushing your luck.'

The Mine Lifting Bag is a massive, bright-yellow balloon. As the clearance divers inflate it, the bomb, crammed with ancient and probably highly unstable explosive, is eased from its grave amidst a swirling cloud of sediment. Several hours later, it has been raised to just below the surface of the water and attached to a RIB. The Bomb Disposal Unit and Harbour Authorities decide to wait till nightfall before making the journey to open sea. There will be less shipping to exclude, and it will give the police time to evacuate all the buildings within 1,000 yards.

Six hours later, shortly before 2100, the divers fire up their outboard motor. A half-moon peeps nervously from behind dark, scudding clouds as they edge forward, with a police launch some 100 yards ahead and another 100 yards behind, blue lights flashing across the black waters of the inner harbour.

To the soundtrack of the whistling wind and raucous calls of circling gulls, the slow-moving convoy passes Gunwharf Quays. Normally buzzing and vibrant, its bars and restaurants lie silent and empty; a police cordon will maintain its evacuation until the danger has passed.

Twenty minutes later, the RIB and launches draw level with the Round Tower at the harbour entrance. Quiz night at the Still and West public house alongside it has been cancelled. The Coxswain reduces speed to less than 2 knots and rides the buffeting waves as he steers his deadly cargo into open water.

It is well after midnight by the time the bomb and its minders reach the location, south of the Isle of Wight, where the detonation will occur. They wait until dawn before deflating the Lifting Bag and lowering its load to the seabed some 7 fathoms below. Two men dive down to pack it with 4 lbs of plastic explosive and resurface with a length of high-explosive cord. The detonator to which they connect it contains a small but powerful amount of RDX high explosive which, in turn, is initiated by a slow-burning fuse. The divers now have ninety seconds to retire to a safe distance. The RIB accelerates away on full throttle.

After 1,000 yards, they turn and stop.

'Ten . . . nine . . . eight . . .' The diving supervisor's eyes are glued to his stopwatch. '. . . three . . . two . . . one . . .'

An ear-shattering blast throws a plume of white water high into the air. And this is only the detonating charge. Moments later the sea seems to lift into a towering liquid mountain that erupts like a volcano as 1,500 kilos of high explosive hurls tons of sand, silt and shrapnel skywards.

Redmere Farm, Ely, Cambridgeshire

Two hundred miles away, Nick Gutfreund's boots are clogged with black Fenland loam, but he trudges on regardless. He heard yesterday that a farmer had hit an underground object the shape of a giant torpedo. He drove here from Somerset overnight.

'My God, Hamish, it's cold. I can hardly feel my fingers.'

'Nearly there, Nick,' his companion replies. 'Next field but one, I think.'

Hamish Low knows all there is to know about bog oak, or what some call Black Gold, one of the rarest and most valuable woods in the world. It's created from the trunks of trees that have lain in lakes, river bottoms and swamps for centuries and even millennia. Deprived of oxygen, the wood undergoes the process of fossilization that would eventually turn it into jet, lignite or coal over many millions of years. At around the 5,000- to 7,000-year mark, it becomes hugely coveted by furniture makers. Gutfreund is desperate to find some for Jerry Kyd's table. He has modern oak from the Royal Forest at Windsor, burr oak from Dorset and birch and walnut veneers from the Salisbury Plain, but he wants to add the rich, dark, almost ebony tones of ancient bog oak to the mix, to symbolize longevity.

'There they are!' Low gestures past a heavily frosted treeline.

'Thank God,' Gutfreund gasps. 'I feel like Scott of the Antarctic.'

Ahead of them, a group of men surround a bulldozer revving loudly and pulling a heavy chain from a shallow crater. Its tracks slip and slide as the chain grows taut, and a mud-encrusted trunk gradually emerges from the ground. It's about 100 feet long and 6 feet in circumference at its base.

'Bingo!' Low says.

He moves towards the ancient timber and rubs its semi-fossilized bark with his thumb. He then cuts into a section with a small saw.

'Brilliant.' Gutfreund shivers. 'La pièce de résistance.'

8. Goodbye, Old Girl

Portsmouth Dockyard, 6 December 2016

Jerry Kyd's emotions are mixed, to put it mildly.

After passing HMS *Victory*, he stops briefly to observe the construction of the Princess Royal Jetty. He can see where the engineers are sinking new piles into the water to support it. He can also see where they're building a state-of-the-art high-security reception area for the QE, and, in the fullness of time, HMS *Prince of Wales* too. He watches with fascination as the dredgers continue to deepen the harbour bed. But this isn't what he's come to see today.

He drives a further half-mile.

'There she is!' he murmurs to himself. 'My God, she looks so sad.'

HMS *Illustrious* has long since been decommissioned, and tomorrow she'll be tugged all the way to Turkey to be broken up. Kyd plans to be at the harbour entrance with the Illustrious Association – all former members of her ship's company – to watch her final departure. Today, however, Kyd wants to spend a few final moments with his old command. He's arranged through the Royal Navy Ship's Disposal Unit to go on board and revisit the ship that holds so many fond memories.

He parks and walks towards the stern gangway. He's shocked once again at how small the old carrier looks compared to the QE. When she was commissioned in 1982, 'Lusty' was herself one of Britain's biggest ever warships.

She had been rushed out of build in order get her into the Falklands War as a relief for HMS *Invincible* and was active in the Adriatic in the early 1990s, helping to impose the no-fly zone during the Yugoslav War. In 1998, she operated in the Persian Gulf, in support of Operation Southern Watch, the Anglo-Saudi-American enforcement of a no-fly zone over southern Iraq. An extensive refit in 2003 prevented her involvement in the Second Gulf War, but in 2006 she was instrumental in the rescue of British citizens trapped by the Lebanon conflict. Following the retirement of her fixed-wing Harrier squadrons in 2010, *Illustrious* operated as a dedicated helicopter carrier until her final decommissioning on 28 August 2014, after thirty-two years' service.

Jerry Kyd climbs the gangway to meet Chief Petty Officer Jon Evans.

'Please watch your step, sir. No lighting on board, I'm afraid.'

'Lead the way, chief,' Kyd says. 'I'm in your hands.'

'Bridge first, sir?'

Kyd nods. 'It's where I spent most of my time . . .'

The two men make their way through the darkened ship, the beam of Jon Evans' torch highlighting swirling clouds of rust-dust as they move through the empty, cavernous hangar.

'Good grief!' Kyd says. 'I've never heard it so silent.'

'Tragic, isn't it, sir?'

'It used to be thunderous in here . . .' Kyd can still hear the roar of engines being tested, the clank, whirr and buzz of avionic equipment and the warning sirens as aircraft were pulled on to the lifts.

'Yes, sir. Would make the ears bleed on a good day!'

They proceed to the main island. Unlike the QE, Lusty's bridge and flight control were connected – side by side, with no more than an open door between them. Kyd steps over discarded papers and threadbare carpet on the bridge. Wiring hangs from the consoles, and the windows are cracked and grime-encrusted.

Lusty's last Commanding Officer looks out across the windswept flight deck and sees in his mind's eye the squadrons of helicopters he had at his disposal – Chinook, Apache, Merlin, Lynx and Sea King. He imagines the Sea Harriers launching off the ski-jump and then 'recovering' by vertical landing.

Kyd winces once more as he recalls the shock news in the 2010 Strategic Defence Review that the Harrier squadrons were to be axed along with the Navy's serving carriers. It was strategic idiocy in his view; he and most of his peers knew that a Royal Navy without fixed-wing capability would be rendered almost completely impotent. A working carrier, he feels sure, would have made all the difference to the way Britain responded to global emergencies. The Libyan civil war was a case in point, and he often refers to it when cautioning against rash political tinkering in military matters. Not only could a Harrier force have helped subjugate the insurgents in the aftermath of General Gaddafi's demise, but a carrier such as *Illustrious* would have been a superb platform for dispensing humanitarian aid during the refugee crisis that followed. A handful of fighter jets from RAF Marham with a few tankers in support had been immensely expensive and really didn't cut the mustard.

The flight deck is speckled white by years of seagull droppings. Kyd climbs the ski-jump to look out over the harbour. The place is alive with endeavour. Alive, that is, apart from the metal carcass beneath his feet.

Turning away as his eyes start to glisten, he spots a group

of tugboats attaching lines to Lusty's bow. They're about to pull the old warship into the tidal basin in preparation for her final journey.

'Time to go, sir,' Jon Evans says respectfully.

Moments later, Kyd steps off HMS *Illustrious* for the very last time.

Wednesday, 7 December 2016

0800

A crowd of about a hundred has assembled atop the ancient Round Tower, the Tudor fortification at the entrance of Portsmouth Harbour. They're shielding their eyes from a bright morning sun still low on the horizon and bracing against a bitter easterly wind. Among the crowd, Jerry Kyd is wrapped in his naval greatcoat against the winter chill. He's standing next to Jonathon Band, the former First Sea Lord, who accompanied Princess Anne when she cut the QE's first steel in 2009 and commanded *Illustrious* between 1995 and 1997.

'I hate saying farewell to my old ships,' Band says, blowing into his frozen hands.

'Civilians don't get it, do they?' Kyd replies.

'They don't, Jerry. I remember giving a speech at the decommissioning of *Norfolk* in 2005. I was her first CO. Not sure how I got through it –'

'Here she comes!' a voice shouts from the crowd. Everybody looks to their right. A tug rounds the corner by Gunwharf Quays, and the familiar grey bow slides into view.

'She still looks the part.' Kyd's voice cracks. 'Even under tow.'

'Three cheers for Lusty!' someone yells as she leaves the harbour. 'Hip hip . . .'

Heartfelt cheers echo around the tower as Kyd stands to attention and salutes. *Bountiful* pulls *Illustrious* through a choppy sea towards a larger tug called *Hercules* that will pull her all the way to the breaker's yard. He watches until she disappears over the horizon.

'Goodbye, old girl,' he whispers.

As he prepares to leave, he turns to the former First Sea Lord. 'Out with the old and in with the new, eh, Jonathon?'

It's a reassuring thought on a sad day.

9. Hold Your Nerve!

Rosyth Dockyard, 12 December 2016

Though still covered with green matting to protect the decks, the QE is edging towards completion, and everyone is counting the days until they can finally move on board and call her their home.

'Listen up, shipmates!' Dave Garraghty, the newly arrived Executive Warrant Officer (EWO) hails the final batch of baby sailors assembled in the main hangar. 'I need to educate some of you lot about what's what.'

Garraghty, now the most senior non-commissioned officer in the ship's company, has salt water coursing through his veins. With the sea trials due to start on 10 March, he's acquainting the newcomers with their new, grey, spartan, utilitarian, no-frills, hard-edged home.

'Just now, I heard one of you referring to the deck as a floor,' he says with theatrical horror. 'Frankly, that's a criminal offence, so stand by to receive whilst I transmit!'

The young sailors shift uneasily as Garraghty launches into a well-practised monologue.

'Floors are called decks or flats, walls are bulkheads, and stairs are ladders. There are no halls or corridors, only passageways. There are no ceilings in a room, only overheads in a compartment. We don't have toilets, we have heads. We have scuttles, not windows – 'cept there ain't any on this ship. Entrances from one compartment to another are called doors – easy one for you. Openings from one deck to another are called hatches. The handles on a watertight hatch or door are called dogs . . .'

While still based at the soulless Lowden Building, the ship's company is spending more working days on board, but access remains strictly controlled by the ACA. Internal construction of some compartments continues, but the enormously complex, computer-controlled firefighting systems are now the principal priority. More than 4,000 sensors are linked to twice that number of sprinklers, in tune with the strictest design and build regulations. When she's laden with fuel, ammunition and explosives, the supercarrier's 1,600 plus personnel will function at the top end of the hazard spectrum, even outside a combat zone.

'You don't close a door or watertight hatch, you secure it . . .'

Now in full flow, Garraghty has his captive audience pinned against the wall. Correction. Bulkhead. Then, 'What the fuck . . . ?'

He stops mid-sentence, suddenly drenched by a torrential downpour.

'Bloody sprinklers!' Garraghty yells. 'You lot. Mops and buckets. At the *double*!'

A hundred men and women are soon busy trying to soak up the water pooling on the deck. Clouds of fine spray fill the air until at last someone manages to stem the flow.

Bob Hawkins appears. 'No fire reported from Ship's Control Centre,' he says. 'Either a spurious sensor or the sprinkler system is tits.'

'Bloody marvellous,' Garraghty rasps, dripping from head to foot. 'State-of-the-art firefighting system, eh? Hope we'll have an army of plumbers on board when we leave the wall . . .'

Lowden Building, 17 December

'Ah, Mr Garraghty . . .' Mark Deller is in the small communal kitchen, dipping a teabag into a chipped mug. 'Any new acquisitions?'

'You bet, sir. Some great bargains over the summer, and a good few over Christmas.' Garraghty is a celebrated aficionado of 1960s and 1970s retro furniture, wall hangings and memorabilia. He already has elaborate plans to pimp up his office and cabin. 'How's the secret-sofa situation?'

'Ha!' Deller exclaims. 'Not outed yet. We keep moving it around, covered in bubble-wrap to confuse snoopers.'

'The ACA got something against it?'

'They said it's not fire-tested. I told them you'd need a flame-thrower just to singe it, but they're not budging.'

'Fuckin' Ada!' Garraghty says. 'They won't like what I've got up my sleeve.'

Deller raises an eyebrow.

'A lovely bamboo-beaded door curtain for the main office, plaster ducks for the bulkhead, and some pink fluffy cushions to brighten the mood.'

Commander Air chuckles. 'Good luck with those!'

Garraghty returns to the office with a piping-hot brew for a now grim-faced Bob Hawkins, who tells him that the captain has been on the line and wants a Clear Lower Deck – that's the entire ship's company assembled – at 1500.

They both know that's not good news.

Jerry Kyd, jaw firmly set, is joined by Darren Houston at the far end of the cavernous hangar. As they approach, Bob

Hawkins brings 673 sailors to attention, then, once the formalities are over, orders them to stand at ease.

Kyd steps up on to a small dais, removes his hat and picks up the microphone and gives it a tap.

'Next year, 2017, is all about getting this ship to sea. All our efforts have been geared to leaving the wall on March 10th.' He pauses. 'Which is why it's important for me to stand here in front of you now, look you all in the eye and tell you . . . we're not going to be sailing on that date.'

There's a collective gasp. Hawkins doesn't flinch, but knows this is going to hit everyone hard. He wonders, too, what the press is going to make of yet another delay, not to mention the British public, who are paying for all this.

'I fully understand your frustration, trust me,' Kyd continues. 'The last thing I want as a sea captain is to sit here in the build basin, tied to the wall. But the truth is, I don't know when we're going to go. The ship's got a whole bunch of new systems, to detect fire and smoke and to smash it down . . .'

He pauses again.

'I look at some of you younger sailors . . .' he says. 'I've got a seventeen-year-old son, and my benchmark, the litmus test for me as your captain, boils down to this: would I put my son in your mess, your bunk space, your work-station and go to sea the way the ship is right now? And the answer is no.'

Before closing, he changes emotional gear.

'Christmas! Enjoy it and be ready to come back refreshed and revitalized. Next year we *will* make history. Don't forget that.'

Kyd leaves the dais, knowing all too well that he needs high morale every bit as much as he needs an efficient fire-fighting system. And that once it is broken, the most vital element for any ship's company can be difficult to fix.

10. All Aboard

0700

The ship's company report for duty before dawn, still downcast by Jerry Kyd's pre-Christmas announcement. But to their surprise, they're instructed to bypass the Lowden Building and head directly to the QE. They will not yet live on board but will, from now on, spend their working days there. This unexpected diversion from 'ship ashore' to 'ship afloat' provides a cheering start to the New Year.

Bob Hawkins, first through the entrance, goes straight to the staff board and slides the wooden indicator by 'First Lieutenant' from 'ashore' to 'on board'.

'It's official!' he shouts.

Hundreds of sailors emerge from the chill, rainswept darkness to queue in the glare of the ship's security lights for their turn to follow him up the gangway.

Executive Warrant Officer Dave Garraghty joins Hawkins for the journey to their shared office on 3 Deck. 'I feel like an eighteen-year-old on my first shift,' he says. 'I know there are tough days ahead, but it's amazing to be the ones to bring this ship alive.'

'Need to introduce you to someone, sir . . .' Grinning from ear to ear, Garraghty extracts a package from under his arm and unwraps a wild-haired, wide-eyed dummy. 'Meet Wilf!' he says gleefully.

Hawkins sighs. 'Car-boot?'

The EWO is a legendary car-boot-sale fanatic as well as an amateur ventriloquist.

'No, sir. Amazon. Car-booty to follow; got some cracking loot over Christmas!'

Jerry Kyd climbs the steps to the bridge on the for'ard island. His private lift isn't yet in commission. He will spend most of his time on the bridge when at sea, so his living quarters are immediately below. His night cabin is two steps across the passageway from his day cabin, also known as the Admiral's Bridge or the Flag Bridge. This spacious, L-shaped room looking out on to the flight deck one way and the sea the other will be one of the best appointed on the entire ship, with plush wall-to-wall carpeting and hand-picked furniture to complement Nick Gutfreund's Rose Table.

Junior Steward Kirsty Rugg will be his aide on a day-to-day basis. She'll not only be responsible for keeping his clothes pressed, shoes polished and meals served but will also ensure his routine runs as smoothly as possible. Once at sea, Kyd will be in command twenty-four hours a day. His time will never be his own, and plans will constantly change as events dictate, so her role is pivotal. They're at opposite ends of the rank spectrum, but their relationship will not be governed by that.

'Now, Steward Rugg,' he murmurs. 'Can you keep a secret?'

'Er, yessir,' she answers nervously.

'I'm partial to the occasional Chocolate Hobnob.'

'Oh, no problem, sir!' The young Mancunian giggles. 'I'll make sure we keep plenty in stock.'

'Excellent. I'm not really allowed them at home. My wife's a doctor . . .'

'Right, sir. Your secret's safe with me.'

Mark Deller has gathered his entire aviation wing, from aircraft handlers and specialist firefighters to air traffic controllers and air engineers.

'Right, fellas, as you know, the most important job on the whole ship is to keep this flight deck clean. FOD, or foreign object debris, is the number-one danger to any carrier. It could be anything from a plastic bag or a screwdriver to a coin – any of these could be ingested and stop the turbines, jam up the propellers and bring an aircraft down, putting everyone at risk – not just the pilots and you lot on deck, but the entire ship's company below.'

Deller most passionately addresses the youngsters straight from training, who've never been to sea before. He needs them to understand that the flight deck, where fully armed warplanes will launch and land, where high explosives and aviation fuel will be commonplace and which will be a natural target for enemy attack, is also a protective canopy for their community.

'Glance behind you at what's being written above the door leading to your locker room,' Deller says, gesturing towards a sign-painter's lettering on the external grey bulkhead. '"Nostris in Manibus Tuti". For those of you not fluent in Latin, it means "Safe in Our Hands". That's your motto. Never forget it.'

Emma Ranson, the Liverpudlian petty officer, nods appreciatively. She takes her job very seriously and can't wait to get her aircraft handlers working properly as a team. It's been a long time coming, but now they can put their little Lego men, cardboard cut-outs and dummy decks behind them. This is the real deal. She scans the vast expanse of deck and wonders how efficiently they'll be able to respond to emergencies. 'Fleet Standard Time to get to a fire is just thirty seconds,' Deller continues. 'And sixty to extinguish it. Usain Bolt would be hard-pressed to meet that challenge across a space bigger than three football fields.'

The young aircraft handlers look at each other uneasily.

'OK. Stand by for the *Queen Elizabeth*'s first ever FOD plod!' Deller yells.

They form a continuous line from port to starboard, and start to walk the length of the deck. Anything they spot, no matter how small, must be picked up and disposed of.

'Every time we go to flying stations, we FOD plod,' Deller bellows. 'We do it at the start of the day, we repeat it every six hours, and then we do it before we start night flying. It's a continual process, a bit like painting the Forth Road Bridge over there. Once finished, it's almost time to start again.'

During flying stations, Deller will be seated in a gallery at the back of Flyco that affords him not only a panoramic view of the deck but oversight of the control room below. The gallery, nicknamed the Papal Balcony, has a sprung leather seat dubbed the Papal Throne in which any incumbent Commander Air or Wings will be firmly anchored. His cabin, just down the passageway, is well appointed, but to his great dismay, too small to accommodate his precious but illicit sofa. After careful consideration he orders his team of loyal smugglers to retrieve it from its hiding place in the empty wine stores and take it, concealed in bubble wrap, to his grander office on 1 Deck. To his relief it fits perfectly, and there it'll now stay, with the ACA none the wiser. Deller has won the battle of the leather sofa through a combination of careful military planning, subterfuge and guile.

In his first Heads of Department (HODs) meeting on board Jerry Kyd entreats his commanders to be encouraging but forthright to their subordinates. 'Explain it this way,' he suggests. 'If you were building a new car or a jet liner or a new mobile phone you would have hundreds of prototypes, each one getting better and better until finally you get what you want – tested to the hilt. You say, "Great, this last model is now faultless, so let's start mass producing and sell it to the customer." You don't do that with ships, of course. It's just too expensive. So, this ship is first of a kind, it's the prototype *and* the finished product, and the one that's going to go round the world for five decades – all at the same time.'

16 May 2017

Jerry Kyd dons his hard hat and heads to one of the dockyard's huge fabrication sheds between HMS *Queen Elizabeth* and HMS *Prince of Wales*. The work being done here is highly classified, so he is quick to show his ID card. Once inside, he stands transfixed. High-pressure hoses are removing layers of protective wax from ten huge, gleaming bronze blades, five for each of the supercarrier's two propellers.

'They're awfy braw, are'nae they?' one of the operators volunteers in a thick Scottish brogue.

'Like modern art,' Kyd says. 'You could exhibit them!'

Top secret in design, they will be capable of generating 100,000 horsepower, enough to power fifty high-speed trains, or to push the QE through the water in excess of 27 knots.

17 May 2017

The blades are transported by heavy loader and crane to the QE's deck but all the time concealed under thick tarpaulins. This is to keep them out of the gaze of Russian and Chinese spy satellites. Knowledge of their precise shape and curvature would provide useful intelligence about the warship's power and propulsion potential and her sound signature in the water. Despite her size, the QE has been designed as a stealth warship, difficult to locate both by enemy radar above the waterline and by sonar below.

The engines have already been tested, along with the transfer of power to the water through the gearing system. To keep the ship stationary, the process had to be conducted without the propeller blades attached to their hubs. The driveshafts stretch nearly a third of the way along the hull, secured by a series of immense thrust blocks that will also absorb the kinetic energy generated by their dynamic rotation. If the fast-spinning shafts were to come loose, catastrophic damage would ensue.

Over the next two weeks the blades will be carefully lowered into position – the first time this has ever been attempted under water. Painstakingly bolted on to their hubs by teams of specialist divers working around the clock, each will be held in place by a total of 114 super-bolts and a multitude of sub-bolts.

ACA Marine Engineer Pat Midgely directs the operation from a floating platform at the stern. Every diver carries a helmet-camera so he can monitor every move via CCTV. There is no room for error.

'Diver two, attach bolt one, blade one,' he says. 'Tighten to three-quarters tension.'

Every bolt will be tightened incrementally, to ensure maximum strength of join. Each propeller will be capable of 190 revolutions a minute and generate the power of 1,000 family cars. If a blade slips or is dislodged by even a millimetre, the ship's ability to move through the water would be compromised.

Bob Hawkins is watching from the quayside with Dave Garraghty. This is the most exciting sign of progress he's seen to date and makes him bold enough to predict that they'll be away by the end of June.

'Next spring tide,' he says. 'I'd put money on it.'

Things are progressing above the waterline too. A white van's just arrived, with Nick Gutfreund at the wheel. Too big to carry on board, the Rose Table has to be hoisted in sections, but within an hour the cabinetmaker is hard at work on the Flag Bridge.

Kirsty Rugg will be entrusted with the responsibility of keeping the classic piece oiled and polished. 'Amazing,' she whispers as it takes shape. 'I'm not sure what I was expecting. But not this . . . I'm frightened to touch it!'

'It's a working table,' Gutfreund says. 'It'll benefit from a few scuffs, scrapes and spillages over the years.' He smiles. 'So don't be frightened of it. It's here to serve you – not the other way round!'

Rugg drapes it in a White Ensign.

Gutfreund takes a deep breath when her boss appears. 'Captain Kyd . . . Meet your Rose Table.'

'Where you'll be having your scran, sir . . .' Rugg gives a wry chuckle as she unveils the cabinetmaker's work of art.

You could hear a pin drop.

The 750 mm concave pedestal resembles freshly gathered

rose stems flaring out dramatically to support its 2,000 mm diameter top, upon which he has inlaid petals of beech, burr oak and walnut veneer. A raised boss at its centre in the shape of a Tudor Rose frames the flagship's red, green, white and gold crest, and the 5,000-year-old Norfolk bog oak provides a dramatic black lip around the table's edge.

'Wow!' Kyd whispers in awestruck admiration. 'Wow, wow, *wow*!'

'There's something else,' Gutfreund says. 'It has a secret.' He lifts off the raised boss to reveal a shallow rectangular cavity, in the centre of which, hinged and locked, is a highly polished brass plate.

He hands over a small key.

Kyd turns it and raises the plate. 'It looks like a letter box . . .'

'That's exactly what it is, captain. But you can only put things in. You can't take them out. It's a time capsule. Any heads of state, visiting politicians or military leaders can post a personal message. The only way to get them out will be to cut open the table at the end of the ship's life, fifty years from now.'

'Genius!' Kyd exclaims. 'Absolute genius!'

'That gives me the shivers, a bit,' Rugg says. 'It's like the table will know things we don't, for all that time.'

'You know who should post the first letter?' Kyd says.

'The Queen,' Gutfreund replies.

'Exactly!' Kyd claps his hands.

The arrival of the table seems like a good omen for Jerry Kyd. His stars are aligning at last.

And so they continue to do.

The ACA confirms that the ship's company can begin to live on board within two weeks. HMS *Queen Elizabeth* is about to become a home as well as a warship.

11. Our Ship Now

Rosyth Dockyard, 1 June 2017

0900

'Rip it all up, lads!' Bob Hawkins shouts. 'I want every scrap off the ship ASAP!'

The First Lieutenant is overseeing the removal of all the protective green matting.

'Fantastic!' He rubs his hands with relish. 'Lots of lovely scrubbing and polishing ahead, fellas. We'll need to keep these flats spotless.'

Hundreds of other crew members are arriving from Pod City and HMS *Caledonia*, laden with holdalls, suitcases and rucksacks. Tonight, they'll be sleeping on board for the first time. At a long line of desks in the hangar ACA reps are giving out 10,000 keys for living, work and recreational spaces. Most of the junior sailors are consigned to eight-man cabins but with 3-feet-wide bunks instead of the standard 2 feet 3 inches. Junior officers will share double cabins, whilst senior officers get their own.

Sailors often call their warships grey villages. The QE is in the process of becoming the Royal Navy's first grey city. All of life is here. Black, white, male, female, gay, straight, the godly and the godless, seasoned veterans with anchors and mermaids inked into muscled forearms, baby sailors fresh from training yet to succumb to the tattooist's needle or even their first tot of rum, senior officers who have sailed the seven seas and young midshipmen who've never spent a night afloat are unpacking clothes and displaying photos of family and loved ones on bulkheads and pinboards – stamping their identity on their ship.

Dave Garraghty steps back to admire his handiwork. 'How does that look, Bobbie?'

'Bit crooked,' Belfast-born Petty Officer Roberta Powell says. 'Needs to go up a bit on the right.'

'Copy that. Stand by.'

The car-boot enthusiast adjusts the bead curtain now hanging in the doorway of the Executive Department's main office, which he will share with Bob Hawkins. Sporting a bespoke sailor's uniform, run up by a former seamstress turned sailor, Wilf the ventriloquist's dummy looks on from a 1960s armchair, surrounded by an array of psychedelic soft furnishing and pop art paraphernalia. Garraghty's favoured decor does not always win the approval of his less flamboyant shipmates, but Hawkins is always game for a laugh.

'Any better?' Garraghty asks.

His long-suffering assistant nods. 'Spot on. Straighter than a straight thing!'

HMS *Queen Elizabeth* is bursting into life around them. Her very own corner shop will soon be open for business. Run by a team of four civilians, mostly ex-forces, the NAAFI is on a passageway named Little Britain. More street-signs are going up in the main thoroughfares, to reflect the ship's particular affiliation with London and Edinburgh, but in the event of emergencies it'll be essential for everyone to pinpoint positions more precisely for damage control and first aid teams. Any spot can be identified by a code comprising one number and one letter, followed when necessary by 'Starboard', 'Port' or 'Midships'. The numbers 1 to 9 indicate the deck and the letters run from Alpha at the bow to Zulu at the stern. 3 Alpha is thus the foremost section on 3 Deck; 7 Zulu the backend four decks below.

Dave Garraghty's office is 3 Foxtrot, and the main galley 5 Mike, where Wes Khan will be working at full blast to produce four meals a day: breakfast, lunch, supper and 'nine o'clockers' – aka heated-up leftovers.

Thirteen washing machines will soon be in use 24/7 in the ship's vast laundry, along with seven tumble dryers, three hydro-extractors, three ironing tables and two general-purpose pressers. When the QE is fully operational they will process 3.3 tons of uniforms, bedding and linen a day, with a guaranteed twenty-four-hour turnaround.

Substantial sections of the ship remain out of bounds owing to ongoing construction, but the ship's company is already becoming the vibrant community that was never possible when spread between HMS *Caledonia*, Pod City and the Lowden Building.

9 June

As Bob Hawkins predicted, the ACA has confirmed that sea trials can begin as early as the next spring tide – less than three weeks from now. The countdown has begun.

But there is one more obstacle to clear.

'OK, guys,' Jerry Kyd says. 'The next few days will be a wake-up call for all of us and probably won't be pretty.'

His HODs are gathered round the Rose Table. Kirsty Rugg is serving coffee as unobtrusively as possible.

'We should hope for the best but expect the worst,' Kyd continues.

The senior commanders glance knowingly at each other.

The QE's dockside energy supplies will be severed tomorrow, leaving her totally dependent on her own engines for the first time. And nobody will be allowed off the ship for six days as she embarks on an arduous journey without moving an inch. The Navy call this a 'test cruise'. Designed to push everyone to the limit, it is not for the faint-hearted.

'It's still a building site,' Kyd stresses. 'And we've a lot of young people who've never lived on a warship before – let alone an untested prototype. Some of them, I know, are quite nervous about what's coming up. But we need to prove ourselves before we go to sea for real.'

He pushes back in his chair.

'We're going to have a few shocks and surprises when we start testing the ship's systems for the first time. Things will get worse before they get better, but we need to shake out any gremlins. If we get this right, we go to sea in the next tidal window. If we don't, we're in trouble.'

The timing of departure has become critical. The summer solstice on 21 June will give Kyd the highest of high tides, perfect for getting out of the basin, and the lowest of low tides, perfect for going under the bridges. These optimal conditions will only last a few days. It would be weeks before the next opportunity, and even then, the long-range weather forecast promises increasingly high winds. The QE's profile will act like a series of huge metal sails, and winds over 15 knots would make her too difficult to handle in such a confined space. If Kyd cannot get out by 26 June he knows he could be stuck here for months to come.

10 June

0800

The gangways remain in place, but every entrance is closed and locked. To all intents and purposes the carrier is at sea.

Almost immediately the general alarm sounds, followed by an urgent announcement. *'For exercise, for exercise, for exercise. Fire, fire, fire. 5 Mike Port side.'*

Fire teams head straight for 5 Deck to overcome a simulated fire – complete with smoke bombs – in the main galley. All exercises are observed and timed by independent adjudicators from the Navy's Flag Officer Sea Training (FOST), who are as meticulous as they are unforgiving.

'Walk, don't run!' Dave Garraghty reminds those who are tempted to pick up the pace. 'Running leads to tripping, falling and causing a pile-up. Which means not only injury but wasting valuable time.'

The relentless stream of punishing fire and flood exercises continues day and night. Nobody knows when or where the next one will occur, but reaction must be immediate. Sometimes several emergencies are called simultaneously. In combat, there will be multiple challenges of this kind, including casualties, and some of the dry-runs include 'dead' and 'injured' volunteers dripping with fake blood.

Unplanned, spurious alarms triggered by faulty sensors are inevitable on a brand-new ship. But these too demand a full and immediate response, until everything's been checked and the relevant sensors reconfigured. No chances can be taken, and the constant need for vigilance and speed of reaction starts to take its toll.

'The boys and girls are bloody exhausted!' Garraghty mutters as they respond to yet another screeching siren.

'New house syndrome,' Hawkins says.

There were always going to be kinks in the system, but false alarms on top of exercises are pushing people hard.

The test cruise continues without let-up. Every scenario is carefully monitored, timed and assessed. If the sailors fail to impress, Jerry Kyd will be forced to delay departure yet again. And then, suddenly and without warning, the weather throws another curve-ball, and the pretence of being at sea has to be temporarily suspended.

Vital food supplies have arrived on the quayside. Not wanting to interfere with the test cruise, Fiona Percival had arranged for them to be 'slung' on board by civilian cranes, but strengthening winds have rendered them inoperable. Bringing on the tons of food by hand is the only option. Which means sailors are required. As many as possible.

Bob Hawkins pipes the ship's company.

'D'ye hear there?' he says in traditional style. 'First Lieutenant speaking. Clear lower deck of all available personnel. Report to the hangar for your best work-out of the week.'

Within minutes a massive human chain, comprising all ranks, stretches along the quayside, up the aft gangway to the storage lifts. Thousands of boxes, cartons, crates and packets are passed along it, hand to hand. Nelson's sailors would have strong-armed sides of salt beef, tubs of fat, barrels of beer, raw sugar and pickled cabbage aboard, not to mention live pigs, goats and chickens. Today it is frozen meats, pre-packed fish and poultry, milk, breakfast cereals, sauces, spices, condiments, cake-mixes and an enormous amount of baked beans — but the essence of the human conveyor belt hasn't changed.

'You know what?' Bob Hawkins passes Fiona Percival a voluminous box of Honey Flavoured Crunchy Nuts. 'Automation's all very well, but there's nothing like rolling up the sleeves and working together for morale.'

She doesn't disagree.

'Butterscotch Angel Delight incoming!'

Within three hours the QE is back 'at sea'. The aircraft handlers and firefighters have just run through a crash-on-deck exercise – well within the required sixty seconds.

Deller beams at his team in Flyco. 'That's an important box ticked. I can put my happy face on now –'

He stops mid-sentence. The screech of another siren is followed by an urgent alert: '*Flood, flood, flood . . . flood in 7 Golf. Emergency party to investigate . . .*'

'That's not good!' Deller says. 'No "for exercise" prefix. This one's for real.'

Marine Engineer Petty Officer 'Big' Bruce Milne is already descending the ladders; 7 Golf is his space – home to one of the four mighty diesel engines. Minutes earlier, he'd been sitting in the Ship's Control Centre (SCC) on 5 Deck when one of his team burst in, drenched and breathing hard. 'Flood in Forward Engine Room!' he gasped. 'Couldn't get through on comms . . . ran all the way . . . water coming in everywhere!'

Ignoring the 'walk don't run' directive, Milne sprinted past the damage control teams already climbing into their dry suits or firefighting overalls. Any water in the Forward Engine Room could be catastrophic. The high-voltage cables, carrying a charge of 11,000 volts, could short circuit and cause a high-intensity electrical arc. The maximum temperature of an arc flash is 10,000 Kelvin – nearly 10,000 °C. With rapidly expanding hot air and the explosive vaporization of metal and insulation material, anyone in the vicinity would be killed or severely maimed.

Lieutenant Commander John Ball, aka 'Damage' (i/c Damage Control), pipes from the SCC to the whole ship. *'D'ye hear there – all training to cease throughout the ship until the Standing Sea Emergency Party has dealt with the flood and fire hazard. Stand by for updates.'*

Wes Khan has left the galley to perform his secondary task as emergency back-up to the firefighters. He helps them pull on their oxygen tanks.

'You'll be fine,' he reassures one young sailor at emergency stations for the first time. 'Your training will kick in, and you'll always be in a team.'

The young sailor nods appreciatively but then starts to suck hard on the regulator of his breathing apparatus.

Khan reaches up to adjust his full-face helmet. 'Make sure there's no gap between face and mask,' he says calmly. 'Try that . . .'

The sailor takes another deep breath and gives a thumbs-up. Wes Khan, also a first aider, will now be on emergency standby until further notice. Marinating the lamb will have to wait.

Torrents of water cascade into the diesel engine compartment as marine engineers frantically cover electrical appliances with plastic sheeting. The main circuit has been switched off, but residual currents may still be live. The threat is far from over as water could be draining into compartments below.

A high-level cooling pipe has ruptured, causing sea water to dam up behind the lagging until the pressure finally became too much to contain.

As the deluge continues, Warrant Officer Dave Perry leads a team to the deck below and starts to unfasten the hatch into another high-voltage compartment. *Danger of Death* is emblazoned across the bright-yellow hazard warning sign, but Perry carries on regardless. Once the dozens of bolts are off, he shines his torch through the opening. 'Water ingressing!' he shouts.

Damage's team in the SCC reacts instantaneously to incoming information over the radio as well as from Dave Garraghty, who's running constantly between here and the engine room in case radio comms should fail.

'Latest sitrep, sir,' he says. 'Electrical circuits switched off in all water-affected areas but water escaping into lower compartments.'

'Thanks, EWO,' John Ball replies. 'Flood sensors activated successfully. Circuits already switched off.'

Ball shouts 'Command huddle!' every few minutes. His entire team form a tight scrum so that everyone can update everyone else on different aspects of the emergency response: electrical circuits, water pressure, damage control teams, casualties and immediate intentions. After every huddle a pipe is made to the ship's company to keep everyone up to speed.

Back in the diesel space, fire suppressant foam has been released and lies like fresh snow beneath the engines. The firefighters wait anxiously outside while the marine engineers continue to wrestle with the flood. Some are attending to the ruptured cooling pipe, while others are either mopping up water or continuing to cover electrical panels and circuits.

After a frenetic hour, the hazard is contained, and the emergency teams are given the order to stand down. Exhausted sailors collapse into heaps along the passageways and are immediately given water before being helped out of their kit.

Wes Khan checks that everyone is OK and not in need of the sickbay. 'This is crazy, man!' He gives his trademark chuckle. 'Testing a brand-new ship's going to be much more difficult than testing an old one. We're in for exciting times!'

22 June

'Ship's Company!' Bob Hawkins yells. 'Ship's Company, stand at ease!'

Nearly 700 sailors have formed a neat square on the flight deck. Following the gruelling test cruise, Jerry Kyd has called another Clear Lower Deck. He's met with the ACA and the FOST observers and wants to deliver news of their decision personally.

'Ship's Company . . . Ship's Company, ho!'

Kyd pauses to survey the hundreds of expectant faces from the dais. 'Right!' he proclaims. 'I won't beat about the bush. We *will* sail on Monday. That's 26 June.'

There is an audible gasp of relief from officers and ratings alike. Murmurs of 'yessss!' ripple through the ranks.

Kyd smiles too, but his tone could not be more serious. 'For those of you who've not been to sea before, there's no cavalry or fire brigade when we move off the wall. We'll have emergencies, we'll have floods. We'll have fires. And casualties too. That's the nature of this business.'

He pauses again.

'But this is our ship now,' he says. 'And don't forget it.'

12. Let Go All Lines

Rosyth Dockyard Inner Basin, 26 June 2017

1000

The tide is high, the winds are light, and the ocean beckons. The pole-mast is being lowered to allow the QE to pass under the land bridges. A small fleet of tugboats has gathered in the build basin to help manoeuvre the QE into open waters.

Jerry Kyd now gives the most significant order of his seagoing career to date. 'Let go all lines!'

'Let go all lines!' the Bosun repeats over the main broadcast system.

All the way down the quayside, dockworkers unbutton constraining ropes and cables from their capstans and cast them into the water. Parties of seamen, working like tug o' war teams, haul them on board, hand over hand.

The tugs on her seaward side start to reverse, and their own lines to the carrier grow taut. Jerry Kyd looks down from the bridge wing and sees the smallest gap open up between his ship and the quayside. 'We're no longer attached to Scotland!' he declares.

The gap continues to grow as the tugs gain further traction on the 65,000-ton behemoth. Until she is in the open sea, this will remain a 'cold' move – her newly attached propellers have yet to make a single revolution. The carrier has to be carefully turned in the harbour basin so that her bow points directly at the sea gate. Its sliding barriers are already open, but with less than 6 inches clearance either side it's going to be a very delicate piece of micro-navigation for all concerned.

And the clock is ticking.

Many of the ship's company are already out on the flight deck taking photographs or filming the departure on their mobile phones. Thousands are watching from the dockyard – mostly construction workers who've helped build her. For those who first started work on her hull sections in Govan back in 2009, she's been part of their lives for almost a decade. These are tough, rugged working men – fabricators, scaffolders, welders and riveters – but more than a few are weeping without shame.

Kirsty Rugg takes a break from polishing the Rose Table and emerges on to the bridge wing to watch the exit through the sea gate. 'We'll never get through that!' she whispers.

Steadied by tugs inside the basin and pulled by others in the Firth of Forth, the QE's bow is perfectly centred as she edges forward. The vast flight deck overhangs the sea wall on both sides so everyone below is cast into her shadow. There's a moment of panic – she is about to smash into a street light – but, to cheers from above, quick-thinking dockworkers dismantle it in the nick of time.

With less than 20 inches of water beneath her and only 14 either side, the QE gradually squeezes out of the build basin. As soon as her stern passes the gate, Jerry Kyd gives his first order at sea. 'A blast on the foghorn, please, Bosun!'

Jay Early obliges, and HMS *Queen Elizabeth*'s mighty foghorn is sounded for the first time. Louder than a rock concert, at 146 decibels, it can be heard 2 miles away.

'Wow!' Wes Khan shouts on the flight deck. 'At sea, at last.'

'Where we should be,' Big Bruce Milne says. 'Now we can really get on with the job.'

The tugs push, pull and nudge the QE towards the right-hand bank of the Firth, where she must drop anchor and wait for the next 6 hours, until the tide falls to its lowest ebb.

2359

The witching hour. The 'cold' move can now become hot.

'Fifty revolutions, both levers,' Jez Brettel intones.

'Fifty revolutions, both levers,' the helmsman repeats as he turns the speed dials accordingly.

The water starts to boil as the vast bronze propellers turn for the first time and the carrier moves forward under her own power. Jerry Kyd, on the bridge with his navigation team, guides her towards the bridges. 'She feels good,' he tells Darren Houston. 'Not vibrating, turning on a sixpence. First signs very positive.'

She passes under the new Road Bridge with plenty of room to spare. Then the old Road Bridge with rather less. Which leaves only the Rail Bridge to negotiate.

'I don't believe it, sir!' Jez Brettel raises his binoculars. 'You could be up for that bottle of port . . . !'

With barely a 6-foot gap between them and the Victorian superstructure, the navigating team look up at the underside of the Edinburgh to Dunfermline train.

'Congratulations, sir!' Darren Houston beams. 'A good omen!'

'Steady as she goes . . .' Jerry Kyd knows full well that good omens, right now, are very welcome.

13. Omnium Gatherum

North Sea, 27 June 2017

0600

It's less than six hours since the QE successfully limboed under the Forth bridges. She's now sailing free off the east coast of Scotland and heading into her proving ground. After years in the build basin with less than 3 feet of water under her hull, she now has many hundreds of fathoms.

Down in the hangar, circuits are underway. Petty Officer Physical Trainer 'Sticky' Vercoe is putting thirty early birds of all ranks through their paces.

'Pick up those knees, shipmates!'

Everyone tries to sustain thirty seconds' running on the spot. It's a regular warm-up exercise but is proving more difficult now than it did in port. The gentle pitch and roll of the ocean is almost imperceptible on a ship this size, but anyone trying to run or balance will feel the slightest lurch or change of incline.

'Five hundred eggs for the fryer. And another hundred to scramble.' Wes Khan is overseeing the preparation of their first breakfast at sea. If he was frustrated in Rosyth with nothing to do, he's now at the other end of the labour spectrum but delighted to be raising his game.

The directive to the ship's company from the Admiralty is

that the carrier's war-fighting capability on its flight deck, bridge, engine room and gunnery positions must be matched by its prowess in all other areas. The chefs must be able to provide food for 1,000 (rising to a maximum of 1,600) in all situations and all weathers. Sailors will require different food types and food groups to the pilots, who will need to eat when they can between flights, especially during combat missions. Next year, Royal Marine Commandos will present a special challenge, expected as they are to consume around 7,000 calories a day – three times the average sailor's. The galleys will also have to switch at a moment's notice to 'action messing' (the production of 'slop' – stews, soups and pastas for rapid consumption – in under three minutes) during emergencies or when at action stations.

Wes Khan and his cohorts must also be able to produce the finest haute cuisine, baking and patisserie for ceremonial and royal occasions. A very substantial piece of floating real estate, the QE will be regarded as sovereign British territory wherever she goes and boast cuisine to match. Her wine and port cellars will also be unparalleled. Beer will come in all brands, including a specially brewed HMSQNLZ label. But for now, the ship remains 'dry', according to ACA diktat. This forced abstinence might be a burden for some, but not Wes Khan. The devout Muslim is teetotal.

'Stand by to raise the shutters!' he bellows. 'First breakfast queue's getting restless . . .'

1100

The navigators peer through a thin veil of sea mist with high-powered binoculars. For many years the only view from this position was of the tree-lined North Deer Park on the opposite bank of the Forth, but now the bridge team is looking at a boisterous, steel-grey ocean through which their ship is slicing with ease. Jerry Kyd, in the captain's chair on the port side, has a good view ahead as well as of the entire flight deck below him. Scott McLaren, the ACA Sea Trials Director, has joined him.

'The first thing's to see how fast she can move,' Kyd says.

'Aye,' McLaren replies. 'It'll be grand to see what she's like at full speed. It feels like she wants to lift her skirts and stretch her legs.'

'We have to rendezvous with HMS *Sutherland* and *Iron Duke* this morning.' Kyd scans the distant horizon through his binoculars. 'But this afternoon we'll put our foot down for the first time.'

Down on 5 Deck, Leading Hand Ricky Gleason, a small but wiry amateur boxer, is sorting through 'gash'. He's an aircraft handler but has volunteered to work additional hours in the pyrolysis plant for an extra £7 a day. The rubbish-processing plant shreds, crushes and ultimately incinerates the ship's refuse. His job is to check that the sacks from the mess decks have been properly sorted — metal, glass or rubber would seriously damage the machinery — and he rules with an iron fist.

'Whadya call that!' he barks at a junior rating.

'Just an old trainer.'

'With a sodding great rubber sole. That'd fuck the machine up good and proper.'

'Sorry. I didn't put it in there.'

The solid waste and final treatment system is one of two on board. Whilst state-of-the-art, it remains untested. The process breaks down the molecular structure of food waste,

bio-sludge, dry solids, waste oil and medical waste by exposing it to temperatures in excess of 800 degrees. The leftover
product, known as char, is stored in drums for disposal
ashore. To further reduce the volume of non-recyclable
waste, the ship is fitted with glass-processing equipment
which crushes and compacts it for subsequent recycling.

Given that the 1,000 people on board will produce upwards
of 9 tons of waste daily, gash management will be vital. Any
failure would quickly reduce her battle readiness, even force
her to exit the battle space to come alongside.

'Any deodorants?'

The hapless sailor holds up another black bag.

'Right, gimme,' Gleason barks. 'At least you managed to
separate that.'

He empties the contents on to his sorting bench and puts
unfinished deodorants on a shelf behind him.

'Me salvage!' He winks. 'Gotta have some perks.'

More lovable-rogue than career criminal these days,
Gleason is the ship's resident bad boy. His past, by his own
admission, was chequered. From a broken home, he lived
on the street and plunged into drugs and petty crime. By
the age of twenty-one he had forty-nine convictions and
served several short sentences at Reading Prison as well as
Feltham, Huntercombe and Low Newton but, determined
to turn his life around, took a job as a bin-man in South
Shields and kept his nose clean. After a few years of honest
endeavour, the Navy gave him the big opportunity he
craved.

'Next!' Gleason bellows at the queue of impatient sailors
outside his sorting compartment.

A hefty and heavily tattooed stoker throws down two large
bags. There's an audible clang as one hits the deck.

Gleason is instantly alert. 'Open up that fuckin' bag, shipmate . . . !'

Jerry Kyd is watching two Royal Navy warships closing fast on his stern. HMS *Sutherland* and HMS *Iron Duke*, both Type 23 frigates, have come out to salute the QE. Two Mark 2 Merlin helicopters are also circling in honour of the new carrier.

Kyd walks out on the bridge wing with some of his junior officers.

'This is the start of the carrier strike journey now,' he shouts into the wind.

'When the QE is deployed operationally, she'll be surrounded by such escorts.

'The combination of different force elements – ships, frigates, destroyers, submarines and aircraft – is what'll really give us our military potency. This is your future . . .'

The three warships sail together for an hour before the frigates diverge. The Merlins give their final salute before returning to Lossiemouth. One of them will be returning in six days to become the first aircraft to land on the QE's flight deck – the moment the ship's company will truly be able to say they are sailing an aircraft carrier.

1330

With the ocean spread out in front of them, Jerry Kyd and Scott McLaren decide it's time for the QE's first speed trial. Working closely with Neil McCallum, Commander Marine Engineering, they divert more power from the ship's two gas turbines and four diesels to her driveshafts, taking them up to 90 revolutions per minute, about three-quarters power.

'Feel that muscle,' Kyd says. The speed dial now indicates 25 knots plus. 'Hold her there. Very smooth. No noticeable vibration.'

Ten minutes later they bring it down to 15.

'She can certainly sprint,' Kyd says.

'I reckon there's even more under the bonnet,' Neil McCullum ventures.

Scott McLaren nods. 'Nay doubt about that, gentlemen. It bodes well. I've nae issue about taking the revs up to 100.'

For two hours the ship is put through her paces on the straight and on the turn. And this is just the beginning. Over the next days and weeks they must push her at varying speeds through as many sea states as possible, both forwards and backwards. It will be an unforgiving test not only of her speed but also her manoeuvrability and robustness. When operational, HMS *Queen Elizabeth* must be able to cover up to 500 miles a day and, with a range of 10,000 miles (on one full tank), should be able to go anywhere in the world at short notice. Once in a theatre of war, she will need to move as fast as possible through the water to generate enough wind across the deck for jet fighters to be able to launch.

These power and propulsion trials are, therefore, critical. It's essential to establish the QE's technical limits and breaking points before the even more critical flight trials with the F-35 next year. Naval and ACA engineers in the SCC monitor her vital signs via the thousands of sensors that feed into their computers. A wall of TV screens give them 'eyes on' most of the high-priority spaces such as engine rooms and other high-voltage compartments. A line of observers, continuously switching between cameras, maintain constant surveillance as more and more strain is put on the ship. She is effectively being tested to destruction.

1600

Black storm clouds are moving in from the north as the QE muscles her way through an increasingly thuggish sea. Waves leap at the ship's sides, whipped up by a strengthening wind, making her glisten in the rapidly darkening day. The flight-deck teams, conducting a routine FOD plod, suddenly turn to the piercing whistle at the stern.

'SOS smoke off the port beam!'

A column of white smoke spirals about 200 yards out, and beneath it an orange lifebelt tossed by the frenzied waves. Within seconds the general alarm siren sounds another alert.

'Man overboard, man overboard, man overboard. Sea boats away port side.'

Everybody on the upper deck and the bridge looks out with growing consternation. The sea-boat crews are quickly lowered. HMS *Sutherland*, which has remained in view, turns towards the QE at full speed and launches her own helicopter for a low-level surface search.

Operation 'Thimble Hunt' is triggered; everyone not on duty must assemble in their mess decks for a full headcount. It's a huge logistical operation overseen by Dave Garraghty and Bob Hawkins, essential to confirm that everybody, including ACA workers, can be accounted for.

Heartfelt concern spreads through the ship's company. Sailors know the hostility of the elements all too well. Nobody will survive in the North Sea for long, even in the summer months.

It takes less than thirty minutes to determine that no one is missing. Only then is the search called off. Investigations show that a spurious alarm triggered the automatic ejection of a safety buoy which, on contact with the water, activated its smoke canister. Jerry Kyd is delighted at the speed of response. Next time it could be for real – and rescue attempts at sea often come down to very fine margins.

Now back at his work station, Wes Khan dons his rubber gloves, in accordance with his Imam's special dispensation. He still has dozens of pork joints to skin and roast before dinner.

Once done, he absents himself from the galley. His third prayer of the day – *Salat al'asr* – is well overdue. When he first moved aboard in Rosyth there was nowhere for him to observe his devotions, but his shipmates immediately agreed that the spare eight-man cabin on his mess deck, earmarked as a quiet area for writing, reading or playing video games, should be reserved for private prayer – touching confirmation of how embracing the Navy can be.

Khan stops at the cabin door. 'Prayer Room' is marked on a Post-it note. He knocks and waits. Some Christians also use it, his own best friend, the Nepalese storeman Ramesh Rai, among them. No one answers. Khan enters, unrolls his prayer carpet, places his Koran on the table and kneels in supplication. He'd normally have to pray towards Mecca, but on an ever-moving warship that's easier said than done. He's decided to always pray away from the door, so he'll be facing in the right direction for at least some of the time.

'*Al u Akbar . . .*' he murmurs, then bows low to deliver his formal exhortations and recitations according to the Koranic scriptures. Finally, he sits back to deliver his own private prayers. He finishes, as always, with an entreaty for the well-being and safety of his captain and shipmates.

1830

'One elephant, two elephant, three elephant . . .' Bob Hawkins barks.

Blowing a Bosun's whistle is also easier said than done. The eyes of the young rating beside him are beginning to bulge, but he perseveres. Originally used to pass commands when the human voice would not carry above the sounds of the wind and sea, it now heralds the senior officer's evening rounds.

'. . . four elephant, five elephant, six elephant . . . keep going . . . seven elephant, eight elephant. OK, that's it!'

The red-faced rating gasps for a breath.

'That's good!' Hawkins slaps him on the back. 'That's how long you need to keep up the pipe as we proceed through the ship, OK?'

'Yessir. I'll do my best.'

'Good man. Let's go.'

The tradition dates back to the time of Henry VIII's navy, when formal visits to every mess deck, every evening, were initiated to both deliver information and hear concerns. Such daily personal contact between Command and the lower ranks has always been deemed vital to morale.

'Sir, Stokers' Mess, 8 Romeo, ready for evening rounds.'

Hawkins thanks the young sailor and returns his salute. 'Lead on.'

About a hundred of his shipmates are sitting shoulder to shoulder and rigidly to attention in the main mess square.

'Relax, gentlemen.' Hawkins takes a seat himself. 'A word of thanks from Command for all the hard work getting us to sea. And a special chuck-up for the excellent response to Thimble Hunt this afternoon. Stay alert, fellas — that won't be our last emergency. Next big thing for us will be first land-ing of an aircraft in six days' time. Flyco's likely to call a whole-ship FOD plod, so if you're free, get up there to give a hand. In return you'll get a gulp or two of fresh air. Right – anything from you?'

A forest of hands punch the air.

'Bloody hell,' Hawkins grimaces. 'Let me have it then!'

A barrage of complaints are delivered at machine-gun speed.

'Sir, the heads are a shambles – half of 'em already blocked . . .'

'Sir, the doors are deadly. The locking levers fall back and crack you on the head . . .'

'Sir, the scran queues go on for ever . . .'

Hawkins tries to remain philosophical while scribbling frantically in his notebook. 'Well, we knew it wasn't going to be perfect from the get go, didn't we?'

1900

'Help . . . !'

Kirsty Rugg's in a spot of bother.

'Hello . . . ! Can anyone hear me . . . ?'

The junior steward was returning from the galley with Jerry Kyd's supper tray. The captain's lift hasn't been officially signed off by the ACA engineers, but she decided to try it rather than climb the numerous stairs to the top of the for'ard island. Just as she was thinking how smooth the ride was in the coffin-sized, one-person elevator, it juddered to a halt between decks.

'Is that you, Steward Rugg?' Jerry Kyd shouts through the lift door outside his cabin.

'Yessir! Stuck in the lift.'

'Are you OK?'

'Yessir. But I have your supper with me.'

'Oh no! That makes it a real disaster . . .'

'Sorry, sir.'

'Only joking! Main thing's to get you out. We'll alert the engineers.'

'OK, sir. Thank you, sir.'

After a quick call to Darren Houston, Kyd returns.

'Steward Rugg?'

'Sir!'

'Have you eaten yet?'

'No, sir. Not yet.'

'Better dig in then. You may be there for some time!'

'Are you sure, sir?'

'Yes. Crack on. While it's still hot.'

Twenty minutes later, the engineers are cranking up the lift by hand.

'Steward Rugg!' Jerry Kyd shouts.

'Yessir!'

'You'll be free very soon. How was my supper?'

'Very nice, thank you, sir. I'll get you some more when I'm out.'

'Don't worry. Leading Steward Munroe's seen to that.'

'OK, sir. That's good.'

'But you're OK? That's the main thing.'

There's a moment's silence. 'Dying for a pee, sir . . .'

'Hold that thought, Steward Rugg. And that bladder . . .'

'Yessir.' Rugg laughs. 'You know what I was just thinking, sir?'

'Go on.'

'The recruitment brochure promised that every day is different in the Royal Navy. Not wrong, were they, sir?'

2130

HMS *Queen Elizabeth* sails across the orange and purple flecked water towards the eastern horizon as the sun sets behind her, carrying a thousand souls fast melding into a community united by common endeavour. She will undergo numerous shifts of character during her lifetime but will always be the product of the here and now – a reflection of those who inhabit her, drive her, maintain her and, increasingly, care for her.

14. Merlin Descends

0600

The wind is up and the sea growing increasingly agitated. Visibility is poor and dark, ominous clouds are looming low over the QE as she enters a thick fog bank. Her external sensors have automatically activated the horn, which is sounding every twenty seconds.

'Let's get out of this weather, Navigator,' Jerry Kyd says.

'Yessir.' Jez Brettel recommends heading due west. 'It's clear 70 miles from here, according to satellite imagery.'

'Concur,' Kyd says. 'Half speed until we're out of this and then put your foot to the floor. I don't want anything holding us up, today of all days.'

Later this morning a Mark 2 Merlin will be coming in from Lossiemouth and will need much better visibility to touch down safely. Jerry Kyd must go in search of clear weather.

Despite the prevailing conditions, the aircraft handlers are already out on deck checking the fire-tenders and executing the first FOD plod of the day. In a few hours they may be called to flying stations for the very first time. For Emma Ranson it's been a long time coming, but her excitement is tempered by nerves. Her team will be bringing the first Merlin in to land. The current weather is not helping her mental preparation and neither is the fact that her safety goggles hurt like hell. Her face is swollen on one side and she's sporting an impressively purpled eye.

'Beautiful shiner, PO Ranson,' Mark Deller says. 'Been annoying the stokers again?'

'No, sir. It was one of the steel doors last night. They're horrendous. I pushed up the lever to open one door and thought it had clicked and locked in the upper position but then it swung back and hit me in the face. They're all calling me Rocky today!'

Deller chuckles. 'Your first war wound on HMS *Queen Elizabeth*.'

'Yessir,' Ranson laughs. 'But I'd still rather be here than sitting back in Rosyth.'

More than a few door-inflicted 'war wounds' have been suffered over the last few days – bumps on the head, black eyes, one cracked tooth and a dislocated finger. Dave Garraghty and his assistant Bobbie Powell are busy checking all the steel doors and marking the ones with faulty locking mechanisms. Each defective door now boasts a sign saying 'Use Alternative Route'.

'This ship was already a maze,' Garraghty says. 'Now it's turning into a black hole. People are going to be sucked into it and lost for ever.'

'You could be right,' Powell says. 'How do we get back to 3 Foxtrot from here?'

'Up to 2 Deck, across and down at the Golf stairwell?'

'We already blocked that!'

'Oh yes. OK. Down to 5 Juliet. Up to 3 Juliet and back down at 3 Delta.'

'We blocked that too.'

0930

Bob Hawkins is on 5 Deck with Petty Officer Sticky Vercoe, who, when not overseeing physical training as the ship's senior Club Swinger, helps the First Lieutenant oversee gash collection and upkeep of the heads.

'Five cubicles in this passageway and only one functioning!' Hawkins is incredulous. 'And it's not much better anywhere else. Not acceptable. What's the main issue, Clubz?'

'People are trying to flush hand-towels as well as the toilet paper.'

'Right, it's a case of head-discipline,' Hawkins rasps. 'Basic hygiene. This is one for evening rounds, daily orders and a general pipe. Gotta sort this out pronto. It could be a real breeder of disease. We have to make these heads out of bounds for public safety.'

'In fairness, sir, I don't think it's our guys. The ACA treat them like public toilets and think they're constantly maintained by cleaners.'

'God help us!' the former bomb-disposal expert snarls. 'I used to blow shit up for a living. Now I have to clear it up!'

They try to move up to the deck above but the door to the stairwell has been taped up.

'Up to the hangar and across?' Hawkins suggests.

'Could try it, sir,' Vercoe replies. 'No guarantees right now.'

1200

Some hard sailing has taken the QE into calm seas under clear skies. The clouds that had enveloped her this morning and threatened today's flying plans now sit harmlessly on the southwestern horizon.

With an hour to go before the first helicopter is due to land, Mark Deller has called for a 'whole-ship' FOD plod, partly to get the ship's company used to flight-deck discipline and to encourage other departments to play a more active role in aviation. Although there are multiple ways out on to the flight deck, safety and security demands that everyone uses only one designated exit and entrance, through the access door under the aft island. Human traffic here has to be monitored and controlled at all times.

Within ten minutes, 150 sailors have assembled in a line that stretches the entire width of the ship. Jez Brettel picks up the bridge microphone.

'D'ye hear there? Navigator speaking. The focus for today is the first landing of a helicopter from 820 Squadron on our flight deck. It's the day we become an aircraft carrier.'

This is the culmination of two years' training for the flight-deck teams, so the sense of expectation and nervous excitement is palpable. And right now, the Merlin is running late.

'Listen up, everyone,' Mark Deller says from his Papal Throne. 'The cab's been held up by the weather we've escaped. It's a pain but points up one very considerable truth about carrier aviation. When we woke up this morning we had Situation Red, really poor conditions, cloud on deck, no visibility whatsoever. It would've put the kibosh on flying. But because we're mobile, we could reposition – something a land-based airfield can't.'

Flying at sea has to be precisely timed. If a planned rendezvous between carrier and aircraft goes awry, there might be nowhere for the aircraft to land before it runs out of fuel or succumbs to battle damage.

Finding a carrier on the high seas isn't easy, and landing on it seldom straightforward. The ship has to be turned into wind, giving an approaching aircraft lift, so landing or launching involves complex choreography between the bridge, Flyco, hangar, deck and pilot. And even more so if there are several aircraft waiting to land as others are taking off.

A full hour late, the Merlin Mark 2 appears on the QE's radar screens.

'*Hands to flying stations, hands to flying stations!*' the ship's broadcast system announces. '*The ship is now at flying stations.*'

The aircraft handlers assemble in their crew room in the aft island. Bringing a 40-ton helicopter on to a moving platform is no mean feat – especially for the first time.

'Right, guys!' Emma Ranson shouts over the excited chatter. 'Nothing's going to happen today that you've not covered in training. Be guided by those who've done this before, and it'll be a walk in the park, OK? Ready for this?'

'Yes!'

'Everyone happy?'

'Happy!'

'OK, let's do it!'

'Have we got visual yet?' Mark Deller asks of his team in Flyco.

Most are scanning the sky.

'Just seagulls, sir.'

'Noted,' Deller says gravely. 'Let the aircrew know we've got birds.'

The high risk of bird strikes provides another major challenge. Gulls, in particular, flock to ships to perch on or find food, and one ingested by a jet engine could bring it down.

'Visual, sir! Seven o'clock.'

Deller briefs Jez Brettel immediately. 'We have visual, Navs. But birds circling the stern.'

'Thanks, Wings. We're monitoring from here too. Am increasing speed to try and leave birds behind.'

'Roger that, Navs,' Deller says. 'In old money we'd probably have got out a shotgun just to let 'em know we were around, but, er, we can't do that any more!'

'No, sir. Definitely not!'

The grey Merlin is closing fast. It swoops down from 1,000 feet, and executes a low-level fly-by down the QE's port side as a salute before circling to land. The helicopter is piloted by twenty-six-year-old Lieutenant Luke Wraith from Yorkshire. He got his wings only eighteen months ago so was surprised but delighted to be chosen as the first rotary-wing pilot to land on the QE. He assumed the honour would go to someone more experienced, but today is all about new beginnings.

Wraith flies halfway down the port side of the ship and slows to a hover. There are six main landing spots on the 4-acre flight deck, but today Wraith will land on 3 Spot right in front of Flyco. A year from now the first F-35 will land on 3 Spot too, but the ship and ship's company have much to prove before that happens.

The immense downdraft from the Merlin's blades scoops a deep crater in the sea below, and a glistening rainbow decorates the curtain of spray rising at its outer edge.

A single aircraft handler beckons the Merlin on to the deck while the others take position in case of emergency. The firefighters are poised. Luke Wraith crabs sideways until he's hovering over the flight deck. The flight director signals him to descend.

This Mark 2 Merlin is an anti-submarine helicopter from 820 Naval Air Squadron, which will be assigned to the QE throughout her fifty-year lifespan. It will also provide round-the-clock maritime patrol and interdiction. Armed with Sting Ray torpedoes, Mark 11 depth charges and the M3M .50 calibre machine gun, the Mark 2 is considered a very capable attack chopper, which will also be used for troop ferrying, casualty evacuation, lifting under-slung loads and, vitally, search and rescue – especially if another aircraft has had to ditch into the sea. The squadron will eventually be joined by Mark 4s from 845 Squadron, which will specialize in inserting Special Forces behind enemy lines.

Holding his aircraft steady against the wind, Wraith gradually descends. The flight director keeps waving him down. Twenty feet, ten feet, five feet. Then rubber meets deck.

Everyone in Flyco, on the bridge and on the flight deck applauds. The flight deck has been christened. Bob Hawkins and Kirsty Rugg witnessed the moment from the Flag Bridge. 'How many aircraft will we eventually have on board, sir?' Rugg asks.

'It'll change from deployment to deployment,' Hawkins says. 'But roughly ten rotary-wing aircraft and up to twenty-four fixed-wing.'

'Wow!' Rugg says. 'Just imagine all those on deck.'

'The time's coming,' Hawkins says.

Jerry Kyd is on the radio to Mark Deller.

'Fantastic, Wings! Many congratulations. I think the Chinese took eighteen months to land their first aircraft on their new carrier. It took your guys four days.'

'Thank you, sir. I'll pass on your kind words.'

His aircraft handlers are cock-a-hoop, and none more so than Emma Ranson. 'It's brilliant for the ship's company to see aircraft on deck,' she tells airwing officer Jim Corbett.

'It is indeed. Especially since a lot of them haven't been to sea before, let alone on a carrier.'

Ranson knows she'll be telling her grandkids about it one day. 'And next year it'll be jets!'

1800

The entire Aviation branch is being organized into seven neat rows. Mark Deller has authorized a team photo to celebrate today's landing – but also to mark another major triumph: the successful concealment of his leather sofa from the ACA.

The epic game of hide-and-seek with the Alliance's Safety Team, forever hunting down 'non-standard equipment', has been a triumph of military inventiveness and teamwork over corporate intransigence. The sofa's been concealed everywhere from the wardroom to the air-stores and even, for a period, in the refrigerated larders. And now he takes his position on the infamous piece of furniture and, with his entire team ranged behind him, leans back and shouts, 'Smile!'

The shutter button is depressed several times to capture the moment for posterity.

2100

Bob Hawkins would normally now read a book or write an email to his wife Trudy. Tonight, however, he's going to watch television. It'll be a bittersweet experience. The ship's internal system, Sovereign TV, shows all the usual terrestrial broadcasters via satellite but also its own bespoke channel. Up to now it's been showing the 1976 BBC naval classic *Sailor*, about life on HMS *Ark Royal*. From today it'll be switching to a 1995 documentary series, *HMS Brilliant*, the story of a frigate on deployment to the Adriatic during the Yugoslav War. It features a young Bob Hawkins as an outspoken Principal Warfare Officer. There are those who say it cost him further promotion. He was a lieutenant commander then and remains one now, over twenty years later.

Hawkins takes an alcohol-free beer from the fridge, lies back on his bunk and prepares for what promises to be a bumpy trip down memory lane. He's also nervous about the reaction to his historic pronouncements by the present ship's company, many of whom would not have been born when he uttered them.

There's a knock on the door.

'Come!' Hawkins can't conceal his impatience.

''Scuse me, sir . . .' Dave Garraghty puts his head round the door. 'Just wanted to check on a couple of things for tomorrow's daily orders.'

'HMS *Brilliant*. . .' Hawkins waves at the screen and invites him in.

'Don't mind if I do, sir. Haven't seen it for years, but I remember your performance!'

Hawkins grimaces. 'A lot of people do . . .'

'Made you famous, sir.'

'Hmm . . . Infamous, more like.' Hawkins gestures to the fridge. 'Help yourself to a coldwet and pull up a pew.'

Hawkins and Garraghty settle back. Following a fast-cut title sequence befitting a high-octane naval adventure, the film settles into its rhythm. Over dramatic aerial shots of the Type 22 frigate slicing through the waters of the Adriatic, its mission to enforce economic sanctions and an arms embargo against the former Federal Republic of Yugoslavia and the warring factions in Croatia and Bosnia is quickly established.

Implementing the blockade carries real risk because HMS *Brilliant* has to patrol within the missile-envelope of the highly volatile Serbian forces. In charge of the frigate's Operations

Room, Bob Hawkins is permanently on the lookout for signs of enemy hostility. The Bob Hawkins of today takes a deep breath as the 1994 version holds forth to a probing camera.

'The greatest thing I enjoy about the Navy is the camaraderie.' Young Hawkins scans radar images of war-torn Dubrovnik. *'There's still a sense of purpose, despite the end of the Cold War, but personally the thing I've had to overcome over the last few years is the idea of women at sea.'*

'Crikey!' Garraghty takes a swig of alcohol-free beer. 'You didn't skirt around the subject, did you, sir?'

Hawkins clenches his jaw. 'Here we go!'

'Because I enjoy male camaraderie in the Navy and I enjoy the aggression of a warship I'm not sure that the fairer sex, as I still like to think of them, have a place here. Quote equal rights to me until you're blue in the face, but they are the fairer sex, they're childbearers, you know? I'm old-fashioned enough to think that we are the people that should protect them.'

Hawkins winces and braces himself.

'Any government who elects to send women to war is morally bankrupt, in my opinion . . .'

'Fuck a duck, sir!' Garraghty gasps. 'Took some balls to say that!'

Kirsty Rugg, viewing the same channel in the aft island, is amazed to see the First Lieutenant on screen and even more amazed to hear what he had to say.

'Wow!' She turns to fellow steward 'Matt' Munro. 'I thought he was presenting his view really well until that last comment. Then he called us childbearers. Like we're growbags, with nothing more to offer.'

'It's a bloody strong view these days, isn't it?' Munro says. 'But that was then, and now is now.'

Many have also been watching in the women's messes. 'I reckon he meant well,' says Danni Hobbs, a warfare specialist. 'And back then women at sea were very new, but I've only ever known a Navy where females do all jobs.'

'But if it did kick off, how would you feel?' one of her messmates asks.

'Simple. I'd be on the upper deck with the guys doing what's needed. It's part of the deal, so you just get on with it.'

Emma Ranson is also quick to voice an opinion in the Petty Officers' Mess. 'Look, I've chosen this career path and it's one I'm really proud of. I absolutely love my job and regardless of whether we go to war or not, I'll never change it. I don't reckon the First Lieutenant would say the same thing now, or even think it.'

'Got to hand it to you, sir,' Garraghty says. 'You weren't afraid to speak your mind.'

'Not a matter of being afraid,' Hawkins says. 'I simply wasn't prepared to say to camera what I thought I *should* say rather than what I really *wanted* to say. One of the freedoms we fight for is freedom of speech, so it was important to be honest rather than spin government policy I didn't hand-on-heart agree with. My personal view was then – and still is, Dave – that it's a very, very difficult thing for any government to send *anyone* to war because it's a vicious, nasty business. But to elect to do that with our female population in particular is still a big dilemma for me.'

'It's a different world, though, sir. Things have changed.'

'Of course. But I can't deny my inner feelings. Gut instincts really. I really value the contribution that our women make. The notion that we don't recruit and train, employ and promote 50 per cent of our population is unacceptable in 2017.'

'Women do a lot of the jobs here better than the blokes,' Garraghty says. 'Especially the radar operators and communications specialists.'

'Damn right! And considering the high-calibre women serving I would hate to be on board without them. We've got the cream of the crop. But I'd be dishonest if I pretended I don't still think it's wrong for our women to go to war.'

Hawkins shakes his head.

'But that's juxtaposed with the fact that I really appreciate the courage, skill and commitment of the women I serve with now. In truth, I wouldn't want to go to war without them. That's the dilemma for me. Frankly, it's unresolvable within my own ethical framework.'

Garraghty nods sympathetically. 'Bottom line is, nobody knows how the public will react until women are brought back in body bags. Or how the government would react, come to that.'

'You're right,' Hawkins says. 'A likely casualty of war would be political correctness itself.'

15. Beauty and Beast Combined

0630

Danni Hobbs, a leading hand specializing in Above Water Warfare (AWW), walks out on deck in helmet and body armour. She carries a general-purpose machine gun (GPMG) under her arm and several belts of 7.92x57 Mauser ammunition over her shoulders.

'Gather round!'

A group of similarly equipped male gunners obey without question.

'OK,' she continues. 'As we're live firing today, I need you all to observe strict health-and-safety regulations.'

Hobbs is an expert in gunnery as well as unarmed combat. Every sailor on board, from chef and steward to stoker and navigator, has to be proficient in small arms firing, including the SA 80 assault rifle. It's Hobbs' responsibility to make sure everyone's up to scratch, and, if necessary, to provide remedial tuition. It's unlikely that many will ever have to take up arms, but a terrorist intrusion might require a lethal response. More likely is a close-quarter attack launched by fast-moving enemy vessels or suicide bombers, and for that reason the QE will have a number of permanently mounted GPMGs on her perimeter. Today Hobbs is overseeing gunnery practice with live ammunition – another first for the QE.

The gunners, under Hobbs' supervision, load their weapons and take aim at bright-orange targets bobbing in the sea. On the order they open fire in short bursts to find their range. The ear-shattering sound echoes across the flight deck as puffs of cordite smoke are carried away by the wind. Once range is established, the gunners extend to longer bursts, testing their arcs left and right as well as up and down. As the ship moves away, red tracer bullets scar the air, helping them maintain accuracy on the diminishing targets, which they continue to shred with a firing rate of 850 rounds per minute up to a distance of 1,000 yards, the limit of a GPMG's killing range.

Yesterday the QE became an aircraft carrier. Today she becomes a warship.

1030

Gunnery drills continue until all the positions are tested, at which point power and propulsion trials are resumed. Scott McLaren, the Sea Trials Director, and Neil McCallum, Commander Marine Engineering, are continuing to push the ship through various configurations of driveshaft revolutions to see how she responds on the straight and on the turn. The 15,000 sensors that warn of fire or flood have settled down and there are now far fewer spurious activations. Today, therefore, they are planning to take the ship to the next level of her propulsive capability.

Jez Brettel picks up the bridge microphone to make a whole-ship announcement. *'D'ye hear there? Navigating Officer speaking. Gunnery drills are concluded, so the big thing for today is to conduct the next of our high-speed trials. We'll be coming up to our top speed for the first time and doing some crash stops in the water as well.*

You'll feel vibration as we make these sudden stops, so it's vital that the ship is properly secured for sea. That is all.'

McLaren and McCallum, monitoring the trial from the SCC, discuss how fast they should spin the driveshafts.

'We've been up to 100 revs per minute,' McLaren says. 'Frankly, I'd be confident up to 150.'

McCallum agrees. 'She seems very stable at speed, but let's see how she responds to an emergency stop.'

McLaren and McCallum order the thrust power to be increased until the ship is speeding through the water at well over 25 knots. Then, at virtually full speed, the ship is 'crashed' into reverse by suddenly changing the direction of spin of the driveshafts. The QE judders violently as her forward momentum fights with the sudden reversal of power and instant deceleration. The two opposing energies create an immense kinetic force that has to be absorbed by the entire body of the ship. But it is the propulsion system that takes the brunt of it, through the huge thrust blocks which attach the shafts to the hull.

The QE shakes and vibrates. Wes Khan has to hold on to a stack of dinner plates in the galley to prevent them hitting the deck, and Kirsty Rugg has to stop the coffee machine in the Captain's Pantry from drenching her. But the crash reverse test is a great success and another major sea trial box ticked.

'Bloody heap of crap!' Ricky Gleason is bristling with frustration. The pyrolysis plant, overheating dangerously, has been shut down until further notice. 'The fuckin' stuff is piling up all down the passageway,' he complains to Bob Hawkins and Sticky Vercoe. 'Bags of bleeding gash, and all we can do is stow 'em.'

'That's our only option,' Hawkins says firmly. 'Stack the gash-bags in spare compartments until we know what's wrong with the plant. We'll have to put food waste in refrigerated containers in the hangar or we'll very quickly have a real health and hygiene problem.'

1400

'Saturday Routine' means a half day, even though it's Tuesday, and a rare opportunity for the ship's company to use the upper deck as a recreational space. Various competitions have been arranged between the messes. At one end there's tug-of-war, touch rugby halfway down and then a naval game called 'bucket-ball'– a cross between netball, rugby and cage fighting – the main aim of which is to lob a ball into a bucket held at either end by a sailor on a raised platform.

The stokers, confident of victory, step out for their knock-out match against the women's mess. Their opponents have different ideas and go in hard from the beginning. Kirsty Rugg, on the bench for the first half, comes on after half-time with the score three-all. Able Rate Lenny Lirret on the stokers' team leaps confidently to catch a long ball hurled down the wing. Rugg inadvertently rams him in mid-air and watches in horror as he spins on his axis and nosedives. With a yelp he puts out his hands to break his fall and impacts the deck with an agonizing thud. He holds his position for a moment, both hands flat against the deck. He then rises, staggers forward and turns up his bloody palms.

'Jesus!' he gasps. 'I've got no frikin' hands left!'

The super-hard, jagged surface, reinforced to resist the rocket forces of an F-35B jet fighter, is more than a match for human flesh.

Players and spectators look on aghast as he stumbles forward, light-headed with pain.

'Sorry, Lenny,' Rugg says. 'I didn't mean to spin you!'

'AB Lirret!' Jerry Kyd bellows in wry humour. 'I hope you haven't damaged my flight deck!'

2100

Silhouetted against the sinking summer sun, the QE seems at once monstrous and balletic. Beauty and beast combined. The day's been eventful and successful, and everyone's buoyed up by the progress of the sea trials. But there's a saying in the Navy: a day in which nothing goes wrong is just a day closer to when something does go wrong . . .

2230

Navigating Officer Jez Brettel is the first to notice that not everything is as it should be. He's having a break in the bridge mess next to the Captain's Pantry.

'Here we are, sir.' Kirsty Rugg places a mug of steaming coffee in front of him.

He thanks her and reaches for it. 'Oh no, not again . . .'

'Oh!' Rugg gasps. 'It's vibrating!'

'And the coffee's rippling,' Brettel says. 'I noticed the same thing earlier with a cup of tea on the bridge. It started just as we reached 90 revs per minute – about what we are now.'

Most people might assume a slight wave motion in their drink was normal on a ship underway, especially if moving at speed. Brettel is more sensitive to the smallest clues that it's not behaving normally. Wobbles and oscillations, indicating instability, tend to get worse, not better.

Minutes later, Scott McLaren answers the phone in the Ship's Control Centre.

'There's a terrible knocking against the hull,' Fiona Percival says from her cabin. 'It sounds like it's about to cave in!'

McLaren glances at the screens to make sure no fire or flood sensors have been activated.

'It's coming from the stern,' she says. 'Sounds like the propellers, or maybe the driveshaft. It's a loud, rhythmic crashing sound. I can hardly hear myself speak . . .'

Neil McCallum goes straight to investigate. As he approaches the hindmost section of the ship (2 Zulu), the Commander Marine Engineering can hear a distant knocking. He descends to the lower decks and the closer he gets to the waterline, the louder it becomes. When he reaches an empty compartment immediately above the driveshaft on the starboard side, it's thunderous, especially adjacent to the starboard propeller. Engineers from both the ACA and the RN are scattered around the compartment, ears cocked against the bulkheads.

'What the hell could it be?' McCallum asks. 'Sounds like something's trying to bash its way in.'

'It's a regular sound,' Pat Midgely, the propeller engineer, says. 'Like a brick in a tumble dryer.'

'But a hundred times louder . . .'

'It's much worse on this side,' Midgely says. 'Hardly any noise port side.'

'I reckon the starboard prop's hit something,' McCallum says. 'Driftwood, or maybe a whale.'

The general alarm adds to the cacophony.

'Fire danger, fire danger, fire danger! Sparking to the starboard driveshaft in 7 Yankee. Emergency party to attend.'

Engineers had noticed sparks flying off the starboard shaft

when it started rubbing against its braking mechanism. They shut it down immediately to avert the fire risk, but the entire compartment is now filled with the stench of burning metal and diesel.

McCallum rejoins Scott McLaren, and they head to the bridge.

'I'm not a panicker,' McLaren tells Kyd. 'With two 30-ton propellers thrashing around at significant speed on a long lever, there isn't a ship in the world that wouldn't make a noise back aft, but now with everything else kicking in we've no choice but to investigate.'

Without hesitation, Kyd stops mid-ocean and drops anchor. The engineers must now execute a fine-tooth-comb inspection of the entire propulsion system, inside and outside the ship. A dive-boat and divers are sent for from Rosyth, but they will not arrive until first light tomorrow.

As night falls over the North Sea, HMS *Queen Elizabeth* lies dead in the water, or at least seriously wounded. Nobody yet knows exactly what her injury is, where it lies or how it was inflicted. They only know it's serious.

16. Lobster Pot Blues

North Sea, 5 July 2017

0600

Highland Fling, a 40-foot dive-boat, nudges up to the QE's stern. Pat Midgely and Scott McLaren are waiting on the transom, the boarding area that juts into the sea. Two burly divers are pulling on their dry suits, helmets and oxygen tanks. A third is readying himself too, in case of emergency.

Midgely and McLaren are shown into a high-tech cabin and seated in front of a TV monitor.

After half an hour of rigorous safety checks, the divers are ready to go. One after the other they plunge into the swirling water. Their bright-yellow helmets bob momentarily on the surface, until they release air from their buoyancy jackets. Their torch beams soon disappear as they swim towards the starboard propeller.

The monitor shows nothing more than an agitated cloud of illuminated bubbles. Gradually the water clears.

'*By the starboard propeller now* . . .' A clear, steady voice through the rasp of an oxygen mask. On screen, a hand sweeps over the bronze surface of a blade dappled by sunlight.

'*Looks OK to me. Nothing immediately out of order. Going deeper.*'

The divers swim past the propellers and start to follow the line of the driveshaft.

'*There are marks here!*' the lead diver announces. '*Scarring all the way down the shaft.*' He points to strange spirals on the red-painted metal. '*Can you see it on camera?*'

'I can,' Midgely says. 'Does it go right round the shaft?'

'*It does. And the metal's scuffed. You can see where barnacles have been scraped off.*'

'Something's violently impacted the shaft,' McLaren says. 'Check the propeller bolts. The blades could've worked loose if the shaft is out of true.'

Markings between the blades and their hub were lined up precisely when attached in Rosyth – to the millimetre. The divers spend three hours measuring them. Nine of the 10-ton blades are in perfect alignment. One on the starboard propeller is out by an astonishing 26 millimetres – a gigantic misalignment which would probably account for the knocking in the aft compartments, the sparking on the driveshaft and the coffee wobble on the bridge.

'What could have dislodged it?' Midgely asks.

'No way of knowing,' McLaren says. 'Mooring buoy? Fishing net? Lobster pot lines more probably, in these parts. But something wrapped itself round the shaft with violent effect.'

There is worse news to come. The engineers examining the propulsion system inside the ship discover a tell-tale crack in one of the huge, load-bearing vices that anchor the driveshaft to the hull.

Midgely and McLaren join McCallum and Lieutenant Andrew Watkis, another marine engineer, to look at the damage.

'You see there's a large crack running here . . .' Watkis points to a jagged black line in the protective resin that cushions the metal thrust block. 'This is replicated on the other side, and there's a start of another crack on one of the other base mounts as well. The block has effectively failed, sir.'

'Vibration caused by the misaligned propeller blade?' McCallum says.

'Yessir. In all probability.'

2000

'A lobster pot!' Jerry Kyd's eyes narrow.

'I'm not a betting man, captain,' McLaren says. 'But I think that's the most likely cause of the damage.'

'Look at these, sir.' McCallum spreads several enlarged photos across the Rose Table. 'You can see the spiralling around the starboard shaft and the impact damage to the anti-rust paint. Odds are this was the result of a rope wrapping itself around it.'

McLaren agrees. 'The force of a rope spinning at 150 rpm could have dislodged the blade, especially if one of the bolts holding it in position hadn't been properly tightened or was faulty in some way.'

'Unbelievable . . .' Kyd picks up a photo for closer inspection.

'Yessir. That would've led to uneven spin, which led to sparking on the brake pads, and ultimately to stress overload and the cracking of the thrust block.'

'I'd be lying if I said I wasn't worried, captain,' McLaren says. 'We don't know how far this damage has spread.'

'We need to go alongside as soon as possible,' Kyd responds.

The ACA Sea Trials Director nods. 'We must realign the

propeller blade and undertake a comprehensive inspection of the entire driveshaft inside and out.'

'OK, gentlemen,' Kyd says. 'We'll head straight to Invergordon. We're scheduled for a four-day stop there anyway to pick up fuel and stores and offload all the gash. Will that be long enough for you?'

McCallum takes a deep breath. 'We'll do our best, captain.'

17. Forever Invergordon

North Sea, 6 July 2017

The entrance to Cromarty Firth, one of the safest and most commodious anchorages in Scotland, is guarded by two precipitous granite headlands that dwarf the supercarrier as she passes through. The craggy inlet stretches 18 miles inland and is lined with huge, ocean-weathered oil rigs waiting to be repaired or broken up. Standing stock-still in a swirling sea mist, they give the place a ghostly aura – until the frolicsome bottlenose dolphins, harbour porpoises and inquisitive grey seals break the surface in apparent celebration of the QE's arrival.

Invergordon, the small but perfectly formed gateway to the eastern Highlands, lies about 5 miles along the northern shore. A natural deep-water port, it was a major base for the Home Fleet until the 1950s.

'Amazing to think it was once awash with our sailors, sir,' says Darren Houston scanning the town through his binoculars.

'Not all to the good, though,' Kyd retorts. 'I was reading last night that the last naval mutiny took place here in 1931. It caused panic on the London Stock Exchange, a run on the pound and ultimately forced Britain off the Gold Standard!'

'Let's hope we don't see history repeating itself, sir,' chuckles Houston.

'I reckon a hotspot or two for the young sailors' wi-fi should be enough to stop an action-replay.'

1400

The baffled engineers continue to grapple with the mystery of the loose propeller blade and crooked driveshaft. They've called in another dive-boat and more divers to check inside the hub while other specialist engineers continue to inspect every inch of the propulsion system.

Above them, Bob Hawkins picks up a main-broadcast microphone as soon as the gangways are in position. *'D'ye hear there? Clear Lower Deck, Clear Lower Deck. All rates – senior and junior plus available officers – report to the hangar. We have gash to get off the ship. All hands stand to.'*

A human chain comprising all ranks from able junior ratings to senior commanders soon stretches from the compartments where the gash-bags have been stowed to the waiting skips on the quayside. They are less happily motivated than they were when passing boxes of shiny red tomatoes, crisp lettuce and free-range eggs for future consumption, but the pyrolysis plant can't be fixed until the sea trials have ended.

'Keep going, people!' Ricky Gleason shouts. 'Otherwise you'll be stuck there hugging bags of minging gash.'

Kirsty Rugg needs no encouragement. Food waste is normally reduced to compressed briquettes before being zapped by the pyrolysis machine, which reduces them to a fine powder.

Gleason hurls a foul-smelling bag to the sailor next to him. 'We 'ave the most modern gash-disposal system of any navy in the world,' he mutters. 'It'd help massively if it actually fuckin' worked. Just sayin'!'

No amount of manpower, however, is going to solve the propulsion problem. The engineers and ACA boffins are still scratching their heads. The proposed four-day turn-around stretches to six and then eight. After ten, the warship is still tethered to the quayside.

17 July 2017

Groundhog Day in Invergordon. With no fixed date for sailing, the ship's company is growing weary of any attraction this small coastal town once held. One small tourist shop sells T-shirts emblazoned with 'Forever Invergordon'. With a couple of strokes of the pen, many of them now read 'Forever in Invergordon'.

By day the matelots clean the ship, bring on stores and go through routine training drills. By night they're allowed ashore to relax and have a drink or two, notwithstanding the ACA's zero-tolerance policy. The Caledonian Bar and the Silver Dollar were drunk dry of beer the first night and had to send for emergency supplies – an order that's been repeated every day since. After three nights, Jay Early, the arm-wrestling Bosun, had beaten every local challenger. Talk among the vanquished about sending for Wee Willie Buchanan to take on the Sassenach sailor with biceps the size of oak trees had dwindled with news that he had dislocated his shoulder tossing the caber in the Highland Games.

The town's been caught out by the arrival of the QE and the sudden demand not only for alcohol, but pizzas, general groceries and hairdressers. Sharon at Sharon's Unisex Hair Salon on King Street, the main drag, has been run off her feet and had to bring in back-up from Aberdeen to cater for the evening queues.

Sailors on shore leave, unless otherwise stated, are allowed to stay out all night, so some who might have got lucky have taken the opportunity of booking cheap hotel rooms. The local boys haven't welcomed the result, and there have been scuffles, but the police, vigilant without being heavy-handed, have kept the peace pretty effectively. More often than not, the warring parties end up buying each other beers and dancing down the street together, singing rude songs.

Overnight shore leave normally expires at 0745 for junior rates, 0750 for leading seamen and 0755 for senior rates. Anyone who fails to report back on board promptly is marked as absent without leave. Arriving even a minute late means punishment.

One sailor four hours overdue was found at an address on the outskirts of town, handcuffed to a bed and completely naked except for his socks. His phone and wallet had gone AWOL, and the working-girl responsible nowhere to be seen. He escaped being disciplined partly because he was the victim of a crime and partly because his acute embarrassment was considered punishment enough.

18 July 2017

There's been a major breakthrough in the underwater investigations early this morning. The divers discovered a mangled rubber seal under the dislodged blade. It must have slipped out of its groove when the propellers were first assembled. This would have prevented perfect contact between the metal surfaces, so the bolts were never as tight as the engineers believed.

The blade only needed a nudge to slip out of alignment – but with hindsight, the much-maligned lobster pot has proved a piece of immense good fortune. The engineers' minute inspection of the entire propulsion system had led to the discovery of the tiny cracks in the thrust block – and the realization that the thrust blocks should have been reinforced from the beginning. It was a disaster waiting to happen.

'Looks like we've clobbered this gremlin at last,' Jerry Kyd tells his Heads of Department at the Rose Table. He wonders what might have happened if the error hadn't been discovered.

'If the thrust block had failed,' Neil McCallum tells him, 'the worst-case scenario is that it wouldn't have been able to hold the driveshaft in place. Rotating at speed, it could've broken free and caused untold damage. It would certainly have damaged or destroyed the propulsion motor. That would have caused a fire in the hold. The stern seal would've been ripped out, leading to a major flood. The locking and braking mechanism on the shaft would also have been ripped out, which could have caused another fire.'

The solution proves remarkably simple. Steel reinforcements, made to very precise specifications, are now being welded in, and the dislodged propeller blade is being rebolted with new rubber seals properly in place.

The ship should be ready to sail tomorrow.

18. Foam Party on the High Sea

North Sea, 21 July 2017

0900

'*D'ye hear there,*' Jez Brettel announces. '*Ship's company is reminded that the ship will continue to roll heavily due to steering gear trials for approximately the next three minutes. That is all.*'

More high-speed power-and-propulsion trials are in train. The QE seems grateful for the opportunity to cut loose again. The navigators need to get her back up to maximum speeds but must first test her stability on the turn in order to put maximum stress on the propellers. The starboard one in particular must be proven fit for purpose.

Propellers, however, are the last thing on Dave Garraghty's mind. He's frantically searching the cupboards in his office.

'Where the hell's Wilf?'

'He was on the chair last night,' Bobbie Powell says. 'The one with the pink cushion . . .'

'That's where I left him when I locked up . . .' Garraghty checks behind the armchair. 'Gone. Disappeared. Some scumbag's stolen him.'

'Probably been float-tested by now,' Bob Hawkins says mischievously.

'Better not have been,' Garraghty retorts. 'He wasn't cheap, you know.'

The ship suddenly lurches as she's put into a tight

35-degree starboard turn. Garraghty takes a seat until the manoeuvre is completed.

'He'd better be returned pronto,' he says. 'I don't mind a joke, but if Wilf's been taken out of spite, I'll be well pissed off.'

Powell grins. 'We could launch a Thimble Hunt . . .'

'Don't think I wouldn't,' Garraghty growls. 'That would serve the bastards right!'

1000

'Ahead both engines, revolution 90.' Jez Brettel gives the order to cease steering gear trials and head further out to sea.

'Ahead both engines, sir, revolution 90.' The helmsman takes the QE to speed with the press of a button. She's back to full performance and her automated best.

Members of her ship's company have gratefully resumed sea routines – not least Wes Khan, who's busy preparing a huge vat of curried lamb for tonight's dinner.

'Can you help me with the poppadoms?' he asks junior chef Tom Pedley. 'We also need to do beef, chicken and vegetable curries.'

'Plenty of time, Wes –'

'Don't count on it, shipmate,' Khan says. 'We could get another flood or fire any moment, and then we'll have to rush off and leave all our lovely scran to spoil! Too much excitement on sea trials!'

2000

Dave Garraghty is dealing with the last of the day's emails when he notices an envelope's been slipped under the door. He opens it to find a message written with multi-coloured letters cut out of magazines and newspapers: 'If you know what's good for you, watch Sovereign TV at 2015.'

'Bastards!' he hisses.

Fifteen minutes later, a small, anonymous compartment appears onscreen, in almost total darkness apart from a green emergency light over a door. Suddenly a torch beam flashes up to reveal a lone figure on a chair, a bag over his head.

'Toe-rags!' Garraghty snaps.

A hand lifts the bag to reveal Wilf, gagged and blindfolded, with a message pinned to his chest.

'Wilf is safe. For now. We will contact you again soon.'

Beneath that is a skull and crossbones etched in black ink.

Garraghty allows himself a sardonic smile. At least he knows Wilf's not been thrown overboard. But he has been kidnapped. Which will mean a ransom demand. Garraghty studies the TV picture carefully for clues to its location. 'Who could be behind this?' he asks himself. The stokers? Maybe. He recently gave them a reprimand over the state of their mess square. The weapons engineers? Logisticians? Aviators? Warfare? Intelligence? He's determined to find out, but for the moment he must wait for the kidnappers to contact him again.

30 July 2017

The sea trials continue.

The Highly Mechanized Weapons Handling System has been designed to transport bombs and missiles from the deep magazines to aircraft on deck – a military version of the stock-moving machinery in Amazon warehouses. Mobile platforms that can move in any direction linked to a network of lifts will be overseen by no more than thirty personnel.

Modern US carriers, using chains, pulleys and trolleys, require ten times that number.

Today's test, however, is an innovative method of fire-fighting on the flight deck. This is a unique 'last resort' should a conflagration rage out of control. It entails covering the entire deck with a vast blanket of fire-suppressing foam which will gush from hundreds of tiny nozzles embedded from bow to stern, linked by miles of pipes and tubes to high-pressure foam tanks below deck. Known as the 'wash-down' system, it's used on US carriers but not on this scale. There's no shortage of things that could go wrong.

Standing on deck, Mark Deller calls his team together to brief them for what promises to be the most visually dramatic sea trial to date.

'Right, close up together,' he shouts over a gusting wind. 'I'm herewith inviting you to the biggest foam party ever to be held on the high seas. Beneath this deck is the most complex plumbing in the universe but if it works the way we hope it will, this could not only save our lives up here but those of everybody on the entire ship. Who's not heard of the USS *Forrestal*?'

Not a single hand is raised.

Forrestal is routinely used as an example of how catastrophically a fire can spread on a carrier. On 29 July 1967, the American supercarrier was engaged in combat operations during the Vietnam War when an electrical anomaly caused a Zuni rocket on an F-4B Phantom parked on the flight deck to fire, striking an external fuel tank of an A-4 Skyhawk. The Avgas ignited, triggering a chain-reaction of explosions that killed 134 sailors and injured 161. The disaster prompted the US Navy to revise its firefighting practices completely.

'Don't forget,' Deller says, 'we're just a floating airfield.

But we can't separate our fuel storage, living quarters and ammunition dumps over a 2,000-acre estate like the RAF; we have all that crammed into a tiny metal box. We might be the biggest warship ever built for the Royal Navy but we're still launching, landing and, God forbid, crashing on the heads of our shipmates living and working beneath us.

'If we don't contain a crash on deck or a missile strike, we could lose the whole ship and everyone with it. The buck stops with us in terms of flight-deck safety, but I hope our new wash-down system will provide us with the ultimate ability to quash a raging inferno.'

Jerry Kyd has invited some of his Young Officers to observe the trial with him from the bridge.

'Do you think we'll ever have a crash on deck, sir?' asks one of the YOs.

'Almost inevitably,' Kyd says. 'But remember that 99 per cent of the time this flight deck will be absolutely fine. It'll be seamless, smooth and safe. Then suddenly something goes wrong and things get out of control quickly and cataclysmically. That is when you don't want panic. You want calm heads. And that comes through drill, leadership, professionalism and state-of-the-art technology.'

Kyd has seen his share of flight-deck accidents and lost close friends in others. Soon after he left the *Ark Royal* in 2003, two airborne early-warning Sea Kings suffered a midair collision in the Gulf. One was returning to the ship at night; the other was outbound under 'silent' procedures. Both crews were killed – seven men he knew well.

The wash-down system is activated from Flyco with a press of the so-called Domesday Button. Hundreds of flush-deck nozzles instantly create an enveloping mist over the entire deck – a 'pre-wet', designed to dampen the deck prior to landing a damaged or flaming aircraft, and wash chemicals or nuclear fallout swiftly over the side.

The emergency siren begins to scream, and the main broadcast bursts into life. *'Crash on deck! Crash on deck! Crash on deck!'*

Fire teams are sent in with hoses to provide the next line of defence. They try to spread foam but are beaten back as the virtual flames take hold. The foam reservoirs are activated, with immediate and spectacular effect. Eruptions of white aqueous film-forming foam spread like lava and get deeper by the second. The AFFF, a unique combination of hydrocarbon and fluorochemical agents, is discharged at 375 gallons per second. John Ball (aka 'Damage') and his team, clad in tight-fitting rubber dry suits, rush in to take samples. They have to check that the foam is the right concentration and consistency to suffocate and extinguish a fire.

Kirsty Rugg watches from the Flag Bridge. 'Come and look at this,' she shouts to fellow steward Matt Munroe. 'It's bloody Christmas on deck!'

After twenty minutes, the foam and pre-wet are turned off, and Mark Deller comes down to debrief his teams.

'A great success!' he beams. 'The plumbing worked like a dream, and the foam concentrations are spot on.'

The wash-down response is very much last-chance-saloon, but they now know it works if they need it. But job done, the AFFF is also extremely corrosive, so they need to sluice it over the side ASAP.

1825

Dave Garraghty and Bob Hawkins are in the Executive Office.

'Sir, this was pinned to the noticeboard.' Bobbie Powell pokes an envelope through the beaded curtain. 'I think it's from the kidnappers.'

Garraghty pulls out a note and flicks on the screen. 'They want me to tune in at 1830.'

Hawkins sits back to enjoy the next instalment of the drama.

The unseen videographer pans round an anonymous compartment to reveal a wide-eyed and tousle-haired Wilf.

A message is held up in front of his face.

'If you want to see Wilf again you must obey the following demands:

1. Packets of Smarties must be supplied to all WO1s [warrant officers first class]
2. EWO must work harder to secure his office for sea. There are too many random objects that need tying down.
3. EWO must wash up for a week in the main galley.
4. The First Lieutenant must stop giving such long pipes and be more succinct.'

'What?' Hawkins exclaims. 'They can't bring me into this.'

Powell laughs. 'They just have, sir.'

Garraghty gets up and heads for the door.

Hawkins raises an eyebrow.

'NAAFI, sir. Smarties.'

He pushes past the bead curtains but pokes his head through a moment later.

'Oh, and sir . . . ?'

Hawkins turns from his desk. 'Yes, Dave?'

'Those pipes are a little on the long side, to be fair.'

19. Appointment with the Past

Northern Isles of Scotland, 2 August 2017

Vital power and propulsion tests remain to be done, but Jerry Kyd is pleased enough with progress to suspend sea trials for twenty-four hours. The QE has an appointment with the past.

Her destination is a stretch of water flanked by the ancient granite Orkney Islands. Scapa Flow, a deep, natural harbour, has provided shelter for shipping since prehistory. Vikings anchored their longboats here more than 1,000 years ago, long before it became the spiritual home of the Royal Navy. It was the primary station for the British Grand Fleet in the First World War and a major naval base in the Second. The Battle of Jutland was fought and won from here in 1916; the German Imperial Fleet was scuttled here in 1919; the hunt for the *Bismarck* was launched from here in 1941, and for her sister ship the *Tirpitz* in 1944.

Scapa Flow was also the base from which Arctic convoy escort ships took vital war supplies to northern Russia in 1945. And it was where, exactly 100 years ago today, RN Squadron Commander Edwin Dunning landed a Sopwith Pup biplane on a moving vessel.

An early-morning breeze ripples the surface of the water, and the sun is rising to a cloudless sky. Approaching from the south, the QE enters the historic waters at 0600. Jerry Kyd guides her towards her deep-water anchorage, close to where Dunning made his landing.

'Five cables to run, sir,' Jez Brettel says.

'Very good.'

'Current depth 35 metres. Expected to anchor in 36 metres. On track.'

'Very good.'

'Bottom type is rock, sir. 6 knots reducing.'

'Happy.'

HMS *Queen Elizabeth* continues to slow.

'One cable to anchorage.' The Navigator keeps an eye on the compass. 'Stand by to let go, Bosun.'

'Aye-aye, sir,' Jay Early says on the other side of the bridge. He picks up his radio and presses the transmit button. 'Stand by, cable party.'

The twenty-strong cable party, at its station around the starboard anchor, raise the 'guillotine' in the fo'c'sle – the massive steel bar that prevents the starboard anchor chain from slipping.

'Let go!' Brettel orders.

'Let go!' Jay Early repeats.

'Off brake!' instructs the cable party petty officer. The brake-man spins the brake-wheel to release the 6-ton anchor. It drops with a thunderous clatter and plummets to the depths, pulling 100 yards of chain behind it. After a few minutes, the QE finds herself tethered to the seabed, anchored in the granite bedrock that's helped secure so many warships before her, including the world's first makeshift carrier, HMS *Furious*.

Later today a formal ceremony on the shoreline will rededicate the monument already built in Dunning's memory. The ship will pay respects, ceremonially, from her anchorage, followed by the flypast of a Hawk from RNAS Lossiemouth.

Groups of sailors and ACA contractors are already strolling in the sunshine, chatting and taking selfies against the dramatic backdrop of Scapa Flow. They look down as they hear the sound of an outboard motor. A RIB has pulled away from the starboard beam and is speeding towards a light-green buoy about half a mile distant.

'Two cables onward, Coxswain!' Hawkins bellows into the headwind. 'The *Oak* lies about 30 metres down, just to the right of the buoy.'

HMS *Royal Oak* was the first Royal Navy vessel to be sunk in the Second World War – a signal to the nation that violence could be delivered anywhere, anytime, even in the safest of sanctuaries. At dawn on 14 October 1939, Kapitänleutnant Gunther Prien's U-boat launched a torpedo which struck the *Royal Oak* at anchor. Never thinking it possible that the enemy would or could attack here, damage control parties were sent straight down into the belly of the cruiser to discover the cause of the explosion. Realizing there was no immediate threat from either the *Royal Oak* or any other surface vessels, Prien returned for another attack. A second torpedo tore a 30-foot hole in the stricken ship, which quickly flooded, capsized and sank. Of the 1,400 crew, 833 were killed. U-47 escaped without detection.

The roar of the RIB engine subsides to a gentle growl. Hawkins stands and ventures forward to the two young men still seated – one a civilian contractor, the other a sailor.

Nathan Logan, technician for BAE, lost his grandfather on the *Royal Oak*, and Leading Hand Henry Charles, Air Department, lost his great-grandfather. By an extraordinary coincidence, the two of them are both aboard today. 'I know we're here to celebrate the exploits of Squadron Commander Edwin Dunning,' Hawkins says, 'but I'm sure he would not

Chris Terrill in Afghanistan.

LBO3 hull section coming under the Forth Rail
Bridge on the way to Rosyth.

Rosyth – the biggest dry dock in the UK.

Pod City.

Goliath astride the *QE* in Rosyth dry dock.

'Gut-wrenching, blood-spattering annihilation!'

A Nelsonian cannon de-barnacled.

A German bomb detonated.

Illustrious beside *Queen Elizabeth*.

Abandon ship! At least the Mass Evacuation
System works.

On board at last – Jerry Kyd celebrates with
chocolate Hobnobs.

Propellers.

The Rose Table in place.

Fire, fire, fire!

Flood, flood, flood!

Squeezing out of the inner harbour into the Firth of Forth.

Lifting her skirts for a sprint.

First aircraft on deck within four days.

Beauty and beast combined.

Mark Deller, his secret sofa and the sofa smugglers.

Diving on the dislodged propeller blade.

Limping to Invergordon.

Testing the 'wash-down' fire-fighting system with aqueous film-forming foam.

Edwin Harris Dunning.

The crew of the HMS *Furious* attempt to reach Dunning's Sopwith Pup aircraft as it veers off the flight deck.

The wreckage of Dunning's aircraft.

The F-35B Lightning at Patuxent River Naval Air Station.

Jak London.

Portsmouth – arriving home for the first time.

HM the Queen commissioning the flagship.

A day to remember.

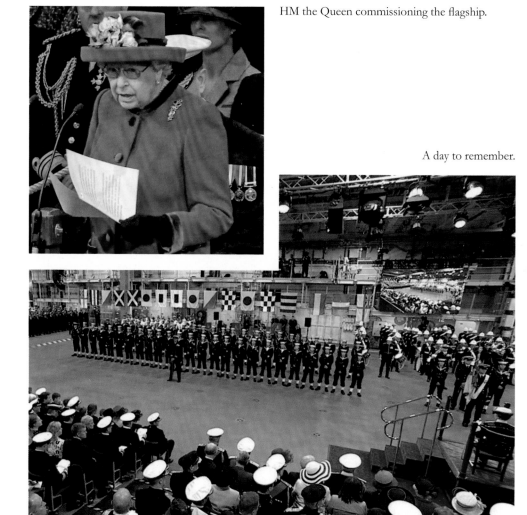

have wanted you to miss the chance of paying respects to your own long-lost relatives.'

'Thank you, sir,' the two men chorus.

'OK, gentlemen. They lie below us at around 33 metres. As a Royal Navy diver, I've been down more than once. Periodically we replace the White Ensign that marks it as a war grave. Nobody's allowed to dive on it recreationally or to disturb it in any way. The superstructure's still intact. She's on her side, but you can see the bridge and gun positions and even the plates, crockery and kitchen utensils in the galleys. The shoes of the sailors who perished are scattered around the seabed. It's now a peaceful place and a tribute to brave men.'

The young men nod in appreciation.

'I think we should now have a quiet minute of reflection in honour of your relatives and all their shipmates.'

They bow their heads. The only sound comes from the bell on the buoy, the lapping sea and distant, circling gulls.

After a minute of contemplation, Hawkins concludes the act of remembrance in true naval style. 'Now, gentlemen, I think we should finish with three cheers for HMS *Royal Oak*. Hip hip . . .'

The cheers echo across the water as the wind causes the bell to ring all the louder.

'God bless them,' Hawkins says finally. 'Happy we were able to make that happen, fellas. You OK?'

'Very grateful, sir,' Nathan Logan says. 'I lost my dad earlier this year. He would've been very happy that I came here to pay my respects to his father.'

'Yessir. Very special for me too,' says Henry Charles. 'I can't wait to tell my nan that I was able to come and see the place where her father is at rest.'

1400

The RIB has returned, and hundreds are now on deck to witness the flypast. Many of them will be thinking not only of Dunning's successful landing on a moving vessel a century before, but also of his fatal crash three days later.

'Honour guard, *ho!*' Darren Houston shouts. 'Pipe the still.'

The young sailor to his right on the bridge wing purses his lips and blows the two shrill, high-pitched notes that signify respect to a senior officer – Squadron Commander Edwin Dunning. Houston and Jerry Kyd snap their right hands to their foreheads in perfectly synchronized salutes. A few hundred yards away on the shoreline, a naval party, including members of the Dunning family, lays a wreath at the memorial by the water.

The message from the War Office to Dunning's parents after his death is declaimed: 'The Admiralty wish you to know what great service he performed for the Navy. It was in fact a demonstration of landing an aeroplane on the deck of a Man-of-War whilst the latter was underway. This had never been done before and the data obtained was of the utmost value. It will make Aeroplanes indispensable to a fleet and possibly revolutionise Naval Warfare.'

Right on cue, the black Hawk swoops low and fast over the sea towards HMS *Queen Elizabeth*. All eyes follow the jet as it screams past on her port side before climbing steeply towards the clouds.

'Sign of things to come, Darren,' Kyd says as it disappears from sight. He returns his gaze to the waters of Scapa Flow, their wind-roughened surface glinting in the sunshine. 'One hundred years ago it was a Sopwith Pup,' he says. 'Today it's a naval Hawk.'

'And next year an F-35 Lightning, sir.'

Kyd nods. 'If our man in America has anything to do with it.'

20. Our Man in America

Three thousand miles away from Scapa Flow, a helmeted figure in full flying gear walks out of a hangar just south of Washington DC. Naval Test Pilot Nathan Gray heads towards an aircraft being readied under a large canvas awning, to protect it from the scorching sun and prying eyes.

Most people's image of a jet-age naval pilot is defined by Tom Cruise's character in *Top Gun*, the square-chinned, slick-haired, womanizing Pete 'Maverick' Mitchell. Gray is taller, leaner, shaven-headed, red-bearded and softly spoken, but there's still titanium at his core. The clue lies in his sharp, bright-blue eyes. Laser-like, they see far beyond their gaze, helping Gray process information as swiftly and efficiently as a chess grandmaster crossed with a Formula One champion. He is not wired like normal men, but he's no automaton. His ready smile, mischievous sense of humour and natural ebullience send that message. But he's also highly motivated and ambitious, driven by a determination and resolve that's made him the perfect candidate to test the most advanced jet fighter in the world.

This sleek, shark-like F-35 could not be more different from Edwin Dunning's short, stocky Sopwith Pup. Nathan Gray, or Nath to his mates, is one of four pilots (three British and one American) who, as part of the Integrated Test Force (ITF), are responsible for the developmental testing of the

F-35B and F-35C Lightning II Joint Strike Fighter. They have been stationed at Pax River, as everyone calls it, for the last two years, in preparation for critical flight trials on HMS *Queen Elizabeth* in about thirteen months' time. Gray will be the first to land an F-35 on her flight deck. It's a singular honour.

He is now about to take his Lightning, codenamed BF-05, for yet another trial, but first he must inspect it from nose to tail. It's mandatory practice, and he does so with an American trainee pilot. Crouching down to check the sturdy undercarriage, Gray looks up into the expansive bomb bays and points to the laser aiming system. 'The hardware is incredible, but the software is off the scale,' he says with genuine, almost boyish excitement. 'Updating it is as easy as updating the software on your mobile . . . sorry, cellphone . . .'

The American nods appreciatively.

'This aircraft's beyond revolutionary.' Gray continues his inspection with obvious pride. 'Sometimes I can't quite believe what it's capable of.'

'Like something out of a sci-fi movie,' the young pilot says.

It's a flying super-computer with deadly electronic warfare, surveillance and reconnaissance capabilities, all made possible by a core processor that can perform more than 400 billion operations per second.

'It's been designed to out-think and out-manoeuvre any other aircraft in the sky,' Gray declares. 'In fact, it's so super-smart it virtually flies itself – releasing the pilot to concentrate on the combat mission. There's never been a warplane like it.'

The F-35 has been branded a fifth-generation fighter, due in part to its 'unprecedented' stealth characteristics. Lockheed Martin say its airframe design, advanced materials and other classified features make it 'virtually undetectable to enemy radar'. The revolutionary but compact machine has a supersonic top speed of 1.6 Mach (1.6 times the speed of sound, or 1,200 mph) and a combat range of 900 nautical miles.

Six 'aperture system sensors' or infrared cameras distributed around its body – two underneath, two on top and one each side of the nose – feed real-time information and images into the pilot's helmet, allowing them, quite literally, to see through the airframe. As if it was not there.

The clincher as far as the QE is concerned is that the F-35B is capable of what aerospace engineers call STOVL (Short Take-off and Vertical Landing). It can take off in less than 350 feet using the ski-jump, and land vertically from a hover. The debate over whether the *Queen Elizabeth* should have employed the conventional catapult and arrestor wire (Cat and Trap) method of launching and landing has been long, involved and at times heated. For better or worse, the final decision was made to go with the STOVL B variant, in the belief that it will be a better fit technically and strategically.

But Gray and his fellow test pilots have still to prove that right. If they fail, the consequences for the QE don't bear thinking about.

The aircraft and ship have never been in direct contact. The pairing, thus far, is purely conceptual, and despite a wealth of computer modelling there are still critical questions over how the ship and aircraft will interact. One concern is the impact of the enormous downward thrust and heat on the flight deck. A second is the impact of the excessive sound of the Pratt & Whitney engine on people's hearing as it launches and lands. And a third is the jet's ability to cope with the wind eddies and vortices that always surround a carrier on the high seas, as Edwin Dunning found out with such tragic consequences. The F-35 may be a technological quantum leap from the Sopwith Pup, but it's still subject to the same laws of physics – the opposing forces of lift, gravity, thrust and drag.

When people ask Gray what it's like to fly, he says simply, 'Like being king of the castle.' He means it. Of all the fighter jets he's known, forty in all, including Harriers, F-15s, F-16s and MiGs, the F-35 makes him feel as if nothing could touch him in combat. But the big questions remain.

Continuing his inspection, he stretches up on tiptoes to peer inside one of the intake vents. He runs his hand along the carbon composite fuselage that helps provide its stealth capability. Then, after checking the underside of the starboard wing, he proceeds to do the same for the port wing before heading to the rear to examine the main jet nozzle.

It's become second nature for Gray to be meticulous to the point of obsession. 'It's the way we have to be,' he impresses on the trainee. 'We have to assume there's a fault. If we can't find one, it doesn't mean there isn't one – it means we haven't looked hard enough.'

The best test pilots, in Gray's opinion, are the pessimists, the worryguts and doom merchants. 'We have to expect the worst, not the best, otherwise we're not on our guard, and that's when we fall over the cliff edge for the dragons to get us. They're always there – lurking.'

He climbs into the cockpit and, after a series of strictly ordered procedures with the control room, closes the canopy and fires up the engine.

Gray knows about cliff edges and lurking dragons from bitter experience. His glittering career has not been without its setbacks, and there are some things he would change in a heartbeat if he could.

Gray's instructor and mentor, back in the day, was Lieutenant Commander 'Jak' London, the most talented fighter
pilot of his generation and a legendary figure in the Royal
Navy. The last time they flew together was on 5 December
2002, at RAF Wittering. Gray was to have gone up with
another instructor, but illness meant someone else having to
step in. London jumped at the chance. He had recognized
Gray's potential as a combat pilot.

Jak London and Nathan Gray took off at 0900 as planned
but almost immediately suffered a catastrophic failure. It
could have been a bird strike or the ingestion of some other
foreign object – either way, the jet blades shattered, and the
engine blew up. Both men ejected as the flaming Harrier
went into an uncontrolled roll. Gray was propelled sideways
but with a slight upward trajectory, so his chute opened just
above the ground. Thanks to landing in a freshly ploughed
field, he only suffered a broken back. London ejected a split
second later, by which time the aircraft was almost inverted.
Gray's friend and mentor, the veteran pilot and Navy ace,
was catapulted straight into the ground and killed outright.

For a while Gray considered giving up, but encouraged by
the Navy to 'get back on the horse' as soon as possible, he
tentatively returned to the cockpit after only three months'
convalescence. With the dedicated help of Gary Langrish
(who was to have flown with him on that fateful day), he
rediscovered his passion for flying. And felt he owed it to Jak
London not to give up.

He went on to prove himself as a front-line fighter pilot in
Iraq and Afghanistan. He was flying his Harrier at around
16,000 feet in Helmand in 2006 when he saw a heavily out-
numbered troop of Royal Marines about to be overrun by
insurgents. Friend and foe were too close to each other for

him to risk dropping bombs or firing missiles, so he went in low and, dropping his air brake, the metal arm that protrudes from beneath the aircraft, scythed through the enemy at wave-skimming height – an altitude of no more than six feet. This was the first of two actions for which he was recommended for a Mention in Despatches for outstanding gallantry – though it's not a plaudit he readily accepts. 'The men on the ground facing the enemy head-on are the brave ones,' he always insists. 'The guys fixing bayonets in readiness for close-quarter combat are the ones who deserve the medals.' It's not false modesty; he genuinely doesn't understand why people are in awe of him.

Now he's lined up on a runway in rural Maryland. Ahead of him is an exact replica of the ski-jump on the QE, built here for the Integrated Test Force.

'Control tower . . .' he says over the radio. 'Lightning aircraft ready for take-off . . .'

There's a short pause before the order that Gray never tires of hearing: 'Lightning aircraft cleared for take-off. Launch jet!'

He initiates the conversion for short take-off. The intake covers rise from the top of the aircraft as it prepares to suck in the air with which it will create vertical and horizontal thrust. BF-05 now looks like a giant Transformer toy in mid-conversion. Then, with a deafening roar, the rear jet nozzle twists downwards, and the aircraft surges forwards with thunderous power. As it gains speed it runs up the 'ski-jump', which helps whip plane and pilot skywards.

After a couple of low-level circuits to burn off fuel, Gray roars back and starts his descent in preparation for landing. Slowing all the time, he prepares to put the aircraft into a stationary hover about 50 feet over the proposed landing spot. Pressing a single button, he activates the seemingly magic conversion from stealth flight to vertical landing.

Intake vents open on top of the aircraft, exposing counter-rotating fans. These suck in air from above and blow it straight down through an outlet valve in the belly, producing some 20,000 lbs of thrust – about half what Gray needs in hover mode. Most of the remaining vertical thrust required is provided by an ingenious but incredibly simple device at the rear: the 3BSM or Three Bearing Swivel Module. This allows the main jet nozzle to pivot 95 degrees downwards in two and a half seconds to divert 18,000 lbs of thrust from the engine exhaust.

With the 3BSM activated, Gray and his aircraft are hovering on two columns of air with a combined force of 38,000 lbs. For stabilization and control, he has two roll posts under the wings that each provide another 2,000 lbs and enable him to finely adjust the hover by controlling roll.

After ten seconds, a blue light tells Gray the transformation is complete and that the propulsion forces are giving him all the vertical thrust he needs to maintain a stable hover.

Gradually reducing power, he descends towards the deck and touches down with the slightest bounce as the hydraulic suspension absorbs the force of contact. But he will have to face conditions when he lands on the QE for real that cannot be replicated here – the variable winds, the swirling vortices created by the ship's two islands; the pitch and roll of the flight deck as it ploughs through the ocean swells.

In the same way that Dunning was breaking boundaries at the end of the First World War, so will the pilots attempting to land the F-35B on the QE.

21. Big Dog on the Block

0700

The 'Call the Hands' pipe alerts the ship's company to the start of another working day. The piercing call from a Bosun's whistle is always performed live via the bridge microphone. Many are already up, but others are only just claiming their place in the shower queue.

The QE is due to sail into Portsmouth for the first time in less than three weeks. Before then, however, she must complete the last of the tests that will allow her to progress to the next stage of her combat readiness.

'*Good morning, HMS* Queen Elizabeth,' Jez Brettel broadcasts. '*Navigating officer speaking. Overnight we met up with the American carrier group of the USS* George H. W. Bush. *They're currently less than 500 yards off our port beam. Later this morning we'll open the flight deck to allow you a look at what is a truly remarkable sight. That is all.*'

Brettel is not exaggerating. Sailing in parallel to them right now is the enormous Nimitz Class supercarrier USS *George H. W. Bush* and several escorting warships. These include two Royal Navy Type 23 frigates, HMS *Iron Duke* and HMS *Westminster*, destroyer USS *Donald Cook*, guided-missile cruiser USS *Philippine Sea*, as well as Norwegian Nansen Class frigate HNoMS *Helge Ingstad*. It is an arresting sight and made all the more extraordinary by the fact that the *George H. W. Bush* looks so battle-weary. She's weathered and battered after spending a year in the Middle East launching airstrikes against ISIL as part of Operation Inherent Resolve, their intervention against the Islamic State of Iraq and Syria. Her rusting superstructure and hull are in urgent need of cleaning and painting, but she looks the part nevertheless, like a boxer coming out of the ring after fifteen gruelling rounds. On her flight deck, hundreds of sailors are already at work, either as seamen tending to the ship or aircraft handlers to a phalanx of F-18 jet fighters – just some of the ninety aircraft she houses.

'Amazing, sir.' Kirsty Rugg is watching out of the Flag Bridge window with Jerry Kyd. 'Gives me goosebumps.'

'Me too,' Kyd says.

Forty minutes later, a helicopter deposits Rear Admiral Kenneth Whitesell, Commander, Carrier Strike Group 2, US Navy, on the QE's flight deck. Hand extended, he strides across to Jerry Kyd. 'Great-looking ship you have, captain.'

'Thank you, sir,' Kyd beams. 'Welcome aboard HMS *Queen Elizabeth*. Come and have some breakfast.'

'So how does the new car drive?' the admiral chuckles. 'Any strange knocking noises?'

'You don't want to know!' Kyd gives an exaggerated shudder.

The American party are served hot bacon butties and English breakfast tea at the Rose Table by Kirsty Rugg and a couple of extra stewards. The atmosphere is informal, and the conversation wide-ranging, but a sense of the 'Special Relationship' pervades this communion of close allies.

'With the QE, I think we'll be able to bring a lot more to the party,' Jerry Kyd says. 'A lot more power, especially with the F-35B as part of our arsenal.'

'We sure need it,' the admiral agrees. 'I guess everyone in this area is getting scared of the Russians' constant sabre-rattling. They'll all want to be your best friend now. You'll be the new big dog on the block.'

It's only an hour before Admiral Whitesell is whisked back to the *George H. W. Bush*, but his visit's been significant diplomatically and militarily. Next time these ships sail together may well be as a part of a joint response to an unfolding global crisis.

2000

Bob Hawkins only piped once tonight – to ask the Ship's Company for names of family and friends who want to attend their arrival in Portsmouth next month. He kept it short and sharp, as the kidnappers directed.

He's now preparing to watch the final episode of *HMS Brilliant* behind a locked door, in the sanctuary of his cabin. He knows how personally upsetting this episode will be.

The frigate is heading back to the UK after seven months in the Adriatic. After a punishing deployment, the young Hawkins is looking forward to getting home for Christmas. Brief stops in Istanbul and Gibraltar precede the warship's arrival in Devonport. The not-so-young Hawkins braces himself for the emotional climax to the series.

He watches himself waving from the deck as the *Brilliant* approaches the quayside. The waiting families include his own two young sons and wife Joan.

'Daddy!' one little boy yells, jumping up and down with excitement.

'Cameron,' Hawkins whispers now, his eyes welling up.

'Daddy, Daddy . . . !'

'Jamie . . .'

The film cuts to the boys' mother, an attractive, smiling brunette.

'I think he can see us . . .' she says. 'Wave, boys. Keep waving so he can see you. There, look! See him at the front there. There's Daddy waving, look, look, look!'

'Joan,' Hawkins murmurs, tears running down his cheeks.

Eleven years after that homecoming in 2005, Bob Hawkins lost Joan to brain cancer. They'd been married just short of nineteen years, and though he's since remarried very happily, he still suffers the grief of her passing. That pain was intensified by seeing his boys trying to deal with the loss of their mother. And this, deep down, is what makes him think the way he does about women serving on warships.

This sense of fundamental, almost primordial loss is somehow crystallized when he ponders the prospect of a mother being badly injured or killed in combat and leaving children behind. He wouldn't want any sons or daughters to lose their father, but somehow the thought of motherhood obliterated by combat is more than he can bear.

The film ends. Hawkins wipes his eyes and collects himself. It's time to think about tomorrow's busy schedule.

22. Pompey Bound

1130

The power-and-propulsion trials in the North Sea are all but done and, despite the issues with burst pipes, pyrolysis plants, propeller blades and thrust blocks, they've proved ultimately successful.

The QE, having sailed over the top of Scotland, is now heading south via the Irish Sea. Her aim is to be in Portsmouth by the day after tomorrow, but there's still work to be done. Today's main exercise, codenamed 'Quickdraw', involves an armed protection force in search of an intruder.

Advancing in line down designated passageways, twelve fully armed sailors methodically clear each compartment, covering each other as they proceed. It's painstaking work; there are many corners and stairwells in which to hide or set up an ambush.

The officer of the day issues a warning over main broadcast in support of the force protection team: '*This is the person in charge. I am addressing this to the person who's forced entry into the ship. We know you are aboard. It's in your interest to contact me by picking up any of the ship's telephones and dialling 999. We can then discuss your grievances. I must warn you that I have armed teams searching the ship to locate your whereabouts. It is only a matter of time before they discover your location.*'

The armed team, having cleared all but one passageway, approach the final few compartments with extra caution.

The first two are empty but the third is not. They go in weapons to the shoulder and quickly secure the space. But the identity of the intruder is a surprise.

One of the team contacts the officer of the day over the radio. 'Quickdraw team-leader with sitrep.'

'*Go ahead, team-leader.*'

'End compartment 7 Tango Starboard. One intruder discovered. Tied, gagged, no apparent pulse.'

'*Description, please, team-leader.*'

'Um . . . About two feet tall, sticky-up ginger hair, and very ugly!'

Minutes later, Dave Garraghty, having finished washing up in the main galley, arrives to escort Wilf back to the Executive Office.

'Any ideas yet who masterminded the dastardly kidnap, Dave?' Bob Hawkins asks.

'No real clues,' Garraghty says. 'But I have my suspicions . . .'

Up in Flyco, Mark Deller kicks back in the Papal Throne. 'Have you noticed that 1L's pipes have been a lot crisper of late?'

'Yessir,' his air traffic controller agrees.

Commander Air allows himself a quiet smile. 'I call that a result!'

16 August 2017

0500

A huge electric-orange sun hovering above the eastern horizon of the English Channel prepares to illuminate the day.

And what a day it promises to be. In a few hours, HMS *Queen Elizabeth* will berth in Portsmouth dockyard.

Jerry Kyd's in no hurry to cut through the glassy waters south of the Isle of Wight. He has to wait for the harbour tugs and wants to leave time for the crowds to gather.

Many of the ship's company are already looking towards the beckoning coastline.

0800

Hundreds of sailors, resplendent in their best uniforms, stream on to the flight deck, where drill instructors march them into pre-arranged positions. Soon, one unbroken line of men and women are ranged along the entire perimeter of the flight deck, facing outwards. Now a purely ceremonial exercise, the Procedure Alpha formation is a traditional sign of peaceful intent from a ship coming into a foreign port – with no one down below to man the cannons.

Five powerful tugboats take station, and once all lines are secure the warship begins her final approach to 'Pompey'.

Massive 'landing lights', erected to help the navigators keep their approach straight and true, gleam behind the Spinnaker Tower, Portsmouth's tallest landmark. Beneath the carrier is a goodly depth of water, thanks to the massive two-year dredge.

As they near the harbour entrance, Jerry Kyd glances down at the famous Round Tower. The cheering crowds are not confined to the old fortification. They spread along the entire length of the harbour wall and fill the streets of Old Portsmouth. From every window of every building, somebody is waving, clamouring, whooping or shrieking.

Kyd has seen the ship's company grow in number and in

confidence over the last fifteen months. He's watched their community evolve and loved the growing sense of pride that now bonds the old salts with the younger sailors. The last gruelling six weeks have imbued them all with that vital sense of belonging and purpose, without which it would be impossible to command.

HMS *Queen Elizabeth* passes Nelson's flagship, which, although in dry dock, remains the oldest commissioned vessel in the Royal Navy. A colour party on HMS *Victory*'s poop deck comes to attention and pipes its salute. The carrier comes to a stop and waits to be turned by the tugs, so she can be tied up with her bow facing the harbour entrance – the naval equivalent of reversing a car into the garage. Bob Hawkins walks out on to the bridge wing as she is berthed alongside the brand-new Princess Royal Jetty.

'We made it, Bob,' Jerry Kyd says.

'Aye, sir,' Hawkins replies. 'And I have to say, despite everything, the boys and girls never lost their pep and zeal.'

'Churchill wasn't wrong,' Kyd says.

Hawkins raises an eyebrow.

'Success consists of going from failure to failure without loss of enthusiasm.'

'Ha!' Hawkins chortles. 'That certainly sums up sea trials.'

23. HMS *Me!*

Four months of maintenance have seen the engineers double-check the driveshafts and thrust blocks, rehang and in some cases replace the doors that had cracked so many skulls and blackened so many eyes and, critically, repair the all-important pyrolysis plants.

Members of the ship's company were given leave, but now most are back on board. Kirsty Rugg, nearly four months pregnant, has moved to a shore job but has returned to the QE for one day only. She's volunteered to help serve the VIPs who'll be arriving to celebrate the supercarrier's official commission into the Royal Navy by Her Majesty the Queen. After twenty years of planning, eight years of construction and two years of training, Britain's biggest ever warship is about to come of age.

The hangar, reconfigured as a vast arena with decked seats on three sides, is already beginning to fill; 3,700 guests are expected today, to enjoy music by the Royal Marines Band and the Portsmouth Cathedral choir. Among them is Nathan Gray, the test pilot, and Nick Gutfreund, the cabinetmaker. He's already caught up with Kirsty Rugg.

'So, who's going to take care of the table now you've got something much more important to look after?'

'Don't worry,' she laughs. 'I've already instructed the captain's new steward how to polish and feed it just like you showed me. His name's Glenroy – Glen for short – and he's fantastic. Your table will be well safe with him.'

1100

The Royal Marines Band are soon followed into the hangar by the entire ship's company, the junior and senior rates marching from the for'ard end and the officers and NCOs from the aft. Once in position, the 100-strong honour guard marches out, each with a bayoneted rifle to the shoulder. Resplendent in perfectly pressed blue uniforms, bright-white gaiters and belts, they take a central position in front of a raised, red carpeted dais.

1130

Her Majesty the Queen is the first to emerge from the black Daimler. Wearing purple with black trimming and a ready smile, she shakes hands with Jerry Kyd, in his Number One uniform with full medals and a gleaming black and gold sword at his side. Princess Anne, the Princess Royal, is wearing the uniform of a vice admiral, as she did nine years ago when she cut the first steel for the warship that now towers over the jetty that carries her name.

Followed by Defence Secretary Gavin Williamson and Admiral Sir Philip Jones, the First Sea Lord, Jerry Kyd ushers the Royal party into the lift which will carry them to the hangar. The Queen inspects the front rank of the honour guard while her daughter inspects the rear, then both accompany the captain to the red-carpeted dais.

The first address is delivered by Naval Chaplain Alastair Mansfield, who will join the QE next year for her deployment to the US. The second is given by Jerry Kyd, who reads out the official commissioning warrant from Fleet Commander Rear Admiral Ben Key, his predecessor as captain of *Illustrious*. Everybody stands for the National Anthem. This is the moment that the civilian Blue Ensign at the stern of the flight deck is lowered and the White Ensign is raised. The iconic naval flag billows proudly in a strong easterly wind as a squadron of Merlin helicopters flies over.

The Queen rises. 'We are gathered here in Portsmouth today,' she says, 'just a short distance from HMS *Victory*, the flagship of our seafaring past, and a reminder of the debt we owe to the Royal Navy, which for more than five hundred years has protected the people of this country and our interests around the world.

'This is the most powerful and capable ship ever to raise the White Ensign,' Her Majesty continues. 'She will, in the years and decades ahead, represent this country's resolve on the global stage. At the forefront of these responsibilities will be the men and women of the Royal Navy, the Royal Marines, supported by the Army, Royal Air Force and by coalition partners.

'As the daughter, wife and mother of naval officers, I recognize the unique demands our nation asks of you, and I will always value my special link to HMS *Queen Elizabeth*, her ship's company and their families.'

Bob Hawkins nods his approval.

'As you prepare to take this country's message of peace, partnership and prosperity across the seas and oceans of the world, the Lord High Admiral, the Duke of Edinburgh, joins me in wishing you well in all your endeavours.'

The formalities over, it's time for the Queen to oversee the cutting of the official cake – a perfect replica of the supercarrier in sponge and battleship-grey icing. This is executed, according to tradition, by the youngest sailor on board, a seventeen-year-old able seaman, who, with the help of the captain's wife Dr Karen Kyd, makes the first incision with a ceremonial sword.

The Queen inspects some of the other cakes made for today by the ship's master-bakers. The one she likes most is covered in pure white icing and features several ranks of marzipan sailors in blue uniforms. The front rank carries a sugar placard saying 'HMS *Queen Elizabeth*'. In the middle of the cake is a marzipan replica of the Queen herself in a bright pink dress, carrying her own placard. It reads 'HMS *Me*'.

Her Majesty is led smiling between two ranks of chefs and stewards who provide a tunnel-of-honour into a bespoke dining area. The tables, draped with white linen and set for a five-course lunch, are located in one of the hangar's machine stores, where hundreds of bombs will await the first flight trials next year.

Wes Khan stands proudly to attention as she passes.

'She's very small,' he says out of the side of his mouth to Ramesh Rai. 'But she has a very friendly smile. Hope she likes the scran . . .'

The Royal party are joined by a select few at the top table. To his astonishment, Dave Garraghty finds he's going to be seated next to the Queen herself.

'What are we going to talk about?' he says anxiously to Bob Hawkins. 'Not sure she'll have attended too many boot sales.'

'Talk about the ship, Dave,' Hawkins says. 'That's what she'll be most interested in.'

'No,' Mark Deller says. 'Tell her about Wilf.'

'I would,' Garraghty says, 'but he's still too traumatized.' He raises an eyebrow. 'Don't suppose you know anything about that little caper, sir?'

'Me?' Deller exclaims. 'Not a thing, EWO. Not a clue. Not a . . . er . . . Scooby's . . .'

'Hmmm . . .' Garraghty treats Commander Air to a level gaze. 'Some might think you're protesting a bit too much there, sir.'

Before Garraghty can quiz him further, he's whisked away to take his seat.

Kirsty Rugg has been sent to the Flag Bridge with a very special envelope. Before posting it in the Rose Table, she holds it up to the light. 'Can't read a thing,' she tells Glen Peters, the captain's new steward.

'It'd probably be treason if you could,' Peters says.

She lifts the central boss, unlocks the shiny brass box and drops it in. 'There,' she says with satisfaction. 'That seems so right, somehow. A letter from the Queen to the Queen.'

Down in the machine store turned Royal dining room, Dave Garraghty is chatting freely to his monarch. She's asking all manner of questions about how the ship works and what the sea trials were like. Emboldened, the Executive Warrant Officer decides to switch the trajectory of the conversation.

'So, Ma'am. Family coming round for Christmas this year?'

'Oh yes,' she laughs. 'They usually do. We have the space, you know!'

2000

It's time for the lowering of the White Ensign. The ceremony is carried out at all shore establishments and on warships when in harbour, on special occasions, like tonight, to the accompaniment of a bugler playing 'Sunset'* or 'The Retreat Call'.

The Officer of the Watch orders two ratings to lower the flag as the bugler's haunting refrain echoes across the harbour and HMS *Victory*, standing only 400 yards away, follows suit. Naval tradition is at a stroke unifying the country's oldest warship (commissioned 239 years ago) and its youngest (commissioned barely eight hours ago).

The Ensign will be raised again on both ships tomorrow at 0800 precisely, in a shorter, sharper ritual known as 'Colours', which will mark the start of the QE's first day as a Royal Navy warship, and the beginning of preparation for her next adventure – a five-month deployment, including her first transatlantic crossing, next year.

Many of the present ship's company will be on board for Westlant 18, a gruelling sixteen-week sea trial that will push ship and sailor to new limits, but not all. It's time for some to move on – the Navy keeps people circulating around the service to keep things fresh. Bob Hawkins, Dave Garraghty, Mark Deller and Fiona Percival will all be taking up new posts elsewhere, and their replacements have already been notified.

* By coincidence the arrangement was composed aboard the first HMS *Queen Elizabeth* in 1932. This was in response to Admiral Sir William Wordsworth Fisher's desire for a 'spectacular show' when it was first performed in 1932 by the Massed Bands and Bugles of the Mediterranean Fleet.

24. The Old Stringbag

1100

Commander Nathan Gray is driving his hire car along the A359 in Somerset. It's a beautiful August morning, but the test pilot is not happy. He slaps the steering wheel with disbelief. 'They've given me a bloody Dinky toy!'

He now regrets opting for 'the compact option'. The bright red Fiat 500 is shiny, but tiny.

It has now been officially confirmed that in ten weeks' time Gray will be the first pilot to attempt landing an F-35B stealth fighter on HMS *Queen Elizabeth*, and today is part of the build-up. He has arranged to take to the air in a particular Royal Navy warplane that he believes will help sharpen his mind, strengthen his resolve and give him heart for the task ahead.

He glances at the decommissioned Sea Harrier permanently parked as a memorial by the main gate of Royal Naval Air Station at Yeovilton and, not for the first time, dwells for a moment on the government decision to axe the seaborne Harrier Force.

He remembers the frantic phone calls back to the UK. Was his job safe? What was a fast-jet pilot going to do if there were no fast jets? Without the Carrier/Harrier combination he and his colleagues felt the Fleet Air Arm had been defanged and the UK's ability to defend itself considerably weakened. Gray initially thought he would have to leave the Navy. But to do what? Become a commercial airline pilot? He shuddered at the thought of ferrying drunken holidaymakers to Magaluf. Having been trained to outwit the enemy in aerial combat, avoid supersonic missiles and dodge anti-aircraft fire, how would he cope with the drudgery of autopilot and circling domestic airports in endless holding patterns?

Instead, he opted for eighteen months of intense training at the elite Test Pilot School in the US. It was the hardest thing he'd ever had to do, but he became one of a tiny cadre of pilots selected for top secret F-35 test flying.

But it is not F-35s or even Harriers Gray has come to see in Yeovilton today. He pulls up to the barrier to show his security pass. An armed guard steps forward to check his ID, takes one look at the Dinky toy and greets him with the broadest of grins.

'Don't say a word!' Gray says.

'No, sir. Not a word.'

The arm rises, and the pilot who flies faster than the speed of sound for a living tucks his little red Fiat into a secluded corner of the visitors' carpark. Half an hour later, after being issued with flying suit, helmet and gloves, he is greeted by Lieutenant Commander Glenn Allison, one of the most experienced pilots in the Fleet Air Arm.

It is pitch-black in the hangar except for the low glow of red exit lights. The smell of aviation fuel is overpowering. Allison goes to a bank of switches and turns them down, one by one. High above them, the main lights flicker then brighten, to reveal every kind of aircraft in the gigantic space. He then walks Gray over to the one they will be flying today.

'Wow!' Gray says. 'Now that's what I call a real warplane.'

He's wide-eyed and open-mouthed. 'Bloody beautiful! Can I touch?'

'Be my guest.'

Gray steps forward and strokes the roughly textured fuselage of the 1941 Fairey Swordfish biplane – the only one in the world still flying. The 'Stringbag', as the Swordfish was affectionately known by its pilots, is a canvas-covered wood and metal torpedo bomber boasting a top speed of 90 knots. It carries three crew in an open cockpit; the pilot sits at the front while the observer and rear-gunner stand behind.

'Exquisite . . .'

Developed in the early 1930s, the Swordfish was all but obsolete by 1939, but a maritime variant proved so capable and durable that it helped change the course of the Second World War. In 1940, a squadron from HMS *Illustrious* made a daring attack on the Italian fleet at Taranto. So many ships were sunk or irreparably damaged that the Italian Navy ceased to be a major threat. In 1941, fifteen Swordfish flying off HMS *Ark Royal* located and fatally disabled the pride of the German Grand Fleet. The damage inflicted was so severe that the crew of the *Bismarck* was forced to scuttle her.

'This was the F-35 of the thirties,' Allison says.

'Swordfish pilots had a much more difficult job to do,' Gray says. 'They had to fly the aircraft with one hand and fight with the other.'

He's right, of course. The F-35 is so advanced that it frees the pilot to concentrate on the battle space. But it does mean that the flying experience can sometimes feel a bit remote. It is to rediscover the visceral nature of traditional flying that Gray is here today. He wants to get closer to the way it used to be, by the seat of his pants.

An hour later, Allison and Gray strap on their parachutes

and climb into the open cockpit. Allison sits in the forward pilot's seat – the only seat in the aircraft. As observer, Gray takes a standing position immediately behind him, and behind him the gunner's position is taken by another crew member, Chief Petty Officer Aircrewman Andy Vanes. He is here for safety reasons. Gray, for all his experience on the world's most modern fighter, is a Swordfish novice.

'OK, sir,' Vanes says. 'This thing is nearly eighty years old, so no ejection seats here. If we have problems and you hear me shout "Jump!" don't hesitate. Leap over the right side and push out with your legs to make sure you don't hit the tail. We'll only bail out above 1,000 feet. Any lower and the chute won't open in time, so stay in and take your chances.'

Two of the ground crew grab the propeller blades and walk them round a couple of times to prime the engine and get the fuel flowing. Then another starts to wind a handle on the left flank of the aircraft. It's an inertia starter, and cranking it spins up a flywheel. It's energetic work and takes around forty to fifty turns to bring the flywheel to speed. This allows the pilot to engage the clutch and the flywheel to impart its energy to the engine. It's a lot of work, but when the Swordfish was operational it was not unknown for the pilot to do the cranking himself before jumping into the cockpit.

The engine bursts into life, and the propeller starts to spin.

Glenn Allison taxis out to the runway, points the Swordfish into the wind and, when he gets the OK from the control tower, lets out the throttle. The nine-cylinder Bristol Pegasus radial engine roars and, spinning the three-bladed propeller at 2,600 revs a minute, powers the aircraft forward.

The Stringbag picks up speed and begins to rise off the runway. Any concerns Gray had about tiny red cars is left behind on the tarmac.

Allison takes the Swordfish up to around 2,000 feet and then follows a course over some of the most beautiful landscape in England. The summer sun, now at its zenith, has added a rich, golden sheen to the patchwork of green and yellow fields below. For anybody else this would simply be a glorious pleasure flight in an iconic and much-loved British warplane, but for Gray it goes much deeper. He is determined to use this unique experience to discover his aviation heritage and connect subliminally with the young pilots who used to fly it into mortal danger.

Allison eases the stick to the left to deflect the starboard aileron. The wing lifts, and the Swordfish responds by falling gracefully into a left-hand turn and then, with a gentle touch on the rudder, he initiates a slow dive towards the farmland below. The aircraft levels out at 500 feet, its shadow darting across fields of ripening wheat. But this pastoral paradise is not what Gray sees. He is imagining the sturdy biplane with its underslung torpedo speeding towards an enemy warship – flying low over a raging sea, through driving wind, rain and the relentless barrage of anti-aircraft guns.

Looking over Allison's shoulders into the cockpit, he reminds himself that flying is never more dangerous than when over the sea. For many, the wide-open ocean is beguiling, alluring and enticing – but naval pilots have a very different perception. They describe it as having a PK of 1 – probability of kill: 100 per cent. A modern precision missile has a PK of 0.8.

Gray shields his eyes from the sun as Allison begins a slow climb to the west, where the sea glints on the far horizon. It is almost as if it were beckoning them on – but that is 'where the dragons be', watching, waiting to strike. Gray prays that the day he lands on the QE they will not come out to play.

He looks down to see the afternoon shadows beginning to stretch over the Somerset landscape. He spots St

Bartholomew's, the Fleet Air Arm church, set in idyllic country-side about 2 miles from the air station. Here all Fleet Air Arm pilots who have died in the service of their country are com-memorated. One plaque means more to Gray than any other.

The one dedicated to Jak London.

1730

Back in his tiny but shiny Fiat, Gray, now heading for the Cotswolds, is buoyed up by today's experience. He feels ener-gized, galvanized, empowered for what is to come. Accelerating up the M5, and passing the time with some mental arithmetic, he calculates that his F-35B Lightning is 1,000 times more powerful than the Dinky toy he is driving, and some 1,400 mph faster than the Swordfish. And that the Swordfish, at £5,500, was half the cost of the Fiat, and some way short of the F-35's £100 million price tag.

Bloody hell! he thinks, as he makes his way to another appointment with the past. *One F-35 could have bought you more than 18,000 Swordfish* . . .

His second destination is Long Newnton in rural Glouces-tershire, where he's going to visit some people he's never met before, despite having a strong spiritual connection.

Gray loses his Satnav signal as he drives deeper into the rolling Gloucestershire countryside. With the help of a paper map he follows tree-lined lanes through endless sheep-strewn fields until he reaches an unsurfaced driveway.

It leads eventually to a large, ivy-covered Cotswold stone house, surrounded by imposing horse chestnut and walnut trees, Turkish hazels and yew hedges which throw their lengthening shadows across immaculately manicured lawns and brimming flower beds. The front door is framed by flowering cherry trees and purple alliums in box parterres. As he reaches for the bell, the sturdy oak door opens.

'Nathan . . .' The smiling blonde woman is probably in her late forties. 'I'm Katharine. We've been so looking forward to meeting you.'

'Likewise,' replies Gray. 'This is such an honour.'

'Come on. You must be gasping for a cup of tea.'

Gray is guided through a spacious, beautifully appointed hallway, and into the kitchen-dining room, where an elderly man sits at a large round table covered with papers and photographs. He is fishing yet more out of an old leather suitcase.

'My father, Michael Dunning,' Katharine says as she reaches for the kettle.

Nathan Gray is delighted to shake hands with the nephew of one of the greatest trailblazers in the history of naval aviation, the father of the aircraft carrier and one of his own all-time heroes.

He then spends an emotional couple of hours leafing through Edwin Dunning's log-books, diaries, letters and personal possessions with Katharine and her father.

Michael Dunning holds up a photograph of Edwin as a boy, with his brothers Gilly and Jack. 'He was always known as "Ned" to his close family and friends.'

Gray reads Edwin's letters to and from his beloved parents, and, perhaps most affecting of all, the great outpouring of love, respect and grief from his friends, comrades and senior officers.

From his captain:

I shall never cease to admire and regret him. He was so keen and full of enthusiasm and such an excellent and capable fellow in every way. Both officers and men serving under him deeply feel the loss of so fine an officer and a gentleman.

From his squadron:

His death has come as a great shock to us – one of the hardest blows of this cruel war. May the thought of what he has done for his country and for us all – his good influence on others – his cheeriness, splendid courage and loving unselfishness help in some degree to heal the wounds of sorrow in the hearts of his dear ones at home and may they feel that his work is not finished: he has passed on to Higher Flights of Glory.

The bonds between Dunning and his shipmates are identical to those Gray has with his own comrades. Katharine hands him a silver hip flask, battered and dented, inscribed with Edwin's name. 'It was recovered from his body after the crash.'

At length, Gray prepares to leave. 'I wouldn't have missed it for the world,' he tells his hosts, brimming with emotion. He bids them farewell and walks out into the dying light of a memorable day.

Before getting back into his car, he leans against a drystone wall, sensing that this is one of those moments when past and future meet. He might fly a very different type of aircraft to Edwin Dunning – or Ned as he now knows him – but the young naval aviator who sacrificed his life for his country 100 years ago would have walked through the same sunshine, felt the same summer breezes, smelled the same fragrant blossom and felt the same dedication to the Navy, the same unquestioning devotion to the men and women with whom he served.

It's been a day of high emotion for Gray and, as he turns the ignition key, he realizes he's even beginning to warm to the little red Fiat that will now take him home.

25. Call of the Sea

1500

The winds are light. The ship's meteorologists confirm the weather is set fair. Jerry Kyd and Darren Houston are at the Rose Table with an array of charts of the Atlantic Ocean. Their arrival in the West Atlantic for Westlant 18 will coincide with the hurricane season, and the captain, though naturally concerned about exposing his men and women to natural hazards, is keen to know what impact heavy seas and high winds will have on his ship.

Glen Peters brings in a tray of coffee.

'Thank you, Glen. Any chance of a Hobnob or two?'

'Yessir. Right away,' the ever-cheerful steward replies in his Caribbean lilt. 'Back in a jiffy, sir.'

'Good man your new steward,' says Houston.

'Absolute godsend,' Kyd says. 'I was sorry to say goodbye to Kirsty, but Glen's meticulous and quite imperturbable. He's a Rastafarian from St Vincent, and nothing seems to faze him. Just the sort of bloke I need on Westlant . . .'

Kyd's ship's company has changed and expanded. The basic complement has increased from just under 700 to just over 800, including a group of sixty very big men in the familiar camouflage uniform of the land forces. But they are not part of the British Army; they are Royal Marines, aka

178

'Bootnecks', the Navy's own sea-soldiers. From Lima Company, 42 Commando, they are here to test the ship's proficiency in delivering a land force to a battle zone using specialist helicopters.

The air wing now comprises flight-deck handlers, firefighters, air traffic controllers and aviators, with many more to fly in once the ship's at sea, and more technicians still to join in the States. Royal Navy clearance divers will keep a watchful eye on the hull and propellers, and there's also the first full Royal Marines military band to go to sea on a warship for fifteen years. The total ship's company now numbers 1,240.

A dark-haired man bearing the rank insignia of commander appears in the day cabin.

'Blackers!' Kyd greets him. 'All good in Flyco?'

'Raring to go, sir,' the newcomer replies.

James Blackmore has taken over from Mark Deller as Commander Air or 'Wings' and will supervise the F-35 test programme. A former fast-jet pilot who flew the last Harrier from the deck of HMS *Ark Royal* on 17 November 2010. His captain then was Jerry Kyd, so to be back under his command for this deployment, which will see the return of fixed-wing aviation to the Royal Navy, is particularly poignant for both men.

'We've come a long way from the axing of the Harriers, Blackers,' Kyd says.

'Absolutely, sir,' Blackmore says. 'New dawn, new beginnings.'

For James Blackmore it's a new dawn in more senses than one. Four weeks ago, the forty-three-year-old father of two was diagnosed with testicular cancer – a massive shock to him and his family. He assumed he would have to pull out of Westlant 18 and face up to the end of his career altogether, but the naval doctors acted quickly. Immediate surgery and a brief convalescence turned the tables on the vicious disease and, now in complete remission, he's delighted to be working with his old friend again.

Together they will oversee the most significant military twinning of warplane and warship in history. Westlant 18, virtually an operational deployment, has to prove Britain's primary conventional deterrent for the next fifty years. If it fails, HMS *Queen Elizabeth* will be dead in the water. Westlant 18 is make or break for the ship; make or break for the Royal Navy; make or break for Great Britain.

Whatever the challenges ahead, the QE, regal in her berth, certainly looks the part. Freshly painted, she boasts striking new crests on her aft tower. About 30 feet in diameter, they portray the Tudor rose of Queen Elizabeth I in red and white, with the letters E and R emblazoned on either side.

The ship may be a primary battle platform, but the intention has always been to use her as a diplomatic one as well. Jerry Kyd is adamant that the power the ship projects should not only be measured by her firepower, but by her ability to influence opinion around the world just by being there. He sees her more as a seagoing Swiss Army knife – capable of as many jobs as she has blades.

Glen Peters returns with a silver tray on which is a plate piled high with Chocolate Hobnobs. 'Leader Peters!' Kyd grins. 'I only wanted one!'

'Sir,' Peters replies, 'it's a fundamental fact of life that one chocolate biscuit is *never* sufficient.'

If the winds allow, the QE will leave on this evening's high tide for a voyage which will offer them the opportunity to display the might of their newest military asset to Britain's closest ally as well as to allow the Royal Navy and US Navy to practise key skills on which they may have to rely in a future battle space. The final dots must now be joined for the QE to be a massive step closer to the day she can be unleashed in anger. And the world will be watching – both friend and foe.

1800

'OK, let's go to America,' Kyd tells his navigation team. 'Bosun, let go all lines!'

The final confirmation of the ship's sailing time was made public very late, so Kyd's been worried there would be no crowds to bid her farewell. Westlant 18 will be his last deployment as a seagoing captain. On his return he will be promoted to admiral, so today is the last time he will ever oversee the embarkation of a Royal Navy warship from a home port.

He looks down wistfully at his ship's company in Procedure Alpha, the familiar thin dark-blue line that edges the entire perimeter of the 4-acre flight deck.

Halfway down on the port side, Frederica McCarthy stands proudly though nervously in her brand-new uniform. 'It's my first time at sea,' the twenty-two-year-old Mancunian admits to the sailor on her right.

'Well, enjoy this bit. The only thing better than leaving harbour is coming back home again.'

'So exciting,' McCarthy says. 'Can't believe we'll be going to New York too.'

'Straight out of training?'

'Yes. I'm a Writer, but I really want to get more involved with the ship if I can. You know, roll my sleeves up and get my hands dirty.'

Chris Trevethan, who has replaced Bob Hawkins as First Lieutenant, takes his own position on the starboard bridge wing for Procedure Alpha. The cheery fifty-year-old, risen from the ranks, has served in the Royal Navy for nearly thirty years, but this is his first carrier. For a frigate and destroyer man, the QE will take some getting used to, and he knows gelling the crew effectively on such a large piece of real estate won't be easy.

'It's only when you leave the wall you really get a sense of how big this ship is,' he tells Dave Hedgecox, the new Commander Weapons Engineering who's taken over from Steve Prest.

Hedgecox nods. 'Like being on top of a tower block.'

Ten senior rates line the front of the ski-jump. At one end, as usual, is Petty Officer Emma Ranson, and next but one is her chief petty officer husband, Paul. They're not the first husband and wife to go to sea with the RN, but it's quite unusual.

A caped figure is about to fill the gap next to him. Alastair Mansfield, the ship's charmingly eccentric new Chaplain (or 'Bish' in Navy speak), walks purposefully up the ski-jump. He's wearing a velvet Canterbury cap, sporting round John Lennon glasses and holding a rough-hewn trident-shaped branch.

'Morning everyone!'

'Good to have you with us, Bish,' Aircraft Handler Scouse Walsh says. 'What's with the big twig?'

Mansfield brandishes his trident proudly. 'I wanted to mark the occasion with something symbolic, so I cut this from a wild thorn tree last night. It represents the land we come from and the land to which we'll safely return.'

'Nice touch, Bish,' Emma Ranson says.

The Royal Marines Band, in full dress uniform, strikes up with 'Sailing', the traditional Navy shanty made famous by Rod Stewart, and marches towards the bow. The giant White

Ensign at the stern, stiffened by the headwind, is waving proudly against a cloudless summer sky.

'My God, look at all the people!' Jerry Kyd says. 'Gunwharf Quays is rammed. And look on the other side – the whole of Gosport must be out!'

The QE already enjoys a healthy following on social media, so part of the responsibility of Arron Hoare and Kyle Heller, the two RN photographers on board, will be to feed the voracious online appetites of Twitter, YouTube, Facebook and Instagram. They are on deck now transmitting live feeds as well as capturing still images for the Navy website and media. Overseeing them is Lindsey Waudby, a perpetually cheerful but ruthlessly efficient Naval Reserve Lieutenant Commander. The former ITN producer and presenter is Head of Media Operations on the QE. For Westlant 18 she'll be responsible for promoting her in the public eye and troubleshooting should things go awry.

Right now, the news is nothing but positive, and Waudby happily directs Arron Hoare as he captures a shot of Frederica McCarthy. Waudby knows a good story when she sees one. McCarthy, fresh-faced and striking, looking genuinely happy and excited on the flight deck of the Navy's biggest ever warship, is good PR in anyone's book.

'Oh my goodness!' says the involuntary star of the moment. 'I've never seen anything like this. Will it be on telly tonight? I hope my parents see it!'

'Two blasts, please, Yeoman,' Jerry Kyd shouts.

The ship's horn is promptly sounded to salute her ecstatic fans.

'This is magnificent,' Alastair Mansfield shouts out loud. 'Those are our people cheering and they care about us. It makes the heart swell.'

HMS *Queen Elizabeth* moves past a packed Round Tower and slides serenely into the Solent. The crowds swell all along Southsea promenade. Jerry Kyd scans the shoreline, wondering why he was remotely worried. He turns his binoculars to the bow, where the Chaplain obstinately maintains his position despite the strengthening headwind, leaning forward at an ever-increasing angle, eyes tight shut and cloak blowing out horizontally behind him.

'The Bish is about to take off, I think,' Kyd says. 'Good man. Completely bonkers of course . . .'

26. Pushing the Boat Out

English Channel, 19 August 2018

0945

Like an athlete before a race, the QE is limbering up. The captain will only strike out across the Atlantic when Neil McCallum, Commander Marine Engineering, is happy that both gas turbines and all four diesels are performing to expectation, and that might not be for another two or three days.

In the meantime, the ship's company must adjust once more to life on the ocean wave. The duty watch in the Ship's Control Centre monitors her vital signs through banks of computers and sensors; down in the engine spaces, the marine engineers scrutinize the pressure gauges and salt water cooling dials; on the bridge the navigation team plots a safe course through one of the busiest sea channels in the world; and in the medical complex, naval nurses and doctors are busy with morning surgery. At one end of the cavernous hangar, aviation mechanics check the rotor blades of one of the ship's Merlin Mark 2 helicopters, while at the other end Royal Marines are subjected to vigorous close-combat training.

The new First Lieutenant is on his morning rounds. Known for being strict but fair, Chris Trevethan is also famed for his career-long habit of calling everyone and anyone 'shipmate'. He freely admits, 'It's a damn sight easier than trying to remember thousands of names.'

Turning a corner from one passageway into another on 3 Deck, he spots a gaggle of sailors cleaning the flats with mops and buckets.

'Don't just dab at it, shipmate!' he booms at an unsuspecting young rating. 'Put your back into it – look like you *mean* it.'

'Yessir,' the hapless sailor squeaks.

'No, shipmate. Not like that . . .'

'No, sir?'

'You're just pushing dirt around the deck.'

'Er . . . I . . . er . . .'

'Gimme the mop, shipmate.'

'Yessir.'

'This might be the most modern warship in the world, but it doesn't do automatic flat-mopping. That's still up to people called sailors. Which is what you are – allegedly! Watch my technique, shipmate!' The genial perfectionist scrubs vigorously at the flat with his commandeered mop before squeezing it out in the bucket with a flourish.

The naval preoccupation with dusting, brushing, washing, mopping, scrubbing, scouring, scraping, burnishing and polishing is not just about order, discipline and instilling pride but also, vitally, concerns communal hygiene and collective efficacy. Germs, disease and illness could spread rapidly in such a closed and sequestered community, and this would have a debilitating effect on the ship's ability to defend itself and wage war.

Lean-manning is a double-edged sword. Even though the ship's slimline crew has been increased following the lessons learned in the North Sea, the overall complement of about 1,200 sailors is still limited. The advantages of automation on the QE are clear to see. The Highly Mechanized Weapons Handling System requires only about thirty sailors to lift and transport bombs and missiles from the deep magazines to the flight deck. An American carrier would need around 300. But, as Trevethan likes to point out, cleaning still requires large dollops of good old-fashioned elbow grease. On USS *George H. W. Bush* the maintenance ratio works out to about 1 sailor per 20 tons of ship. Here it is 1 sailor to every 65 tons. Ergo, British sailors on the QE have to work three times harder than their American counterparts to keep their ship clean.

'You see,' Trevethan says, 'a nice long, strong action, and then rinse . . . !'

'Yessir!'

'OK, shipmate. Carry on.'

Wes Khan is overseeing lunch preparation in the main for'ard galley. 'Today we've six main course choices,' he announces to his trainee assistants. 'One is cheesy hammy eggies, which people love, so we'll be making hundreds.' His eyes sparkle. Next on the list is another Navy favourite – trainsmash, a tomato-based casserole. 'Quick to eat. No chewing. Straight down the hatch!'

The new Commander Logistics, Jenny Curwood, who's replaced Fiona Percival, is giving Lindsey Waudby a guided tour of the ship's two vast larders down on 8 Deck. The Head of Media Operations wants to issue a press release to spark public interest in the warship's mighty housekeeping challenge.

'Most ships have just one food store.' Curwood pushes through a vast steel door into a space that stretches across the entire width of the ship. 'But we have one aft, this one, and another for'ard. Together they contain enough food to sustain us for up to sixty days.'

'Wow . . .' Waudby makes notes in perfect shorthand. 'Is the other one this big too?'

'Exactly the same.'

The stores are replicated as part of the ship's risk management, and located as far away from each other as possible so that if one is destroyed by flood, fire or enemy attack there's another to fall back on.

'They're the largest dry-food stores and fridges in the Royal Navy,' Curwood says with pride. 'To feed everyone breakfast, lunch and supper, our budget's £3.11p per person per day.'

'That's less than for a police dog . . .' Waudby keeps scribbling. 'That's a story right there!'

'People might be interested in our milk situation,' Curwood says. 'Fresh milk for cereals, tea and coffee directly impacts on ship's morale, but it's got very limited "survival time", so it's the first thing to be resupplied when we come into port. We get through 360 litres a day. Nobody's happy if we have to resort to Long Life milk or, God forbid, powdered milk – that's knocking on the door of a full-scale mutiny!'

Waudby laughs. 'We take things like that for granted shore-side, don't we?'

'We certainly do. But so much of what we do here's about efficient use of resources. Essential to economy and efficiency is the need to minimize waste and to reuse appropriate foods in stews, soups or salads. We're first and foremost a war machine, so we always have to keep that primary purpose in mind – even in the galleys.'

The QE, like any warship, must not be forced offline when operationally immersed. Food and fuel must be constantly sustained, and not just at landfall. Royal Fleet Auxiliary tankers and store-ships will transfer thousands of tons of fuel and stores, via a perilous operation known as replenishment at sea (RAS), which involves coming close alongside often in raging seas. She will attempt both RAS and VertReps (vertical replenishments via helicopter) on this deployment.

'Even if we're at war,' Curwood continues, 'we must maintain a balanced and healthy diet and continue to cater for all – vegetarian, vegan, gluten-free, dairy-free, halal, kosher and allergies. Food's about morale – and that's at a premium on a warship, especially if people are trying to do you harm and sink you. Amazing what a square meal can do to keep up the spirits.'

Jenny Curwood is a vivacious and indefatigable forty-five-year-old mother of three, responsible for keeping the ship not only fed and fuelled but also supplied with ammunition, engine spares, uniforms, medical supplies and even beer and wine. You name it, Curwood will not only find a way of acquiring it from anywhere in the world, but also transporting it and getting it on board whether at sea or alongside.

'It's not easy,' she admits cheerfully to Waudby. 'But I usually manage to keep the ship supplied with most things. Although I'm not quite so efficient in my personal life. I buy chocolate for my kids from different parts of the world, but it never seems to make it out of my cabin. For a supply officer, chocoholism's a slippery slope . . .'

The gash teams are busy sorting through the rubbish in the pyrolysis plant and separating it according to the strict rules previously implemented with such gusto by former bad boy Ricky Gleason. He has left the ship along with many of the previous gash-team volunteers, so new ones have stepped forward. One of them is Frederica McCarthy, the baby sailor who trained as a Writer but wanted to get her hands dirty. She works in the ship's office on a half-shift and does six hours a day as a gash-girl.

'Why do you want to do that?' enquire her incredulous messmates.

'For an extra seven pounds a day,' she says simply. 'It'll come in very useful when I hit those shops in New York.'

McCarthy has to wear voluminous, dark-blue overalls and thick yellow rubber gloves, with her hair piled up on top of her head, but the shapely Mancunian is still turning heads. More than a few Royal Marines are bringing their gash to be sorted with surprising alacrity and some might say suspicious regularity.

1015

The ship's broadcast system buzzes and clicks – an indication that someone's about to make a general address. *'D'ye hear there?'* says a disembodied but familiar voice. *'If you like sweets and don't mind receiving them from a rather strange man then come to the quarterdeck at 1030. That is all.'*

Alastair Mansfield, laden with Haribo, Maltesers and Quality Street, is preparing for the first service of Westlant 18 in his own inimitable fashion. 'Call it blackmail if you like,' he chuckles to Lindsey Waudby as they proceed along one of the main passageways. 'But everybody likes sweets, and I've no problem helping people to associate church with something nice.'

They push open a heavy steel door to the wide-open quarterdeck at the stern. Sheltered from the wind but open to the sea, it's a naturally peaceful place which affords a great view of the ocean and the long, snaking wake that permanently trails behind the QE.

'Wonderful!' The Chaplain fills his lungs with sea air. 'This place provokes thought and encourages contemplation. Perfect for my line of work.'

The flight deck is now strictly out of bounds to everyone except the air wing, so for the next four months most on board will be restricted to their own dedicated live and work spaces in the ship's belly. Daylight for the vast majority of the ship's company will be in short supply.

Fifty-eight-year-old Mansfield, married with a teenage son of fifteen, is a deep-thinking man, but a life in the Navy has also heightened his sense of the absurd. Naval humour, distinct and culturally ingrained, is a coping mechanism that most career sailors learn to employ with some proficiency, but few more so than he.

'What made you sign up for this, Bish?' Waudby asks. 'I often wonder why men of the cloth opt for a military career.'

'I really did hear the call of the sea.' Mansfield gazes out over the grey-green waters of the English Channel. 'I was attracted by the romance of it, and the challenge too.'

'But what triggered it?'

'Well, when I was a young priest working in a London parish I was frustrated and uncertain about which direction I should go. I suffered a crisis of confidence, I suppose, and confided in a wonderful old priest called Robin Morrell who'd been a naval gunnery officer in the Second World War. He simply said, "Al, I think you'd learn more about faith in a warship than anywhere on land." I wrote to him before he died and said, "Robin, you remember what you told me about warships – you were right."'

He picks up the microphone to address his expanding and expectant congregation. 'Queue up and get your sweeties here, people . . .'

1030

A lone musician is about to start practising below deck. Frank Rochford, a twenty-four-year-old Scot from Campbeltown, is a musical prodigy. He plays clarinet in the marching band, but also, as a gifted soloist, the violin and the instrument of his beloved motherland – the bagpipes.

After a lot of trial and error, Rochford has found the ideal rehearsal space. It's not a bespoke music room but a cramped store stacked from floor to ceiling with super-soft, ultra-absorbent toilet rolls. 'Absorbent' is the key word here, as it makes the room acoustically ideal.

There's not a lot of scope for the bagpipe enthusiast in a military band, but there's already the thought that Rochford might play his from the top of the ski-slope when the ship enters New York Harbour. 'It might be wishful thinking,' he tells his bandmates. 'But just imagine. What a way that would be to come into New York!'

Well beyond the reach of Rochford's bagpipes, Glen Peters is in the Captain's Pantry, ironing shirts and singing along to 'Natural Mystic' by Bob Marley on his iPod.

'Hey, man, I love my music,' he tells anyone who questions whether he should be listening while working. 'It keeps me goin', soothes me, and the captain don't mind, an' that's the main consideration.' Swaying to the infectious calypso-reggae beat, he takes another shirt from the pile, spreads it over the board and picks up the steam iron. 'I like ironing,' he freely admits. 'It's relaxin'. Helps me to think and meditate.'

A committed Rastafarian, Peters wears his hair in dreadlocks (tied in a bun when in uniform), worships Haile Selassie, meditates, neither drinks nor smokes and lives a life of peaceful endeavour. But his wayward background is something he freely admits to. He's as proud of having turned himself around as he is of being a Royal Navy sailor.

'I was outta control back home,' he will confide. 'An angry young man, had five kids by five ladies and in trouble with the police. If I hadn't changed paths, I'd be dead by now. For sure.'

It all changed for Peters when he responded to a RN recruitment drive in St Vincent. Peters is one of around fifty Caribbean nationals on board, at least six of whom are from St Vincent, although none can boast quite as colourful a past.

Peters' endeavours are interrupted by the ring of the pantry phone.

'Hello, Leader Peters here ... Ah yes, thanks, Chief Blunt ... I'll collect it tomorrow ... around 1600? Great ... No, he doesn't!'

It's Jerry Kyd's fifty-first birthday tomorrow, and he thinks no one knows.

1830

All the Heads of Department, from War, Logistics, Aviation and Weapons to Marine Engineering, Intelligence and Medical, are filing into the captain's day cabin. One by one they take their seats at the Rose Table to await Jerry Kyd's arrival. Every evening throughout Westlant 18 the HODs, plus Darren Houston and Chaplain Alastair Mansfield, will meet here for a Command brief. This gives everyone the opportunity to report on their department and highlight any issues or problems that may have arisen over the last twenty-four hours. It also allows the captain to speak openly about his current concerns and future intentions.

One by one, the HODs will summarize their day – briefly, succinctly and to the point.

'Jenny – you first,' Kyd says. 'Sustainability?'

'Three weeks' fuel and sixty days' food, sir. No outstanding needs.'

'Thanks, Jenny. Bish?'

Alastair Mansfield leans forward in his chair. 'Chapel all in order, captain. The Royal Marines Band is a fantastic addition and will provide us with great supporting music for our Sunday services. I'm currently looking for a space for an all-faiths prayer room.'

'How many faiths on board, Bish?' Kyd asks.

'Not sure yet. Christianity, obviously. Several denominations. Muslim, Rastafarian, Hindu and Judaism. Maybe more.'

'Must be somewhere amongst our 3,000 compartments?'

'Yes, captain. I've got my eyes on one possible space on 2 Deck.'

'OK, Bish. Let me know how you get on. Wings?'

'All good, sir,' James Blackmore says. '820 Naval Air Squadron embarked. Three cabs. All serviceable. CO is Grassy Knowles. He'll oversee anti-submarine training plus search and rescue during our Atlantic crossing. We'll pick up 845 Naval Air Squadron in a couple of days when we're in the southwest approaches. Bob Bond will bring in three more Merlin Mark 4s plus his full complement of thirty-nine pilots, crew and technicians. Ready for sea, sir.'

'Thanks, Jim.'

Jerry Kyd turns to Neil McCallum.

'OK, "Engines". How many wheels on the wagon?'

'Sir, I'm happy to say that we have all six burning and turning. Four diesels and both gas turbines.'

'Excellent. Anything from you, Darren?'

'No, sir. All good,' says his second in command.

'OK. Thanks, everyone. Just a few words from me then before dinner . . .' Jerry Kyd pauses momentarily to refocus everyone's attention.

'Guys, it's vital we settle into our routines ASAP. Things are going to get much more complicated soon, and it's all going to happen very fast. When 845 Squadron join us the number of aircraft on board will be doubled . . .'

Jerry Kyd points out of the windows to the four 820 Squadron Merlin Mark 2s already on the flight deck.

'The paradox of an aircraft carrier in my experience is that the more aircraft you have, the easier things get. It forces you to be more organized and on top of things. I wager, as we fill up with rotary-wing and eventually jets, we'll find things on deck and in the hangar getting easier as people get busier and more attuned. So, before we start across the Atlantic, please all make sure that your ducks are in a row in every department. My hope is we'll commence the Atlantic transit in twenty-four to forty-eight hours. OK. That's it guys. Have a good evening.'

The officers head for their dining room, where they'll sit down together for a three-course dinner, followed by coffee and cheese in the wardroom next door. This is their time to relax, but above all it's a chance for them to spend time together and bond in a non-work context. It's also a chance to share a bottle of wine or a few beers. Now that HMS *Queen Elizabeth* is commissioned, she has automatically become a 'wet' ship.

The captain stays in his day cabin, where he will, as usual, sit down to eat alone. Glen Peters sets his place for one at the now vacated Rose Table, while Kyd enjoys a glass of alcohol-free beer and a packet of Walkers salt and vinegar crisps – his hors d'oeuvre of choice. It's not that Jerry Kyd is antisocial, frugal or unduly abstemious, but as a Royal Navy captain this degree of social isolation simply comes with the job.

'Don't you ever feel you'd like to be dining in the ward-room with the officers, sir?' Peters asks.

'They call it the loneliness of command, Glen.' Kyd grins. 'But I don't see it that way. There needs to be an element of separation between me and my officers. The last thing they want is for the grumpy old boss to invade their space, and it's the last thing I want to do too. At the end of the day, I really like to wind down on my own.'

'To the extent you can wind down, sir.'

'True, Glen. No rest for the wicked. Or naval COs.'

Kyd is on call twenty-four hours a day, which is why his cabin is just under the bridge and why he will never touch alcohol at sea. On a warship anything can happen at any time, and the buck will always stop with him.

'Dinner is served, sir,' Peters says. 'Prawn cocktail. Shep-herd's pie and veg. Negative duff. Cheese and biscuits.'

'Excellent.' Jerry Kyd takes his place at the Rose Table.

'Another alcohol-free beer, sir?'

'Why not. Let's push the boat out!'

Peters opens another bottle of San Miguel oo and pours it expertly into the captain's glass.

'What was that music you were playing in the pantry just now, Glen?'

'That was "Boombastic" by Shaggy, sir.'

'Hmm – it was great. I'm really getting into this reggae of yours.'

'Nutt'in wrong with that, sir.' Peters gives him a megawatt smile.

27. Us Watching Them Watching Us

English Channel, 20 August 2018

Kyle Heller, one of the ship's photographers, walks out on the starboard boat bay to check if he can still get a mobile phone signal as the QE scythes through the grey waters just off the Cornish coast. He becomes vaguely aware of a high-pitched sound in the vicinity.

'Can you hear that?' he asks a nearby sailor.

'What?'

'That sort of . . . twittering sound?'

The sailor tilts her head.

'Oh yeah . . . something electrical, maybe?'

'I think it's coming from up there . . .' Heller points at a ledge about 10 feet up.

He pulls out a GoPro from his camera bag, attaches it to a monopod and raises it to film whatever might be there.

Lieutenant Commander Lindsey Waudby's phone rings.

'Ma'am, Kyle here. I'm in the starboard aft boat bay. I think you'd better come down. We've found something.'

Five minutes later, Heller is showing her the GoPro footage.

'Chicks! What are they? Seagulls?'

'No, ma'am. We think they're baby pigeons.'

'Pigeons!'

'Yes, ma'am. They must have hatched back in Portsmouth, but the mum couldn't follow us out to sea.'

With the help of a ladder and a dabber, the two chicks are gently retrieved and placed in a cardboard box, then taken to the Media Office for safekeeping.

Waudby peers down at the two balls of fluff, who look back at her with wide, unblinking eyes. 'What do baby pigeons eat?'

Before anyone can answer, an urgent request comes through for Heller to report to the starboard bridge wing with his most powerful telephoto lens. A Russian warship has been spotted in the near distance so needs to be officially photographed and identified without delay.

In the Operations Room, the ship's nerve centre, Lieutenant Commander Pete Davies, Principal Warfare Officer (Communications), picks up the main broadcast microphone to address the ship's company.

'D'ye hear there. Due to the proximity of a Russian Federation warship we need to minimize our emissions and transmissions. So personal mobile phones may not be used until further notice. Information from intercepted emissions could be collected and exploited for long-term military use and could compromise you, your family and friends. Those found wilfully contravening this order will face disciplinary action. Assume River City State 1. That is all.'

The 'River City State' code-word indicates various levels of communications regulation and restriction, ranging from 4 (normal) to 1 (maximum restriction). The ship also switches automatically from 'Area Risk State White' to 'Area Risk State Purple' – the highest level of concealment and lockdown – to make sure the ship's own GMS transmissions are minimized and that no maritime or aviation procedures of a strategic nature are practised whilst in direct view of a potential adversary.

To reduce her electro-magnetic footprint, HMS *Queen Elizabeth* must immediately adjust her normal posture and adopt a strategic silence until further notice. It is Pete Davies' job to keep eyes on the Russian frigate and to ensure the communication blackout is maintained until she moves away.

'Fairly routine stuff, guys,' he announces to his junior colleagues. 'This is a standard defensive measure to ensure the Russians can't gather information and track us. We might not be on a combat footing but as a top-secret military asset we don't want them to know how our own instrumentation works or for them to gain any access to information about our personnel.'

Quite apart from the ship's own electronic signature, 1,200 mobile phones would act as a very significant loudspeaker to a listening enemy. Not only could personal calls be intercepted, but social media accounts could be hacked. This can have serious security implications at the best of times, but right now, in such close proximity to a Russian warship, the potential to unwittingly supply useful information to their intelligence service is significantly increased.

Kyle Heller, on the bridge wing, takes a series of photos of the Russian warship intermittently visible through the thickening sea fog. It's soon confirmed as the *Admiral Makarov*, a highly capable frigate with a ship's company of 200 and armed with Kalibr long-range cruise missiles, torpedoes and a rocket launcher. With the help of the Norwegian Navy, the RN has been tracking the *Makarov* since her departure from the Baltic a week ago en route to her permanent Black Sea base of Sevastopol on the Crimean Peninsula. Shadowed by HMS *Hurworth*, a Portsmouth-based mine-hunter, and, at some distance, by a Wildcat helicopter from 815 Naval Air Squadron, it may be entirely coincidental that the Russian frigates route has brought her this close to HMS *Queen Elizabeth*, but it's afforded the Russians their first close-up glimpse of the world's most advanced carrier, which they may one day have to engage in combat.

While some are attending to stowaway pigeons and others monitoring the inquisitive Russian frigate, Leading Chef Wes Khan is climbing the steep stairwells from 5 Deck to 2 Deck, where he has an appointment with the Chaplain.

'It's a long way up from the galley, Bish,' he says, breathing hard. 'Time to start early-morning circuits and lose some of this.' He rubs his ample stomach.

'Well, don't lose too much,' Mansfield replies. 'You know what they say – never trust a thin cook!'

The Chaplain ushers Khan into an empty office about 30 feet long by 15 wide. 'Wes, this is part of Air Department's domain, but currently unallocated, so for now it's going to be our All Faiths Prayer Room.' The spare cabin he prayed in last year has been reassigned for accommodation.

'That's fantastic, Bish.'

'Anyone can use this, of whatever faith or persuasion,' Mansfield says. 'Just needs softening a bit with some carpet and something on the walls. I'll put in a small table and a Bible.'

'And I'll put a Koran in here. A prayer rug as well.'

The two men stand back and admire the vacant space now commandeered for supplication, contemplation and reflection.

'Hotwet, Bish?'

'Excellent idea, Wes.'

The Muslim chef and the Christian Chaplain head to the junior galley for a well-earned cup of tea.

The *Admiral Makarov* is about 3 miles out, on the port bow. Jerry Kyd is surrounded by six of his Young Officers, who've come up to the bridge to have a look for themselves. The Cold War was in full swing back in 1985, when Kyd joined his first ship as a young midshipman. 'Back then, if the balloon had gone up, we were very much the dominating force at sea against the Soviet Navy,' he tells them. 'That's not so much the case these days. The Russians have been busy improving their armed forces, especially their Navy, and now field a range of extremely effective weaponry, such as supersonic guided missiles. They're busy and increasingly capable and really trying to test us in the Atlantic and the Mediterranean.'

He knows only too well that the Russians have been pushing their luck in recent years and regularly making both surface and subsurface sorties into waters around the UK, and probing British airspace with their warplanes. 'It's continuous shadow-boxing – us watching them watching us.

'Even as would-be adversaries, we remain strangely bonded as fellow sailors. There's always a shared respect amongst mariners operating in often pretty treacherous conditions. But we must never get complacent and forget that the Russians are still a potential enemy.'

'How much of a threat are they, sir, realistically?' a female sub-lieutenant asks.

Kyd pauses. Schooled as a naval officer in the Cold War, he is above all a pragmatist and recognizes grave similarities between then and now. 'The Russians are showing clear intent again,' he says. 'Just look at what's happening in the Ukraine, and recently much closer to home with the Novichok incident in Salisbury. These are continuous and profound reminders that we cannot let our guard down – ever. Our armed forces provide the nation's ultimate insurance policy, and I mean across all the services, not just the Navy. We enjoy prosperity and freedoms that most of you young people take completely for granted these days. But our security, I'm afraid, is veneer thin.'

Jerry Kyd is well aware that the greatest threat from a potential foe is not a nuclear strike. He knows the West is very vulnerable now. The Russians could easily attack with missiles and target critical national infrastructure like power stations. Chaos and social unrest would likely consume the UK within a matter of days.

'It's vital we maintain control over our sea-space and air-space at all times.'

Though optimistic by nature and always measured in his strategic analysis, Jerry Kyd is nonetheless as convinced of the Russian threat as he is steely in his resolve to counter it.

'Bridge, please, Officer of the Watch . . .' Glen Peters seeks permission to enter with a silver tray.

'Yes, please,' comes the immediate response.

Jerry Kyd takes a sip of coffee before raising his binoculars once again. 'The Russians were very dismissive about the QE at first,' he tells his YOs. 'Their response to the prospect of this ship being built was openly contemptuous. They said, "It's just a large, convenient target for our missiles", and that they could "send her to the bottom of the sea". I'm rather more confident in our ability not only to stay afloat but to prevail. In reality they'll be very worried about what we can do and what we're generating here, especially with the F-35s on board and our latest destroyers and nuclear submarines coming online.'

Kyd has every confidence in the QE as a strategic asset – a huge, sovereign, sea-based battle platform that will pack a massive punch from anywhere on the planet.

He also knows that while the Russian Navy does pose a threat, it doesn't have much to compete with the QE. The

Russians have several ageing helicopter carriers, but their main fixed-wing carrier, the *Admiral Kuznetsov*, built in 1985, is currently out of service. They're planning a new 100,000-ton, nuclear-powered Shtorm Class carrier, but even if they go ahead with the build it is unlikely to be laid down until 2025 or even 2030.

'There's no doubt about it,' he says, 'with the QE Class carriers we and the US will be way a head of the rest of the world. This is a twenty-first-century ship, and that's why the Russians, the Chinese and the North Koreans will be watching us with concerned interest.'

He takes another sip of coffee. 'If I were a betting man, I'd put money on our first operational deployment being in the Far East, and even the South China Seas – to let us show mutual intent with our key allies.'

The Russian frigate, enshrouded in sea fog, is now hardly distinguishable from the grey sea and sky that frame her.

'Squawk, squawk!'

'It mustn't be too thick, but quite liquidy ...' Dave Hedgecox, the new Commander Weapons Engineering, is mixing a cup full of oats and water.

'I think they know they're going to be fed,' Lindsey Waudby says. 'They're going crazy!'

'Squawk, squawk, squawk!'

The two pigeon chicks, all downy fluff and sprouting feathers with gigantic beaks they have yet to grow into, are bouncing round their cardboard box like a couple of cage-fighters.

'What a racket!' Kyle Heller has returned from his mission to photograph the Russian frigate. 'I could hear them all the way down the passageway.'

'Breakfast coming up.' Hedgecox spoons oat-mix into a plastic syringe which he pushes into a finger cut from a blue latex glove. He then snips off the fingertip to allow the porridge to seep out – emulating the way the chicks feed from their parents.

'Right, thanks to Google, I'm now a mother pigeon,' he says proudly.

'Look at 'em go!' Waudby says. 'They love it! You're wasted on weapons, sir!'

Though delighted at this display of naval enterprise, Waudby remains concerned about the chicks' future. There's no possibility of keeping them until they can fly because by then they'd be halfway across the Atlantic. If they were released at sea, they'd perish. She knows the chances of their survival are remote.

1800

'*Sir, the naval escort, HMS* Hurworth, *is diverging, and the* Makarov *is heading south and away from us.*'

'Very good. Thank you, Officer of the Watch.'

Kyd puts down the receiver and goes to the window of his day cabin to watch the frigate disappearing into the distance. He can now order his ship to revert to a normal communication stance.

'That's what I love about being at sea,' Kyd says. 'You can plan till you're blue in the face, but the unexpected will still unseat you.'

''Twas ever thus, sir,' Houston agrees.

'Let the Russians watch and wonder.' Kyd grins. 'But at a distance, if you please, Mr Putin.'

A deep drone sounds just outside. 'What on earth is that?' Kyd says.

The volume increases alarmingly as the door opens. Glen Peters appears with a small but highly decorated cake, made in secret by Aaron Blunt, the captain's chef – a chocolate sponge, covered in a riot of white and pink icing and boasting a single lighted candle. And now Frank Rochford marches through the door to unleash the bloodcurdling skirl of his Highland pipes in a hearty rendition of 'Happy Birthday'.

'Many happy returns, captain,' Peters says. 'Thirty-one today, isn't it, sir?'

28. Furious Flight

0840

'Can't see a bloody thing!'

Jim Blackmore is peering through his binoculars from the Papal Balcony in Flyco. A white haze hangs heavy in front of him: a swirling, diaphanous sea mist that's triggered the ship's automatic fog horn, which is now blasting out intermittently but insistently to warn of her encroaching presence.

Blackmore is looking out for three specialist helicopters coming in from Yeovilton. Once Furious Flight, part of 845 Naval Air Squadron, is embarked, and as long as Jerry Kyd is happy with the ship's propulsion, the QE will leave territorial waters to commence her Atlantic transit.

Hopefully sometime tomorrow.

Lindsey Waudby peeps into the box containing the stowaway pigeons. 'Good morning, babies,' she says softly. 'What are we going to do with you?'

She's asked the aviation department to let her know of any last-minute flights ashore before the Atlantic transit gets underway. She knows she can't possibly request a special flight to transport what many would regard as vermin.

She replaces the lid and starts her working day.

The Head of Media Operation's job is far from

straightforward. Much about the ship is classified or even top secret, so the best stories are simply not for public consumption. Nevertheless she has to spark press interest and feed the voracious QE social media platforms. The public interest in war machines and battle technology is less vigorous than in human stories – and not only the feel-good ones. Waudby not only needs to promote the positive but also suppress the negative. She is part publicist and part firefighter.

845 Naval Air Squadron's Furious Flight is a helicopter squadron with a great deal of history but completely new to carrier operations. That could tick the right boxes. She starts to draft a press release.

Flying in convoy through a lifting fog bank, the three Merlin Mark 4s head towards HMS *Queen Elizabeth* but are arriving later than expected. Bob Bond, piloting the lead helicopter, is a highly accomplished naval pilot and Commanding Officer of 845 Naval Air Squadron. A highflyer in every sense of the word, he's also an incorrigible action man who, like Nathan Gray, won his own Royal Marines Green Beret to add to his coveted Wings. In 2008, he volunteered for special duties and became involved in hush-hush specialist reconnaissance in a variety of locations around the world, including Afghanistan. This Commander Bond is not short of 007 parallels, and he's quick to enjoy the resulting banter.

'Cerberus to Furious – you're cleared to close. I now hold you 20 miles to the north west.'

'*Roger, Cerberus – approaching your control zone.*'

'Roger, Furious Flight . . . oh, and, er, Commander Bond, the captain has been expecting you . . .'

Bob Bond laughs. He's heard all the wisecracks a thousand times but would be disappointed if they dried up.

'On radar now, sir,' calls an air traffic controller. 'Furious Flight inbound.'

'Excellent.'

Jim Blackmore's screen shows three dots in a line coming in from the north. Furious Flight is part of the Helicopter Commando Force. Nicknamed the 'Junglies' after their work in Borneo and Malaya in the 1950s and 1960s, they specialize in dropping Royal Marines and Special Forces behind enemy lines. Whilst part of the Royal Navy, they have always been land-based – until now. Their ultra-modern Mark 4 Merlins have been specially refitted and upgraded to work from a sea platform.

The airframe and avionics have been 'marinized', optimized for ship-borne amphibious operations. They have folding tails and rotor heads that allow them to be stowed more easily, and extra communication equipment and improved buoyancy should they crash into the sea. Unlike the Mark 2 Merlins of 820 Squadron, which specialize in anti-submarine warfare and air-sea rescue, the Mark 4 Merlins of Furious Flight will concentrate on more covert work in enemy territory.

'*Visual, Cerberus!*' Bob Bond says. '*See you now. Coming in low at 200 feet.*'

'Welcome, Furious. We see you too,' the QE's control tower replies.

Bob Bond leads the Merlins into a low flypast in salute to the Navy's future flagship.

'*Furious on a run down your port side, Cerberus,*' he says. '*Stand by to recover three cabs coming home to Mum.*'

'Cerberus ready and waiting, Furious.'

The three grey helicopters circle in preparation for landing. Bob Bond and his crew can see the yellow-helmeted aircraft handlers moving into position on the flight deck to guide them in.

Leading Aircraft Handler Scouse Walsh prepares to guide

in the first of the Junglies to 3 Spot, halfway down the flight deck. His broad grin is suddenly replaced by tight-lipped concentration. With clear, precise arm signals he directs Bob Bond into a hovering position over the sea on the port side, then beckons him in sideways towards the centre of the flight deck. Once wheels are on deck, Walsh raises his crossed arms to knock wrist against wrist, confirming a successful touchdown. On his next signal, four waiting handlers move forward to tie down the Merlin with restraining straps as it powers down.

Scouse Walsh has been in the Navy long enough to have worked on the Harrier fleet that flew off *Illustrious*, *Invincible* and *Ark Royal*. He never thought he'd see the return of fixed-wing flying, so this deployment is a dream come true. He's counting down the days to the first F-35B landing.

Jim Blackmore strides out across the flight deck.

'Hello, Bob – what time do you call this?'

'Sorry, Blackers. Bloody fog at base!' Bond grasps Blackmore's outstretched hand.

'Well, you're here now.'

'Most of us,' Bond says. A number of aircrew have been stranded in Yeovilton, so an aircraft has to go back and pick them up.

Blackmore brightens. 'Oh really? May have a couple of passengers to go ashore, if that's OK?'

'Sure. Plenty of room. Who are they?'

'Er . . . aviators, Bob. Trainee aviators.'

Dave Hedgecox is preparing the chicks' midday feed in Lindsey Waudby's Media Office. The weapons engineering specialist is delighted with his two charges' healthy addiction to warm porridge. He has started to administer another helping when there's a loud knock on the door.

'I've come to see your stowaways,' Jim Blackmore says. 'Just in time for tea.'

Jim Blackmore peers into the box. 'Have they got names?'

'Yessir,' Waudby says. 'That one's F-35, and the other is Lightning.'

'Excellent,' Blackmore says. 'Now listen, I've got good news. There's an empty cab going, but it leaves in an hour . . .'

In less than five minutes, after a frantic Google search, Waudby is on the phone. 'Is that West Hatch Animal Rescue Centre?'

Within the hour, she's in the Flight Crew Room, handing over a box marked 'live animals' to Scouse Walsh.

'Pigeons?!' He puts his ear to the box. 'Bloody hell, I can hear them! They'd be better in a pie if you ask me, but I'm here to obey orders. So let's go!'

Walsh walks briskly across the flight deck and hands the box to one of the camouflaged commando aircrew on the Merlin, who places it carefully on a seat and secures it with a double harness.

Moments later, Hedgecox and Waudby watch the helicopter take off, sweep round the bow and head north for the Dorset coast, along with the luckiest pigeons in history flying to safety even before they can fly themselves.

HMS *Queen Elizabeth* has successfully executed its first 'humanitarian' undertaking.

'I'll miss them,' Waudby says wistfully. 'Our very own carrier-pigeons.'

1900

Commander Darren Houston picks up the microphone to deliver his routine end of day sitrep.

'*Good evening, Elizabethans. It's been a busy day. We encountered a Russian Federation warship, hence the constraints imposed on our communications. Sorry about that, especially as we won't be in signal for much longer. We welcomed 845 Squadron today; it's very good having them on board. Finally, you may have heard we had a couple of stowaways. They've now been safely delivered to an animal welfare centre ashore, where they will be looked after until ready to be released. Tomorrow, you'll be pleased to hear, we start our long passage to Florida. Have a very good evening.*'

29. Weather Watch

0900

In the early hours of this morning, to everyone's surprise, the QE was ordered to divert from her transatlantic course to a northerly one. In a highly classified development, she was directed by the Admiralty to turn right at Cornwall and head towards the deep waters off the northwest coast without delay. So sensitive was this sudden tasking that the reason for it was not released to the general ship's company let alone the press and wider public.

Gossip on the mess decks has been rife, and the rumours generated, in all cases, wide of the mark.

'Bet we've got a technical problem.'

'Westlant 18 is cancelled – we're going in for repairs.'

'One of the propellers has fallen off.'

'We're going back to Rosyth for a rebuild.'

The real reason for the deviation is that a Russian submarine has been identified by another Royal Navy asset – not on official transit – so this needs to be dealt with quickly, efficiently and secretly. Even though she's still on sea trials, HMS *Queen Elizabeth* has her own sophisticated means of subsurface surveillance and the ability to work in tandem with frigates that specialize in underwater warfare. She also carries the specialist anti-submarine Merlin Mark 2s of 820 Naval Air Squadron.

As a highly classified episode, it's not possible to divulge further details other than to say that intelligence was soon received that the recalcitrant submarine made good her departure and headed away before the QE reached her position. It can be reasonably supposed, however, that the Russians had no taste for a confrontation with Britain's biggest warship on her home ground.

This incident has provided an unexpected but fascinating glimpse into the future when the QE, fully armed and primed, will be able to provide considerable muscle in the protection of British territorial waters, not only to deter hostile vessels but also to fight them off if necessary.

In a debriefing to his HODs, Jerry Kyd is very clear about the importance of reacting to events like this without delay. 'That's two separate incidents in as many days where the Royal Navy had to be seen to act and respond quickly with a range of measures to counter Russian armed forces operating in our back yard — we must always be ready to meet them and show our muscle.'

1000

With all rogue Russian submarines seen off, all helicopters embarked, all known stowaways landed ashore and all engines continuing to whir and purr, Jerry Kyd has finally given the order to strike west. Right now, he and Darren Houston are standing on the bridge wing waving enthusiastically to another Royal Navy warship closing on the starboard side. HMS *Monmouth*, a Type 23 frigate, will accompany the QE throughout Westlant 18 as her dedicated bodyguard.

'I have a soft spot for the *Monmouth*,' Kyd smiles. 'She was my first command back in 2004.'

'You'll have to fly over at some point during the deployment, sir,' Houston says.

Kyd nods to his new Navigator, Lieutenant Commander Sam Stephens, who gives an immediate order to the quartermaster at the helm.

'Half ahead both engines. Revolutions nine zero.'

The port and starboard driveshafts are taken to 90 revolutions a minute. The two mighty bronze propellers start to turn, and the ship moves forward with the grandeur and majesty that befits her immense scale and regal name. Accelerating eventually to a 20-knot cruising speed, the QE glides out of British territorial waters. The huge frame of the ship flexes under the strain imposed by the deep Atlantic swells which she must now straddle. But with the retractable stabilizers deployed, the motion of the ocean is hardy discernible to those on board.

Jerry Kyd and his navigators have decided against taking the shortest route to America. The *Great Circle Route* follows the curve of the earth's surface and at 3,200 miles to Florida could not be more direct, but it takes shipping through the Grand Banks of Newfoundland, a group of underwater plateaus attached to the North American Continental Shelf. The Grand Banks are infamous for perennial fog, icebergs and, in 1912, the loss of RMS *Titanic*. It is not for fear of hitting an iceberg that Jerry Kyd has decided against it, but because poor visibility and the natural caution required to navigate its waters might slow his progress too much. Instead, he's decided to take the longer 'rum line' or straight-line route between the southwest of England and Florida, which will take them further south in a sweeping arc through the Azores and across to the Caribbean. It will add 300 miles to the journey, but the currents and more clement weather (average temperature is expected to be around 30 degrees) will make for an easier passage. And they will be more likely to encounter the trade winds that will help in the continuing trialling of rotary-wing aircraft, something they'll be doing almost every day en route.

Ahead of the QE, then, is a 3,500-mile voyage to her first destination, the US naval base at Mayport, Florida. On the way the ship will undergo some preliminary warm-water trials in the Caribbean to make sure the cooling systems work in tropical climes, but the master plan is for her to be in Florida no more than two weeks from now for refuelling and revictualling, before heading up to Norfolk, Virginia to start the F-35 trials in early to mid September.

'As you know, hurricanes could be a big problem for us.' Lieutenant Commander Dan McMahon, the head meteorologist, is talking to his small but specialist team of weather watchers.* 'We want high winds for our flight trials, but not 150 knots . . .'

The screens in front of them show computer-generated weather maps which are being continually updated with live data streaming from orbiting and geostationary satellites. There are already indications that the hot air and low-pressure cells coming off the Sahara into the eastern Atlantic are beginning to form tropical storms. Many of these will be short-lived, but some, further energized by warm currents and spun by the rotation of the earth, may grow in stature and start to move across the Atlantic. If they continue to gain strength, they may mature into full-blown tempests that could strike the area the QE is heading for.

---

* A ship's meteorologist is nicknamed the 'weather guesser' or, because he/she is practising what is considered a dark art, the 'weather wizard/witch'.

'Our job will be to inform Command, especially the CO and Commander Air, of all developments day by day, and sometimes hour by hour,' McMahon emphasizes.

Lindsey Waudby lets out a howl of delight as she scans the internet.

'Look at this,' she says to her team. 'The pigeon story's all over the news. It's been picked up by the *Telegraph*, the *Times*, BBC and ITV.'

'Wow!' Kyle Heller says, looking over her shoulder.

'That's a result, ma'am,' Arron Hoare echoes.

'Certainly is!' Waudby claps her hands.

There was some concern among her bosses back home that the pigeon story might make too light of the QE's tasking and they initially blocked it. The animal shelter announced the story to local journalists themselves, and the news soon spread.

Waudby continues to scroll through the coverage on her computer.

For the former ITN reporter, this is a big win on the hearts and minds front.

'I mean, no one is going to think that pigeon rescue is the primary purpose of our most powerful warship. This story's given us a human face, and it'll appeal to a different audience that might not otherwise take any notice of us.'

Jenny Curwood is on the phone to Northwood Joint Force Headquarters in Hertfordshire, responsible for all command and control functions for the Navy, Army and RAF. Having swapped her regulation office chair for a large blue power ball to help her posture, she's at her desk, gently bouncing with the motion of the ship. She needs to check on the next consignment of human blood.

It has a short shelf life, so has to be resupplied every twenty-eight days, wherever the ship happens to be. There is a large medical complex on board, complete with a GP service, a dentist and two general surgeons, so fresh blood is essential in the event of accident or surgery. This will be even more vital once the flight trials start, as an accident on the flight deck could see serious casualties.

The blood sent from the UK has to be delivered within forty-eight hours and must be kept refrigerated. At the moment, the plan is to have the next supply delivered to Norfolk, Virginia.

For the Air Force and the Army the logistics of supply, whilst complicated, are not nearly as challenging as they are for the Navy. Warships are perpetually on the move and often have to change routes at the last moment for operational reasons.

Curwood is assured that the blood will be delivered on time.

Chris Trevethan, meanwhile, is on his morning rounds or 'walking the estate' as he likes to describe it. He's currently trudging the length of 5 Deck, ostensibly to check the cleanliness of the flats, but for Trevethan his daily tours are as much to help him keep his finger on the emotional pulse of the ship's company.

'Good morning, shipmate,' he says repeatedly. He has learned to be very sensitive to mood – collective and individual. Most people find a natural support network among their own peers, but not in every case, so Trevethan's always looking out for signs of isolation or loneliness. Social sensitivities apart, he is also quick to reprimand when required.

'Shipmate!' he bellows at a young female sailor with her

hair hanging more loosely than regulations allow. 'Tame that hair if you please. You have a choice – cut it or bun it!'

'Yessir,' the flustered sailor splutters as she pushes the unruly strands under her beret.

Trevethan is strict, sometimes grumpy and occasionally impatient, but his innate bonhomie and quick wit make him a great favourite with the ship's company – even the ne'er-do-wells who step over the line. Maybe it's because he's climbed the ranks himself that he has natural empathy with the junior ratings. That and the fact that he knows all the tricks, ruses, ploys, scams and dodges. 'Oh yes,' he will readily admit. 'I'm well aware of their wheezes and wangles. I invented a good many of them.'

Continuing his walkabout, Trevethan decides to head up to the flight deck no longer readily accessible to the general ship's company. The helicopter crews from 820 and 845 Naval Air Squadrons are already training round the clock, which leaves next to no access for recreational purposes. The vast majority of sailors and marines must live and work within the belly of the ship – on any one of the nine lower decks, none of which have access to daylight. To give everybody a sense of the outside world, Channel 13 on the TV network, the Electric Porthole, provides a permanent view of the flight deck from a fixed camera on the aft island. It's not much, but reminds everyone that there is a world out there, and lets them know when it's day and when it's night.

Having sought the necessary permissions, Trevethan climbs to 1 Deck from 2 Deck and then pushes through the heavy steel doors of an airlock compartment to the outside world. 'Cor blimey!' He shields his eyes from the sudden glare. 'I can't be up here for long,' he gasps. 'Five minutes of fresh air and I go a funny colour!'

1900

Finishing his duties for the day, Glen Peters puts his head round the door of the captain's cabin. 'Sir, I'm heading off, if that's OK.'

Jerry Kyd is still ploughing through official signals on his monitor. 'Goodnight, Glen.'

'Goodnight, sir.'

The captain's steward and right-hand man, tired and ready for bed, must now make his way from the top of the for'ard island to his mess way down on 7 Deck. It's a long haul, but the first part is made easier by his privileged access to the command lift, which imprisoned Kirsty Rugg during the first sea trials. There's barely room for more than one person in the tight cubicle, but it does go down to the hangar level, the equivalent of six storeys, so provides welcome relief to tired feet and aching legs. 'Only top people are allowed to use the lift,' Peters likes to tell his friends when pointing out the official notice on the door:

COMMAND LIFT

Only the following personnel have permission to use the command lift

HMTQ
CO
CDR
BRIDGE MESS STEWARD

'You see, it's for the captain, the Commander, me . . . and Her Majesty the Queen. Reserved for Royalty and a Rasta.'

Ten minutes later he is in his 'gulch' – a cabin for eight

sailors. He's changed into shorts and T-shirt and unleashed his dreadlocks. Lying back in his bunk or 'rack' with the curtain pulled against the outside world he relaxes into his tiny cocoon of solitude, kisses his forefinger and places it on the smiling face of his young son Emmanuel looking down at him from a photo stuck to the bedhead. He puts on his beaten-up old headphones, which only work on one side.

'Gotta get some new ones in New York,' he tells himself before shutting his eyes and settling back to listen to 'Rain from the Sky' by Delroy Wilson.

Succour to his soul.

0300

The supercarrier cuts through the dark Atlantic swells. Most of the ship's company are asleep, but not all. On the bridge the duty watch guides the QE safely onwards; those in the SCC constantly monitor the ship's vital signs, in particular the performance of her diesel and gas turbine engines; duty emergency parties stand by, ready to react to any eventuality.

Down below, six bakers work through the night to produce all the bread and patisseries needed for the next day.

Suddenly the relative serenity is shattered by the ear-splitting wail of the general alarm. Three long electronic blasts of the high-pitched siren shriek down every passageway, bouncing off every bulkhead.

'*Flood, flood, flood!*' announces a disembodied but insistent voice. '*5 Zulu Starboard. Access is Port side only.*'

All hands will now be awake, although only the duty-watch emergency parties actively react to the pipe. Everyone else can stay in their quarters, being fed regular updates through the main broadcast system in case the situation becomes more acute. Within seconds, a small army of sailors is making its way to the scene of the emergency. Some, already in thick rubber wetsuits, look understandably nervous, but this does not inhibit the speed of their actions.

Having arrived at the steel door leading to the quarterdeck they can hear the sound of loud gushing. They push through and immediately find themselves wading through fast-flowing water cascading across the deck and down the stairwell. There's only emergency lighting to see by, but it's enough to illuminate a powerful horizontal jet. 'It's a salt water cooling pipe,' someone shouts. 'Fractured at the main valve. We need to lock it off, pronto!'

Without warning, the general alarm sounds again – three more long blasts. This time it's signalling a new threat. *'Fire danger, fire danger, fire danger!'* announces the same urgent voice. *'Fire and emergency parties to DG1, 8 Delta.'*

Sensors have indicated a fuel leak in one of the engine rooms. An advance party of marine engineers and firefighters climb down to DG1 – one of the four diesel engine rooms. They open the first steel door into a holding compartment and enter four at a time. Before opening a second door into the engine space itself, they close the first behind them to maintain air tight integrity should there be an explosion or a fireball. The immediate area might be destroyed and everyone killed, but it's essential to ensure that fire and particularly smoke are not allowed to spread.

The emergency party enters the second door, closing it quickly behind them. First in is Leading Hand John Ball, known to all as 'Itchy' – for obvious reasons.

'Fuck me!' he says. 'What a stench.' The floor of the engine room is awash with slimy, straw-coloured liquid. The acrid fumes betray it as aviation fuel – a highly flammable kerosene-gasoline blend.

'Itchy!' A voice from deep inside the engine space. 'Fuel leak on the for'ard bulkhead – it's a gusher!'

Ball moves forward tentatively, flanked by two firefighters armed with foam extinguishers.

'It's the Avcat pipe to the flight deck,' he shouts. 'The pump valve's failed!' He points to a large silver pipe on the upper bulkhead.

'Lay foam!'

The fire-team immediately activates the fixed-foam fire-fighting system. A push of a button instantly lays down a white carpet over the free-flowing fuel. Itchy Ball sets about stemming the leak while others with foam-hoses stand by ready to react if anything sparks. The flashpoint of Avcat, 38 °C, is lower than diesel, and in an engine space like this, where hot combustion gases are constantly being generated, the peril is very real. Damage control has to be immediate and uncompromising.

0500

The flood on the quarterdeck, caused by a corroded valve, has been quelled, and the fuel leak in DG1, the result of a failed bearing in the pump, is now plugged.

'Just another night on a warship.' Itchy Ball grins at his exhausted team. 'Living the dream, serving the Queen!'

So far tonight, in the time it's taken to quell a flood, deny a fire and bake bread and croissants for 1,200 sailors and marines, HMS *Queen Elizabeth* has moved nearly 200 miles nearer to the USA.

30. Starry, Starry Nights

0630

'Gimme ten burpees!' the chief physical training instructor (PTI) bellows.

There's a collective groan from the thirty sailors who've turned up for Sticky Vercoe's early-morning circuits in the hangar. Most are already asking themselves what prompted them to get out of perfectly warm and comfortable beds for this painful ritual.

'Make that twenty for hesitating,' their torturer bawls gleefully. 'Go!'

The hapless volunteers drop to the floor on both hands, kick their legs out behind them, touch their chests to the floor, push up, leap into the air and clap their hands above their heads.

'That's one. Nineteen to go. Keep time, stay together!'

Everybody obeys, but despite the PTI's edict some proceed at a faster pace than others. One of the slower contenders is Mohamad 'Wes' Khan. The ever-cheerful, popular and hardworking chef is increasingly conscious of his spreading midriff. A sylphlike 67 kilos when he joined the Navy eighteen years ago, he's nearly 95 kilos today – a lot to carry for a man under 5 feet 7 inches. As a twenty-six-year-old recruit he was fit and fast, played a mean game of hockey at centre forward and boasted an impressive six-pack – something his shipmates now find hard to believe.

'Honest,' he tells them, 'my stomach was like a washboard!'

'Of course it was, Wes. In your dreams, maybe!'

'It was,' he insists. 'Still is, under all this!'

'Well done, Wes!' Vercoe shouts. 'Chest all the way to the ground, shipmate.'

Khan's been attending circuits every morning since leaving Portsmouth and intends to keep it up until the ship returns in early December. His target is to lose 15 kilos.

He completes his final burpee with a groan but has no time to rest.

'Straight to sit-ups, people.' Vercoe is unforgiving. 'Gimme fifty!'

0900

The QE is travelling at an average speed of 23 knots. The going is good, the sea state benign, and the winds set fair. Jerry Kyd, perched on his leather captain's chair, is in ebullient mood. Never happier than when surveying the wide-open ocean, he's overseeing tactical manoeuvres with HMS *Monmouth* and using the opportunity to school some of his Young Officers (YOs) in carrier-strike tactics.

'Gather round, guys.'

Two sub-lieutenants and two midshipmen form a semi-circle round their CO.

'OK, watch carefully as we reposition in relation to each other. *Monmouth* is more fleet of foot so will do most of the hard yards, because her job's all about protecting us from threat.'

On a full operational deployment, the QE will be the

Queen Bee in the centre of a carrier battle formation. Her escorts, protective warships, including Type 23 frigates, Type 45 destroyers and Astute submarines, will form her defensive shield and react to air, surface and sub-surface threats as they arise.

'Frigates such as the *Monmouth*, specializing in anti-submarine and anti-aircraft warfare, will run around us like faithful guard dogs,' he explains to his YOs. 'And it's some of those rapid tactical movements we're beginning to practise today. It can involve complex choreography, and working so closely always runs the risk of collision. The key is timing, agility and skill.'

HMS *Monmouth* moves fast astern as part of a move to defend the carrier in the event of air attack from the rear. The Type 23 frigate, on a tight turn and leaning hard to starboard, carves a white, frothing scar into the dark-blue sea as she sprints into her defensive position.

'There, you see,' Kyd says. 'Brilliantly in position and we didn't have to alter course once.

'We can't do this on a wing and a prayer and couple of patrol boats,' he tells them. 'We don't have to be the aggressor, but we do have to be the robust defender of our country and what we believe in.'

The captain is no warmonger. He's a rationalist, a strategist and deep-thinking pragmatist, firmly rooted in the real world, who likes to quote Thucydides, the great Athenian historian and general: 'To be happy means to be free, and to be free means to be brave. Therefore do not take lightly the perils of war.'

Jerry Kyd is well aware that war is nearly always the worst option, but he grows impatient with ideologues who think that peace does not have to be defended. He accepts that the democratic liberties he would die to defend come with all manner of freedoms he would not personally endorse, but he accepts it as his God-given duty to defend them. This includes preserving and upholding the rights of the indignant pacifists who would like to hound him out of his job and relieve him of his responsibility to protect them.

The manoeuvres with HMS *Monmouth* may be a glimpse into the future of high-tech task-force operations, but surprisingly both warships are currently resorting to very traditional operational methods. Communications between the two modern warships are being conducted by flashing lights from the bridge wings – the Morse code first used by the Royal Navy in 1867. The ability to communicate by the even more anachronistic use of semaphore flags is also something Jerry Kyd attaches huge importance to; something he wants to impress on his Young Officers. 'We might boast hugely advanced technology, but never forget the core traditional, basic skills, because it's these that'll keep us alive in the next war if all else fails.'

Kyd beckons them on to the bridge wing to watch the continuing choreography more closely. 'We've just seen the importance of maintaining radio silence from the *Admiral Makarov* incident. But our enemy doesn't have to be close by – it could be an enemy spy satellite, so keeping a warship hidden is a key part of any deception plan that a crew will operate at sea, especially when part of a large Task Group.'

HMS *Monmouth*, making speed from behind, overtakes the QE on the port side and, making another sharp turn to starboard, moves fast across the bow of the carrier to take station on her starboard quarter.

The adoption of 'strategic silence' could keep HMS *Queen Elizabeth* alive in any future conflict against an enemy with sophisticated monitoring equipment. Flashing lights and flags mean that she'll still be able to talk to her escorts without emitting giveaway electrical impulses. And if combat damage knocked out the ship's communications system, she'd still have a means of exchanging vital information with friendly forces. It's surprising how many navies around the world have dispensed with this basic form of seamanship and communication, but it remains Jerry Kyd's firm conviction that traditional methods will give him the edge – even over fifth-generation warships such as his own.

Close ship manoeuvring, a crucial element of Task Group operations, has not been practised in the Royal Navy for nearly ten years. After *Ark Royal* and *Invincible* were withdrawn from service back in 2010, and *Illustrious* became a helicopter carrier, the seagoing skills needed to keep a Task Group active, effective and safe have atrophied. These will need to be relearned and honed over the next thirty-six months before the QE's first active deployment in 2021.

'OK, guys,' Kyd says. 'That's all for now. See you this evening for astronavigation.'

While the warships continue to manoeuvre, the embarked helicopters go through their own training evolutions. The Merlin Mark 2 aircrews must perfect their anti-submarine warfare skills and in particular their tactics for Carrier Strike Group operations – the complex process of defending and fighting a large seagoing force.

1900

The sun reddens as it descends and throws a long, glittering reflection across the water, giving HMS *Queen Elizabeth* an unlikely pinkish hue. Then, with one final, extravagant gesture it projects a magnificent red and yellow fan against the deepening blue sky before it drops out of sight below the horizon.

A group of Young Officers report to Jerry Kyd on the bridge. 'Follow me,' the captain says. 'The first of the planets should be out soon.' He picks up a varnished wooden box and leads everyone on to the starboard bridge wing. 'Right, this is a state-of-the-art navigational aid. Well, it was in 1767, when it was invented.'

Kyd pulls out a triangular metal contraption with a complex array of lenses, mirrors and a small telescope.

'This, as you'll know, is a sextant,' Kyd tells his attentive students. 'Its design has remained unchanged for over 200 years, but if we go to war, like those flashing lights and flags, it could keep us alive.'

The sextant calculates the distance between two physical objects. Its primary purpose is to measure the angle of an astronomical feature with the horizon for the purposes of celestial navigation. Through simple trigonometry, it allows the observer to plot their position, and if GPS and radar were to be knocked out in combat, it would allow a ship to find its way to safety, or even to continue the fight.

Jerry Kyd scans the darkening canopy. 'Look out for Venus,' he says. 'That'll be the first planet out, and long before the stars – it'll pop up as if someone has switched on a light about eighteen degrees above the horizon.' The YOs peer into the heavens, each one eager to spot Venus first. Kyd doesn't even try to compete. He knows their strong young eyes will beat him to it. Besides, he wants them to take the initiative.

One sub-lieutenant points skywards at a faint pinprick of light. 'There, sir.'

'Excellent!' Kyd raises the sextant to his right eye. 'I'll check the angle while you keep your eyes open for Jupiter and Mars – they'll be next up.'

Within half an hour, they are busy calculating their position using their own measurements of planetary angles, together with an almanac of astronomical tables.

'Take great care with your initial readings and the subsequent mathematics,' Kyd tells everyone. 'You should be able to find our position to the nearest 2 miles.'

After half an hour of fevered calculation, the Young Officers have established their latitude and longitude.

'So, there you have it.' Kyd is delighted. 'Thanks to the stars, your eagle eyes and a bit of mathematics, you now know more or less exactly where you are on the earth's surface, and that could be vital to your survival. OK, that's enough for tonight. Tomorrow we'll consider Polaris or the North Star.'

He points again. 'It's not bright and can be difficult to spot, but it always sits above the North Pole.'

The YOs narrow their eyes.

'It's almost motionless,' Kyd says. 'All the stars of the northern hemisphere appear to rotate around it, and using an easy maths equation it'll give you your latitude.'

'Thank you, sir.'

2300

The quarterdeck at the stern is only dimly illuminated. Wes Khan allows his eyes to adjust to the half-light and then moves carefully towards one of the exposed sections that overlook the frothing white wake.

He's finished his twelve-hour shift, completed his holy ablutions and delivered his final prayers. Now he wants to enjoy a few moments of quiet contemplation before 'racking out'. He's only going to get about five hours of precious sleep before dawn prayers and sunrise circuits. His stomach muscles are aching from this morning's burpees and crunches, but he's holding firm.

Khan raises his gaze to the heavens, to the silver glow of a half moon and the million glittering stars beyond it. '*Alhamdulillah*,' he whispers.

The Muslim chef is always entranced and humbled by the sheer enormity of the black satin firmament in the middle of vast oceans. He has no immediate interest in luminosity, nautical almanacs, lunar distances or perpendicularities. He's looking to the celestial sphere for spiritual rather than navigational guidance.

'*Alhamdulillah*,' Khan repeats before heading to his cabin.

And HMS *Queen Elizabeth*, watched over by Orion, Andromeda, Cassiopeia, Centaurus and the Pleiades, continues west into the ever-darkening night.

31. No Sun, No Sea, No Sky

0900

'It's bloody redders!' Scouse Walsh squints against a dazzling mid-Atlantic sun.

'Sweltering,' Paul Ranson agrees, taking a long swig from his water bottle. 'But it's gonna get a whole lot hotter the nearer we get to Florida.'

The veteran aircraft handlers, standing on an exposed, shadowless flight deck, are wearing thick, fire-retardant over-alls, eminently practical for the work they do, but uncomfortable and constraining in this weather. From underneath their pro-tective helmets rivulets of sweat are running down glowing, florid faces.

'Stunning day, all the same,' Paul Ranson says, looking towards the shimmering horizon. 'And look at that swell. It's mega.'

Paul Ranson and Scouse Walsh are just two of twenty air-craft handlers and firefighters on deck waiting for the return of three helicopters. The Merlin Mark 2s have been away for over an hour, practising anti-submarine tracking techniques.

Almost halfway across the Atlantic, the carrier has reached the Horse Latitudes, between 30 and 35 degrees north of the equator, and is well into the Azores High – a sub-tropical zone of high atmospheric pressure where the conditions are consistently warm, dry and sunny.

If HMS *Queen Elizabeth* were a cruise ship, everybody would be lounging in deckchairs, sipping cocktails and gazing across the sun-kissed sea prior to an evening of fine dining and dancing under the moonlight. But the vast majority of the ship's company, imprisoned within, are completely oblivious to the tropical tranquillity that surrounds them.

The weather is perfect for flying, which is ramping up as the ship proceeds across the Atlantic. Bob Bond, CO of 845 Squadron, and Chris 'Grassy' Knowles, CO of 820, both want to take full advantage of the persistently high winds that are another feature of the Azores High in these latitudes.

The Mark 2s are concentrating on low-level tracking of 'enemy' targets with depth charges and Sting Ray torpedoes at the ready. The Mark 4 Junglies are engaged in search and rescue training and the tactical transportation of heavily armed Royal Marine Commandos, for whom this mainly involves practising complicated boarding procedures, 'scrambling' from the bowels of the carrier and negotiating a circuitous Assault Route to the hangar, where they 'kit up' and 'weapon up' before moving on to the lifts that raise the aircraft to the flight deck. They are then escorted by naval assault guides in snaking lines to the helicopters, which are 'burning and turning', ready for an immediate launch.

The marines must be ready to deploy quickly and efficiently at a moment's notice, day or night, especially if an F-35 fighter is downed in enemy territory and the pilot needs rescuing – a highly specialized task, and perilous in the extreme. For the elite of Lima Company, the training starts now. Later in the deployment, they will be flown ashore to practise fast insertions into 'enemy' territory on the US mainland, allowing them to perfect their rescue procedures under much more realistic conditions. But for now their task is simply to assemble and get airborne as fast as possible.

All day, every day, and most nights, the rotary-wing crews are in the air. Their vital training is constant, rigorous and exacting. Even though the ship is still working up her operational capability and battle-readiness, they will need to react to real emergencies. When the F-35 flight trials begin in just over three weeks, a Search and Rescue (SAR) helicopter will be permanently in the air.

So often the ship's lifeline, helicopters must be ready to launch and recover twenty-four hours a day. One fringe benefit is that the crews and deck handlers get to enjoy the fresh air. Having said that, there is 'fresh air' and there is 'fresh air'. Depending where they are in the world, it could be anything from raging winds in tempestuous, storm-driven seas to the driving, stinging rain of tropical typhoons or the freezing, debilitating sleet and snow of a sudden violent squall or blizzard.

On the other hand, it could be, as now, the cloudless blue skies, warm sunshine and fresh breezes of the Azores High.

1300

'Sorry I'm late, captain. Got a bit lost on 2 Deck!'

'Happens to the best of us, Bish,' Jerry Kyd says. 'Sit down, sit down.'

Jerry Kyd frequently invites the cleric for lunch or supper, partly because he's exceptionally good company and partly because he helps keep the captain's own finger on the emotional pulse of the ship.

Mansfield shares nothing of a personal nature that's been confided in him by those seeking pastoral care or support, but he's able to advise Kyd from his perspective as a sort of ecclesiastical psychologist-cum-social worker. The two men sit at the Rose Table while Glen Peters serves sandwiches and soup.

Mansfield looks out over the ocean. 'Wonderful views today, captain.'

'Truly,' Kyd agrees. 'But I do worry that, with the current flying programme, the ship's company isn't able to go top-side to see all this for themselves. How are people feeling down below?'

Mansfield nods. 'You're right to worry, captain. I think people are beginning to feel a little deprived of sunlight and fresh air.'

'I'm not surprised. But we have to complete the flying programme before we get to America.'

'The boys and girls understand the F-35 situation, captain. But there are a few mutterings, like "I didn't realize when I joined the QE I was signing up for the submarine service!"'

Of the 1,200 souls on board, around 1,100 are more or less permanently contained within the ship and live an electrically illuminated, air-conditioned, subterranean existence. Below deck, time has become shapeless. A clock or watch will indicate the hour, and a calendar will reveal the date, but there is no ready way to determine whether it's morning, noon or night, or to keep track of the passing days. To confuse things even more, when the QE reaches America's east coast on 5 September, she will have turned the clocks back by a total of seven hours – one for every 428 miles.

The ship's company might be frustrated by their current existence, but they are nevertheless fired by a sense of duty, purpose and comradeship, which helps them apply their energies and initiative to the tasks in hand, and also prompts a very inventive, energetic and creative approach to time off.

There are televisions, DVDs, computers and PlayStations of course, but sailors have a hive mentality. They prefer communal recreation, and a plethora of leisure activities, some long established, some spontaneously invented, are helping them to unwind and relax in this strangely secluded world.

Fitness classes are a big attraction, and at least three energetic circuits are held each day (0600, 1130 and 1645), usually in the hangar. The seven gyms are well attended, and so is the dedicated boxing training area with its full-sized ring. And on this deployment, there is a spectacular additional option for the fitness freaks provided by Lieutenant Colonel Roly Brading of the Royal Marines. His daily CrossFit class is based on a fitness regimen and philosophy that combines aerobic exercise with calisthenics, Olympic weightlifting and gymnastics. One of the UKs leading exponents of Cross-Fit, Brading is superhumanly fit and charismatic, but as unrelenting in his coaching style as he is fervent in his belief of its benefits. He is intent on creating as many supermen and superwomen as possible by the end of Westlant 18, and his small but expanding following is becoming Messianic in its dedication to the cause.

One of his most earnest disciples is Harrogate-born Rob Rouston. Neither man likes to be beaten, so their sessions are fast becoming showdowns, friendly but fiercely fought. The two men push themselves to levels of mental and physical endurance that's already the talk of the ship.

For those who prefer to exert their energies in more creative and contemplative ways, Alastair Mansfield hosts painting classes in the ship's chapel twice a week. Others are studying for GCSEs and A-levels in a range of subjects from French to the History of Art, or Open University degrees in mathematics, biology and even philosophy. And upwards of fifteen devotees report for ukulele practice at 1530 every afternoon in the medical complex.

'Get your sheets out for "Hotel California", everyone.' Naval nurse and ukulele virtuoso Petty Officer Matt Hicks' ambition is to put on a concert for the whole ship before the end of deployment – possibly on the return trip across the Atlantic just before Christmas.

1830

Every HOD has provided Jerry Kyd with a succinct sitrep in this evening's Command brief, and only Jim Blackmore's update remains.

'Sir, ladies and gentlemen,' he begins. 'We've completed initial training in search and rescue and anti-submarine tracking. 820 Squadron is on course, and so is 845. In fact, we're ahead of schedule, so I can confirm that next Sunday will be a maintenance day for all aircraft. No flying. That's conclusion of brief, sir.'

'Thanks, Wings.' Jerry Kyd knows he's fortunate to have some of the finest officers in the Royal Navy as his appointed Heads of Department. He never fails to be impressed by their dedication and grateful for their unwavering loyalty. His job is to ready this ship for war, and nothing will stop him achieving that, but he always has the welfare of his men and women at heart. Kyd's very conscious that a warship, no matter how state-of-the-art, is next to useless without a steadfast, committed and devoted ship's company.

'Right, ladies and gentlemen. In that case, next Sunday will be a "Saturday Routine", and we'll open up the flight deck to all. Games, BBQ, the works. Let's get some sun on our sailors.'

'We could get the new blow-up cinema screen out after sundown,' his second in command says.

'Film night, Darren. Brilliant!' Kyd says. 'My goodness, the boys and girls deserve it, and we'll be asking a hell of a lot more from them soon. Let's make it happen. What film do you suggest?'

Houston will need to check, but thinks he has the perfect answer.

2 September 2018

1400

The specified attire for the flight deck this afternoon is 'sports rig', although it's not long before most of the men have stripped to their shorts. Many of the women are also keen to minimize body cover, and while 'itsy-bitsy, teeny-weeny' bikinis are strictly prohibited, there are more than a few pushing the boundaries. In a little over a week the Florida beaches will beckon, so this is a chance for the Vitamin D-deprived troglodytes to kick-start the tan and get into body-beautiful mode.

The QE is now 2,000 miles from home and 1,000 from the USA. With no mobile phone contact and no social media opportunity, the ship's company is a closed world where time seems to have stood still. With no other shipping visible, the sense of isolation is complete. Even the purpose of the deployment has been temporarily forgotten.

'Wow! Look at that!' A huge waterspout no more than 100

yards off the port bow betrays the presence of a whale coming up for air. Everyone gathers to watch in awed silence and
then, as if it had been waiting for an audience, the magnificent creature breaches the surface. The fine young humpback
slowly arches its glistening grey back and, as a final flourish,
waves its immense tail before diving back to the depths.

Some go back to reading in the shade or rubbing in copi-
ous amounts of sun-block, as the flight deck transforms
itself into a recreation ground, featuring all manner of
American-themed sports from baseball and basketball to
volleyball and clay pigeon shooting off the stern.

Jerry Kyd aims to bag a few clays himself, but first wants to
take this rare opportunity to mingle with his ship's company.

'Afternoon, ladies,' he greets a group of Wrens spread-
eagled on towels within easy reach of their iPod speakers.
'What are you listening to?'

'"Freaky Friday", sir,' they chorus. 'Lil Dicky and Chris
Brown.'

'Of course it is!' He gives them a wry smile. 'Though I'm
more of a reggae man, myself . . .'

He moves to join the group cheering a frantic volleyball
game outside the aft island. 'Who's winning?' he asks the biggest man he's ever seen on a warship.

'Marines, sir.'

Kyd gestures at the elaborate skull and anchor tattoos
covering every inch of his titanic chest and back. 'No need to
guess who you're supporting . . .'

'No, sir. Sergeant Dirk Nel, sir.'

'South African, perhaps?'

'Yessir. Durban. Natal. But my mum's from Sunderland.'
He treats his captain to the world's biggest grin. 'And the tats
are from Plymouth.'

Kyd reckons Sergeant Nel can't be a fraction less than 6 feet 7 inches and 265 lbs. *'Thank God he's one of ours . . .'* he thinks.

Despite playing an essential role in the Royal Navy, few career sailors really understand what makes the Bootnecks tick. But Jerry Kyd does. In the early 1990s he spent time in Northern Ireland, initially as a lieutenant on HMS *Cygnet*. The patrol boat provided him with his first direct experience of the elite shock troops and changed the course of his career.

He eventually became the Boarding Officer, heading up a team of eight commandos. During what he describes as his 'James Bond' days, they rode in fast-moving RIBs, mostly under cover of darkness, targeting vessels suspected of gun-running or people-smuggling. Clad in black, tight-fitting dry suits and sporting Heckler & Koch MP5s, they'd board via long rope-ladders. When they were ready to leave, they'd leap off the back end into the frothing wake 50 feet below. With hindsight he knows it was complete madness – like being catapulted into a giant washing machine – but it built his confidence and strengthened his resolve as a leader. Most importantly, it taught him to trust his men.

And to trust himself.

2100

The Royal Marines Band's jazz quintet is in full swing. 'Lazy River', 'Mack the Knife', 'St Louis Blues' and 'Sweet Georgia Brown' flood across the flight deck as all manner of delicacies sizzle on a vast BBQ on the leeward side of the aft island.

Over 1,000 hungry sailors, marines and aviators wait patiently in line, now dressed in the compulsory 'Banyan' rig – where anything remotely stylish is off-limits. The more garish, gaudy and lurid the Hawaiian shirt and shorts the better. There's nothing stealthy about HMS *Queen Elizabeth* tonight.

2200

Most of the ship's company are now happily replete and sitting on cushions and rugs from their mess decks. Many have also brought up their daily beer rations to help enliven the occasion.

The sun sinks below the horizon. The lights dim. The projector flashes. The screen between the islands flickers, and the speakers burst into life. Everyone settles back in eager anticipation as a powerfully percussive riff rises to a crescendo. Two words, in stark white lettering, leap out of the black background.

TOP GUN . . .

Everybody cheers.

Tonight, F-14 fighter jets will roar across the QE's flight deck, celluloid precursors to the thunderous blast of Nathan Gray's real life F-35B scheduled to land in just under three weeks.

HMS *Queen Elizabeth*, for one night only an oversize, floating outdoor cinema, sailing under another star-studded sky. As the credits roll, the Oscar-winning theme tune, 'Take My Breath Away', pounds across the restless, swirling waters of the Atlantic. The good guys have won, of course, and the hero got the girl. The audience cheers once again.

This has been an extravagant few hours, enjoyed by all who must now return to their subterranean lairs. Next time they can be released for an extended period will be landfall in America.

32. No Ripped Jeans

Atlantic Ocean, 4 September 2018

America's Sunshine State is an exciting prospect for everyone. Sovereign TV has been feeding as many details as possible about Naval Station Mayport's many facilities – including a private beach, cinema, bars and fully equipped gyms – and its immediate vicinity.

Many have already booked online. Some will be venturing to Disney World and Universal Studios in Orlando, while others have opted for adventure packages, including skydiving, horseback riding, surfing and hiking. Most have decided, however, to settle for the delights of Jacksonville, the nearest big town. They plan to sun themselves by day on the nearby Atlantic Beach and immerse themselves in the pleasures of the town by night – especially on Atlantic Boulevard, famous for its bars, clubs and restaurants.

Frederica McCarthy, baby sailor, Writer and itinerant gash-sorter, is particularly excited. She plans some serious partying and lots of dancing on her first run ashore. She loves to dance. The extra money she's earned through her gash work will come in useful, though she wants to make sure she has enough left for New York. She plans to go to Orlando at some point but will spend most of her time off in Jacksonville.

1900

'Who's piping for evening rounds?' Chris Trevethan asks.

'Me, sir,' a junior rating replies.

'Done it before?'

'No, sir, not on rounds.'

The First Lieutenant is preparing to set off on his nightly tour of the mess decks, accompanied by a junior officer and a naval regulator. He has vital information to impart before arriving in Florida tomorrow, and this is by far the best way to disseminate it. Notices pinned to walls, broadcasts on Sovereign TV and pipes broadcast around the ship are all very well, but they don't reach everyone.

'Better have a go before we start, shipmate,' Trevethan says.

The young sailor cups his right hand nervously round the silver Bosun's whistle, raises it to his mouth, takes a deep breath and blows hard. A piercingly shrill but intermittently discordant warble fills the air.

'That sounds like a strangled cat!' Chris Trevethan screws up his face in mock agony. 'Has no one ever shown you how to pipe?'

'No, sir,' the rating murmurs. 'Taught myself.'

'Hmmm. Moot point, shipmate. Hand it over.'

Reddening with embarrassment, the sailor does so.

'Grip it firmly in your right hand,' Trevethan says. 'No limp wrists. Strong grasp. Like this.'

'Yessir.'

'Wrap your lips around the mouthpiece. Nice tight seal. No gaps.'

The young sailor nods.

'Then blow. Long, sustained, relaxed. *Comme ça.*'

A constant, high-pitched note cuts through the ambient hum of the air-conditioning.

'That's the way to do it, shipmate.' Trevethan looks pleased with himself. 'Big breath and controlled exhalation.'

'Yessir.'

'Military precision. Nothing fancy. You're not Herb Alpert.'

'Who, sir?'

'Careful, shipmate!' Trevethan hands back the whistle with an exaggerated frown. 'Or I'll put you on punishment for being too young! OK, let's go.'

Led by the novice, now whistling as if his life depends on it, the First Lieutenant and his team head to the Stokers' Mess.

'OK, shipmates, listen up!' Trevethan addresses the attentive sixty-strong assembly. 'Let me start with a question. How many here are under twenty-one?'

A dozen raise their hands.

'Right – know that you're underage when it comes to buying alcohol in the US of A. Don't try and get away with it because they'll ask for ID.'

There are a few mocking guffaws from the over-twenty-ones.

'You've been able to drink legally in the UK since you were eighteen, but abuse the law in the US and you could be arrested.'

Trevethan lets his words sink in.

'And from a wider perspective, the rest of you watch out too – American cops see the world very differently to your average bobby and will have a much less lenient attitude to British matelots out on the piss. Step out of line and you could be CS gassed, Tasered or shot. And if you end up in jail, there's not much I'll be able to do to get you out.'

The stokers raise their eyebrows.

'Don't load up before you go ashore either,' Trevethan warns. 'That'll lead to tears. Public drunkenness is greatly frowned upon in the States.'

He looks down at his notes and purses his lips.

'Right, lastly and most importantly . . .' The First Lieutenant is now deadly serious. 'Make sure you always go out in groups. Never alone. Adopt the "Shark Watch" routine. One of you must be on watch *all* the time. He must not drink but keep his eyes on things and stay alert. Take it in turns to be the shark-watcher. Above all, go out together, stay together and come back together.'

Everybody nods.

'Has anybody here *not* heard of Timmy MacColl?' Trevethan asks.

A few tentative hands are raised.

'Right, for those who don't know, he was a British sailor serving on HMS *Westminster* in 2012. They stopped at Dubai, where, one night, he went ashore by himself. He was seen getting into a taxi, and that was it. He was never seen again.'

Trevethan heads for the door but turns before he leaves. 'Stay together, fellas – I don't want to be writing letters to your parents back home.'

He delivers the same sobering message to every mess, male and female.

One further warning is given to the younger sailors in particular. It relates to rig ashore, and on this point the First Lieutenant is again emphatic.

'No Union Jack shorts! No football shirts! Nothing risqué, ladies!' He pauses. 'And no ripped jeans, please, shipmates. Or, if they have to be ripped, because I understand that is the current fashion, please keep the denim-to-flesh ratio sensible!'

33. Pulling Out the Pin

1000

'Big day, Darren,' Kyd says to his right-hand man.

'Yes, sir.' Houston smiles. 'We've come a long way from Rosyth.'

As the ship edges ever nearer to the beckoning coastline, the bridge team prepare for their entry into Mayport. It's a hot day, with only a gentle offshore wind to worry about, but any sudden gusts, notorious in this part of the world, could cause havoc in a heartbeat. HMS *Queen Elizabeth* will be coaxed in very gently, as always. Jerry Kyd has never pranged a warship in his life and has no intention of starting now.

Procedure Alpha has been activated. Today, because of the high temperatures, everyone is dressed not in navy-blue serge uniforms but light, white cotton 'tropical rig'.

The skies are not cloudless. Cumulonimbi are towering into the upper atmosphere on the eastern horizon. The hurricane season is well underway, but so far no significant storms have made it all the way across the Atlantic. This year is forecast to be below average for major storm systems, but nobody, least of all the QE's meteorologists, is feeling complacent. The season's climatological peak falls six days from now.

Jerry Kyd looks up at the distant storm clouds and makes a mental note to talk to Dan McMahon as soon as possible.

1200

The QE and HMS *Monmouth* have berthed next to each other, opposite the massive USS assault ship *Iwo Jima*. Florida beckons, but the ship's companies still have work to do. On the carrier's starboard side, closest to the quay, food stores are arriving in huge American juggernauts. On the port side, facing the water, a floating tanker is pumping her semi-depleted tanks full of diesel.

Jenny Curwood is overseeing all the storage operations, and, as is usual for Logistics Officers, time alongside is even busier than at sea. She has to liaise with the ship's agents, the port authorities and the military authorities both here and back in Britain. Some spare parts ordered for the engines and helicopters are due to arrive as soon as they've cleared US customs.

The refuelling will take all morning and even though the tanks are only being topped up, Curwood expects to take on at least 3,500 cubes (aka tonnes) of diesel – enough to fill 55,000 average family cars.

1800

The main broadcast system crackles before delivering the pipe everybody's been waiting for.

'Secure! Everybody's reminded that return to ship must be by tomorrow morning, 0745 for able rates, 0750 for leading hands and 0755 for senior rates.'

Within minutes, hundreds of the ship's company, mostly in their glad-rags, are heading down the gangway. Frederica McCarthy, in a light summer dress with her long auburn hair hanging loose, is one of the first off. Jacksonville is 10 miles away, so dozens of coaches are waiting to shuttle the sailors into town.

The only person looking out of place in the exuberant queue is Wes Khan. Still in his galley uniform and carrying a bag of gash to a waiting skip on the quayside, he'll not be spared galley duties today, as the ship's company continues to need feeding. 'See you lot,' he chuckles. 'And don't worry, I'll have breakfast waiting in the morning!'

2100

Ocean Boulevard is alive with music and raucous laughter.

At Lynch's Irish Pub on 1st Street North, Frederica Mc-Carthy and her messmates are ordering rounds of Corona beer. The dance floor's heaving to live music from Zero Double 8, an energetic hip-hop band, and it's not long before McCarthy joins the mêlée – hip-swinging, laughing and care-free. This is a long way from gash-sorting on 3 Deck.

The pub is thronging with British sailors and marines. For the first time in over three weeks the female sailors are able to liberate their locks from the tight buns that are *de rigueur* on duty. Make-up completes the transformation from military constraint to civilian vivacity.

Some are doing shots at the bar, where rows of flaming Drambuies light up laughing faces. One by one, they knock back the fiery liqueur then bang the empty glass on the counter for an instant refill. Frederica McCarthy, onstage and dancing with the lead singer, pumps the air triumphantly with a clenched fist as friends from the dance floor chant: 'Fredd-ie! Fredd-ie! Fredd-ie!'

This *joie de vivre* is all part of the bonding process and, in its way, as important as any professional duty or training regime. At sea, all hands are effectively on duty round the clock, in relentless, sometimes monotonous, often dangerous work. In the civilian world, everyone gets a Friday night once a week. For serving sailors they are few and far between.

They laugh and cry with their shipmates, they may even squabble and fight, but they would also die for each other if called upon to do so. Bob Hawkins, former First Lieutenant and legendary party animal, always maintained that nights like this are an essential part of being a serving sailor – with one caveat: 'It is fine to hoot with the owls, as long as you're prepared to soar with the eagles the next day.'

The strict 'no touch' rule that governs behaviour at sea does not apply when ashore and off-duty, but few are flaunting their affections publicly. Some who've become couples prefer others not to know, as it can introduce an unsettling dynamic. The unattached are free to concentrate their efforts on local well-wishers, whether that takes the form of canoodling under the palm trees or something a bit more intense elsewhere.

A handful of the local women are showing a strictly professional interest in the proceedings, mostly at street corners where love is for sale.

0030

Whether on the hunt for carnal pleasures, drinking to excess, high-kicking in Irish pubs or just enjoying the company of friends in a restaurant, over a thousand Royal Navy personnel are still living it up. A few have started to head back to the ship and are somewhat unsteadily climbing aboard the shuttle coaches.

The action at Lynch's Irish Pub is getting increasingly boisterous, and, although it is still good-natured, police cars patrolling the strip are keeping a close eye on things. They're used to rowdy sailors in this part of town and have their own way of dealing with things if they get out of control.

Lieutenant Commander David Marshal (Air Engineer Officer), Lieutenant John Shuttleworth (Deputy Air Engineer Officer) and Lieutenant John 'Jack' Hendren (Squadron Logistics Officer) are draining their beer glasses and settling the bill about 2 miles away, at Poe's Tavern on Atlantic Beach.

The three officers take a moment to enjoy the warm, tropical night and breathe in the fresh sea air before climbing into the Uber they've booked to take them back to the ship. Bonnie Ginter, the driver of the red Honda Jazz, is looking to finance her college degree, so works all the hours she can. Her husband's a veteran, so she's pleased to be driving the British sailors but she has bad news for them. 'Sorry, guys, one of my headlights has blown, so I won't be allowed on to the base. I'll drop you at the front gate, but then you'll have to walk. And I'll have to finish for the night.'

'Haven't you got a spare?' Marshal asks.

'Yeah, in the glove box. But they're impossible to fit. I'll take it into the shop tomorrow.'

'We could have a go . . .'

'Yeah!' Jack Hendren says brightly. 'Even air engineers should be able to change a lightbulb.'

The officers soon realize it's a much bigger job than they'd bargained for. Access to the headlamp is not straightforward, so what seemed like a simple bit of DIY has turned into a major challenge. David Marshal seeks guidance from Google on his iPhone and is advised to remove the front bumper.

'Hmmm, I'm not so sure . . .' He strokes his chin. 'I reckon we could get in from the side if we took off the wheel arch.'

'We'll need tools for that,' Shuttleworth says.

'There's a gas station close by,' Bonnie Ginter says.

'Let's go.' Marshal now has the bit firmly between his teeth.

The gas station is closed, but they notice a twenty-four-hour auto parts store across the road. 'That's all very well,' Shuttleworth says. 'But we don't want to buy a load of kit we'll never use again.'

Marshal agrees. 'Jack – you're the logistics wizard. Go and do what you do best – acquire equipment!'

Hendren jumps to it and, with well-practised charm and his most disarming British accent, manages to convince the proprietor to lend him the necessary tools.

Half an hour later, wheel arch removed, Shuttleworth manages to work his magic.

'Thank you so much!' Bonnie Ginter is delighted. 'I'll be able to work on tonight after all. But please let me give you your money back,' she pleads. 'I can't stop your payment on account, but I can give you cash back.'

The officers refuse, but Ginter shoves some dollar bills in David Marshal's hand as soon as she's dropped them back at the ship.

0130

The bright green, white and red neon lights of Atlantic Beach Drive gaudily proclaiming the names of bars, clubs, restaurants and taverns, have been joined by flashing electric-blue and the blare of police sirens. Several bruised and bloodied young men are being handcuffed outside Lynch's Irish Pub and bundled into the back of three squad cars.

They are all British sailors.

34. Storms A'brewing

0730

Lieutenant Commander Lindsey Waudby is not happy. She's scrolling through the overnight newspaper headlines in both the US and the UK. None of it makes good reading for the officer whose responsibility is to promote the ship in the public eye.

'British sailors arrested after drunken shore leave in Florida . . .'

'Florida Police use Tasers on drunk and disorderly British sailors . . .'

'HMS *Queen Elizabeth*: Six "drunk" British Royal Navy sailors arrested . . .'

The media are having a field day, even though details of what actually happened last night remain sketchy. All that Waudby knows is that six sailors, two from HMS *Monmouth* and four from HMS *Queen Elizabeth*, were arrested and jailed for 'alcohol-related crimes', ranging from fighting and jaywalking to trespass and resisting arrest. She's also been informed that they will appear in court later this morning. If they're not released before the QE sails they'll have to pay their own way to the next stop in Norfolk, Virginia. There they could face extra punishment, probably hefty fines and extra duties, for being AWOL for the whole period they were away from the ship.

The American morning papers have been quick to pick up on the story from initial police reports, and although the news came in too late for the British press, most of them are already revelling in it online. It's certain to be on their front pages tomorrow.

Waudby shakes her head as she scans yet more damning accounts. They refer to only six sailors yet somehow give the impression that the entire ship's company was on the rampage last night. But the ship in question is HMS *Queen Elizabeth*, and her ship's company the cream of the Royal Navy. It was always going to be a big story. Waudby will have to advise her colleagues back in the UK as best she can, but not before discovering more 'ground truth' herself; what the military call *situational awareness*.

First reports from witnesses amongst the crew are suggesting a degree of 'police overreaction', but Lindsey Waudby needs facts – unbiased facts. There are some uncompromising individuals in the Royal Navy, and hard men and hard drinkers too, but, in her experience, out-and-out louts are few and far between. Hoodlums and yobs tend not to last long in the service. They are rooted out pretty quickly, partly by the disciplined nature of the organization but mostly by those serving in the ranks. The Navy is remarkably self-regulating.

Another headline arrives on her screen, this time from the *Sun*: 'BAD BUOYS. First pics of drunk Royal Navy sailors Tasered by US cops'.

Not only has the story spawned an inevitable *Sun*-pun, but the paper has published the police mugshots of the 'Mayport Six' complete with names and ages. The hitherto anonymous drunken sailors now have a very public profile on both sides of the Atlantic.

As things stand, the situation could hardly be worse for the incarcerated sailors, for HMS *Queen Elizabeth*'s international reputation and for that of the Royal Navy as a whole.

Waudby dials Darren Houston. 'Sorry to bother you, sir. I've been through all the papers. But they keep coming.'

'I was afraid of that,' the Commander says. 'Much detail on the alleged offences?'

'Some, sir. Based on police reports, but a lot of hearsay too, I think.'

'Tabloids are hoovering it up, I imagine.'

'Yes, sir. Broadsheets as well, I'm afraid. And some TV news reports. They've got the mugshots, so I need to help the individuals lock down their social media accounts for their own protection.'

0740

Most of the ship's company who went ashore last night returned to the ship in the early hours. All those on duty today will already be up and about – monster hangovers or not. Four, of course, are languishing behind bars in a Jacksonville holding cell with their two colleagues from HMS *Monmouth*. A few other hardliners are sprinting down the quayside to beat the deadlines for being back on board.

0759

Down in the junior rates' dining hall, breakfast is in full swing. To mark the first full day in Florida, the chefs have added American pancakes to the morning menu, complete with the best maple syrup. And everybody claims to have seen something or heard a rumour.

'I saw two cops wrestling one of our blokes to the ground . . .'

'They were out for us. Brit-bashing it was . . .'

'Mind you, our blokes were well pissed . . . completely rat-arsed . . .'

'He went down like a ton of bricks and smashed his head on the floor . . .'

'Saw one big stoker gobbing off at a cop . . . She didn't think twice – just zapped him with her Taser . . .'

The First Lieutenant is grim-faced. Not only has he got four sailors facing trial, but he's just taken a call from Si Moule, the Master-at-Arms, to be told that another one's gone missing. He walks down the passageway to see Dave Smith, the Executive Warrant Officer.

'Better stand by, shipmate,' he says. 'One blighter AWOL. ET Alex Davies. First time at sea. Last seen putting away beers at the Irish Pub but not seen after midnight, and he's not one of the villains arrested.'

'OK, sir.' Smith resigns himself to an even more challenging day than he'd expected. 'Once he's more than four hours adrift we'll issue a missing persons bulletin and contact his family.'

'Hopefully he's sleeping off a hangover on a park bench somewhere.'

'Indeed.'

Neil McCallum finds Jerry Kyd on the bridge wing.

'Excuse me, sir. Have you got a moment? I'm afraid DG4's down.'

'Not operational at all?'

'No, sir. The fuel injection governor's faulty. And we've got issues with DG2 and 3 too. The ventilation supply fans have failed.'

'Is that it?'

'Afraid not, sir. The aft gas turbine is overheating too.'

The QE's two gas turbines and four diesel engines had been running well, but the transatlantic crossing seems to have been more punishing than expected. When the ship goes back to sea in a few days, she will be heading straight for Norfolk to pick up all the equipment and personnel needed for the two months of F-35 trials in the West Atlantic. They'll need maximum power to launch the jets.

'How long to fix?'

'Not long once we get the parts, sir. They've been ordered from the UK.'

'How many days? Worst case.'

'Worst case, seven, sir. But we'll aim for less.'

1200

There's a definite 'morning after the night before' feeling on board. Today isn't going to be easy for anyone. Far from it. Chris Trevethan has just initiated Operation 'Cleansweep', a 'whole-ship evolution' in which everyone works together to deep-clean all the main living areas and thoroughfares. It's a nautical spring-clean, extremely thorough but very democratic. No rank is spared this duty, so everyone from able rate to commander is wielding a mop, duster, squeegee or dustpan and brush. At any other time, even Jerry Kyd would be brandishing a broom but he's currently deep in conversation with meteorologist Dan McMahon. Charts, graphs and satellite photos are spread across the Rose Table.

McMahon has become increasingly worried about a tropical storm crossing the Atlantic. It's been gaining strength and is already exhibiting the classic circulation pattern of an anticyclone. Its wind speeds now exceed 39 mph, which means it's already powerful enough to have been named by the World Meteorological Organization. Only significant events are named, so 'Florence' is demanding attention.

'So, Florence is strengthening, Dan?'

'Significantly, sir. Drawing energy from the warm seas all the time.'

'Her ultimate strength?'

'Could be a Cat 3 or 4, sir. If so, she'll pack a punch.'

'Her possible track?'

'She could veer south into the Gulf of Mexico or she could strike the Florida Keys. Or she could swerve north and impact the US somewhere between Mayport and Norfolk about two weeks from now. Exactly where we'll be, according to the current programme, sir.'

Kyd scans the satellite photos.

'OK, Dan. Keep your eye on things. The question is, do we stay here and hunker down or get out of harm's way? That's if we have the engines to do so.'

Jerry Kyd has always maintained that life on a warship is much easier on the high seas than when tied up alongside. Whatever the oceans throw at a ship her crew will generally find a way of dealing with it. Ships are meant to be at sea, and so are sailors. In harbour for too long can undermine efficiency and erode morale. Things have a habit of unravelling. It's when the gremlins come out to play.

1500

The Mayport Six have returned from their incarceration. After an uncomfortable night behind bars, the British sailors attended court this morning, where, dressed in green overalls, handcuffed and with chains around their ankles, they were marched in front of a district judge. The State of Florida provided them with a defence attorney, who entered pleas of guilty to being drunk and disorderly, offered nominal mitigation (three weeks at sea) and proffered their abject apologies.

The judge found them all guilty of 'alcohol-related misdemeanours' and sentenced them each to one day in jail, which he said they had already effectively served by being locked up overnight. He then promptly waived their fine, saying they could return to their ships, where he accepted they might be subject to further naval discipline. The four shamed QE sailors are back on board. Three have gone straight to their messes and one, Jamie Lutas, has sought out Alastair Mansfield.

'It was a really horrible experience, Bish,' he tells the least judgemental man on board.

'What happened, Jamie?'

'I was in this bar when I heard this sickening crack. One of the guys from the ship had fallen off his stool and hit his head on the floor. Blood everywhere.'

Mansfield grimaces.

'I went straight over to help him but as I bent down an arm grabbed me from behind. I instinctively resisted and pushed the arm away.'

'Don't tell me,' Mansfield says. 'The arm had a policeman on the end of it.'

'Yeah, a bloody big one. Before I knew it, I was pinned to the ground, handcuffed and hauled off to a police wagon.'

'Roughly handled?'

'Well, they weren't using kid gloves. I mean, hands up, Bish, I'd had a few and was probably a bit mouthy, so I'm not saying I was totally innocent, but they shouldn't have used that degree of force.'

'It's America, Jamie. Different way of doing things.'

'Yeah, but I was just doing what comes instinctively and helping a shipmate in distress. I don't even know him that well – but he was from the ship, and we look after each other, don't we?'

Jamie Lutas and the others admit they were the worse for wear but that's no excuse, Stateside. Boisterous behaviour in public might pass muster on a Friday night in Portsmouth or Plymouth, but it doesn't impress in zero-tolerance USA.

One of the sailors had been caught crossing a road unlawfully against the lights. Jaywalking is not a crime in the UK, so, fuelled by booze, he remonstrated with the police officer, who ended up discharging her Taser into the man's leg. Another two were arrested for fighting each other and even though they made up and were having a beer together, they were arrested for public disorder and intoxication. A fourth, having been ejected from a bar for being drunk, lay in the road out of protest and refused to move. He finished his protest in jail.

'We were locked up with some real bad guys, Bish,' Lutas says. 'There were about twenty of us in that overnight cell – some proper scary dudes.'

Alastair Mansfield listens to Lutas with growing sympathy for a young man who at best was in the wrong place at the wrong time and at worst a victim of his own high spirits. As an authority figure without rank and outside the chain of command, the Chaplain is a safe haven for troubled people to confide in. Mansfield does not take this responsibility lightly but he's no soft touch either and knows that in time this current trauma will become a quality 'dit' or war story to be shared down the pub on a Friday night.

To everyone's relief, Alex Davies is no longer AWOL. He returned to the ship over nine hours late and is now sitting in the Royal Navy Police office looking very sorry for himself. After drinking all last night and most of today, he remains very unsteady on his feet.

'Can I go to sleep, pleesh?' he asks the Master-at-Arms.

'You can sleep as soon as we get you back to your mess,' Si Moule says. 'I've ordered you an escort. You've caused a lot of people a lot of worry – do you realize that?'

'Am I in trouble?'

'A whole world of it, shipmate. You can't rock up here when you feel like it. For all we knew you were lying in a gutter with your throat cut.'

Davies starts to say something but thinks better of it.

The fact is, the young engineering technician had gone on a massive bender and woke this morning to find himself on the floor of some stranger's apartment in downtown Jacksonville. Hardly able to move, he lapsed into a coma-like sleep until after midday, when, too frightened to return to the ship, he panicked, cast his fate to the winds and started drinking again at a beach bar. Eventually he was spotted by another crew member, who persuaded him to go back and face the music.

The Master-at-Arms decides that Davies is still too inebriated to make a statement or even much sense, so, as soon as the escort arrives, he orders him back to the Stokers' Mess. After a somewhat wobbly 'walk of shame', Davies climbs into his bunk to sleep off the alcohol still surging through his bloodstream. A guard is placed on him to make sure he stays lying on his side, and doesn't risk choking on his own vomit.

It now remains to be seen what fate awaits the Mayport Six. On paper their crimes are greater than Davies', so it'll be up to the captain to decide how they are to be dealt with. Jerry Kyd is the ultimate arbiter of right and wrong on the QE and is expected to come down very hard on the wayward sailors. No one envies the erstwhile jailbirds as they await whatever punishment the captain deems appropriate.

1800

'The captain!' Darren Houston announces.

The officers at the Rose Table fall silent and sit to attention as Kyd takes his seat.

'Right!' he says. 'I want us all to keep perspective over these arrests and bad publicity. A lot of what I'm reading online is misinformed and distorted reporting from a few rags back home. The Bish has seen most of the guys involved – that's right isn't it, Alastair?'

'That's correct,' the Chaplain says. 'They're all OK. One black eye and one relieved of a tooth, but otherwise very embarrassed and apologetic. They just want to move on.'

'And so do we all,' Kyd says. 'I don't want this to assume any greater significance than it should. There were well over a thousand sailors out on the town last night, and so four of them from here and two more from *Monmouth* falling foul of what I'd call zealous local policing is an astoundingly good result in my book. I reckon the cops wanted to make an example early on so went in hard. I'm not saying our guys didn't deserve what they got, but that's it as far as I am concerned. They have been punished enough.'

Jerry Kyd has thought long and hard about how to handle his recalcitrant matelots and, after seeking advice from his legal advisers on board and back in Portsmouth, he's decided to draw a line under the proceedings. He is unforgiving of mindless, loutish behaviour or anything that brings the Royal Navy into disrepute, but pragmatic enough to know that sailors on the razzle will never be totally upstanding members of society. And he certainly wouldn't want them to be shrinking violets.

A Commanding Officer considering penal options for transgressors will aim for consistency but make allowances too. These same sailors may one day go to war. They'll have to fight together and maybe even die together. If the ship is hit by a hypersonic missile, there will be mass casualties, and sailors will have to carry their injured shipmates to safety whilst ensuring that the ship's still able to fight. It is the ability and willingness of a crew to work together selflessly and altruistically that could make the difference between victory and defeat. There's nothing more unforgiving than combat at sea because there's no obvious escape route. If the bombs, bullets, choking smoke and immolating flames do not claim you, the raging ocean probably will.

'The question we have to ask ourselves,' Jerry Kyd says, 'is what sort of sailor would we want to go to war with? The automaton who obeys every rule, plays it safe and never takes chances? Or the free spirit who pushes his luck, ventures into unknown territory and breaks the odd rule?'

No such lenience will be shown to the hapless Alex Davies. Going AWOL is an unforgivable breach of discipline and can never be forgiven or overlooked. For the wayward stoker, only two things are now certain. The first is that in the fullness of time he, unlike the Mayport Six, will be 'called to the Table' where he'll be tried and sentenced for his sins. The second is that he'll wake up tomorrow with a headache from Hades.

'Moving on,' Kyd says to his HODs. 'We have a strength-ening storm system crossing the Atlantic and possibly heading in our direction – maybe striking the mainland somewhere between here and Norfolk. So, we're keeping eyes on that should it affect our programme. We also have a problem with DG4 and need to get that sorted before we leave the wall. I'm not prepared to start flight trials without all the wheels on the wagon, and neither am I prepared to head into hurricane-driven seas with anything less than full power at my disposal. There's a chance we might have to delay before we go back to sea, but I hope it'll be a short one. We don't want another Invergordon.'

The HODs nod their agreement.

'One piece of good news to finish,' smiles Kyd. 'Lindsey Waudby heard this morning that our two stowaway pigeons have finally been released to the wild. They are now flying solo somewhere over Somerset. Courtesy the Royal Navy.'

35. Hobnobs versus Oreos

Mayport Naval Station, 13 September 2018

As she heads for the mouth of the harbour, a powerful off-shore wind wraps itself around the QE's superstructure like a boa constrictor and tries to wrench her off course. The Navigator, Lieutenant Commander Sam Stephens, is taking evasive action. Speaking through the radio, he's giving a constant stream of clear, concise orders to the American tug-masters who are nudging, coaxing, pushing and pulling the giant British warship past the heavy, concrete sea walls. Jerry Kyd, standing on the starboard bridge wing, has delegated the leaving-harbour responsibility, but he's watching every move like a hawk. If things go wrong, it's Kyd who'll be answerable, but he has every confidence in his very capable Navigator.

The ship glides out into the St Johns River estuary without mishap.

'Can't pretend I'm sorry to be leaving, Darren,' Kyd says.

'No, sir,' Houston says. 'I think we can say we've done Mayport and got the T-shirt.'

An additional week alongside meant the captain's worst fears had been realized. Now a fully fledged Category 4 hurricane, Florence will make what promises to be a very destructive landfall in the next forty-eight hours, somewhere between Mayport and Naval Station Norfolk about 700 miles to the north.

Yesterday, North Carolina, South Carolina and Virginia issued mandatory evacuation orders for their coastal communities. Thirty American warships have already evacuated Naval Station Norfolk to take sanctuary in the Caribbean.

Jerry Kyd knows very well that the most dangerous part of a hurricane is its northwest quadrant, where the anti-cyclonic winds are always the most ferocious. For that reason, he will now take the *Queen Elizabeth* south until it's safe to head back towards Norfolk.

Despite the imminence of a major hurricane, everybody's pleased to be back at sea. Even the most committed party-animals have had their fill of the pubs, clubs and bars of Atlantic Boulevard. And there are at least four on board the QE and two more on *Monmouth* who are very happy to be waving goodbye to the local police.

It is partly a money thing too. Most of the ship's company are overspent and need to start earning valuable sea pay again before arriving in New York in November. Records at the ship's Cash Office show that over £800,000 were exchanged for dollars whilst in Mayport. Taking card payments into account as well, it's likely that they injected around £1 million into the local economy in less than a fortnight. Around £800 is nearly three weeks' wages for an able rate.

Whilst everyone is looking ahead and consigning Mayport to the 'been there done that' column in life's log-book, there is one final reminder that at least one Floridian was sorry to see them go. Copies of a letter sent to the ship have been pinned on noticeboards on every mess deck.

To the Command of the HMS Queen Elizabeth,
I am not anybody of great importance and I don't have a high position of authority or anything of that nature, I just work in the transportation business as an Uber driver part time while I am finishing my college degree.

Therefore, what I am going to inform you about concerning three sailors on your ship is pretty special since they had nothing to gain for what they did. First, let me say that everyone that I have given a ride to who are sailors on HMS Queen Elizabeth were exceptionally kind and very respectful to me, and I find it to be very sad that our media here in Jacksonville, Florida only reported on negative circumstances that happened with a small percentage of sailors on your ship.

That is why I want to make sure that you know about these three sailors that helped me out, while expecting nothing in return. I had received a call from Neptune Beach to pick up a man named David and two of his friends to take them back to Mayport Base. But when I went to get them I lost one headlight which meant I needed to replace it or else quit working for the night until I got it fixed.

David and the other two sailors (I never got their names) told me they worked in the Engineering Dept. on your ship and that they could fix the light for me.

I was amazed they would consider taking the time to fix something for someone they didn't know at all. They were pretty skilful even though it was not an easy job in the dense humidity and heat. They were pretty uncomfortable and sweaty, yet without one complaint, they gave their time to help out a stranger and I will never forget their kindness.

I want to say thanks to the Command of the HMS Queen Elizabeth, for having such excellent sailors on your ship.

Sincerely, Bonnie Ginter

Mayport fades from sight as the QE heads out to sea and for most the city will fade from the memory too. Only one sailor on board has yet to face the consequences of his misdeeds ashore. Alex Davies is likely to be called for summary trial by the First Lieutenant in the next few days. He's already had to face the wrath of his mum over the phone and he's still reeling from that.

The QE sails south, away from the expected track of Hurricane Florence. As evening falls, the sky darkens, but no stars appear – just black, billowing storm clouds on the northern horizon, backlit by intermittent sheet lightning. The roar of the ocean is drowned out by the deep rumble of distant thunder and the occasional clap that sounds much nearer. Florence is making her final approach to the US coast far to the north but her impact is being felt far and wide.

West Atlantic, 15 September 2018

Florence made landfall in the early hours of this morning as a Category 1 hurricane. Although downgraded from Category 4, she struck North Carolina with winds in excess of 90 mph and heavy rainfall. A massive storm surge resulted in widespread flooding, major power outages and, so far, fifty-four fatalities. HMS *Queen Elizabeth*, safe in her southern sanctuary, dodged a bullet and this morning resumes her northerly course towards Norfolk.

Meteorologist Dan McMahon still has his eye on the hurricane spawning grounds off the West African coast. They remain extremely active. It looks like Florence will not be the last of the season. In the meantime, the seas, charged with kinetic energy, are frenzied and confused. The waves are chaotic and muddled. The QE pushes over the seething, crumpled ocean like a massive steam iron, leaving a smooth wake behind her. It is as if she is trying to press the wrinkled water flat.

This is exactly what Electrical Technician Marine Engineer (ETME) Alex Davies is doing to his tropical Number One trousers down on his mess deck. The communal iron hisses as he slides it carefully over the white fabric. Normally he'd be in his overalls, working down in the engine spaces, but today he has to be in his smartest dress uniform. In half an hour he goes to Table.

Davies pulls on his newly pressed kit, adjusts his collar and lanyard and glances in the mirror to check his hat is on straight. He has to walk half the length of the ship and climb three decks to get to the First Lieutenant's office, so is leaving himself plenty of time. Being late for Table would not be a good start to proceedings.

Back on course and driving north through the restless waters, the ship is abuzz with activity. Frederica McCarthy is in the Writer's Office sorting out pay-cheques but this afternoon will revert to her voluntary job as gash-sorter in the pyrolysis plant. Rob Rouston is in the aft gas turbine compartment changing a leaky valve on a fuel-compressor but looking forward to his next CrossFit session with Roly Brading. Appropriately gloved, Wes Khan is skinning pork joints in the galley. In St Paul's chapel, Alastair Mansfield is tending to a tearful young sailor who's missing home. On the bridge, Jerry Kyd, sextant in hand, is teaching astronavigation to another batch of Young Officers, and one deck below, Glen Peters is scrubbing out the pantry sink prior to making the captain's mid-morning coffee. After an extended stay in Florida, HMS *Queen Elizabeth* is restored to normal life – or as normal as life ever gets on this floating Little Britain.

Things seem decidedly abnormal for Alex Davies as he walks down the crowded 3 Foxtrot passageway. Some of the sailors he passes smirk knowingly; others nod sympathetically. Everyone knows there's only one reason a sailor is dressed in freshly pressed Number Ones at this time in the morning.

The 'Table' is a simple, upright polished wooden desk, upon which Chris Trevethan is currently leafing through his notes on the case. Beside him is a female sub-lieutenant who's been assigned as legal adviser. After a few minutes' consultation, Trevethan indicates to the duty RN police officer that he's ready to proceed.

The accused can feel the beads of sweat forming on his upper lip when the door opens.

'ETME Davies!'

The young stoker snaps to attention and marches smartly into the office-turned-courtroom and comes to a halt in front of the Table.

'Salute!' the police officer orders.

Davies obeys.

'Remove headdress!'

'ETME Davies,' Chris Trevethan says sternly. 'You're charged with being Absent without Leave. Being nine hours and thirteen minutes adrift. And returning to the ship drunk and incapacitated. Do you understand the charge?'

'Yessir . . .'

Trevethan looks up from his notes.

'ETME Davies – do you plead guilty or not guilty?'

'Guilty, sir.'

'Have you got mitigation?'

'Yessir. CPO Carr, sir.'

'Call him in.'

The RN police officer opens the door. 'CPO Carr!'

Chief Petty Officer Carr marches in to present a character reference from Davies' branch.

'Sir. ET Davies is on his first deployment, but his branch says he's an able worker and has the making of an effective marine engineer. He's willing and keen to learn. He's very embarrassed about the situation he finds himself in and will accept any punishment awarded.'

Chris Trevethan says nothing but fixes the young stoker with a level stare. Alex Davies shifts uneasily on his feet.

'ET Davies,' Trevethan says at last. 'You put a lot of people to a lot of trouble. Do you understand?'

'Yessir.'

'Do you have a problem with alcohol?'

'No, sir.'

'If you do, we can help.'

'I don't, sir.'

'I'm just saying . . .' Trevethan says. 'If ever you feel you do, 'fess up, and the Navy will do all it can to sort things out for you.'

'Yessir.'

'ET Davies, I fine you ten days' loss of leave. You'll stay on the ship throughout our stop in Norfolk, you'll do extra cleaning duties and you'll muster three times a day in different rigs. Understand?'

'Yessir.'

'I don't want to see you in front of me again.'

'No, sir.'

'If I do, you will get a much harsher punishment. Consider this a warning.'

'Yessir.'

'And lay off the sauce in New York.'

'Yessir.'

West Atlantic, 17 September 2018

0900

In a few hours the QE will arrive at Norfolk Naval Station. Ahead of her is a week of intensive preparations prior to the first F-35 landing, now scheduled for 25 September, two days later than originally planned. The extended delay in Mayport and the impact of Hurricane Florence have disrupted the original programme. After years of preparation, a forty-eight-hour postponement does not sound like much, but any change in plans at this stage could have far-reaching consequences. There are 250 scientists and technicians to be boarded in Norfolk, test pilots have to be embarked and prepared. Plans are also in place to helicopter on VIPs and senior representatives of the Royal Navy and the US Navy to witness the event. And the arrival of the F-35s themselves will require split-second coordination with Pax River. Any sort of delay at this stage is going to be very frustrating for both Jerry Kyd and those in the aviation wing who'll be personally involved with the landings.

A group of yellow-helmeted handlers are sheltering in the lee of the aft island. None is smiling.

'Right, lads, listen up!' Paul Ranson calls over the wind howling across the flight deck. 'I know you're disappointed. I'm threaders too. It's just the roll of the dice. So take it on the chin.'

It's been confirmed that because of the delay to the schedule, Paul Ranson's Starboard Watch will not, as originally planned, be on duty for the first landing of the F-35. The two air-handling teams, Port Watch and Starboard Watch, alternate their shifts daily.

'Don't worry, guys,' Ranson says. 'We'll have months of landing and launching the aircraft. You'll all get your turn.'

The handlers nod half-heartedly. They know Ranson's right, but the simple fact is, they're not going to be the very first team to land a fixed-wing jet on HMS *Queen Elizabeth*.

'Rub it in, fellas,' Scouse Walsh says. 'It means we can all have a lie-in instead.'

'Exactly,' Ranson laughs. 'Silver lining, lads!'

Paul Ranson is just as dispirited. But delighted for the leader of Port Watch – Emma Ranson, his wife. And he'll not be lying in on the day. Off duty or not, he'll be there to witness that landing come what may.

1130

The QE edges neatly into her berth in Naval Station Norfolk – the largest naval base in the world. Once her securing lines are buttoned to the quayside, the Union Jack is raised at her bow. Either side of her, for as far as the eye can see, are US warships: aircraft carriers, troop carriers, helicopter carriers and massive supply ships.

As soon as the gangways have been craned into place, a high-ranking delegation from the US Navy climbs on board. It's led by Vice Admiral Bruce Lindsey, Deputy Commander US Fleet Forces Command. He and his entourage are escorted to the Flag Dining Room at the stern, where he is received by Jerry Kyd and many of his most senior officers.

'How was the crossing?' Vice Admiral Lindsey asks.

'Good,' Kyd replies. 'Though Hurricane Florence tried to spoil the party.'

'Same here. We evacuated Norfolk, but everyone's back now.'

'Could be more storms on the way,' Darren Houston ventures.

'I guess you're big enough to plough through pretty lumpy seas.'

'Hope so.' Kyd smiles.

'You looked great coming in,' Lindsey says.

They touch upon the forthcoming F-35 development tests.

'I'll tell you something,' the admiral says. 'As the only Level 1 partner in the programme, you Brits have the lead right now. Twinning a fifth gen' carrier with a fifth gen' fighter – the world's never seen this sort of firepower together. On your first deployment in anger you'll have the USA with you, believe me. We're watching what you're doing with great interest and learning.'

Lindsey speaks for many in the US Navy and US military generally. American carriers are powerful warships and though nuclear-powered they are based on legacy designs – even their latest, the massive USS *Gerald R. Ford*, derives from a 1970s design. She still has to prove herself, but the QE, with her stealth characteristics and high degree of automation, is leading the way.

1600

Sitting alone on the bridge, Jerry Kyd looks out on the impressive array of American warships on either side of his own and considers Vice Admiral Lindsey's words. The geo-strategical 'Special' relationship between the UK and the USA has become increasingly asymmetric since the First World War, as the US Navy grew in size and firepower. That's never going to change, but Kyd knows that his supercarrier is a potential game-changer nevertheless. She's poised to become Britain's most powerful non-nuclear strategic deterrent, and a major force in the global power game. Perhaps more potent and persuasive than anything the Americans have or plan to have – even with the *Gerald R. Ford* fresh off the blocks.

Kyd will be forever grateful to the US Navy for keeping the Royal Navy on the boil until it's ready to resume its carrier strike role. But he also knows that it's still a long road back to where they used to be. The RN has been asleep for a while. If they are spot-checked by the enemy, they need to be ready, not only with the right technology and equipment but the right people – trained and ready for the fight. Not for the first time, he feels the weight of a nation's hopes on his shoulders.

Glen Peters appears with a cup of tea and a plate of chocolate biscuits.

Kyd's brow furrows. 'What on earth are those, Glen?'

'Chocolate Oreos, sir,' comes the apologetic reply. 'They're American, sir. We're out of Hobnobs until stores arrive tomorrow.'

Kyd looks askance at the dark-brown biscuit wafers with white crème fillings.

'Try one, sir?'

Kyd picks up one of the 'sandwich cookies' and takes a tentative bite. His eyes widen in surprise at the unbridled sweetness. He continues to chew, but for him the Oreo doesn't have the honest crunch of a Hobnob, nor the fulsome flavour of its jumbo rolled oats.

'Thanks, Glen. I'll . . . er . . . wash it down with the tea.'

Peters leaves the bridge, and Kyd looks down at his half-nibbled Oreo, reflecting on the delights of the sturdy British biscuit. His comparative contemplations turn naturally from biscuits to boats.

By sheer strength of numbers and firepower the US Navy would certainly outgun the Royal Navy. He knows that. But naval warfare is also about tactics, strategy and, vitally, the quality of your manpower. Imagining a modern sea battle, he sees HMS *Queen Elizabeth* at the centre of a Task Group taking control of an oceanic battle space. She would be covered from air and surface attack by escort destroyers and her own fighter jets. The sub-surface threat would be countered by her frigates and submarines. She would be further protected by her own stealth design, meaning an enemy would find it more difficult to locate her in the first place, but if they did, she could unleash her own Phalanx anti-aircraft system, which will shoot out a wall of lead to take out any incoming missiles. She would also have a long-range radar, capable of identifying an incoming object the size of a tennis ball travelling at supersonic speed from over 2 miles away . . .

The character of war and the way it is waged have changed and are continuing to change at an ever-faster rate. It's getting increasingly difficult to keep up with the technology of combat: artificial intelligence, space and cyberwarfare, miniaturization, robotics, quantum computing. All this is going to change the way Kyd and those who will succeed him fight wars. He wonders what sort of ship HMS *Queen Elizabeth* will become over the duration of her service life. What sorts of new technologies will be invested in her? What future generations of fighter jets will fly off her?

Kyd prays that when locked and loaded she will never have to be triggered in anger, but how likely is it, he asks himself, that his warship will only ever be a teeth-baring deterrent? In her prospective fifty years of duty he knows that she'll have to snarl ferociously and pounce with deadly intent. And he does not need reminding that his core business is also about dealing with the death and destruction of his own.

Kyd's mission is to prepare the QE for active duty. Future captains will take her to war. He wonders what sort of man or woman will command her on her final deployment in 2070.

'Sir, good news!' Glen Peters calls from the bridge door. 'The NAAFI have found another box of Hobnobs!'

Kyd gives a quiet smile as his world settles back on to its normal axis.

36. Bullets, Bombs, Baked Beans and Blood

0900

The quayside is a hive of activity. A convoy of trucks is queuing with urgent deliveries. Huge Arctic juggernauts, refrigerated transporters, are bringing hundreds of tons of food stores – enough to sustain 1,500 people for twenty days at sea. Squeezing past them are open-top trucks laden with dozens of GBU-12 inert bombs for the F-35 flight trials. More compact, hard-covered lorries are bringing small-arms ordnance for the ship's GPMGs and rapid-firing mini-guns.

Commander Jenny Curwood, overseeing the loading, is trying to organize more cranes to lift on ninety pallets of fresh food into the ship's fridges as quickly as possible. Dry stores and tinned foods must wait, so hundreds of boxes of cereals, sacks of flour, tins of cooking oil and enough baked beans to sink a battleship are being stacked neatly in temporary ramparts adjacent to the gangway. More trucks are arriving all the time, so Curwood's working fast.

There's one perishable commodity she's looking out for in particular – the all-important delivery of fresh blood for the medical centre. A consignment, planned for weeks ago, was sent from the UK the day before yesterday and should have arrived by now but could have been held up at customs. The ship's current stock of blood is almost past its sell-by date, so must be replaced. The usually cheerful Commander Logistics looks worried. The ship cannot sail without the blood.

A lone figure is walking purposefully through the frenetic quayside activity. Shaven-headed and with a close-cropped red beard, he's carrying a large hold-all and wearing beige civilian chinos, a pale-blue button-down shirt and the broadest of smiles. 'Pax' is only about 100 miles to the north of Norfolk, so Nathan Gray has driven down this morning to drop off his luggage. There's little room in an F-35 cockpit for personal possessions. He'll sleep on board tonight and head back tomorrow to prepare for the flight.

Importantly for Gray, today is also his first chance to see the ship in the flesh. He had a brief glimpse inside the hangar when he attended the commissioning last December, but there's no ceremony now, no pageantry, no pomp and spectacle. Frills, bells and whistles have been stowed as the ship is readied for what will be her longest period at sea since construction. Gray watches the activity around him with mounting exhilaration. It's humbling to the naval test pilot that all this activity, all this effort, is aimed at landing him and his F-35 safely on the flight deck.

Gray continues towards the aft gangway, where, according to his 'joining papers', he should come aboard. As he gets closer, he sees a familiar figure.

'Blackers!'

'Welcome, Nath!' James Blackmore strides towards him with arm outstretched. 'Good to see you.'

The old friends grip hands.

'Excited?' Blackmore already knows the answer.

'I thought I was excited driving down from Pax River this morning,' Gray says. 'But when I came into port and saw the

QE and the Union Jack waving over the bow, my heart went into overdrive. What a sight.'

'Been a long time coming, Nath.'

Still chatting, the two men head up the gangway.

'I see you made the headlines in Mayport.' Gray's blue eyes sparkle.

'Not just in Mayport, I'm afraid,' Blackmore says. 'We went global!'

'I know. My wife read about it in the *Stoke-on-Trent Sentinel.*'

1000

Three large coaches, horns blaring, negotiate their way carefully through the narrow channels left by the lines of delivery trucks. After parking up near the for'ard gangway, their automatic doors slide open to release a small army of men and women on to the quayside. They take a moment to inspect the vast warship in front of them before unloading endless suitcases, rucksacks and grips.

The 150 new arrivals are from the Integrated Test Force – set up specifically to oversee the testing of the F-35. The mostly American contingent will embark with the ship for the duration of the flight trials. Though employed by the military, most of them are civilians, so few are in uniform. Many are old hands in the aviation industry and come in a range of distinctly non-military shapes and sizes. There are intense, bespectacled scientists, besuited, crop-haired administrators and smart-looking officials in highly badged white overalls and hard hats.

The ones in well-worn emerald-green sweatshirts are dedicated F-35 maintainers and mechanics. Gum-chewing, grizzled and gruff, they look like reconstituted Hell's Angels. Large bellies abound, and so do long pony-tails, but these men are supreme specialists, at the top of their game.

The assorted members of the ITF 'family', a sort of 'Little America', will now take their place on Little Britain. This new cultural mix will add considerably to the diversity of custom, language, tradition, outlook and attitude on board and stand as testimony to the two nations' interoperability.

One of the maintainers, tall, well built and with a military air, stands back from the crowd to gaze in awe at the towering ship and its unique twin islands. Forty-nine-year-old Robert Salerno IV, known to all as 'Turbo', served in the US Navy for ten years, so is well used to ships and shipborne living.

This will be the first British vessel he's ever worked on. He's elated by the prospect, but harbours private misgivings about understanding the local accents. After a few minutes he throws his rucksack over his shoulder and runs to rejoin his compatriots.

Once registered at a huge table in the hangar, the American newcomers are given temporary ID cards, a preliminary health and safety brief and then shown to their cabins. They'll be provided with guides for the first few days until they learn their way around the massive piece of floating real estate that will be their home until late November.

A sprightly Cockney able rate welcomes another group of waiting Americans. 'If y'd loike ta foller me, lays'n'ginelmen, Ah'll showya to yer gaffs.'

'What did that fella just say?' Turbo asks with some consternation.

Nathan Gray has moved all his gear into a single cabin on the officers' accommodation deck. Though typically spartan in its decor, it's a 'luxury' Head of Department's cabin, so more spacious than most. He's brought nothing with him to personalize the space other than a small photograph of his wife Lucy, which he pins to the empty noticeboard above the desk.

After checking out the en-suite shower and toilet he lies back on the wider-than-average bunk to contemplate the moment. He knows that the next couple of months are going to involve relentless, unremitting missions in a range of wind and weather conditions. 'Eat, sleep, fly, eat, sleep, fly,' he murmurs to himself. Lucy smiles down at him from the pinboard. He smiles back. He misses her. He always does, and, not for the first time, thanks God their stars eventually aligned.

Having first met when he was twenty-one and she eighteen, they became pals, good friends, but there was no spontaneous ignition. No immediate romance. But they made a pact that if neither had married by the time they were thirty they'd become an item. When Gray was twenty-nine he broke up with his then fiancée at roughly the same time as Lucy also finished a long-term relationship. Lucy texted her 'backstop boyfriend', and after a few dates they invoked their fall-back option and were married within a year. They have just celebrated their tenth anniversary.

Gray always knew it takes a very special woman to understand and handle a fast-jet pilot – let alone a test pilot – always dicing with death and, perhaps as a result, more determined than most to extract every last drop of adrenaline from life.

He knows he must be exhausting to live with sometimes, not to mention infuriating, exasperating, irritating and maddening in equal measure.

Lucy soon proved herself more than equal to the challenge, and whilst able and willing to encourage his ambitions, reinforce his self-belief and embolden his spirit, she could also bring him down to earth when needed and keep his feet more or less on the ground. Sometimes Gray regrets they didn't act on impulse earlier and tie the knot in their twenties. But he also recognizes that they were probably not ready for each other. His near-death experience with Jak London was something he had to get through on his own. Its shock, trauma and pain helped shape the man he was to become.

His focus moves from Lucy to the back of the cabin door, where his name's been scrawled on a laminated accommodation card in black marker pen: 'Cdr Nathan Grey.'

'GRAY!' he bellows.

Everybody misspells his name. Underneath is his designation, 'Test Pilot', and the dates of his proposed time on board: 'Developmental Test Trials: September 18th 2018 – November 25th 2018'.

Gray might miss his wife but, looking around his plain, stark, unadorned cabin, he knows there's nowhere else he would rather be right now. For all its clinical austerity, this, to him, is the much-anticipated conclusion of what has often felt like an interminable journey. He reminds himself he still has one more hop to make before he can say he has truly arrived, and that will not be for another five days. He looks up and feels a surge of anxiety. The dragons are out there. Then he hears Jak London's voice. 'Nath, always remember: if things are too easy, they're probably not worth the effort.'

Gray hauls himself out of his bunk and changes into his

uniform. His stomach knots again. Nerves or excitement? 'Both,' he tells himself as he closes the door behind him.

Ten minutes later, having only asked the way twice, he has managed to locate the wardroom for 'Standeasy' – midmorning coffee. He's looking out for three friends who were also due to join the ship today and sees them as soon as he enters the crowded room. Squadron Leader Andy Edgell of the RAF, Pete 'Wizzer' Wilson of British Aerospace Systems and Major Michael 'Latch' Lippert of the US Marine Corps are the other test pilots who'll share the testing over the next couple of months. Latch is accompanied by his wife Amanda and their six-month-old son Adam. Amanda and Adam will not be sailing with Latch, but they have an appointment with Alastair Mansfield. The Bish has promised to perform a very special ceremony for them before the ship departs.

1230

The lunch queue is growing in the main dining hall.

'More chips!' Wes Khan yells from the servery. 'And quickly!'

The ship's company is getting through an average of 250 kilograms of chips a day, and Khan knows that any delay in keeping the trays topped up will lead to a massive tailback. Reinforcements appear from the deep-fat fryer, and Khan watches the sailors heap them on to their plates. 'We're meant to be eating healthy!'

'Starting tomorrow, Wes!' they chorus.

'That's what you said yesterday! Think of your beach body.'

'You mean like yours, Wes?'

'I'm getting there . . .' Khan breathes in sharply.

1430

Three more gigantic refrigerated trucks full of fresh food have arrived on the quayside, but all the available cranes are lifting the inert bombs into the hangar. Curwood reaches for her radio. 'Commander L calling 1L. Channel 2. Over.'

Chris Trevethan, sitting in his office, responds immediately. *'1L receiving, ma'am. Over.'*

'1L, we have a problem,' Curwood says. 'There are no cranes available and several tons of fresh food to get in to our fridges ASAP. Manpower needed, I'm afraid. Over.'

'We were about to announce Secure,' Trevethan says. *'But no worries, ma'am. Leave it with me. Out.'*

Trevethan walks purposefully out of his office, descends two decks to the entrance of the for'ard gangway, where he picks up the main broadcast microphone.

'D'ye hear there?' his voice booms through the ship. *'There are several large trucks on the quayside full of lovely fresh food – and it's all for you. We have negative cranes to bring it on, so muscle is required. I can't pipe leave until this is done, so the sooner we crack it, the sooner you can go ashore. Clear Lower Deck. Clear Lower Deck of all personnel!'*

The response is immediate. Within minutes a human chain stretches from the trucks to the refrigerator compartments. Jenny Curwood watches with satisfaction as it works to an almost metronomic rhythm. 'Just like I tell my children,' she says to her assistant, Gordon Clarke. 'Tidy your rooms and you can go out!'

1600

Most of the food is now on board. The sailors have been released and are making their way ashore when a single white van draws up in front of the aft gangway. A sentry checks the manifest and takes possession of a large white box marked with a red cross.

The fresh plasma is taken straight to the medical complex, where it's unpacked and transferred to the medical fridge.

'Good job this didn't get mixed up with the food stores,' one of the medical staff remarks. 'Could have been on the menu tonight.'

1800

Although many have gone ashore, the supper queue in the main dining hall is a long one. Members of the ITF survey the array of mainly British dishes with keen interest but no little suspicion.

'Hey, buddy, can I ask you something?' A worried-looking American turns to the Royal Marine behind him. 'Toad-in-the-hole. What in the name of good God almighty is that?'

'A great British favourite,' the marine replies helpfully. 'Battered amphibian.'

'Battered . . . amphibian . . . ?'

'Mmm. Delicious. They breed them on board.'

'You have a choice,' pipes up another. 'Boned or deboned. I prefer boned. More crunch!'

And so starts the cultural assimilation of Little America with Little Britain – two nations delightfully divided by a common language, sense of humour and, tonight, palate.

21 September 2018

1100

Major Michael Lippert, the US Marine Corps test pilot, is standing on the quarterdeck in full dress uniform, complete with medals. His wife Amanda serves in the US Navy too and is dressed to match. Nathan Gray, Alastair Mansfield and six-month-old Adam Thomas Lippert complete the set. The ever-genial Chaplain is about to anoint the baby with holy water held in the inverted ship's bell.

Nathan Gray notices the tiny but tell-tale ripples on the surface. 'The bell's toppers with oggin!'

'Translate, please, Nath.' Latch Lippert is still learning the intricacies of Jackspeak.

'Full of water.'

'You guys call water "oggin"?'

'What else?' Gray grins. 'Though Holy Oggin today, naturally.'

Latch Lippert has been training with Gray for the last eighteen months at Pax River, and the two men have become close friends. It was Gray's suggestion that Adam be baptized on board the QE, and Lippert leapt at the opportunity. With pleasing symmetry, he was himself baptized on his father's ship some thirty-four years ago.

Lippert Junior remains blissfully unaware of the significant events unfolding around him. Even when a brass quartet from the Royal Marines Band arrives and strikes up with 'Eternal Father', he simply turns his head from one side to the other without opening his eyes. But all that changes when the ceremony itself begins, and, yelling at the top of his voice, he becomes the only American so far to be vigorously unimpressed by Britain's biggest warship and, in particular, by her historic bell.

1300

Nathan Gray, now in flight overalls, is on the way to his mandatory Flight Deck Acquaint. Lieutenant Commander Spike

Hughes is waiting for him outside the aircraft handlers' locker room and the two Fleet Air Arm officers set off for a tour of the 4-acre space. They check markings, illumination lights and the exact positions of the six dedicated landing spots in relation to the aft and for'ard islands. Gray and his fellow pilots will soon be testing and measuring the wind vortices and general turbulence created by the islands, and how they impinge on the aircraft.

Sophisticated tracking cameras are being positioned to monitor the aircraft as they launch and land. A huge anemometer mast is being erected near the bow to collect wind velocity and air-flow data.

Gray bends down to feel the deck. 'So this lighter area is TMS?'

'Yessir,' Hughes says. 'It's only been laid down at the six landing spots.'

Thermal Metal Spray, the uniquely British invention that bonds aluminium and titanium at the molecular level, has been applied to the areas of the deck which will sustain most heat and thrust from the F-35B in vertical-landing and short-take-off mode. It's been tested under laboratory conditions, but Gray will be the first to do it for real.

He knows from his Harrier days that the integrity of the flight deck is all-important. It provides both the pilots' platform and a shield for those living below. RAF pilots operate from runways located some distance from people's working and living quarters. Naval pilots launch and land right over their heads. When Gray brings in the F-35 next week, he will be doing so directly above a community of 1,500 people.

The two men stop at 3 Spot, directly in front of the aft island. 'This is where you'll land for the first time, sir,' Hughes announces cheerfully.

'Yup,' Gray nods. 'Something I've done a thousand times in the simulator.' He looks up to the huge windows of Flyco – the panoramic control tower. 'But that place will be rammed on the day,' he laughs. 'All back-seat pilots shouting at me!'

Hughes grins. 'If they could do any better, sir, they'd be the ones flying, wouldn't they? Shall we head up the ski-slope?'

Moments later Gray is standing at the very apex of the bow, looking down at the water some 80 feet below. 'Blimey, it's a lot higher than our replica deck at Pax,' he says. 'Don't want to end up dropping off here in a brand-new F-35.'

'Best not prang it if you can help it,' agrees Hughes.

The two men shake hands. Hughes heads down the flight deck, leaving Gray on the ski-jump. Turning to survey the vast ship bathed in warm September sunshine, he imagines himself swooping in low to hover over the sea next to 3 Spot. He sees himself crabbing over the ship, ready for his final descent. He sees himself touch down and taxi to his parking spot before de-powering the engine, opening the canopy and climbing out of the cockpit. There are other less comfortable scenarios, but he is not allowing himself to imagine those. He has to think positively and is pleased to have walked the deck before he has to land on it, that his feet have touched it before his wheels. When he does come in to land it will feel more like coming home than arriving somewhere for the first time.

1900

Nathan Gray salutes as he steps off the ship with RAF pilot Andy Edgell. Latch Lippert and Wizzer Wilson will sail with the ship tomorrow. Gray and Edgell must now return to Patuxent River Naval Air Station, as they'll be the ones to bring in the two F-35s. Thereafter all four pilots will share flying duties over the two three-week test periods. Developmental Testing Phase 1 (DT1) will take place before the QE's visit to New York, and DT2 will come immediately afterwards.

Squadron Leader Andy Edgell is disappointed that he won't be the first to land on the *Queen Elizabeth*. He knows it's more appropriate for a naval pilot to be given that honour, but he can't help feeling slightly hard done by. RAF and Fleet Air Arm pilots would fight to the death for each other in combat but are, nonetheless, driven by a healthy sense of competition and a less than healthy antagonism.

The FAA always resented the RAF's dominant role in the Joint Force Harrier programme. Intended to establish a fully integrated fighter wing, it faltered because the RAF was not prepared to allow its pilots to live and work at sea for months at a time, which led to the axing of the Harrier squadrons altogether – and thus the early decommissioning of the Illustrious Class carriers. Because the RAF 'own' all fighter aircraft, the collapse of the Joint Lightning Force for similar reasons remains a lingering but unspoken concern.

The fact that Nathan Gray will be the first pilot to land an F-35 on deck is a feather in the Fleet Air Arm's cap, but the RAF will claim some kudos on the day. The plan is that Edgell will come in straight after Gray, and then, after refuelling, will be the first to launch off the ski-jump. So, honours even – at least in theory.

37. Lightning Is Forecast

Naval Station Norfolk, 23 September 2018

0900

It's time for HMS *Monmouth* and HMS *Queen Elizabeth* to head for the classified location chosen for the top secret F-35 landings, just forty-eight hours from now.

Monmouth is the first to leave her berth. With full power astern, the Type 23 frigate powers out backwards and takes station in the adjacent sea channel. Under Jerry Kyd's careful guidance, his carrier edges away from the wall. There's no room to turn her in the harbour, so Kyd must also reverse. He knows that as he leaves the protective shield of the other warships tied up nearby, the wind will impact on his two islands with greater force. He must use this to his advantage and not let it rotate him dangerously. He also knows that as soon as his stern hits the sea channel he'll have to increase power and punch out fast, before the current takes control.

He monitors every move of the guiding tugs and remains sensitive to every vibration, tremor and hum of his ship. He knows her moods as well as he knows his own.

'You know, Darren, it's very strange, this, for me,' he tells his second in command. 'Here I am, still ticking off lots of "firsts" for the QE – first transatlantic crossing, first visit to a foreign port, first fixed-wing landing – and yet at the same time I'm ticking off lots of "lasts" for me. Today's the last time I will ever take a ship to sea.'

Jerry Kyd will be handing the QE to Captain Nick Cooke-Priest in New York. He'll be moving on to even greater things, but it won't be easy. Sailors get very close to their ships, and commanding officers even more so.

Back in the Atlantic swell, he notices immediately that the sea is heavy and confused and the cloud cover extensive, thanks to Hurricane Florence. Inside the QE, the community is gearing up for the challenges ahead. The ITF contingent are finding their sea legs. Wes Khan is marinating lamb joints for tonight's curry. Scouse Walsh is testing his made-to-measure earplugs in readiness for the F-35s. Chris Trevethan prowls the lower decks to ensure the duty watches are cleaning the flats to good effect. Rob Rouston and Roly Brading are in the gym, lifting impossibly heavy weights and trying to pretend to each other it doesn't hurt like hell, while Alex Davies is mustering for inspection in his Number Ones, as part of his ongoing punishment. Glen Peters is ironing shirts in the Captain's Pantry. Alastair Mansfield is in Saint Paul's chapel, overseeing a painting class, and Frank Rochford is in the toilet paper store on 2 Deck, practising his bagpipes.

James Blackmore, meanwhile, is in Flyco, poring over plans for the historic landings. He's now focusing on the numerous helicopter flights – some to collect VIPs from shore and others to oversee their evolution as search and rescue aircraft, should there be a crash. He's also ordered continual FOD plodding over the next two days.

Vigilance is vital.

24 September 2018

Lieutenant Commander Dan McMahon, the meticulous meteorologist, is worried. Until last week, he had been busy tracking Hurricane Florence through the Caribbean and coastal USA but now he's trying to put together an accurate forecast for tomorrow morning's landings. 'The most critical thing for the F-35s will be the height of the cloud base,' he tells his team while scrutinizing satellite imagery of the upper atmosphere. 'They'll need at least 1,000 feet of clear sky for everything to go to plan tomorrow. If the clouds are lower than that, we'll be in trouble, and either have to cancel or move to another area – as long as it's not too far away.' The QE will have to stay within striking distance of a land base in case of emergencies.

After further analysis of the data, McMahon's prognosis is mixed, as he tells Jerry Kyd an hour later. 'Sir, I'm concerned about a low-pressure system moving towards Pax River. If we have a problem with the weather tomorrow, I reckon it'll be there, not here.'

Kyd is now anxious that the weather might have the last say after all. 'Keep your eye on the ball, Dan, and let's make a final decision in the morning but let's assume it's still a "go".'

No military commander wants to change a well-worked strategy at the last minute but dealing with the unexpected is the nature of life and, more to the point, the nature of war. 'No plan survives first contact with the enemy,' he reminds himself yet again. And right now the enemy comes once again in the form of mischievous weather gods who seem intent on spoiling the party at every opportunity.

Out on the flight deck, the aircraft handlers and firefighting teams have gathered around Petty Officer George.

'Right, lads and lasses,' the gruff Brummie begins. 'Never forget that a flight deck is an unforgiving place, and that'll be even more the case with jets on board. We'll have them blasting away as well as rotors burning and turning. Be safe and look after each other. Tomorrow will be a first-time experience for all of us. No smally hand-signals. Be bold. Look good and be professional. Set the standard for the weeks that follow, when we will be launching and landing all the time. Never get complacent.'

The young men and women look serious but determined.

'OK. Get below. Have some scran and then get your heads down. Come up tomorrow with your game faces on.'

Scouse Walsh walks towards the exit with Emma Ranson. 'The youngsters are looking a bit nervous,' he says, taking off his helmet.

'It's a big deal for them,' Emma replies. 'Me too, though. It feels like my whole career has led to this!'

'Yeah. You're lucky, Emms. To get the first landing I mean. Is Paul gutted?'

'He'll be disappointed,' she says. 'But he won't admit it. He just wants it to go well for the ship.'

'Aye,' Scouse nods. 'He's a real team player, for sure.'

'Anyway, you'll all get your chance to move those jets around the deck,' Ranson says. 'We have weeks of flying ahead of us.'

'Hope so, Emms. As long as that flight deck holds up. Otherwise we're straight back to Portsmouth tomorrow . . .'

1930

Darren Houston climbs to the bridge and delivers his customary evening pipe: *'Good evening, Queen Elizabeth. Commander here. Tomorrow's an historic day for the ship as the first fixed-wing landings will take place at 0930. So, rest well tonight, because whatever your job and wherever you work, you'll be contributing to the effort. If you're not on watch, you're all encouraged to watch on closed-circuit TV because – make no mistake – tomorrow we become a fully fledged aircraft carrier. That is all.'*

38. Lightning Strikes

0500

The night sky is in full retreat as the sun stirs below the eastern horizon.

'Call the Hands' will not be made for another two hours, which means most on board remain asleep. But not all. Deep inside the belly of the ship, a steward is making his way from the Aft Galley on 5 Deck to the crew room on 1 Deck. He's moving cautiously, particularly on the ladders, because he's carrying a huge tray precariously stacked with freshly made bacon butties. Wrapped in silver foil to keep them warm, they're for the aircraft handlers, who've also risen early.

'Here you are, fellas,' he says cheerfully. 'Plenty for everyone. Dig in.'

The normally effusive, wise-cracking team do as directed but in near silence. They're pensive and preoccupied. This will be a big day for all of them. A day to remember – and hopefully for all the right reasons.

Patuxent River Naval Air Station, Maryland

0530

A hundred miles away, Commander Nathan Gray and Squadron Leader Andy Edgell are going through their final flight-briefing. It will not be long before they pull on their pressurized flying suits and don their bespoke flying helmets.

Both pilots have landed on HMS *Queen Elizabeth*'s flight deck a thousand times in the simulator, but even the most complex algorithms are unable to allow for a bolt from the blue.

The briefing concludes. On his way out of the door, Gray is handed an official signal just received from Commander Air, Jim Blackmore: 'Nath – the captain sends his fondest felicitations but asks you make sure you arrive at 0930 Charlie Time as planned. Don't be late. Start as you mean to go on. Remember the world is watching!'

Gray smiles at the tongue-in-cheek reference to pilots' timekeeping.

The two of them reach the kit room. Their flying gear is laid out in two neat piles: pressure suit, life jacket, flying gloves and helmet. But before they start to pull it on, the phone rings. They must go to the Meteorological Office immediately.

0930

HMS *Queen Elizabeth* is in her assigned position. One of the Merlin Mark 2s has just returned from Norfolk with several high-ranking British and American Navy and Air Force officers who are coming to witness today's events. The cloud base is at 1,200 feet, and the surface conditions are benign. The ship is ready, but Pax River is in the grip of the low-pressure system Dan McMahon forecast. They've called for a delay of at least forty-five minutes for the F-35 departures.

The Flyco air traffic control team settle back in their chairs but keep a watchful eye on their radar screens. The navigating team on the bridge also relax momentarily, whilst ensuring the carrier maintains a course into the prevailing wind. The vast majority of the ship's company is below deck and so not able to see the landing in the flesh. All those not working, however, are waiting impatiently on their mess decks to watch it on Sovereign TV. Chris Trevethan has been overseeing the inflation of the ship's big blow-up screen in the hangar, which will also carry a live feed. Now he is having to manage the expectations of about 400 restless sailors and marines.

'Listen up, shipmates!' he booms. 'There's a short delay because of gopping weather at Pax River. Patience, please. Normal service will be resumed as soon as possible!'

The man who has most reason to be frustrated is in fact the most relaxed. The affable and unflappable Commander Air makes himself comfortable on the Papal Throne. Today has been a long time coming, so having to wait simply gives Jim Blackmore an extra three-quarters of an hour to savour what is to come.

Jerry Kyd scans the horizon from his captain's chair.

'At least we can blame the Americans for the weather, sir,' Darren Houston says, doing his best to ease the tension.

Kyd focuses his binoculars on the waves breaking dramatically over the *Monmouth*'s bow as she takes station on his port beam. The Wildcat helicopter on her flight deck is poised for air-sea rescue. He prays nobody will need it. He'll never forget one particular Harrier GR7 malfunction on HMS *Invincible* during operations in the Med nearly twenty years ago. The pilot overshot the flight deck, hit the waves at 90-plus knots and failed to eject.

Kyd can still see the eruption on impact in his mind's eye. He still doesn't know how the man survived. And he has no desire to see Nathan Gray or Andy Edgell sign up for membership of the Goldfish Club today.

1000

Nathan Gray is in the kitting-up area at Pax River, checking his helmet connections for the hundredth time, when Andy Edgell appears.

'It's a go, Nathan,' he says. 'Cloud base is above 1,000 feet. Time to make history.'

'Let's do this thing!' the naval pilot replies quietly.

According to procedure, both go straight to the heads to drain their bladders. They've been sipping water constantly all morning. Dehydration in the cockpit is always a danger, but a full bladder makes it difficult to concentrate. An F-35 provides its pilot with incredible attack capabilities, super-smart, cutting-edge defensive systems and innovative stealth technology, but only a pee-bag packed with an absorbent sponge if they are caught short in the cockpit.

It's time to kit-up, something Gray is very superstitious about. The G-Force pants must go on before anything else, and he always does up the right-hand buttons before the left. Then the right zip, followed by the left. It must be in that order. The flight jacket goes on next, right arm first, then

297

left, then one fluid movement of the zip. Finally he connects the hoses in order from top to bottom. Most pilots carry their helmets and gloves to the aircraft. Not Gray. He pulls on his $400,000 helmet and then his black leather flight gloves in the kit room. Only then is he good to go.

Their aircraft are waiting on the apron outside their base HQ. Edgell's is codenamed Lightning 64. Gray's is Lightning 65. They both greet their individual ground crews, who are waiting alongside. Gray makes a point of shaking hands with every one of them before proceeding with his checks. Again, superstition demands that he start on the left-hand side and walk clockwise, examining everything as he goes.

Once both pilots are happy, they climb their ladders and strap themselves in. Gray feels the muscles in his stomach clenching. 'This is it,' he whispers to himself as the canopy closes. He's trained for this moment for nearly three years, but it was always something that was going to happen some-time in the future: next year, next month, next week. Now the time has come.

Andy Edgell gives him the thumbs-up. Gray reciprocates and initiates the starting procedures. A simple three-switch operation. First the battery. Then the integrated power pack to start the engine and the cooling system. Finally, he switches on the engine itself. It starts as a low whine but gradually builds in volume as it spools up. He initiates an automatic systems check with the press of a button. In ninety seconds, the aircraft self-tests almost every one of its thousands of functions. Finding no problems, it declares itself ready for flight. Gray checks his fuel, turns on his helmet-mounted display and signals to Edgell once again.

Together they taxi out to the runway, accompanied by an F-18 chase plane (codenamed Salty-Dog-Chase) as an overseer and an F-18 tanker (code-named Salty-Dog-Tanker). They only have 100 miles to travel to the ship, so neither aircraft is carrying full tanks, but if they hit a fog bank and have to wait to land on the carrier or turn back to Pax River they'll need to take on more fuel. If Gray crashes on landing and destroys part of the flight deck, or the flight deck proves unable to withstand the powerful thrust forces, Edgell will need to refuel to return home. Every eventuality has been considered. Although the pilots follow strict protocols, today is anything but routine.

All four aircraft take off and climb to 16,000 feet.

ETA to the ship is in thirty minutes.

1035

'Jets in the air,' shouts the air controller in Flyco. 'Good to go!'

The team around him is alert and ready. The aircraft handlers take position on deck. The firefighting teams stand ready. A Merlin launches in readiness for search and rescue. HMS *Monmouth* takes up her own position about 1,000 yards off the port beam. The frigate could provide an extra helicopter landing deck either for search and rescue or for transfer of casualties. Lindsey Waudby and her photographers are poised to capture this historic moment for the world's press.

Jerry Kyd is keeping a watchful eye on a hundred spinning plates from his captain's chair. Lieutenant Commander Sam Stephens, the Navigator, gives a sharp, precise and very significant order over the bridge radio.

'*Yeoman Navigator, Flag-Foxtrot port outer yardarm – close up hoist.*'

The Yeoman, Leading Hand Tom Nettleship, immediately hoists a tightly packed bundle to the top of the for'ard island. Once in position, he pulls on the halyard to release a large flag showing a bright-red diamond against a white background. It catches the headwind instantly. This is Flag-Foxtrot and indicates to all other shipping that fixed-wing flying is in operation. The last time it was hoisted on a Royal Navy aircraft carrier was in 2010, when Jim Blackmore piloted the final Harrier off HMS *Ark Royal*, commanded by Jerry Kyd. The emotional symmetry of today's events is lost on neither of them.

All over the ship, above deck and below, sailors prepare to watch the long-promised first landing. Officers not on duty crowd around the flat screens in the wardroom; the hundreds in the hangar jostle for the best position to see the blow-up screen; night-watch chefs emerge to switch on their bunk-room TVs, and in the anteroom to the captain's day cabin, Glen Peters looks down eagerly over the flight deck. In the event of battle damage to Flyco itself, this small balcony would serve as an emergency position for Commander Air and his close team. There is only room for half a dozen people but it has a panoramic view of the flight deck.

1055

The radar screens in Flyco indicate two aircraft approaching at speed from the west. Everybody's searching the sky with their binoculars.

'*Sighted. Two o'clock!*'

The air traffic controller has spotted two black specks on the distant horizon, growing rapidly as they hurtle towards the ship.

'*Here they come*,' Jim Blackmore says. '*On time. Sort of! Good luck, everybody.*'

Gray and Edgell, in formation at 11,000 feet, are closing on the ship at 500 knots. The aircraft handlers and firefighting teams of the Port Watch take their positions. '*Be safe guys*,' Emma Ranson says. Jim Blackmore puts on the headphones that link him to the captain and the Navigator on the bridge. Sitting next to him is Fleet Commander Vice Admiral Ben Key. He is here in his own right, but also to represent Rear Admiral Keith Blount, the head of the Fleet Air Arm, who has asked to be informed the moment Nathan Gray is safely down.

'Will I be able to make the call to Admiral Blount from here in Flyco?' Ben Key asks.

'No problem, sir,' Blackmore says. 'We can patch it through to my cans as soon as Nath is on deck.'

Momentarily chastizing himself for tempting providence, Blackmore hopes to God that the phone call to Rear Admiral Blount will be to report success and not failure. Banishing any negative thoughts from his mind, he raises his binoculars again. Standing behind him are the other two test pilots, Wizzer Wilson and Latch Lippert. 'I'm pinching myself that we're actually here,' Lippert says. 'Oh, we're here,' Wizzer Wilson says. 'And we're going to remember this moment for the rest of our lives.'

1059

Nathan Gray speaks to the ship for the first time. '*HMS Queen Elizabeth – this is Lightning 65. Request join.*'

The response is immediate. '*Lightning 65. Clear to join. The deck is yours . . . Come to Mum.*'

Gray smiles. It's the first time in eight years that he's heard a British voice speaking to him from a carrier – and, after so long in America, he's delighted to be invited to come to 'Mum' instead of 'Mom'.

With a mile to go, and having come down to 1,000 feet, Edgell gives Gray another thumbs-up and breaks away. The RAF pilot takes Lightning 64 up to 8,000 feet and begins to circle at 300 knots with Salty-Dog-Chase. Salty-Dog-Tanker stays 3,000 feet above him.

Gray guides Lightning 65 into a slow, curved descent towards 'Mum'. As he dips his port wing he looks over his left shoulder at the sea, the very real sea. Not the placid, pixelated sea of the simulator but the surging, savage ocean that will claim him in a heartbeat if given a chance, as it did Edwin Dunning 101 years ago.

He sets up his helmet-mounted display to show the correct landing parameters. The first and most important thing is to recheck his fuel load; if too heavy, it would compromise his ability to sustain a stable hover. He's marginally overweight, so to burn off fuel he immediately embarks on a series of fly-throughs – landing approaches without landing, followed by the circuits to bring him round again. This also allows him more time to check the ship from stem to stern and assess if there are any unusual air wakes present, or visual illusions that the simulator hadn't managed to replicate. So far, so good.

1110

Satisfied that he's sufficiently reduced his fuel load, Nathan Gray brings his aircraft down to 600 feet and starts his final approach. This time he activates the landing gear. Three green lights glow in the cockpit, confirming that the wheels have deployed. He converts the aircraft from her sleek, stealth mode (Mode 1) to vertical landing mode (Mode 4) and slows to about 180 knots.

The upper-lift fan door opens just behind his cockpit, activating the Rolls-Royce fan that sucks in the air to produce massive downward thrust. Gray feels the vibrations surge through his body. The rear jet nozzle swivels from horizontal to vertical. He holds his breath for ten seconds until he sees the green light confirming the transformation is complete. His Lightning is now in full hover mode – hanging in the air, though still maintaining some forward movement.

'*Lightning 65 abeam to land,*' he calls.

The Landing Signal Officer in Flyco replies, '*Lightning 65 – clear to land 3 Spot. Wind Red 10 at 15 knots. Dedicated flying course 160. Mum is making 10 knots.*'

Gray approaches the most dangerous part of the landing process – the point at which he will slow to a halt about 150 feet above the sea, just off the port beam. He looks over at the expansive flight deck and thinks of the 1,500 souls gathered below. If he gets this wrong, his F-35B Lightning could turn into a massive flying bomb. *This doesn't happen in that goddamned simulator*, he thinks to himself.

Lightning 65 is now half plane, half rocket as Gray continues to coax it down the port side. He is still over water and slowing in the hover: 50 knots . . . 40 . . . 30 . . . 20 . . . As soon as he draws level with 3 Spot, almost exactly halfway down the ship, he stops still, virtually static in mid-air.

He can see Jim Blackmore in the Flyco gallery, immediately opposite, overseeing the landing with his customary poise. They are almost on a level. Eye to eye. Gray is reassured to see Blackers in command. This is a mighty long way, he reflects, from the time they drowned their sorrows together on the announcement of the axing of the Harrier force. Back then, they were convinced it was the end of their careers as fast jet pilots. 'Look at us now!' he thinks with quiet satisfaction.

Gray holds the hover for about a minute, with the massive downdraft sending up clouds of spray that generate a host of tiny, evanescent rainbows.

'*Feet wet.*' The air traffic controller confirms Gray is still over water.

The stealth jet, the ultimate 'transformer', starts to crab sideways.

'*Feet dry,*' the controller says the moment it is over the ship.

Gray edges towards the figure 3 painted on the deck beneath him. Thanks to the sensors on the outside of the aircraft, images are beamed into his helmet, allowing him to see right through the airframe beneath his feet. X-ray vision is just one of the super-powers the F-35 bestows on its pilot.

Gray holds position no more than 100 feet above the deck, then starts his final descent. With in excess of 40,000 lbs of downward thrust and a temperature from the rear nozzle of over 1,400 degrees, he's aiming a supercharged blow torch at the *Queen Elizabeth*. Her specially treated flight deck is about to be truly tested for the first time.

Lightning 65 is seconds from landing. All over the ship, people are braced for the moment of contact.

Twenty metres to go, 19, 18 . . .

Everyone is holding their breath. There's silence in the hangar, silence in Flyco, silence on the bridge.

Ten metres to go, 9, 8, 7, 6, 5, 4, 3, 2, 1 . . .

Touchdown!

The wheels make contact. Almost immediately, the roar of the Pratt & Whitney subsides, and the air intake covers close. A brief pause to savour the moment is followed by a loud cheer in the hangar. Sailors punch the air in excitement. Everybody on the bridge and in the wardroom rises to their feet. An emotional Jim Blackmore gives Gray a double thumbs-up. The pilot responds by raising his arms like a F1 driver who's just taken the chequered flag.

Nathan Gray is immediately directed by the aircraft handlers to the section of the deck in front of the for'ard island known as the 'graveyard', where he will refuel prior to launching after Edgell. As soon as he moves from 3 Spot, two BAE scientists, Richard Lawrence and Nimali Amarathunga, rush to inspect the flight deck surface. The Thermal Metallic Spray designed to dissipate heat and withstand thrust seems to have held up. It will be subjected to far more rigorous testing in the coming weeks, but so far so good. The two scientists give huge grins and a thumbs-up.

Fleet Commander Ben Key dials the head of the Fleet Air Arm. The phone rings repeatedly before being picked up.

'*Blount.*'

'Keith, Ben Key here. I have the great pleasure to inform you that at 1130 Eastern Time Commander Nathan Gray landed his F-35B Lightning safely on the flight deck of HMS *Queen Elizabeth.*'

There is the briefest of pauses as Admiral Blount ponders the moment.

'*Thank . . . fuck for that!*' he says at last.

Ben Key laughs out loud.

'*I've been like a cat on a hot tin roof,*' Blount continues. '*I am so delighted. Please extend my hearty congratulations to all concerned — especially Nathan Gray . . .*'

*

It is now Andy Edgell's turn.

He looks down at the flight deck 8,000 feet below.

'*HMS* Queen Elizabeth – *this is Lightning 64. Request join.*'

'*Lightning 64. Come aboard. The deck is yours.*'

The RAF pilot breaks out of his holding pattern and descends towards the waiting supercarrier. Within minutes he too has landed with the same poise, control and courage as his naval compatriot, triggering yet more applause.

It is now past midday, so Emma Ranson's Port Watch stand down, and Paul Ranson's Starboard Watch take over. Scouse Walsh, eager to get involved, plants his customized ear protectors, pulls on his helmet and dons his heavy-duty goggles. Back to his fulsome and ebullient best, he heads out to help guide the jets to their launch positions. 'F-35s?' he says. 'Piece of piss!'

But Walsh speaks too soon. It's suddenly clear from Andy Edgell's body language that all is not well. He's shaking his head angrily and drawing his fingers across his throat – the signal to abort. There's an immediate conflab between the pilot, Flyco and the ITF scientific team monitoring the aircraft electronically. The on-board computers are indicating an anomaly in the automatic self-testing procedures. It's probably spurious, but nobody's taking any chances. The RAF pilot is furious, but there's nothing he can do. He proceeds to park his aircraft prior to exiting the cockpit. His flying is over for the day.

Nathan Gray is given the order to launch.

'That's not the deal,' he tells Jim Blackmore.

'It is now, I'm afraid,' Commander Air says firmly. 'We must have a launch, Nath.'

The ship's Command know that a launch has to follow the

F-35 and Lightning.

Procedure Alpha into Mayport, Florida.

The first landing – view from Flyco.

Nathan Gray and Andy Edgell approach HMS *Queen Elizabeth*.

Touchdown!

Nathan launches for the
first time.

Hurricane Michael arrives.

Refuelling in storm-driven seas.

The perfect pilot.

Royal Marine Commandos 'rescue' a downed F-35 pilot from behind enemy lines.

Steady, steady . . .

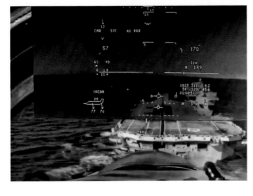

Wizzer's eye view.

The first SRVL – mission accomplished.

Captain Jerry Kyd

Chaplain Alastair Mansfield, 'The Bish'

First Lieutenant Chris Trevethan

Dave Garraghty and Wilf

Derek 'Scouse' Walsh, Leading Aircraft Handler

Petty Officer Emma Ranson

First Lieutenant Bob Hawkins

Frank Rochford, Royal Marines Bandsman and Piper

Frederica McCarthy, Writer and Logistician

Glen Peters, Captain's Steward

James 'Blackers' Blackmore,
Commander Air

Jenny Curwood, Commander
Logistics

Kirsty Rugg, Captain's
Steward

Lieutenant Colonel Roly
Brading, Royal Marines

Waseel Mohamad Khan,
Leading Chef

Pete 'Wizzer' Wilson, Test Pilot

Commander Nathan Gray,
RN Test Pilot

Rob Rouston, Marine Engineer

Robert 'Turbo' Salerno IV,
Integrated Test Force Maintainer

(*Left*) New York beckons.

Crew line up on deck, facing Manhattan.

Jerry Kyd departs.

Rob and the man in the pink tutu.

Remembrance Day.

Home again – a circle completed.

Families greet the returned crew.

landing to complete today's historic test. Only then will the Secretary of State for Defence be able to declare the mission a complete success in his announcement to the House of Commons in two days' time.

'Sixty-four is tits, Nath. 65 must go. Prepare to launch.'

Gray does so, but has no doubts about how much this is going to hurt his RAF colleague. Edgell is a dedicated, passionate and emotional man who, as a lead test pilot, openly admits to cancelling his life for the developmental testing of the F-35 Lightning. He and Gray have worked diligently and effectively together, two alpha males at the top of their game, driven by the same deep determination to be the best.

But that is not the only problem.

The Navy taking first launch as well as first landing could cause ructions at a higher level. Today's plans were meant to help establish a closer working relationship between the two services, not fan the flames of an historic rivalry.

It occurs to Gray to suggest they swap aircraft, but he knows it would be an empty gesture. With a strict flight programme to observe, fluctuating weather conditions and a host of VIPs on tight schedules, to do so would involve a prohibitively long delay.

Less than an hour after his landing, Gray edges forward and, carefully guided by the flight-deck marshals, moves towards the launch position. On land such marshalling instruction is advisory; on carrier operations, it is mandatory, because there is so little space to play with, and direction is critical. Gray makes a tight U-turn and heads towards the 400 feet take-off mark. Paul Ranson is waiting for him, a simple green flag in his hands – a signalling device worth no more than a pound or two, about to be used to launch an aircraft worth £100 million.

Eyes on the amber launch lights, Gray lines up dead centre on the ski-jump tramline. So far, all flying communications between aircraft and carrier have been through hand signals and lights. The aircraft's powerful radio emitters have been muted to protect the ship's own receptors from being 'frazzled'. So-called EMCON Silent is regarded as the height of perfection in flight deck practice, with everything achieved through established procedure, exact timing, impeccable planning and strict execution.

Finally, the radio does burst into life as Flyco speaks to Gray through the 'hot' mic to check procedures.

'*Test, launch distance 400 feet, exit speed 95 knots, minimum rate of climb 300 feet per min.*'

'*Test reads back 400/95/300,*' Gray replies.

'*Test readback correct, on launch conditions, go STO sequence.*'

'*Copied, Control, go STO sequence.*'

'*Lightning 65 up and ready with 10.5k pounds fuel.*'

After the briefest of pauses, Jim Blackmore gives an order the Royal Navy hasn't heard since he himself flew the last Harrier off HMS *Ark Royal* eight years ago.

'Launch the jet!'

The lights on deck turn from amber to green. The Flight Deck Officer (FDO) gives Gray the signal to convert. The pilot presses the button to initiate transformation for short take-off. The lift fan behind his head gives a reverberating roar, and the rear nozzle swivels downwards, combining horizontal and vertical thrust. Gray gives a thumbs-up to indicate 'ready for launch'.

Paul Ranson brings the green launch flag from above his head to the deck.

Gray concentrates resolutely on the end of the ski-jump – the exact point at which he expects to leave the deck. If his focal point is too near, he runs the risk of over-controlling the steering while he tracks his front wheel down the white centreline. If it's too far, he will not be quick enough to react to any deviations caused by air vortices or ship motion.

'*Control – test, slamming in 3-2-1 . . .*'

Gray actuates full power via the throttle in his left hand. The thrust and noise are intense, but he holds the brakes. This is a critical moment. If he releases them too early, he wastes 'deck run'. Releasing too late could cause the wheels to skid and burst the tyres.

'Hold it,' he tells himself. 'Hold it!'

He takes a deep breath.

'Now!'

Releasing the brakes as evenly as possible to avoid any swerve, he unleashes the jet. Lightning 65 lurches forward, pushing Gray sharply back into his seat. Whatever happens now, he is committed to the launch. Even if the aircraft's sensors activate a warning and caution lights illuminate on his display, there is no longer time or distance to react and stop the aircraft. Gray has less than 300 feet to get airborne and knows that once the jet gets to the end of the ski-jump it will either fly or plummet into the sea. Either way he will be heading skywards, in his aircraft or his ejection seat.

As the F-35 passes the for'ard island he adds a few extra inputs on the left and right pedal, sensing the influence of the air wake deflecting off the superstructure. He makes another small adjustment on the pedals as he reaches the base of the ski-jump and feels the vortex from the front of the ship sweeping across the runway. He gives the right brake a small tap to maintain the centreline. Fleetingly, subconsciously, sublimely, he sees a flash of himself as a ten-year-old kid hurtling over rough ground on his beloved BMX. He hits the base of the ramp and feels the forces propelling him upwards.

His calls over the hot mic echo around the control room. 'Airborne!'

And now he has to stay that way.

He reads out his rate of climb in hundreds of feet.

'Six, five, five, five, four, four, three, three, three, four, four, five, six, seven . . .'

The cadence and tone of his voice are vital signals to the ITF test team buried in the bowels of the ship. They are monitoring all aspects of the aircraft's progress, and that includes the performance and welfare of the pilot.

Based on the experience of hundreds of previous land-based ski-jump tests and simulator work, they know that if Gray's speech becomes uncharacteristically hurried or the pitch suddenly changes, this could indicate potential problems, especially if his rate of climb is falling. They might have to urge recovery actions if he has not already taken the initiative.

The ultimate recovery order is the unmentionable E word – 'Eject!' – but as the test pilot, Gray owns that action.

It was at this point in that fatal launch back in 2002 that the main engine in his Harrier blew up. He was over land then, when he had to eject along with his friend and mentor, the legendary Jak London.

'Come on, Jak,' Gray whispers to himself. 'Take us up, mate.'

'*Climb rate good 65*,' the control room reports.

'Staying out of the loop,' Gray replies. 'Off the controls . . . seeing how the aircraft responds . . . passing 200 feet and 120 knots . . . Lightning 65 climbing away!'

*

Jerry Kyd sees the F-35 rise slowly towards the sky and nods his head in quiet satisfaction. There's a great deal of work for the ship and the aircraft to complete over the next eleven weeks. But that work has now started. And so far, apart from a spurious computer alarm on Lightning 64, the day has been a success.

'You have to feel sorry for the RAF, though, don't you, Darren?'

'Oh yes, sir!' The phlegmatic Commander gives him a wry grin. 'And I will continue to feel that way for at least the next ten seconds!'

Gray has retracted his undercarriage, converted to stealth mode – as far as operational safety precautions allow – and flown several wide circuits to burn off fuel. After ten minutes he makes one dramatic fast flypast, right over the top of the carrier, before coming round to complete his second landing.

Half an hour later, with the aircraft fully tethered, the cockpit canopy rises. Gray unstraps himself and climbs down the ladder to be greeted like a rock star. Aircraft handlers, Flight Deck Officers and ITF technicians crowd round him. Everyone wants to shake hands with the first man to have landed and launched from HMS *Queen Elizabeth*. Jim Blackmore is in the throng, and so too is Jerry Kyd.

Gray has a folded White Ensign in his hand – the only luggage he carried with him. Some months ago, he suggested that he should present it to the youngest member of the ship's company to boost morale. The idea was eagerly endorsed by Jerry Kyd, who now witnesses the presentation.

As Gray steps towards the seventeen-year-old rating in the Anti-Air Warfare branch, he notices the name on his shirt.

'My God!' he says. 'I don't believe it! Your name's Dunning?'

'Yessir. Aaron Dunning.'

His great-grandfather, he tells Gray, served on HMS *Hermes*, and his grandfather was a submariner. He professes no knowledge of Edwin Dunning, or any immediate family connection.

'Well, you have a great naval name,' Gray says. 'Be proud of it, and Google Edwin Dunning.'

'Yes, sir. Thank you, sir. I will.'

Nathan Gray turns to Jerry Kyd.

'It's an omen,' the captain says. 'And a bloody good one too.'

39. Do Not Feed the Birds

0700

Major Latch Lippert of the US Marine Corps is taxiing to his point of take-off. Three earnest-looking figures in blue helmets and white overalls march purposefully across the flight deck and take position near the fire-trucks at the base of the for'ard island. Carrying small, wind-protected microphones, they are scientists from the Institute of Naval Medicine and here to measure the noise levels of the F-35 around the ship. Its Pratt & Whitney F135 engine is as loud as it is powerful and could pose a very real danger to people's hearing. On a shore base, the jet would take off and land far from the ground-crew, but the QE can't offer that luxury. Flight-deck workers already wear custom-made earplugs (with encased earphones) under heavy-duty earmuffs. Of course, it helps that to minimize the need for the spoken word, all the main communication between aircraft handlers and pilots is achieved through a series of strictly encoded and well-practised hand signals that have been used since the Second World War.

Scouse Walsh, positioned on the take-off spot, beckons the roaring F-35 towards him with fluent, bold, self-assured arm and hand movements. Lippert edges his aircraft towards its launch position. Once his front wheel hits the 350 feet marker, Walsh motions him to stop.

The American waits for the ship to adjust its position in relation to the natural wind. Moving through the water at 12 knots, the QE is sailing into a prevailing wind of 17 knots, so the total wind across the deck is 29 knots.

Once the wind-speed and direction are right and Lippert has converted the aircraft into launch mode, James Blackmore gives the all-important order from the Papal Throne.

'Launch the jet!'

The F-35 surges forward in a dramatic cloud of spray as 40,000 lbs of thrust impacts the rain and sea water that has collected on the flight deck overnight. Accelerating into the headwind, the F-35 whips off the ski-jump and soars skywards.

The men with microphones check their hand-held computers and record the sound levels from their position at the base of the for'ard island. A whisper is about 30 decibels. Normal conversation is 60. A motorcycle engine is around 95. Noise above 70 decibels over a prolonged period of time would start to damage hearing. Loud noise above 120 can cause immediate harm to the inner ear. Latch's F-35 has tipped the scales at 120. They move closer to the ski-jump, ready for the next launch. Wizzer Wilson is already edging towards the same take-off position.

The aim is to complete at least 100 flights before New York, and another 100 afterwards. Every launch and landing will push the safety envelope incrementally to establish the F-35's operational limits in ever more challenging weather conditions. The prevailing local winds currently vary between 5 and 20 knots. Kyd can add another 25 by powering through the water at full speed. He's confident, therefore, of testing the aircraft up to around 40 knots, but finding sustainable winds of greater strength will be a challenge.

The plan this morning is for both pilots to launch and land at least four times into gradually increasing wind speeds, from a variety of different directions. Andy Edgell and Nathan Gray will complete another eight flights between them this afternoon. From next week they'll have to start flying at night as well.

Lippert, now circling above the carrier, likens test flying to a man crossing a rickety footbridge over a raging river. He moves forwards, testing its integrity step-by-step. When it begins to creak, he'll take smaller, more cautious steps, trying to judge how far he can safely advance, but always ready to retreat before there's no going back. Of course, there's always the chance he'll leave it too late . . .

Their simulators, through computational analysis and fluid dynamics, can suggest the margins of risk, but no one will know for sure until both aircraft and pilot are exposed directly to the elements. Pushing the aircraft to the edge of safety and possibly a little bit beyond enables them to write the definitive report for front-line pilots – an operational bible that will establish the Lightning's technical, mechanical and aerodynamic limits.

'Launch the jet!' James Blackmore orders once again.

Wizzer Wilson's F-35 surges forward. The men with microphones, crouched by the ski-jump, only yards from the point of take-off, are practically blown off their feet as the jet rockets skywards. Their monitors register an ear-shattering 160 decibels.

0945

'Wow! Look at that baby fly!' Glen Peters is polishing the Rose Table but can't tear his eyes away from the action on the flight deck. 'The view's better from here than Flyco,' he tells his assistant, Junior Steward Joshua Hanks.

'It's deafening!' Hanks holds his hands over his ears.

'Sure is,' Peters says. 'At least we're behind the glass.'

The two stewards lean against the sill and watch the two F-35s circle above the ship.

'Lot of birds . . .' Hanks says.

'Yeah,' Peters says. 'Those little green and yellow ones are everywhere.'

Over the last few days increasing numbers of migratory birds have been using the QE as a welcome mid-ocean perch. Most are common yellowthroats and blackpoll warblers on their way from Canada to South America. They're intermittently joined by an assortment of herons, gannets and seagulls that swoop down to rest their weary wings.

The more soft-hearted sailors have been leaving breakfast cereal for the winged visitors on the quarterdeck. Big mistake.

1543

Nathan Gray is coming into the hover just off the port beam.

'*Slowing for vertical landing . . .*' he reports as he prepares to guide his aircraft on to 3 Spot. '*Steady in the air.*'

'*Birds all over the place,*' he suddenly transmits.

Moments later, a tiny blackpoll warbler appears in front of him. It flies over his cockpit towards the upper intake fan which has opened up behind the cockpit. The bird has no chance against the massive suction forces and instantly disappears. It's vaporized in a nanosecond, but the aircraft is taken out of service at once. It will not fly again until it's undergone a complete internal inspection. It might outfly or outwit the most sophisticated heat-seeking, supersonic missiles, but today the formidable F-35, or at least this highly sensitive test variant, has been brought to its knees by a tiny creature weighing less than one millionth of its heavily armoured bodyweight.

1800

'*Good evening,* Queen Elizabeth,' Darren Houston announces via the main broadcast system. '*Commander here. Just one notice tonight but an important one. You may have heard that one of the aircraft ingested a bird today. Luckily there was no damage other than to the unfortunate bird, but it could've been different. Bird strikes could potentially bring down an aircraft. Despite your best intentions, please do not feed the birds. Anything that encourages them to flock here could prove disastrous not only to the aircraft but the ship itself. So I repeat — do not feed the birds. That is all.*'

2000

Both Lightnings have been taken down to the hangar for the night, but off the starboard bow some frantic flying continues. A bloody but spectacular display of aerial combat is unfolding in silhouette against the setting sun.

A powerful and fast-moving bird of prey swoops from altitude, and the panicked yellowthroats scatter in all directions. The predator locks on to its chosen target, strikes with ruthless accuracy and disappears into the open quarterdeck to devour its victim and find a sheltered perch. It has chanced across a well-stocked feeding-station and probably has every intention of sticking around.

40. The Black Duke

28 September 2018

1130

'Cheerio, Glen,' Jerry Kyd says. 'Look after the ship while I'm gone.'

'Goodbye, sir. Have a good day.' Peters hands the captain his flying helmet.

Kyd is making an official visit to HMS *Monmouth*. He's officially handed over command to Darren Houston for the period he'll be away. Even though it will only be for a few hours, the ship cannot be deprived of leadership for even a minute.

Already in a khaki flying suit, Kyd makes his way to the Westland Wildcat waiting for him on the flight deck. He asks the pilot if they could do a couple of circuits round the QE before heading over to the frigate. He's never seen the carrier from the air. Minutes later, looking down on his command from a height of 500 feet, he feels an overwhelming surge of sadness. He has just twenty-six days left as captain.

Having circled the QE twice the Wildcat breaks away in a curving trajectory towards the *Monmouth*, sitting about half a mile away on the QE's port beam. Jerry Kyd smiles as he approaches the frigate he commanded over twelve years ago when still only a commander.

He has extremely fond memories of the ship affectionately

known to all as the 'Black Duke'. The Duke of Monmouth led a rebellion against James II of England in 1685, for which he was executed and had his coat of arms blacked out. Even today the ship which bears his name is the only one in service to have her name painted in black rather than red, and to fly a plain black flag in addition to the White Ensign. Jerry Kyd, well aware of her dubious historical associations, is always quick to point out that – living up to her motto 'Fear Nothing but God' – she also carries the most Battle Honours of any vessel currently serving in the Royal Navy.

The pilot circles the ageing frigate. Commissioned in 1993, she is 60,000 tons smaller than the carrier she protects, but sleeker, faster, and packs a more powerful punch. She bristles with Sea Wolf anti-air missiles, Harpoon anti-ship missiles, anti-submarine Sting Ray torpedoes, and a 4.5-inch naval gun on her bow. Kyd is struck by his old ship's diminutive size but reminded of the wonderful crew of 180 sailors he commanded on her between 2004 and 2006. Unusually there were no women on board, which, in Navy parlance, made *Monmouth* a 'Stag Ship'. But Kyd has always maintained that his all-male crew was one he would have gladly died for.

They had many testing operations in the Baltic and secret intelligence-gathering missions in the Mediterranean as well as numerous policing patrols around the world. Stealth and guile had been their stock in trade, and in every case their missions were accomplished.

The Wildcat touches down lightly on the small flight deck at her stern. Jerry Kyd is greeted by the ship's commanding officer, Commander Will King. The two shake hands warmly and head for the CO's quarters for an early lunch.

'Nothing has changed!' Kyd says on the way into his old

cabin. 'Nothing has changed at all. Not even the carpet. God, it's good to be back!'

1300

After fish and chips with mushy peas, Jerry Kyd is on the starboard bridge wing of the *Monmouth* looking at his own ship about a mile away to the south east. 'My goodness, what a sight,' he breathes as an F-35 launches off the ski-jump. In his mind's eye, he can see twenty-two of them ranged around the deck and launching in quick succession.

Suddenly, the *Queen Elizabeth* flashes her signal lamp towards the *Monmouth*. A message is being sent in Morse code.

'Decipher, please.' Will King nods towards a signalman who gets busy with his notepad.

'A message for Captain Kyd,' he says nervously. 'From Commander Houston, sir.'

Kyd reads the message and looks up grimly.

'Problem, sir?' King asks.

'A major problem, I'm afraid.' Kyd hands King the notebook.

The CO of *Monmouth* bites his lip before reading it out loud. '*Hope having good time. All good here. Have eaten all your Hobnobs.*'

Kyd scribbles his reply and hands it to the signalman. It's a brusque and uncompromising message. '*You can take a man's ship, but never his Hobnobs. I'll be back!*'

A nostalgic tour follows, during which Kyd's constantly reminded how small and confined it is on a frigate, and how part of him misses close-quarter living, with everyone knowing everyone. He is finally taken to the wardroom, where a dozen nervous Young Officers are waiting to greet him. Will King has asked him to give them a pep talk over coffee.

He immediately sits among them, to put them at their ease. 'Right, let's go round the room – name and job,' he says. 'I'll start. Jerry Kyd. Captain, *Queen Elizabeth* . . .'

'Great,' he says when the last of them has followed suit. 'You people are at the beginning of your career at an amazing time in the Royal Navy. You're going to see some extraordinary changes, and you'll be part of the effort to drive those changes through.'

Kyd pauses to accept a cup from a midshipman probably in his teens.

'Make no mistake, though,' he continues. 'We're approaching a time when we might be called to arms once again, to protect the nation and the nation's interests globally.

'We're not a big navy any more. But we are an effective one, and about to become even more so, with a new carrier strike capability.'

'How do we shape up against say the Chinese, sir?' asks a young female sub-Lieutenant.

'Good question. Last year I spoke one-to-one with a very senior Chinese admiral, and he told me, "We gauge our own standard of preparedness by deciding whether or not we could defeat you at sea. Not the US Navy, but the Royal Navy."'

Kyd's audience is gripped. They're not often privy to the inner thoughts of senior admirals in the Republic of China Navy.

'He recognized that we bring hundreds of years of tradition and experience to the way we operate and run our ships and train our people.'

Another Young Officer raises his hand. 'Sir, if we had to cross swords with one of the big boys, how would it go?'

'Well, we would almost certainly fight in coalition with our NATO allies. Certainly the Americans. But with the QE Class of carrier we'd bring something pretty amazing to the party. Make no mistake, though, we want to avoid confrontation if we can. We need to show our potential enemies that they shouldn't mess with us, and step back a pace. Because if it kicks off, it won't be pretty. War is brutal. And war at sea is particularly unforgiving. But you have great ships, and you're the best-trained sailors on the planet. We would very quickly make the enemy's eyes water. I can assure you of that.'

His audience shifts in their seats.

'When the night's dark, the sea rough and you're facing the enemy – it'll be terrifying. But it's the same for them. They're also terrified. And they don't have your background. Your Nelsonian heritage is not misplaced historical romance. It's real. It's part of your DNA. So be the best you can. Observe the highest standards in everything you do.'

'Do you think the QE will go to war, sir?'

'The *Queen Elizabeth* will be in service for the next half century. She's our primary conventional strategic deterrent. Having said that, I'm virtually certain she will see combat. I hear people saying there'll never be another war so why do we need armies and navies. That frustrates me. They're living in cloud cuckoo land. Do they all cancel their insurance if they've not been burgled for five years? Of course not. Look at the world we live in. Political crisis, environmental crisis, global warming, burgeoning populations and migration out of control. Increasing poverty on the one hand, and spiralling wealth on the other. It's a recipe for disaster. Armed conflict is inevitable, either because of ideological discord, revolutionary zealotry or hostile and belligerent competition for scarce resources.'

Kyd takes a sip of coffee before resuming.

'Is state-on-state friction decreasing? No. Are terrorist threats on the decline? No. It's naive to think that none of this will result in confrontation on a global level. Deep folly. If I was a betting man, I'd say that you young people will see combat.'

'It's why we joined, sir,' says a self-assured sub-lieutenant barely out of his teens.

'Be careful what you wish for,' Kyd replies.

41. The Perfect Pilot

1000

'Watch and learn, people!' James Blackmore gestures out from Flyco.

The air traffic controllers gaze in admiration at a demonstration of flawless flying off the port beam.

'Brilliant . . .' Nathan Gray is watching through binoculars. 'Rudder control, superb.'

'He could teach you a thing or two, Nath!'

'No arguments there, Blackers. I hear he performed an impeccable hover over 3 Spot yesterday.'

'He did. Steady as a rock. Plus, he was flying into a strong headwind . . . while eating a bird!'

Everybody's in awe of the American peregrine falcon that's been feeding off the songbirds which have plagued the flight deck and put the aircraft at risk. The predator is now regarded as an essential member of the ship's company (Fleet Air Arm, naturally).

1200

Lieutenant Colonel Roly Brading is the fittest man on board, but right now he's struggling to walk 60 metres. Surrounded by cheering CrossFitters, he has covered about 40 but is breathing hard and beginning to wobble.

'Steady, sir. Pace yourself!'

'Twenty to go, sir!'

'Don't give up, sir!'

Brading is not carrying any extra weight, and there are no obstacles to hinder him, but it's worth pointing out that he is entirely the wrong way up. The muscular marine prides himself on his ability to walk on his hands. It's a challenge, though, especially for a big man, which demands great power and immense cardio-vascular fitness.

He grits his teeth. He just makes it to the finishing line before falling on to his back. His biceps and shoulder muscles are gleaming with sweat and look like they are going to burst.

'You giving it another go, sir?' Marine Engineer Rouston asks. 'I reckon you could add another 10 metres . . .'

'No, not today. Lima Company have a JPR exercise today. Going in as observer.'

'JPR? Serious stuff.'

Joint Personnel Recovery will be one of the main responsibilities for the Royal Marine commandos when the QE goes into combat. If an F-35 was to come down behind enemy lines, the pilot would need to be recovered, dead or alive, and the wreckage of the jet would have to be destroyed to prevent its secrets falling into the wrong hands.

1400

Seventeen commandos in full fighting order have boarded two Merlin Mark 4s. Eight in each cab, plus Roly Brading. They sweep round the bow and head west towards Quantico, Virginia, some 300 miles to the west. Set in deep sub-tropical forest, the US Army base will represent hostile territory.

Commander Bob Bond, who's piloting the lead aircraft, has been at the forefront of bringing the Mark 4 into active service. So far on this deployment they have been used mostly for search and rescue duties. Today is the first time they are fulfilling the specialist role for which they were primarily designed – low-level fast insertion into enemy territory to deliver a small force of elite commandos or Special Forces for covert operations.

The Mark 4 has been adapted for maritime conditions so has greater buoyancy as well as being easier to escape from once immersed. It also gives a very smooth ride.

The flight time to Quantico is just under three hours. The marines sit back, collect their thoughts, contemplate their roles and wait.

The aircraft handlers also have to wait. Fast jet flying is on hold for maintenance, and the Mark 4s will not be back for hours, so the Starboard Watch are enjoying a rare morning to themselves in their locker room. Some are drinking coffee, some are chatting, some are giving their helmets and visors a good clean. Scouse Walsh is on the phone to Flyco.

'How many tubes do you need, sir?'

'We have one to replace but get two. Always good to have a spare.'

At 2.4 metres in length, the fixed wipers on the massive Flyco windscreen are purported to be the biggest in the world. It's vital for the Aviation Team to have good vision over the flight deck in all weathers, and one is not functioning as it should. The rubber washer-liquid tubing has perished and must be replaced urgently.

'OK, listen up, people,' Walsh calls. 'I need a volunteer to get some stores.'

There is no reaction.

'You lazy bastards!' he bawls. 'Right, I'm going to ping someone. OK, Walshy. You're the chosen one.'

'Not again, Scouse!' Michael Walsh (no relation) is a popular member of the watch, but this is his first time at sea, so he tends to get pinged more than most.

'Nip down to General Stores, shipmate, or maybe Warfare Stores, and get some tubing for the Flyco windscreen wipers.'

'What are they called?'

'Dunno,' Scouse says. 'Just ask for –'

'Fallopian tubes!' shouts a voice from the back of the Crew Room.

'Oh yeah, that's right,' Scouse Walsh says. 'Ask for Fallopian tubes.'

'Fallopian?' the unsuspecting junior says. 'OK.'

'You'll need a NATO stock number.'

Walsh grabs an order sheet and scribbles in the appropriate box: 'ID:IOT 985933265'.

'There you go, Walshy.'

The Merlins, swooping in fast and low, skim the treetops as they approach their objective. Ready to deploy as soon as their cabs touch down, the marines are fully briefed about the mission: an F-35 pilot has ejected after being hit by a heat-seeking missile. His parachute deployed safely, but, having commandeered a car to make good his escape, he crashed in a remote, forested area. Trapped in the car and badly injured, his emergency beacon activated automatically. It will be a race against time to reach him before the enemy does – in the form of US marines.

The helicopters touch down just long enough for the rear door to open, and the commandos to exit at speed. Seconds later, they are back at altitude, where they'll circle until called in to evacuate the rescue team.

Michael Walsh, frustrated and flustered, has returned to the Crew Room.

'Nobody has any of these blinkin' Fallopian tubes,' he complains to Scouse Walsh.

'Are you sure?' the Liverpudlian says.

'I've asked everywhere. People just smirk and say they're fresh out.'

'Have you tried any of the women's messes?'

'No . . .'

'You should. I heard they had loads.'

'Why?'

'Dunno, mate. It's just what I heard.'

'Do I really have to?'

'They'll go spare in Flyco if we can't get any.'

On his way to the messes, Michael Walsh bumps into WO Jenny Scrivener, the most senior female NCO on board.

'Excuse me, ma'am. Do you know where I could get my hands on some spare Fallopian tubes?'

'Sorry?' Scrivener can't quite believe what she's heard.

'Fallopian tubes, ma'am,' Michael Walsh repeats brightly. 'We need 'em for the windscreen wipers in Flyco. I was told there might be some in the female messes, but I can't go in unaccompanied.'

'Oh, I see . . .' The warrant officer grins. 'I believe they do have some, yes. In fact, I have a couple myself. But I'm afraid I need them.'

'With respect, ma'am, I think Flyco might need them more . . .'

*

The marines have located the airman, streaming blood, trapped under the devastated bodywork of a saloon car.

'Cutters!' a corporal shouts. 'Now!'

The teeth of a cordless saw grind through the door frame, and several marines attempt to crack open the carcass of the vehicle while another administers morphine to its badly injured occupant.

Then, without warning, automatic gunfire adds to the cacophony.

'Incoming!' a sentry yells from a nearby ridge.

The enemy are advancing from the treeline by the road. The marines spread out to provide cover to the rescue team, and a ferocious firefight follows. Roly Brading stands back, noting tactical errors and suggestions for improvement. He will share these with his men in a rigorous debrief later, but overall he's pleased with their controlled aggression and ability to adapt to an ever-changing situation.

Still under heavy fire, they stretcher the injured pilot to open ground and haul him aboard a Merlin to make their escape. Once they've lifted off, he's unceremoniously hurled through the entry hatch, to be buffeted by the vicious downdraft before he plummets to the ground. He lands with a sickening thud and lies there, motionless.

The dummy is US government property and cannot be removed from Quantico.

Michael Walsh is back in the crew room, empty-handed and bemused. His namesake takes him to one side and treats him to a rapid lecture in obstetrics, after which he looks at the order form with new eyes: 'ID:IOT 985933265,' he says. 'Oh, bloody hell! You got me good!'

'You were so determined to find the things, we were

starting to worry you would come back with an armful of 'em for real!'

'Well, at least I now know what Fallopian tubes are.'

Scouse Walsh claps an arm around his shoulders. 'Every day's a school day, shipmate.'

2300

Dan McMahon is working late. The Meteorological Officer, preparing a long-term forecast for the ship's arrival in New York, is keeping a close eye on a nascent storm system moving towards the Gulf of Mexico. Whilst intensifying, it's not yet big enough or sufficiently organized to have been named by the National Hurricane Center. *Hopefully it'll stay that way*, he thinks. He glances at the list of names chosen for significant storms this year. The next name to be allocated is 'Michael'.

42. Let's Ride a Hurricane

'Michael's a big boy!' Dan McMahon is glued to his computer screen.

'And growing fast, by the look of it.' Lieutenant Commander Richard Payne is peering over his shoulder.

The two meteorologists are watching live satellite images of the storm system they've been monitoring over the last few days. Forty-eight hours ago, with winds in excess of 42 mph, it became substantial enough to be named, then moved westwards and clipped Cuba yesterday, where mountains ripped a hole in its underbelly. Like the Incredible Hulk, it reacted angrily and, energized by the warm waters of the Caribbean, has become an even more monstrous version of itself. Michael now fills the 600,000 square miles of the Mexican Gulf as a full-blown Category 4 hurricane – the second-highest classification on the Saffir-Simpson Scale, with wind speeds of up to 156 mph.

'It'll hit land as a Cat 5.' McMahon hauls himself out of his seat. 'Better tell the skipper.'

The flight trials have hit a brick wall. The pilots, desperate to push the F-35s to greater limits, have so far found nothing stronger than 20 knots of natural wind combined with another 20 knots generated by the forward movement of the ship. Jerry Kyd and James Blackmore would like natural winds in excess of 60 knots, and so far, they've been impossible to find. But a full-blown hurricane may be more than they had bargained for.

ITF maintainer Robert 'Turbo' Salerno IV is tending to the F-35s in the hangar. They are powered down and chained to the deck, sleeping contentedly as their keepers check their vital signs. Turbo climbs into one of the cockpits to examine the electrics and canopy integrity. He sits in the pilot's seat as he does every day when the technicians go through their checklists. To get so close to the jet on a regular basis is one of the great privileges of his job. He never tires of it.

Turbo is a devoted family man with deep religious convictions, so like Alastair Mansfield he has to believe that the F-35 will help keep the peace. But, conscience aside, Turbo loves the aircraft for what it is – an astonishing piece of aeronautical engineering.

'Not sure we'll be flying tomorrow,' Andy Edgell says from the hangar floor. 'Or even the day afterwards.'

'Weather, sir?'

Edgell nods. 'Hurricane on the way.'

'Rats for the programme, sir.'

'Yeah. Could scupper it altogether.'

At tonight's Command briefing Nick Gutfreund's Rose Table is covered by dozens of charts of the US eastern seaboard.

'Met Officer, please.' Kyd beckons to Dan McMahon.

'Sirs, ma'am . . .' The head meteorologist points to the southwestern Caribbean. 'Hurricane Michael originated from a broad low-pressure area that formed here on 1 October. The disturbance became a tropical depression on 7 October . . .' He tracks its progress with a fingertip and explains its gathering intensity. 'It's expected to move north-east, hitting land as a Cat 5 hurricane tonight or tomorrow.'

'What wind strengths, Dan?' Kyd asks.

'156 mph and above, sir.'

'And then where will it go?'

'The expectation, sir, is that it will cross the southern states, where it'll diminish in strength but re-emerge into the Atlantic and re-energize as a tropical storm. Michael is likely to come very close to us if we stay on our present course.'

'Wind speeds?'

'Difficult to estimate, sir, but I'd guess at around 70 mph on its outer edges.'

'Wave heights?'

'Thirteen to twenty feet, sir.'

'OK, so that's 60 knots of wind in a Sea State 6.' Kyd looks over to James Blackmore. 'Wings, what do you think? Could you fly into that?'

'It's on the limit, sir,' Blackmore says. 'Bumpy but doable if we regulate our own speed.'

'Navs?'

'Well, sir,' Sam Stephens says, 'US warships are evacuating to the southern Caribbean to tuck in behind the islands, but we don't have time to get down there. We could go further out to sea, or stay put and hunker down.'

Kyd considers the charts.

'All six wheels on the wagon, Engines?'

'Yessir,' Neil McCallum says. 'All prime movers good to go.'

Kyd sits back in his chair.

'Right,' he says. 'We'll stay put, take position in the south-west quadrant of the storm and ride the winds.'

Blackmore nods his agreement.

'Darren, make sure we're secured for sea,' Kyd says. 'We've never been in a Sea State 6. Ever. So warn people to tie everything down.'

'Yessir.'

'And tell the Medical Centre to break out the seasick pills. They're going to have some customers.'

'Excuse me, sir,' Chris Trevethan interjects.

'Yes, 1L?'

'We're due to RAS with USNS *Supply* in forty-eight hours. Should we postpone?'

Kyd pauses. The plan is to take on 1,000 tons of fuel from an American tanker. An RAS, involving a close coupling of a warship and a tanker, is dangerous enough in calm waters.

'You know what?' Kyd looks round the table. 'It'll be a good test of our mettle. Let's see what we're made of.'

Overnight, Hurricane Michael shifts out of the Gulf of Mexico and does indeed head northeast. As it approaches the Florida Panhandle, the superstorm reaches Category 5, with peak winds of 160 mph just before making landfall near Mexico Beach, Florida. Both here and in Panama City, catastrophic damage is being reported. Reports are coming in of numerous homes destroyed and trees felled. Nobody knows how many casualties so far but power outages are widespread.

A gust of 139 mph at Tyndall Air Force Base has caused devastating damage. Vehicles have been tossed through parking lots like toys and large hangars severely damaged. An F-15 has flipped on to its roof. Vast swathes of forest around its perimeter are almost entirely flattened, while trees that remained standing are completely stripped and denuded.

As Michael moves inland, it weakens but veers towards Chesapeake Bay, very near Naval Station Norfolk. It's expected to head back into the western Atlantic, where it is likely to be reinvigorated.

Michael is not finished yet.

10 October 2018

0800

A lone figure battles his way up the ski-jump as his carrier rides the deepening troughs and rising peaks of an increasingly agitated ocean. The higher he staggers up the slope, the more forcefully he is beaten back by the strengthening headwind. But the captain is nothing if not determined, so he perseveres until he's made it to the top. Eyes watering and anorak billowing, he looks down on the crashing bow waves. Half an hour ago, watching all this from the comfort of the bridge, he was gripped by a sudden, visceral urge to meet it head on.

Having cut a swathe across the southern states, Michael has so far left fifty-nine dead. Weakened by his rampage overland, he was momentarily downgraded to a tropical storm. But now, feeding rapaciously off the summer-warmed waters of the eastern seaboard, he has grown once more into a powerful extratropical cyclone. HMS *Queen Elizabeth*, positioned as planned in the southwest periphery of the storm system, is bracing herself.

Kyd squints at the cloud-clogged horizon and lowers his right shoulder into the oncoming wind and rain like a prop forward preparing for a head-on tackle. Before long, it will be impossible to stand anything like upright on the ski-jump, but he's not deterred. In time-honoured fashion, he respects the elements, but seeks to harness them too.

He turns to look at the aircraft handlers and ITF maintainers tending to the F-35s chained to the deck – checking them, nurturing them, caring for them. The stealth jets have functioned well so far but within relatively safe parameters. Soon they'll be taken well out of their comfort zone – to the outer limits of their performance envelope. Only then can they be presented for operational duties.

1000

Storm clouds are gathering like an angry mob intent on violent disorder. The tempestuous sea is possessed of a seething new energy. The growl of distant thunder fills the air as towering cumulonimbi, discharging their lightning bolts, do battle in the upper atmosphere.

Before long, wind-driven rain thrashes the flight deck as aircraft handlers and maintainers brace for a series of savage squalls with waves exploding over the bow. The eye of the storm is far off, but Michael's reach is a long one, and he's not pulling his punches.

Through the veils of spray and a 60-knot barrage of horizontal rain, a shadowy form advances up the centre line of the flight deck. The glistening jet stops at the 350-feet marker and waits, snarling with intent. Latch Lippert can't see the end of the ski-jump, let alone the sky beyond, but the laid-back American has faith in the technology and methodically goes through his last-minute checks and procedures. He presses the button to activate the air-intakes. The main vent on top of the aircraft yawns open and starts to suck in the swirling air that will soon be converted to vertical thrust.

336

The crossed red lights on Flyco change to amber and then to green.

'Launch the jet,' James Blackmore says.

Paul Ranson drops his green flag to the deck. Lippert presses a single button on his control panel, and the rear nozzle swivels downwards. Rain smashing ferociously against its canopy, the F-35 surges forwards. The upward lift off the ski-jump is immense, and the rate of climb faster than the American pilot has ever known on the QE, but the aircraft automatically adjusts to the conditions.

'Six, six, six, six, five, five . . .' Lippert reports. 'Some turbulence,' he adds as he initiates a left turn at 500 feet. 'Adjusted . . . Climbing away nicely.'

Nathan Gray follows in the second jet to the same good effect. Both pilots complete a number of circuits at height to burn off fuel and then swing round for recovery. Gray comes in first, riding the wind. Buffeted by the airflow, his aircraft rocks gently but adjusts around its own centre of gravity to achieve the balance it needs to touch down – which it does perfectly.

More launches follow.

And more landings.

The carrier increases speed, and the F-35s handle it well.

By the end of the morning, the aircraft's operational envelope has been considerably expanded. The risk has paid off.

1400

The approaching tanker is massive and grey but she looks no bigger than a child's toy on the surging ocean.

'USNS Supply. This is warship Romeo Zero Eight. Over,' Sam Stephens says.

'*Romeo Zero Eight. This is* Supply,' comes the immediate response.

'You will take station on us,' Stephens says.

'*Romeo Zero Eight. Affirmative. Course 120 degrees at 12 knots.*'

If the test pilots' task today was perilous, what these two ships are about to attempt is off the scale. Replenishment at sea is one of the most dangerous manoeuvres for any vessel, even in calm waters. The QE plans to take on 1,000 tonnes of diesel, which means they will have to sail in close parallel, no more than 30 yards apart, for several hours. One wrong move could lead to a collision serious enough to sink one or both, but when in action she will have to refuel whatever conditions might prevail, so it will be good practice, according to Jerry Kyd's 'train hard, fight easy' approach to life and survival.

'*Special Sea Duty Men, close up!*' the main broadcast system echoes.

Dozens of sailors in blue hard hats with black chin-stays and eye-protecting goggles make their way to their allotted stations – many for the first time in their naval careers.

The smaller ship (a mere 48,000 tons) lines up on the QE and slowly moves towards her from the stern on the starboard side. As soon as they are in parallel, they close to within 30 yards whilst maintaining the same speed through the water. The sea, now funnelled between them and further agitated by the constriction, erupts with fresh fury. Gigantic, convulsing waves rise high in the air, their explosive plumes cascading repeatedly over both vessels. It's like looking down into the cauldron of an active volcano; if anyone were to fall in, they'd be consumed in a heartbeat. The navigators and helmsmen on both bridges work hard to maintain the gap between them, countering the natural urge for two large objects in such close proximity to collide.

'Line-man, stand by to fire!' Chris Trevethan bellows.

The sailor beside him grips a compressed-air launcher. If all goes well, the nylon line attached to its rocket-shaped projectile will provide the first solid link between the two ships.

The First Lieutenant blows a whistle three times as a signal that he's about to fire. A three-whistle reply signifies the USNS *Supply* is ready to receive.

'Fire when ready!'

The line-man takes aim. A loud blast is followed by a burst of smoke as the projectile is launched. It makes it about half-way across before being overpowered by the wind. It is quickly hauled back in, and the line-man reloads.

'Fire when ready,' Trevethan repeats after another exchange of whistles.

This time the line-man aims higher, and the projectile soars safely across the divide. The nylon line hauls across a thicker line, which in turn links the QE's RAS station and the outlets on USNS *Supply*. A huge fuel pipe is then pulled across the load-bearing tightrope by a tug-of-war team. And thus two of the most modern ships in the world have been coupled by a 200-year-old method for transferring goods while underway. In strategic terms this allows a warship to become very 'long-legged': by reducing the need to come along-side, its endurance and stamina are considerably enhanced.

The huge metal probe on the end of the fuel pipe finally slams into the mouth of a copper receiving bell set in the carrier's side.

Meanwhile, one of the QE's Merlins proceeds to transfer goods, mostly spare parts for the Aviation Department, from

USNS *Supply* in huge underslung nets. The combination of RASing and VertRepping could theoretically allow the QE to stay at sea indefinitely.

Jerry Kyd, standing on the rain-lashed starboard bridge wing, is quizzing two young navigation officers about the tactical implications of RASing.

'What would you do if you came under attack while re-fuelling like this?'

One doesn't hesitate. 'Disengage, sir.'

'Exactly.' Kyd nods. 'As fast as possible.'

They'd need to steer rapidly clear of the tanker, he tells them, to open up all radar and weapon arcs. Incoming threats travel at Mach 2 and above, affording little time between detection and denial. Conventional RAS Standard Operating Procedure (SOP) is to order an emergency break-away, disengaging lines and hoses before moving forwards on full power.

'Once you've opened up the range, you can start shoot-ing,' Kyd says. 'But how long do you think that would take?'

'Five minutes?' the other Young Officer ventures.

'At the very least.' Kyd dips his head against the stinging rain. 'If a sea-skimming missile is incoming from the same side as the tanker, you may not get clear quickly enough to take it out.'

'Is there an alternative, sir?'

'Actually, there is,' Kyd says. 'When I was on *Monmouth* in 2006, I decided that the quickest way to open weapon arcs was to go hard astern on the main engines, ripping out the fuel lines as the tanker continues forwards.'

Kyd moves closer so his voice can be heard over the roar of the wind.

'You'd have to balance the ship's attitude with the rudder and engines so you don't hit the tanker's stern with your bow, but you'll be able to shoot in all directions within about ninety seconds of the initial alarm. And because you're not heeling the ship on a great swerve, your missiles and radars have a more stable platform.'

'That's fantastic, sir. Why wasn't it already Standard Operating Procedure?'

Kyd explains that when you're RASing at 30 metres' separation from the tanker, every bone in your body is telling you not to drop back, in case you get sucked in alongside and collide. 'So it's not for the faint-hearted, but it could save the day.'

'Have you ever tried it, sir?'

'I trialled it with my frigate and a stopwatch against some friendly fast jets. It worked a treat. It needs a worked-up bridge and seamanship team, but it's in the book now, for wartime usage.'

'Does it have a name, sir?'

'It does, actually.' The captain pauses for a moment before heading back inside. 'It's called the Kyd Manoeuvre.'

2100

High winds continue to howl round the forward and aft islands as night falls. The VertRep Merlin sits alone on the flight deck, securely tied but with blades still 'burning and turning', as they have done for the last eight hours. If they turned off the power now, the aircraft could be destroyed or badly damaged. The centrifugal force of the blades neutralizes the wind-strength by cutting through it. Suddenly stilled blades would instantly twist and buckle, and the cab could turn over and be hurled into the sea. The Merlin must maintain its own downdraught until the wind subsides.

The crew and the aviation wing can do nothing but watch and wait.

After causing seventy-four deaths and $25 billion of damage across Central America, the Caribbean and the southeastern United States, Michael is having the last laugh.

43. You've Just Made History

'How are you feeling, mate?' Nathan Gray asks.

'Buzzing.' The only civilian test pilot in the team grins. 'It's been a long time coming.'

'Sure has,' Gray says. 'Good luck, Wizzer. I'll be watching from Flyco.'

The two men shake hands, and Wilson makes his way to the kit room to collect his flying gear and helmet. Today will be the culmination of a long and eventful career. What he's about to attempt could revolutionize carrier aviation in the modern era.

One of the reasons naval Harriers were axed was that they needed to ditch unused weapons and fuel before landing on their carrier. High temperatures – in the Arabian Sea and Persian Gulf particularly – inhibited engine thrust. The F-35's vertical hover performance presents a similar challenge, because it too requires the aircraft to be as light as possible during its approach.

Even the QE, despite its size, carries limited fuel and munitions. Ditching those munitions – at a cost of hundreds of thousands of pounds – would be needlessly profligate, and constant resupply is dangerous and strategically nonsensical. The husbandry of resources, especially when confronting an enemy, is vital.

Shipborne Rolling Vertical Landing (SRVL) might be the answer.

A purely vertical landing involves no forward velocity. The aircraft hangs in the air at zero mph, and the pilot depends totally on his jet-borne thrust to touch down – like flying a rocket in reverse. Coming in horizontally at speed has one great advantage – wind over the wings, so if the fusion of vertical (jet-borne) and horizontal (wing-borne) flight could be achieved, it would give significantly greater lift and allow the aircraft to land with up to 7,000 lbs of extra weight – more than a full weapon load. And because it would still be semi-hovering, it should be able to stop using its own brakes well before it runs out of flight deck. But up until now, it's been regarded as too dangerous to attempt.

Combining horizontal and vertical thrust is easier said than done. The two forces are not readily compatible, and the slightest mistake in approach speed and alignment could have catastrophic consequences. The extra forward momentum would give the wings more lift, but without the braking assistance provided by arresting gear there's a real danger of crash-landing or overshooting into the sea. It's been practised in simulators but never in the real world. Some tentative testing was done with the Harrier, but the results were not convincing.

Wizzer Wilson is going to be the first man to attempt a full-blown Shipborne Rolling Vertical Landing. He has been working on its aerodynamic and engineering implications for almost seventeen years and achieved in excess of 2,000 simulated landings. But as Nathan Gray was well aware when he executed the first vertical landing on to the QE, there is nothing quite like doing it for real.

There is a frisson of excitement and apprehension as Wilson walks towards his jet. James Blackmore is in his usual position. Nathan Gray, Latch Lippert and Andy Edgell are standing alongside him. Jerry Kyd is working with his navigators to position the ship into the prevailing wind. The SRVL will need a minimum 8 knots of true wind, and at the moment it's four short, so they're moving further out to sea in search of a stronger airstream.

The duty aircraft handlers have prepared his F-5 with their usual dedication. The BAE pilot shakes hands with every one of them. Turbo Salerno is the last to bid him well before he climbs the ladder to his cockpit. Scouse Walsh stands ready to direct him towards his take-off point.

A couple of handlers are touching up a couple of large orange squares painted near the stern which indicate the ideal touchdown spot. For Nathan Gray, these makeshift targets seem to hark back to the low-tech days of Edwin Dunning, when pioneering procedures were more or less made up as they went along.

Wilson closes his canopy and starts the engine. Scouse Walsh waves him from his parking space just under the for'ard island towards his take-off position at the 350 feet spot. The F-35, ready to burst out of its blocks, lines up facing the ski-jump. The anemometer on the bow is now showing a wind speed of 9.5 knots and rising.

'Everything is go,' Wilson says. 'Let's do this thing!'

Below deck, most are oblivious to what's going on above their heads, unaware of the significance of the unfolding drama. Most are diverted by their own duties, preoccupations, concerns and worries. Wes Khan is dealing with a feeding crisis – there's been yet another run on chips.

'The Americans are the worst,' he tells Rai, the Nepalese storeman. 'They have chips with their pasta!'

'Shall I get more boxes of frozen chips from the deep-freeze? Each box is 25 kilos.'

Khan does a quick calculation. 'Better get three. Or we'll have chip riots.'

'Heaaaaaaave!' Rob Rouston yells to his regular training partner. They're in the gym on 2 Deck, and Roly Brading grimaces as he pulls himself up for his tenth full-arm chin-up. To make things harder, he's wearing a 15 kg weighted waistcoat with a 20 kg dumb-bell gripped between his legs.

'Go on, sir!' Rouston encourages. 'Six more inches and you're there!'

Biceps and lat muscles straining, Brading shudders as he stretches his neck to touch the underside of his chin on top of the bar. He drops to the floor exhausted.

'Go on, Rob,' he gasps. 'Your turn. Gimme ten good ones.'

Rouston picks up the 20 kg dumb-bell and reluctantly squeezes it between his knees. He spits into his hands, looks up to the bar and leaps to grab it.

'Here goes nothing!' he laughs. 'I'll be happy with five, sir.'

The marine grins. 'You matelots are such lightweights!'

A dozen sailors wait in the medical centre. Nothing serious today – the normal scrapes, cuts, abrasions and bruises that sharp-edged warships tend to inflict on their citizenry. There's an impacted wisdom tooth for the dentist to attend to and, in the case of one worried-looking young man, a suspicious rash of a personal nature that he thinks he might have picked up in Mayport.

In the main ward, currently empty of patients, Matt Hicks is methodically restringing and tuning the ship's ukuleles, ready for this evening's practice. Further along 5 Deck, Chris Trevethan is buying shaving soap and a packet of mixed nuts in the NAAFI while one deck below Alastair Mansfield is laying out the hymn books and service sheets in readiness for the afternoon service. The workaday routines continue.

'Wind speed up to 11 knots, sir,' an air traffic controller reports.

'Stand by to launch,' James Blackmore says from the Papal Throne.

Paul Ranson holds his green launch flag high above his head.

Blackmore, now standing, looks up and down the flight deck below him.

'Launch the jet.'

Paul Ranson drops the flag with a flourish.

Wilson surges forward into the head wind. He has no need to consult the panel in front of him for speed, trim, altitude, horizon, air intake and vertical thrust power; his visor display shows him all he needs to know. He takes the jet up to 1,000 feet and, at a speed of 200 knots, flies in a wide circle to burn off excess fuel, then makes two practice approaches from the QE's stern at a height of about 100 feet, testing for wind vortices and general turbulence. Finally, as happy as he can be with the landing conditions, he circles in readiness for what he hopes will be the world's first Shipborne Rolling Vertical Landing in a fifth-generation fighter.

Wilson lines up for his final approach. He is 2 miles to the carrier's stern, at a height of 500 feet. Reducing his speed to about 70 knots, he balances his forward momentum with the vertical thrust provided by both his central fan motor and the rear nozzle and flies, half rocket, half plane, towards the beckoning flight deck. He will descend on a seven-degree glide path, twice as steep as an airliner coming in to Heathrow, but at a final approach speed of only about 35 knots relative to the ship – exactly the same as Edwin Dunning's when he landed his Sopwith Pup on HMS *Furious* in 1917.

An emotionally charged silence descends on Flyco as Wilson closes. He's on course and moving steadily 'down the hill', maintaining the critical seven-degree angle of approach. If he comes in too high and overshoots the mark, he could end up in the sea. If he comes in too low, his rear nozzle could strike the deck and he would flip. He is now only 400 yards short of the stern. In seconds he will be too low to pull out of the landing.

'Two hundred feet . . . 100 feet . . .' he says calmly into his helmet mic. 'A bit high . . .'

'Too steep,' Nathan whispers to himself from the Papal Pulpit. 'Pull out, mate, pull out,' he wants to shout but restrains himself.

Wizzer Wilson does not need telling.

'Wave off, wave off!' he says at the last moment as he accelerates and climbs back into the sky.

Everyone in Flyco breathes a sigh of relief but, like Wilson in the cockpit, remains calm. Panic does not sit well among aviators.

'OK . . .' Wilson says. 'Going round again.'

Nathan Gray raises an eyebrow at Andy Edgell. The RAF squadron leader nods but quickly looks away. His emotions are raw, and he doesn't want to show it, but Gray knows exactly what he's going through. He feels the same. The SRVL is a brave new frontier to these men, and they are all willing Wilson to succeed but, above all, to keep safe.

The F-35 sweeps round in another wide circle and approaches the ship's stern once again from 2 miles out. This time Wilson comes in slightly lower, adjusting all the time to the wind, which is now gusting up to about 12 knots. He follows the tramlines on his helmet display and aims the aircraft towards the flight deck for the second time.

The aircraft handlers and fire teams are poised, ready to respond to any emergency.

Everybody in Flyco can hear Wizzer Wilson as he talks himself down. '*Coming in steady . . . slight buffeting from the right . . . orange target boxes in sight . . . three seconds to point of no return . . . two, one . . . committed!*'

The F-35, following the QE's wake, draws level with the stern and comes in over the flight deck at a height of 40 feet. Clouds of spray explode into the air as the vertical thrust of the jet nozzles blasts the water puddled on its surface. The aircraft, straight and steady, comes down precisely on the orange markers and rushes forward on all three wheels towards the ski-jump. There's nothing to stop it apart from its own brakes, which Wilson applies immediately. The F-35 comes to a smooth halt within 150 feet of touchdown.

Flyco erupts.

'That was surreal,' Wilson says. 'Did that just happen, or was I dreaming?'

'That happened, Wizzer,' James Blackmore says. 'Well done, my friend. You've just made history.'

The SRVL will have to be perfected and pushed beyond its current limits, but it's no longer just a conceptual possibility. It's another addition to the extraordinary list of achievements – which include the angled deck, the cat and trap, the ski-jump and the mirror landing sight – from the pioneers of seaborne aviation, and other navies, both friendly and hostile, will be seeing this as the way forward. The F-35/ *Queen Elizabeth* combination is already beginning to pay dividends.

*

Nathan Gray is waving frantically at Wilson and giving him double thumbs-up signals. Andy Edgell is weeping openly but smiling through the tears. He might be an RAF pilot on a Royal Navy warship, but today is not about partisan loyalties. It's a joint service achievement, and it seems entirely appropriate that the man in the hot seat is a civilian pilot who has served with both the RAF and the RN.

Wizzer Wilson remains in his cockpit for some time, savouring the moment. 'You know what, guys?' he says over the hot mic. 'That was fun. Can I do it again?'

17 October 2018

Fuelled by yesterday's excitement and powered by her two mighty Rolls-Royce gas turbines and four Wärtsilä diesels, the QE is heading north towards New York. The port visit everyone's been looking forward to is only two days away. But there's still a great deal to achieve beforehand.

The first phase of Developmental Testing of the F-35B (DT1) is almost complete, and tomorrow the jets will fly back to Pax River for a week of maintenance and downtime for the pilots. They will return to the ship for the second period of testing after the New York visit. Before leaving, however, they have one final, vital challenge – to fly with full bomb loads on their wings for the first time to start monitoring and measuring how the extra weight affects the aerodynamics of the aircraft on launch. Most of these experimental runs will be made during DT2, but Jerry Kyd and James Blackmore are keen to get ahead of the game. They want at least four fully laden launches to be completed today.

The weapons to be used are inert versions of the GBU-12

Paveway II laser-guided precision bomb. Their main body is solid concrete, but in every other respect they are identical to those used in anger.

Latch Lippert will be the first to launch with two on each wing, an extra payload of 2,000 lbs. He's settled into his cockpit and is preparing to execute yet another first for the QE. Scouse Walsh stands in front of the fully laden F-35, ready to direct the American pilot to his take-off position on the 400 feet marker. Lippert tests the air-intakes and rear jet nozzle before he gives the thumbs-up. The ITF handlers move in to unchain the aircraft, but a muffled explosion stops them in their tracks.

'Bloody hell!' Scouse Walsh says. 'Look up there . . .'

Everybody stops to watch clouds of acrid black smoke mushroom angrily out of the funnel housed in the for'ard island and cast swirling shadows across the deck. A shower of burnt fabric and peculiar wool-like particles rains down, soft, fibrous and hot to the touch. Emma Ranson, leading a long line of aircraft handlers, combs the flight deck in a con- certed FOD plod to pick up every last scrap, but flying is immediately cancelled until further notice.

The Paveway bombs are promptly detached and returned to the hangar while a full emergency is declared and an inves- tigation launched. It is not only the aviation engineers who are worried but also the marine engineers. An exhaust prob- lem suggests an engine problem. This is more than just a glitch.

Up in the Captain's Pantry, oblivious to the dramas unfolding on the flight deck, Glen Peters reaches up to the top right- hand corner of a whiteboard, wipes out the red figure 3 and replaces it with a 2.

'New York, New York,' he says to Lieutenant Gary Smith, the Captain's Secretary. 'I've been counting the days since leaving Portsmouth. It started as sixty-one and now it's down to two. Forty-eight hours!'

'Excited, Glen?'

'Half and half, sir. Two days closer to the captain leaving.'

Smith nods. 'It's going to be strange without him, for sure.'

'End of an era,' Peters says. 'And as soon as he goes, I return to general duties below deck.'

Even though he understands his replacement by a new man is part of a natural rotation to keep command positions fresh and dynamic, he's dreading Jerry Kyd's departure. To avoid the potential awkwardness of transferring his allegiance from one captain to another, Peters will reallocate to the wardroom and look after the officers en masse. He'll lose his privileged position as the captain's confidant, but also a friend for whom he feels intense respect and loyalty.

'It's bloody sweltering back here!' Marine Engineer Rob Rouston shouts. 'Everything's very hot to the touch.'

The bearded fitness fanatic from Ripon has crawled up the back of the for'ard gas turbine engine room, to the base of the billowing funnel. 'Temperature's well over the limit, guys,' he calls to other marine engineers watching from below.

They need to find out why it started smoking, and what's belching on to the flight deck. The first clue is that the engine has shut itself down.

'It's just got too bloody hot for the Gazzy in here, fellas,' Rouston says. 'The engine's tripped itself. Something's overheating somewhere.'

The Rolls-Royce MT30 gas turbine is based on the

Rolls-Royce Trent 800 aero engine that powers Boeing 777 airliners. One of two on the ship, it's capable of generating up to 36 MW of power and produces a great deal of heat from its exhaust, which is channelled through heavy stainless-steel trunking to the funnels. But if the ambient temperature in the engine compartment rises to above 80 °C, the power plant is programmed to turn itself off automatically.

Petty Officer Mikey Fyans, head of the for'ard gas turbine engineering team, climbs up next to Rouston with a high-powered torch, and together they investigate the lower section of the funnel and the exhaust trunking.

'Look!' Rouston says. 'The starboard trunking has split wide open along the welding. I can see your torchlight coming through.'

'That's where the heat is escaping from,' Fyans says. 'And look at the insulation lagging around the bottom of the funnel. Completely burned away.'

'So it's not the engine overheating, it's the exhaust system,' Rouston says. 'And the insulation's fucked!'

The two engineers sweep the torch across the area. The steel trunking, a rectangular exhaust pipe about 6 feet long, 2 high and 3 across, has split intermittently along its lateral welds. The hot exhaust gases generated by the MT30 have escaped and, at very high pressure, blown straight on to the canvas-covered fibre-glass wool insulation lagging wrapped round the lower part of the funnel.

'There's a lot of missing lagging,' Rouston says. 'No wonder the temperature rocketed. So that's the FOD on the flight deck – bloody burnt lagging . . .'

The marine engineers will need to pull a very significant rabbit out of the hat. Whatever repairs they can effect will take time and certainly cannot be achieved before New York.

And New York will not be much help either. It's not a dedicated naval base, so there'll be no expertise to call on and none of the necessary materials required for a more comprehensive repair.

Without the for'ard gas turbine, the QE will be deprived of at least 25 per cent of her power, so will not be able to attain the speed required to create sufficient wind across the deck for the F-35s to launch with full weapon loads. If it cannot be fixed on board, which seems likely, the only other option will be to head straight to Naval Station Norfolk after New York for repairs.

There is little or no leeway to the timing of DT2 either. The window of opportunity is severely limited, not only because of the restricted availability of the F-35s themselves, but because the American ITF personnel need to return home to their families in time for Thanksgiving – always the fourth Thursday in November, a sacred and immoveable holiday fixture in the national calendar. If the final flight trials are not completed by then, they'll have to be abandoned until next year. That in turn could lead to an early return to the UK, and an admission to press and public that the F-35 test mission had not been successfully completed because of a technical failure on the ship.

'It's nuts!' Rouston says. 'A multi-billion-dollar ship and a trillion-dollar jet fighter programme brought to its knees by a bit of dodgy welding.'

The ship continues under the power of her remaining gas turbine and four diesel engines. The flight deck has been cleared of FOD, so at least the F-35s will be able to head back to Pax River first thing in the morning. It will also be safe for the helicopters to fly again, which is just as well because tomorrow three of the Merlins and their crews will face their biggest challenge to date.

18 October 2018

0900

'Stand by to start the VertRep,' Jenny Curwood tells her team of logisticians. They are standing on the secondary bridge on the aft island, looking out across a relatively calm sea to the mammoth American supply ship 200 yards off the port beam.

Curwood is about to oversee another major RAS. In the next few hours, 140 pallets of dry and refrigerated produce, enough for 96,000 meals, will be taken on board by helicopter. Three from the QE and one from the American vessel will be used in a major evolution that's been in the planning for five months.

To the onlooker it might seem strange to go to all this trouble only a day away from the Big Apple. But today's operation, which should take no more than eight hours, would take a week or more to complete in a city not geared up to resupplying warships. And the QE needs to be able to prove that she can achieve a major VertRep whilst underway.

Jenny Curwood is ready to start not only the largest Vert-Rep the QE has ever undertaken, but probably the largest ever attempted by the Royal Navy in support of a single warship.

Two Merlins, one from 820 Squadron and one from 845, sweep in a wide arc towards USNS *Supply*. An American Sea Knight takes off for the QE, and the three aircraft start an unremitting round of pick-up/drop-off flights. Every three minutes, underslung loads are gently deposited on deck, where handlers rush to unhook them. Deck tractors and forklift trucks transfer the pallets to the aft flight-deck lift, to be taken down to the hangar. The complex choreography requires split-second coordination from deck crews and air crews alike, and the helicopters have to perform a hazardous aerial ballet. The rhythm of the operation is metronomic. With so many moving parts, the potential for disaster, including mid-air collision, is ever-present.

After nearly eight hours, the VertRep is complete. Food supplies sufficient to sustain the ship's company for the next three weeks are safely stowed below. Perhaps above all it has demonstrated the vital interoperability between the two navies.

1830

'OK, shipmates! New York tomorrow, and it's going to be a busy visit.' Chris Trevethan is delivering the same message to all messes. 'Lots happening over the week we're there. In our role as a diplomatic platform we'll be host to the American political, business and military elite. It's the task of the ship to cement and reinforce Anglo-American relations and that means you'll all have a role to play. If it's not a direct role like the stewards or the Royal Marines Band, just make sure you're on your best behaviour, be polite to all who come on board. Civvies will get lost very quickly – be your charming, helpful selves and guide them to where they need to go.'

Trevethan, working through a scribbled list of briefing topics, gets to the thorny issue of 'running ashore' and once again stresses the importance of looking after each other.

'Same will apply in New York as it did in Mayport and Norfolk,' he says firmly. 'Go ashore together, stay together and come back together. It's a big, exciting city. But it has robbers, pickpockets and muggers who would love a chance to duff over a British matelot with a wallet full of dollars. If you come across any of your shipmates the worse for wear, get them back on board ASAP. We can deal with them and look after them better here than if they stay ashore. Don't let your shipmates down, please, shipmates!'

2300

Glen Peters crawls into his bunk, exhausted. His worn-out headphones are now held together with tape and string, so listening to some morale-restoring reggae on his computer is an increasingly complex mission. He wants to buy a replacement set in New York but knows he'll have to ask his wife Claudia if she minds him spending a couple of hundred dollars on the ones he'd really like.

He opens up a downloaded brochure and smiles as they appear on screen: *Beats Headphones, $299.99. Wireless Bluetooth Over-Ear Phones with Pure Adaptive Noise Cancelling and Mic/Remote.* He decides on the bright-red ones, then instantly recoils from that sort of outlay. The exchange rate is not great, and Christmas gifts for the family must come first. He falls asleep listening, or half listening, to Bob Marley and the Wailers singing 'The Redemption Song'.

44. Manhattan Ahoy!

North West Atlantic, 19 October 2018

It is a fresh autumn day, breezy, bright, crystal clear but cutting cold. HMS *Queen Elizabeth* moves sedately through the grey-green waters of the New Jersey Bight. She is heading towards the Hudson Estuary, sea gate to New York State and front door to New York City. Once again, Britain's biggest warship is an instant attraction to the local dolphins, which surf playfully on her bow waves while squadrons of seabirds wheel and reel across her stern. Gulls, terns and kittiwakes scream hysterically in the hope of snatching anything tasty thrown up by the churning wake.

Jerry Kyd rolls up the charts of the local waters and reaches for his binoculars. Adjusting the focus, he smiles as the most famous skyline in the world begins to take shape on the near horizon.

'Manhattan!' he murmurs. He is instantly transported back to 1985, when, as a young midshipman on HMS *Ark Royal*, he first sailed past the Statue of Liberty. Little did he know, as the most junior ranking officer on board what was then the Navy's biggest warship, that he would command her a quarter of a century later, then take the helm of HMS *Queen Elizabeth*, a carrier three times her size.

The 'Mighty *Ark*', like 'Lusty', continues to hold a special place in Kyd's heart. He's still haunted by the moment in November 2010 when he witnessed the last Harrier leave her flight deck, piloted of course by James Blackmore. And he'll never forget having to tell his ship's company that she was to be decommissioned. After calling a Clear Lower Deck in the hangar, he didn't try to hide his anger at a political decision he has never forgiven. 'We will go out with style and dignity,' he urged. 'Hold your heads high and never let your chins drop.' His words were met with spontaneous applause from all those present. 'The *Ark* is a great ship, and that is down to you – every single one of you,' he added, his voice beginning to crack. The applause continued as he hurled the microphone across the deck and strode back to his cabin, where, even though it was only 11 a.m., he poured himself a whisky. A large one.

When Kyd became CO of the QE, he determined that, come what may, he would bring her here in memory of the *Ark Royal*. He wanted his last run ashore to be in the same place he enjoyed his first and now feels both privileged and proud to be back, at the opposite end of the rank spectrum.

In less than a week he will hand over command and fly home. He shakes his head in disbelief at the idea that his tour of duty is nearly done. Next year he will start a whole new chapter as Rear Admiral, Commander United Kingdom Maritime Forces. But never again will Jerry Kyd command his own warship.

He continues to scan the iconic New York skyline until he reaches the gap where the Twin Towers once stood. Lowering his binoculars, he is haunted once again by the imagery of that fateful day when, against the backdrop of an impossibly clear blue sky, they were felled in billowing clouds of smoke and dust, sealing the fate of both the blameless and the blameworthy. He can't quite believe that half the sailors on board are too young to remember it. There are at least a dozen who had not even been born in 2001. Kyd has always recognized that, as brilliant in its execution as it was abhorrent in its objective, 9/11 altered the course of history, and of his own career.

Sam Stephens is fixing the ship's exact position by taking bearings of visible landmarks with a horizontal sextant.

'Navs, what are you fixing off? Empire State Building?'

'Yessir. Plus the Coney Island Tower and the west bank transit marker.'

'Ha! That's one for the log-book.'

Jerry Kyd climbs into the captain's chair and greets his second in command, who's also surveying the coastline through binoculars. 'Morning, Darren. Let's have a blast of the ship's horn when we're closer to land. Tell the Yeoman to stand by.'

'Yessir. Couple of blasts?'

'Why not?' Kyd grins. 'Might as well announce ourselves in style.'

One of the 820 Squadron Merlins prepares to land. It's collected the American harbour pilot who will help bring the carrier to her anchorage. He's accompanied by two American journalists who'll cover the carrier's arrival and Robert Wood Johnson IV, whose great-great-grandfather founded the Johnson & Johnson pharmaceutical giant in 1886. 'Woody' Johnson also happens to be the mega-philanthropist and billionaire owner of the New York Jets, the NFL team he bought in 2000, and the US ambassador to the United Kingdom.

The QE progresses along the main Ambrose shipping channel to Lower Bay at the mouth of the Hudson River. Although still 10 miles short of her anchorage near the Statue of Liberty, the ship's company is given the order to assemble in full Procedure Alpha. Over a thousand British sailors, marines, airmen and airwomen march to their positions and, standing to attention in Number One uniforms (no longer tropical whites), form a striking, dark-blue margin around the supercarrier's perimeter. The Royal Marines Band, in full ceremonial uniform, strikes up with the evocative and stirring 'Sarie Marais', a folk song from the Boer War, and marches in perfect slow step down the flight deck towards the White Ensign waving vigorously at the stern. Two press helicopters are circling above them, beaming back live pictures to American morning TV audiences.

An armada of yachts, motor cruisers and pleasure craft is forming beside and behind the QE, to accompany her on her final approach. Amongst them there's even a Norwegian Viking longboat about to complete her own transatlantic passage. Jerry Kyd, suitably impressed, walks out on the starboard bridge wing to hail the crew. He waves enthusiastically, and they wave back.

'Just so long as they have no intentions of boarding us!' he murmurs.

Woody Johnson, delighted and excited to be on the bridge, does not underestimate the significance of the ship's high-profile visit to the US. 'It's all about the relationship between our two countries,' he declares to the journalists. 'There's an urgent need for the US and the UK to stick together in an ever more dangerous world.' He gestures to the flight deck. 'This ship and the F-35 which it's been trialling will stand the free world in good stead. It's great for this fine ship to see New York, and it is great for New York to see this fine ship.'

The journalists scribble dutifully and then take photographs.

The ship's company is locked into position for Procedure Alpha on the flight deck. Climbing to the top of the ski-jump to take his own place in the ceremonial formation is the familiar figure of Alastair Mansfield; his velvet Canterbury cap is pulled low over his ears and he is once again clutching his talismanic blackthorn branch. The stiff headwind that always curls and whips over its lip is strengthened today by a vigorous westerly from the mainland, and an icy one at that, so it takes longer for the Bish to summit the incline.

Once in position, he stands with feet wide, facing forward, chin raised, chest out and cloak flapping as the ship edges further up the Hudson. Frank Rochford is now fighting his way towards the Chaplain's side, playing 'Scotland the Brave' on his trusty bagpipes. The ship's company, resigned to at least an hour of increasingly chilly conditions, is grateful for the Bish and the piper's diverting entertainment. The ski-jump tableau is so utterly British in its idiosyncrasy, eccentricity and theatricality that it absolutely befits their arrival in this most American of destinations.

Rochford pauses for a moment, breathing hard.

'Morning, Bish!'

'Welcome, Frank. Bit breezy up here . . .'

'Ach, a wee bit,' the piper replies. 'But nothing to worry a boy fra' the Highlands!'

Mansfield's eyes are watering profusely, and not just from the relentless airstream. 'I'm welling up, Frank. Very emotional, your playing. And entering New York this way is unheard of. The locals will never have seen anything like it, I'm sure.'

He's right. US supercarriers aren't allowed to enter the harbour because their nuclear power plants would present a major environmental threat. No carrier this size has ever sailed so near to New York City, let alone one with a thousand sailors lining its perimeter, a full military band marching the length of its flight deck and a Scottish piper in full flow standing alongside a cloaked, weeping Chaplain wielding a branch of Sussex blackthorn at the very tip of the bow.

On one level this is pure pomp and circumstance, but for Alastair Mansfield it is far more than that. Here he is, standing proudly at the forefront of the Royal Navy's most powerful warship heading towards one of the world's great cities. But it is not the ship he's thinking about, not its scale or power, not its ground-breaking technology or its military potential. It is the priceless freight of human life on board; a myriad individuals, all with their own stories, their own frailties, strengths, dreams, fears and hopes. He loves the diversity of his flock – over twenty nationalities with a range of beliefs and non-beliefs, contrasting cultural mores, sexualities, political attitudes and ambitions. And he loves their underlying unity, a fundamental harmony and accord born of duty and dedication to a common cause – *each other*.

Proceeding at a regal 5 knots, the QE is joined by tugboats and a pillar-box-red fireboat of the New York City Fire Department. Its eight high-pressure hoses fire plumes of water high into the air in celebration of the warship's arrival. Jerry Kyd chooses this moment to order the horn to be sounded. Two long, loud blasts reverberate across the water – a salute to New York, New Yorkers and the US of A.

Eventually, with less than half a mile to the anchorage, the ship's company is given the order to fall out of Procedure Alpha. The neat blue thread quickly unravels as everyone rushes to capture the moment of arrival on their mobile phones.

'Bloody amazing,' Rob Rouston says, texting his dad back in Yorkshire. 'Not many folk get to do this, do they?'

'Sixteen years I've been in the Navy,' Scouse Walsh says, dispatching a photo of the Staten Island Ferry to his young family back in Liverpool. 'I've been waiting for this day to come – arriving in the Big Apple by "Grey Funnel" cruises. Doesn't get better than this!'

The ship drops anchor less than 1,000 yards from the Statue of Liberty. The flight deck resounds with the clank of the colossal chain falling 50 feet to the harbour bed.

And so begins what everyone expects to be a very special foreign visit, especially for the young sailors who have never been here before. But it's no jolly. HMS *Queen Elizabeth* must now transform from a battle platform to a floating embassy, and there's a crowded programme ahead. Over the next week she will host a number of ambassadorial and consular functions as well as a major forum for hundreds of prominent delegates. The chefs, while continuing to feed the ship's company, will also have to provide the fancy canapés, patisseries and fine wines for a range of VIPs and high-ranking naval officers, as well as laying on cocktail parties for the great and the good of New York.

And the Royal Marines Band must provide musical entertainment for the receptions and cocktail parties as well as the pageantry that always so impresses international visitors.

There will also be a rota allowing most of the ship's company to get ashore – to see the sights, eat their fill, shop till they drop, let their hair down and for some, no doubt, to 'pull out the pin'.

While the hangar is cleared and cleaned ready for its transformation into a state-of-the-art multi-purpose indoor arena, a huge floating platform is attached to the stern for the liberty boats to pick up and set down passengers.

As evening falls, those of the ship's company who venture to the flight deck are rewarded with their first unimpeded panoramic view of the Manhattan skyline at night. The soaring skyscrapers provide a vivid display of glittering golds, neon pinks and greens augmented by the blue, white and red of the Empire State Building, a towering urban lighthouse, all perfectly mirrored in the Hudson River.

45. Rob and the Pompom Girls

0745

The sea fog that crept in overnight lingers on the Hudson. Glistening in the fine, diaphanous drizzle, the QE sits comfortably at her anchorage. Manhattan looks more subdued without her night-time neon make-up and somehow doesn't seem quite as tall.

After another intoxicating, high-kicking night, the city that never sleeps seems to have slipped off her high-heels for a moment and sunk into the carpet of mist at her feet. Like some of the sore-headed sailors who ventured ashore last night, she could probably do with her first coffee of the day. All are back on board, and none have broken the curfew.

'*Fifteen minutes to Colours!*'

The main broadcast alerts the ship's company to the imminent start of the new day.

'*Ratings as detailed, close up.*'

The colour-details – two sailors at the stern and two at the bow – are already in position. For Morning Colours six weeks ago in the summer sunshine of Mayport, Florida, the required rig was the light, white tropical Number One uniform. Now, however, with summer long gone and the ship at a much more northerly latitude, the sailors are back in their thicker serge navy-blue uniforms. Standing at ease but statue-still, they cradle the flags already attached to the halyards ready for hoisting and wait patiently for the top of the hour.

The only other people on deck are two early-morning runners, heads down and arms pumping. Their work rate is evident from the puffs of condensation that form every time they exhale in the cold morning air.

Below deck in the main dining room, breakfast is well underway.

'It was a hoofing night,' Rob Rouston informs the queue to the servery.

'Looks like you had a skinful, shippers!' someone says.

'Yeah!' laughs the bleary-eyed stoker. 'Got trollied. And I warn you, beer's crazy expensive. About nine dollars a pint.'

'*Whaaat?*'

'Gen. And an American pint's smaller than ours.'

'Suck it up, mate.'

Rouston reaches for the porridge. 'Getting pissed is an expensive evolution here. On the bright side, the food portions are massive. The burger and chips I had was enough to feed yer average British family for a week!'

'*Five minutes to Colours . . .*'

The officer of the day stands at ease on the flight deck, and from behind him comes the sharp, rhythmic sound of boots in marching formation. The Royal Marines Band in full ceremonial uniform will play the anthems of the UK and the USA when the colours are raised. Jerry Kyd, with ceremonial telescope under his left arm, is also now present on parade. This will be his final Colours ceremony before he hands over the Captaincy in three days' time. The pride and emotion of the moment show in his eyes.

At the strike of eight o'clock the bridge flag is jiggled up and down by a Yeoman. This is the visual prompt for the Officer of the Watch to start proceedings.

'Colour party . . . *Ho!*'

The detail slam their feet together with a sharp crack of the heels. The sudden movement and sound startles the large seagull that has just perched on top of the flagstaff. It flies off, squawking angrily. Unconcerned, the officer gives the next order: 'Pipe the still!'

A sailor to his side sounds the high-pitched Bosun's whistle, the signal for the colours to be raised.

The main broadcast sounds once more. '*Attention on the upper deck. Face aft and salute. Colours!*'

The two heavy-breathing runners stop in their tracks. Standing upright and with feet together, they turn to the stern of the ship.

The White Ensign and the Union Jack are slowly raised as the band strikes up with 'God Save the Queen'. Nathan Crossley, the tall Drum Major, salutes smartly, as does Jerry Kyd. The rising Ensign hangs limp at first but starts to flap as it is hoisted higher until, at the top of the staff, it billows in the stiffening breeze. The Union Jack at the bow also stretches out as the wind fills its folds. The band segues seamlessly into 'The Star-Spangled Banner', a much longer anthem, but all the while Jerry Kyd holds his salute. Firmly. Respectfully.

As if in response to its own rousing anthem, the Hudson shakes off its blanket of morning fog to reveal Manhattan, heels back on, standing tall, proud and ready for the new day.

When the band is done, the Officer of the Watch executes a smart about-turn and marches purposefully towards Jerry Kyd.

'Colours complete, sir. Permission to carry on?'

'Yes, please,' Kyd says. 'Carry on.' The band plays 'Life on the Ocean Wave' in honour of their outgoing captain, who takes the salute as they march past him.

'That's it,' he says resignedly to Darren Houston. 'My final salute at Colours on HMS *Queen Elizabeth*. I did them in Rosyth, Invergordon, Portsmouth, Mayport, Norfolk and now New York. Not a bad place to do the last one.'

He watches as the band marches towards the aft tower, where they re-enter the ship.

'Right.' He blows into his hands. 'Cup of tea!'

Jerry Kyd turns to walk off the flight deck himself.

'Morning, guys!' he calls. 'Morning, sir!' the two runners respond, back in their stride.

Rob Rouston, re-energized by his porridge, has dropped into the for'ard gas turbine room to see fellow engineers Mikey Fyans, 'Dickie' Davies and Valric Sargeant. Still agonizing over the failed welds on the exhaust ducts, they've tried closing up the gaps with metal stapling pins but to precious little effect.

'It's a right bugger!' Rouston strokes his beard thoughtfully. 'We just have to hope it can be sorted in Norfolk. Meanwhile, just enjoy New York, fellas.'

'You going ashore today?' asks Mikey Fyans.

'I am, shippers.' Rouston claps his hands. 'The ship's been given a load of free tickets to see the New York Jets. Never really got me 'ead round American football but should be an experience to see it live. We're goin' in rig too.'

'Rig run?' (A run ashore in naval uniform.)

'Yeah, an order from on high. "Number Ones for all." Thought that was a no-no these days [since 9/11] as it turns us into targets, but suppose there's a method to the madness.'

*

368

Alastair Mansfield is sharing a pot of tea with Wes Khan in the junior rates dining hall on 5 Deck. They have developed a close friendship, and he's keen for the leading chef to contribute to an all-faiths commemoration of the Armistice Centenary three weeks from now. 400,000 Muslim soldiers died in the Great War and deserve to be remembered.

'I'm going to visit the Ground Zero memorial the day after tomorrow, Bish,' Khan tells him. 'People forget that innocent Muslims died that day too.'

'They do indeed.'

Khan hesitates. 'I wouldn't be saying a prayer, though . . .'

'I'm thinking more of a statement than a prayer.' Mansfield points to the draft service sheet. 'Take a look.'

Khan tentatively reads the words out loud.

'*Let us offer our thanksgiving to Almighty God . . . for victories achieved at sea, on land and in the air . . . and for the liberation of so many from cruelty and oppression.*

'*Let us give thanks for the heroism and courage of those who have served in the armed forces, in civil defence in hospitals and relief agencies.*

'*And let us pray for those who endured captivity, torture and death . . . that others may be free . . .*'

'I'll think about it, Bish,' Khan says. 'I promise.'

Mansfield nods. He completely understands his friend's concern about openly conflating Islam and Christianity in an increasingly intolerant world.

The two men sip their tea in thoughtful silence, relaxed and fortified in each other's company.

1100

About 200 sailors muster at the stern on 3 Deck, waiting for the liberty boat to take them ashore. Most, dressed in civilian clothes, are going in to explore Manhattan, but about 100 are dressed in their smart dark-blue Number One uniforms with gold-embroidered rank insignia and branch badges. All the suits have been freshly pressed, and black boots newly polished. Hats too have been cleaned, so are gleaming white. They're going to see the New York Jets. Their billionaire owner, Woody Johnson, has gifted the ship's company 100 free tickets for today's crunch match against the Minnesota Vikings. And for most of them, like Rob Rouston, it will be their first taste of American football live.

The big double doors open, and everyone steps on to a floating platform en route to *Lady Sea*, a Hudson River ferry boat. The sailors chatter and laugh as they leap aboard. Some go straight inside to grab a seat in the warm while others, braving the biting wind, climb to the open upper deck. Rob Rouston is happy to face the elements. 'Aye, it's a bit parky,' he concedes, inhaling a lungful of chilled fresh air. 'But it's nought to what the North York Moors throw at you of a winter!'

'Matelots never say no to a freebie,' Lindsey Waudby laughs. The QE's media officer is helping oversee today's junket. This is her last official duty before heading home to the UK in a few days. Her time on the QE, like Jerry Kyd's, was always to end in New York, and coming to see the Jets is a wonderful way of bowing out. She's well aware, however, that, as the ambassador's guests, today's visit is as much diplomatic as recreational. They'll be very much on show today and flying the flag for Britain. That's why, counter to the current, post-9/11 ruling, a rig run has been sanctioned.

The *Lady Sea* takes a short detour to give everyone a closer look at the Statue of Liberty but reaches North Cove Yacht Harbor in Lower Manhattan in just over thirty minutes. Everyone disembarks, and all those in civvy-rig first have to prove to the jetty sentries they're carrying ID before being officially allowed ashore. The uniformed party decants into three luxury coaches laid on by the Jets, complete with an escort of two NYPD police cars and four motorcycle outriders.

The convoy sets off, and everyone settles back for an 8-mile drive that first takes them through the heart of the city. The police escorts, flashing red and blue lights, cut a swathe through the thick, slow-moving traffic, which allows the coaches to motor unobstructed all the way to the Lincoln Tunnel in midtown Manhattan.

'So this is what it feels like to be a celeb!' Rob Rouston says. 'It's like we're in a blinking movie.' The 1.5-mile tunnel takes them under the Hudson to Weehawken, New Jersey, where they're able to speed up until they cross the Hackensack River and arrive at the immense Meadowlands sports complex – their final destination.

Everybody gasps as they see the MetLife Stadium for the first time – at $1.6 billion, the most expensive ever built. 'It looks like a bloody great spaceship . . .' Rouston takes a photo on his mobile phone that he immediately posts on Instagram.

The coaches set the naval party down outside one of the many entrances. There are still two hours to kick-off, but thousands of football fans are already streaming through the turnstiles. Some sporting the white and green colours of the Jets mingle with others in the gold and purple of the Vikings.

'Like a rugby match back home,' Rouston says. 'No aggression or segregation like at our football matches.'

Every sailor is given a special security pass that will give them free access not only to the stadium but to a dedicated VIP suite.

'Free sandwiches, lads!' Rouston shouts. 'But get out your cheque books if you want a beer.'

Led by Jets officials, they file up the escalators leading to the arena and become increasingly aware of people cheering them.

'Thank you for your duty!' one woman shouts.

'We're grateful for all you do,' someone else bellows.

'God bless you,' another calls.

They soon find themselves moving through a spontaneously formed tunnel of Jets and Vikings fans applauding and offering hands either to be shaken or high-fived. The delighted sailors respond by grasping or slapping open palms to the left and to the right, prompting the crowds to cheer all the more.

After posing for a lot of selfies with American fans, the 'VIP matelots' are taken on to the field itself to watch the teams warming up.

'They're big lads for sure,' Rouston concedes. 'Mind you, I'm not sure how they'd fare against the Bradford Bulls or the Leeds Rhinos without all that padding and them big biker helmets.'

Once the players run off for final team talks, the sailors are accompanied to their VIP suite. After a long climb, mostly by escalator, they're ushered into a plush reception room with an open-air balcony overlooking the pitch. A long table down the centre of the room is loaded with huge paniers of breads, pastries and cakes. There are large heated containers of steaming hot food: curries, stews, risottos, pizzas and pies. At the end is a gigantic chafing dish of golden-brown French fries, another of baked potatoes and yet another of bubbling baked beans. On an adjacent table countless bottles of sauces, condiments, pickles and relishes are lined up in multi-coloured rows. To cap it all there is an ice cream bar at one end of the room and beer and wine at the other. All free.

'Bloody hell!' one wide-eyed sailor gasps. 'I've died and gone to scran heaven.'

'It's a dream,' another says. 'Talk soft. I don't want to wake up!'

Everyone queues to fill their plates. Every time containers or platters start to empty they are immediately replaced or refilled by an army of attentive waiters.

Sailors gradually spill out on to the balcony to watch the action on the pitch – athletic, precision-dancing displays by a phalanx of pompom-brandishing cheerleaders. Their smiles are as wide as their legs are long, and the crowd roar their approval of the routine that precedes the appearance of their football heroes. The British sailors join in. It's difficult not to be carried away by the collective energy of 80,000 football fans intent on celebrating this most all-American of sports. And the game itself is yet to come.

After more razzmatazz, which includes marching bands and fireworks, the national anthem is sung by a busty soprano with big hair and a long red dress. The entire crowd stand and, placing their right hand across their heart, join in with emotional gusto. The QE contingent stand to respectful attention and salute.

The players run on to the field through an explosion of coloured smoke and flashing lights. The sailors watch in mystified fascination. Once the whistle blows, many are torn between trying to work out the complex plays and tactics and replenishing their plates and glasses. The decision is made a great deal easier when six of the cheerleaders arrive to pose for photos. The queue that forms is a long one. 'Best run ashore I've ever had,' Rouston grins, his arms round two of the pompom girls. 'They never mentioned this in the recruitment office!'

At the end of the first quarter, all the sailors are ushered on to the balcony, where an in-house TV crew is waiting to film them for a live-feed to the huge stadium screens. First a thirty-second film is screened showing HMS *Queen Elizabeth* at sea and an F-35 Lightning taking off from her flight deck. Over the top of pounding percussion a deep American voice booms out.

'*HMS* Queen Elizabeth *is the Royal Navy's brand-new aircraft carrier, the biggest ship ever built for the British fleet. She's currently undergoing trials off the east coast, flying F-35 stealth jets and exercising with the maritime services of her biggest ally, the United States of America. Please show your appreciation to our friends from Great Britain!*'

'Wave! Wave to the camera!' screams the TV director. 'Smile! Smile and wave!'

Everybody obeys, and their response is relayed to the huge stadium screens: 80,000 people rise as one in tribute to the Royal Navy.

'Keep waving, keep waving!' the director shouts.

Cheering fans immediately below the balcony turn to chant: 'Nave-eee! Nave-eee!' whilst pounding the air with clenched fists.

'It does make you right proud.' Rob Rouston gives the crowd a thumbs-up. 'Bit overpowering, though, isn't it?'

Now front-line ambassadors for Queen and country, the British sailors spend the rest of the match between the VIP suite, the viewing balcony and the numerous souvenir and gift shops. Right now, everybody from the QE is a dedicated New York Jets supporter.

On the way back in the coaches, everybody sifts through their mobile phone photographs for immediate posting to social media sites. 'Ha! I've already got twenty-two likes for me with them pompom girls,' Rob Rouston says. 'I only put it up five minutes ago.'

The Jets were thrashed 17 points to 37, but it's been a triumphant day for the Royal Navy.

Back on the ship, a lone figure is leaning on the rails of the starboard bridge wing. Glen Peters is oblivious to the huge orange sun sinking behind the skyscrapers. He went ashore this morning but came back after an hour, telling his friends, 'My mind's elsewhere right now. I have to be on board until the captain's gone. He may need help to pack and stuff.'

The disconsolate steward goes to press the captain's uniform for the last time. He unfolds the ironing board, plugs in the steam iron and turns on his trusty iPod for an invigorating burst of Peter Tosh.

'You and your music!' Joshua Hanks, his assistant, laughs.

'I can't listen to this in my cabin any more because my earphones have almost completely packed up,' Peters mourns. 'I'd really like to get a pair of those Beats headphones, but they're so expensive. Not sure Claudia would approve of me spending over two hundred pounds on cans!'

'Glen, mate, just do it,' Hanks says. 'Treat yourself. Might cheer you up a bit . . .'

Peters says nothing but turns up the volume on the next number – his favourite, 'No Obligation' by Bugle. The infectious beat, powerful syncopation and insistent lyrics work their magic, and soon Peters is not only ironing in time to the music but singing too.

'Great song . . .' He presses hard down on the iron to ensure the sharpest of creases in Jerry Kyd's uniform trousers. 'The captain likes it too. He's into his reggae now. I seen to that!'

46. Better Than in Nature

Unusually, Wes Khan is not on duty today. He rose early nonetheless, at least an hour before 'Call the Hands'. He wanted to beat the morning rush for the showers to give him plenty of time for ablutions and prayers before packing his bags. Khan goes on leave today and, along with his friend Ramesh Rai and three other chefs, will enjoy three days at a hotel they've booked in Queens. Well wrapped against the biting wind, they watch with anticipation as the *Lady Sea* makes its final approach to the landing platform.

'No cooking for seventy-two hours,' Khan says wistfully.

'What shall we do today?' Rai asks.

'It's beautiful weather,' Khan says. 'How about Central Park?'

Everyone nods their agreement.

'And then Ground Zero,' he adds. 'I really want to see that.'

Once everyone's on board, the *Lady Sea* casts off and heads towards Manhattan. As she leaves the boarding platform, several other ferries appear to deliver delegates for today's Atlantic Future Forum – a high-level summit on cyberwarfare and artificial intelligence. Over the next two hours, 150 scientific experts, technical innovators, industrialists, politicians, military representatives and other shadowy figures in dark suits begin to assemble in the hangar. Most of them seem to know each other, which suggests that the inner circle of the cybersecurity community is a small one. A tight one. And when it needs to be, no doubt, a clandestine one.

This inaugural meeting will focus on both the opportunities and threats presented by developments in cyber-technology and the world of artificial intelligence (AI) and will result later today in the signing of the Atlantic Future Forum Accord, to ensure that the UK and US remain the world's leading partnership in futuristic military technology.

Lieutenant Colonel Roly Brading has been helping to devise and organize this event for months, but after walking half the length of the hangar on his hands, he reckons choreographing an international forum inside it is relatively small potatoes.

A distinguished-looking man in the uniform of a Royal Navy admiral takes his position in front of a perspex lectern. 'Good morning, ladies and gentlemen,' he says brightly, as the HMS *Queen Elizabeth*'s crest flashes up on vast video screens behind him.

'Welcome to Great Britain's latest flagship, and the inaugural Atlantic Future Forum on cybersecurity and artificial intelligence.'

Admiral Sir Philip Jones, the First Sea Lord, Chief of the Naval Staff and head of the Royal Navy, has flown over especially for today's event – an indication of its significance.

'The armed forces of the United Kingdom and the United States of America share a special bond that has stood for generations; a bond forged in the heat of operations spanning the world. In today's deteriorating global security climate, faced with the breathless pace of technological advance, there's never been a more important time for our great nations to work ever more closely together.' He pauses as spontaneous applause ripples round the hangar.

'I hereby declare the Forum open,' he pronounces. 'I look forward to some enlightening presentations and discussions throughout this auspicious day. This evening I hope you'll all stay for the official cocktail party – the first of many this fine ship will host in her long lifetime.'

A series of expert headline speakers provide cutting-edge analysis of the latest in cyber-technology and sobering discourses on the future of warfare. Everyone, whether from industry, politics or the military, lays down stark warnings about the terrible consequences of falling behind in the cyber-race.

A shaven-headed man in a black suit steps up to the podium to talk about drone-swarm technology. He speaks chillingly about the ability of drones to make autonomous decisions based on shared information. 'This has the potential to revolutionize the dynamics of conflict,' he says. 'And we're inching ever closer to seeing this potential unleashed. In fact, swarms will have significant applications to almost every area of national and homeland security. Swarms of drones could search the oceans for adversary submarines. Drones could disperse over large areas to identify and eliminate hostile surface-to-air missiles and other air defences. Drone swarms could potentially even serve as novel missile defences, blocking incoming hypersonic missiles. On the homeland security front, security swarms equipped with chemical, biological, radiological and nuclear detectors, facial recognition, anti-drone weapons and other capabilities offer defences against a range of threats.' His expression is grim. 'There's another side to the coin, of course, ladies and gentlemen. If the bad guys start operating drone-swarms we could be in a whole heap of trouble.'

Jerry Kyd, standing at the back in the shadows, listens with a mixture of fascination and foreboding. Cyberwarfare might be in its infancy, but he knows very well it's going to transform combat in the twenty-first century and beyond. The decision link, the time it takes to unbridle and release a cyber-attack, smart missile or, God forbid, a drone swarm, is growing ever shorter. The military strategists and more importantly the front-line operational practitioners will increasingly struggle to cope with the threats posed by miniaturization and artificial intelligence.

HMS *Queen Elizabeth* might be Britain's biggest warship, but she is also, as the Russians have delighted in pointing out, Britain's biggest military target. Her own defensive systems and those of her escorts could well protect her from the latest hypersonic missiles and smart torpedoes, but just how susceptible will she be to malicious cyberattack on her sophisticated software systems? Plans are in place to have her software systems rigorously tested against this ever-evolving threat. Next year, she will take a central role in Information Warrior, a massive Navy-led exercise which will simulate attempts to bring down networks and jam satellite communications, to ensure the fleet remains able to combat the increasing technological advancement of hostile states.

Kyd is aware that high-tech warfare is only ever as good as the high tech at one's fingertips. He realizes too that opposing sides in a modern conflict will very quickly endeavour to block, neutralize or infect each other's computer systems, whether they relate to weapons, communications or navigation. The navy with the best and most adaptable fall-back procedures will win the day. Kyd is no Luddite, but he takes comfort from the knowledge that his ship's company will also be able to depend on traditional skills – such as semaphore, Morse code and astronavigation – which will remain immune to cyberattack.

Jerry Kyd continues to listen to the keynote speakers as they elaborate on cyber options in the battle space, when a familiar figure approaches with a tray.

'Excuse me, sir, brought you some coffee.'

'Thanks, Glen. Surprised you could see me hidden away back here. You not going ashore?'

'Er, no, sir. Not today.'

After exploring Central Park Zoo, the chefs are on the subway south to Lower Manhattan. They get off at Rector Street and bump into Scouse Walsh and another couple of aircraft handlers as they climb the steps towards street level.

'Hi, guys,' says the cheery Liverpudlian. 'Any idea which tube goes to Central Park?'

'Get the line to Columbus via Penn Station and Times Square,' Khan says. 'You can walk from there.'

'Gotta visit Strawberry Fields,' Walsh says. 'Pay my homage to John Lennon. It's right alongside the apartment block where he was shot in 1980.'

'Hope it's good for you, mate.'

'Yeah. Well, you know, us Scousers have to stick together. How about you, Wes?'

'We're going to visit Ground Zero.'

'So we're all on a pilgrimage today,' Walsh says. 'See you later, shipmates.'

Khan and his friends continue up South End Avenue to Liberty Street and cross the main West Street highway to the now sacred space where the Twin Towers were felled.

Back on the QE, the Atlantic Future Forum is gathering pace. Some delegates have retreated to anterooms to discuss classified and secret information. Others, like Jerry Kyd, continue to listen to leading cyber experts who are talking not only about how to defend against cyberwarfare but how to attack with it as well. It's prompted the captain-soon-to-be-admiral to contemplate warfare at a very profound level. Once promoted, Kyd will be head of UK Maritime Forces and Surface Ships, and his authority, in terms of allocating British naval resources, including manpower, to future conflict zones, will be considerably enhanced. It will be a huge responsibility that will put great demands on his professional instincts, his sharp intellect and perhaps, more than ever, his need to square duty with conscience.

Kyd has always viewed the practice of warfare from the perspective of a rules-based international order and the liberal Western values that embody it. This is how he's been able to justify the deadly trade and dark art he is engaged in. He's a deep-thinking man but no bleeding heart. He accepts that it's his duty to neutralize the nation's enemies if necessary or, more precisely, to arrange for lethal violence to be inflicted on any who threaten the same against Great Britain and her allies. Up until now, war has been an essentially human endeavour. It's involved strict discipline, formal chains of command and, for the most part, as far as Britain has been concerned, a respect for rules of engagement and a deference for treaties and conventions designed to limit the excesses of kill-or-be-killed combat.

But things are changing fast. The human component is being usurped by neoteric technologies. And taking a human being out of the decision-making process, Kyd thinks, will revolutionize combat – and not in a good way. How do you fight an enemy which uses AI and leaves men, women and children out of the loop? New 'instant kill' weapons, cyborgs and DNA warfare suggest a type of unrestrained conflict that will ask difficult if not impossible questions of existing ethical codes. Kyd is very much of the opinion that the superhuman strength bestowed by superhuman weapons must be matched by an attempt to control it through super-human reason. This is a big ask of military leaders who, like those they command, are still ordinary people called to do extraordinary things. They do not always get it right, but at least they try to wage war within a moral framework.

The Western military tradition is rooted in the teaching of Aristotle, who, as early as the fourth century BC, said that soldiers, as citizens themselves, would and should exhibit emotions as long as their feelings were controlled and balanced. Consequently, he prescribed that armies should train their soldiers in such a way that their characters became *better than in nature*. It was precisely because soldiers were invested with the power and authority to kill that he felt they should be bound by an even higher moral standard than the rest of us.

Kyd, a student of philosophy, understands that conventional warfare can be unforgiving, but for all the 'visceral nastiness' and 'gut-wrenching, blood-spattering fury', it is something that can be comprehended and, to a degree, controlled. He believes that, in the context of cyberwarfare and smart technologies that bypass human decision-making, the dangers are profound and potentially overwhelming.

He fears that there may be few leaders who will be strategically, emotionally or ethically equipped to deal with the horrors that lie ahead as conflict shifts its paradigm. It also strikes him, not for the first time, that the futuristic QE/F-35 combination, whilst representing an extraordinary advance in the Royal Navy's capability, is also the thin end of the wedge for politicians and military commanders alike.

Is the F-35 stealth fighter that thinks faster than the man who flies it a stepping stone to pilotless warplanes? Kyd wonders what mind-blowing super-technology will be housed by the QE in fifty years, when she's due to be decommissioned. He will never know, of course. Only the very youngest sailors on board will see that time for themselves. What sort of world will the QE see before it is time for her to be replaced? The US is already planning to build a 'ghost fleet of drone warships' that will be completely unmanned. Carrying sensors and weapons alone, they will give the fleet greater firepower than ever before, inflicting enormous destruction as automated killing machines.

But what of now? Their worst nightmare is that the terrorist fraternity continues to develop a more sophisticated ability to harness the lethal potential of cyberwarfare and artificial intelligence. New Yorkers need no reminding of what fanatics and zealots, willing to die for their beliefs, will resort to.

Wes Khan and his friends look down into the square pool hollowed out of Ground Zero. Water cascades into it from all sides, forming liquid curtains that cover each sheer wall of the perfectly engineered quadrangular void. It is a faithful but ghostly outline of the footprint of the Southern Tower. Amid the hundreds of specially planted swamp white oak trees that stand like guardians in the 9/11 Memorial Garden, an identical cuboid cavity lies nearby – it's where the Northern Tower once stood. People are ranged along each side of both footprints – some in groups, some in couples and some standing alone, but all looking down thoughtfully, sorrowfully, mournfully into the glittering, rippling, reflecting pools.

Most of those gathered here will be strangers, but all of

them are united by their contemplations; combined with the deliberations and meditations that this place prompts and stimulates. The beautifully imagined Memorial Garden is a lasting testimony to a suffering beyond easy comprehension and a human tragedy beyond simple explanation. The names of the 2,977 people killed on the morning of 11 September 2001 are inscribed on the parapets that surround the pools.

It is also a solemn reminder of man's inhumanity to man, so whilst there's a sense of peace about the place, it's restless, even edgy. A silence enshrouds the memorial site too, but it is a loud silence. The gushing water is intended to mute the sounds of the surrounding city, but the distant drone of traffic and the occasional insistent echo of a police siren intrude now and again. It is a constant reminder to all that this is in the middle of Manhattan – and life goes on. And maybe that is what everyone wants to be reminded of. Otherwise the dark, suffocating tragedy of the place would be too much to bear, too stark to endure.

Khan is quiet as he thinks back to that fateful day, when he was going through his naval training. He and his fellow cadets watched the TV in horror as the deadly attacks were launched. In the days that followed, he was immediately aware that people had changed in their behaviour towards him, becoming more suspicious and apprehensive in his company. For a while the authorities even segregated him and other Muslims for their own safety. It was a bad time for Khan, when he even considered leaving the Navy, but he persevered with training and through sheer force of personality and generosity of spirit re-established himself as 'one of the guys'.

His initial fears that everyone would turn against him were unfounded. It had been a post-9/11 blip, and ever since he's been constantly reassured by the Navy's natural tendency towards inclusivity and acceptance. It is the way it has to be on close-knit warships, and it didn't take long for people to realize that, whilst Wes Khan is a devout Muslim, he is no fundamentalist. In fact, many sympathized with him when he explained that sixty innocent Muslims were killed in the attacks – a frequently forgotten minority, because most only consider Muslims to be the perpetrators.

'This place makes you think,' Ramesh Rai says quietly.

'It does,' Khan agrees. 'It's very tranquil. Unlike the day it happened.'

'What's your view of the people who did it?' Rai asks.

'What they did was not Islamic,' Khan answers. 'We're taught that to save one person's life is to save all humanity, and to take a life is to kill all humanity. These people will be called to account by God on the Day of Judgment.'

1800

After a day of presentations and high-level discussions, the Forum's delegates take their seats to witness the signing of an accord between the US and the UK – a pact to encourage closer and lasting interaction between the two countries in the development of cyber capabilities in the short and long term.

Several representatives from both countries, including Dr Liam Fox, the British Secretary of State for Trade and Industry, sign it in front of their crossed national flags. The agreement commits both countries to an annual forum and a free flow of information and intelligence.

Everybody now accepts as inevitable that future battlefields will be shaped in the cyber domain, so it's entirely appropriate that such a far-reaching and visionary agreement should be secured on the most modern aircraft carrier in the world. The Atlantic Future Forum has reinforced the determination of both nations to stand shoulder-to-shoulder against the new generation of weapons that threaten to destabilize it.

Once the accord is signed, the delegates stand and applaud warmly before being invited to an adjacent section of the vast hangar. In the space that until a week ago was reserved for two F-35 stealth fighters, the guests now mingle in a place of soft lights and relaxing small talk. Royal Marines musicians, led by Frank Rochford on his bagpipes, play a moving rendition of 'Highland Cathedral', a popular Scottish anthem. Then other band members play foot-tapping jazz as stewards stream in with silver trays, and the mood shifts from hard power to soft.

There will be precious little in the way of cocktail parties on any future ghost fleets of drone warships. And certainly no bagpipes.

47. Farewell, Captain Kyd

0900

The entire ship's company apart from those on watch is called to the hangar. Over a thousand sailors in four ranks form three sides of a neat square. One side comprises the officers, another the senior rates, and the third the junior rates. The fourth is open, but in the middle stands a dais with a wooden lectern.

Jerry Kyd enters the far end of the hangar, accompanied by Darren Houston, and is met by Chris Trevethan.

'Clear Lower Deck ready for your address, sir.'

'Thank you, Number One. Lead on.'

The three officers march to where the assembled sailors are standing at ease.

'Ship's company!' a drill petty officer shouts as Jerry Kyd approaches.

The waiting sailors stiffen in readiness for the order to come.

'Ship's company. *Ho!*'

Obeying as one, a thousand sailors now stand in respectful silence as their captain climbs to the lectern. He picks up a hand-held microphone and nods to the duty petty officer.

'Ship's company!' the PO booms. 'Stand at ease!'

The sailors relax – feet now apart and hands behind their backs.

'Thanks, everyone, for turning out now for my final Clear Lower Deck,' Kyd says. 'This is my last day, and I want to say my final goodbye to you all now before I take my leave of the *Queen Elizabeth* family.'

He pauses to clear his throat and take a deep breath.

'Guys, we're in the business of naval aviation and power projection. It's our job to get aircraft in the air to do the bidding of our government, whether that's to confront our enemies or to bring humanitarian aid to the needy. It's also our job to deliver soft power, as you've been doing so brilliantly in New York this past week. But this ship's more than a vessel to launch and recover aircraft, more than a floating embassy, more than an amphibious conference centre. It's a home to some of the finest young men and women it's been my privilege to lead over the last two and a half years.

'This afternoon I'll move on to make way for new blood, and that's good for the ship and it's good for you. New ideas. New approaches. New ways of seeing. This is how we keep our ships fresh and dynamic.'

The assembled sailors listen with rapt attention to the man who's commanded them from the beginning.

'During my time as CO, I've tried to keep a light hand on the tiller. A job made easier for me by my Heads of Department, who do so much of the heavy lifting in terms of running this incredible ship. And so do all of you. Every one of you I'm looking at right now. It doesn't matter what work you do – marine engineering, logistics, intelligence, warfare, seafaring, navigation, aviation. You're all as important as each other, and together you're more than the sum of your parts. If this ship goes into combat, and I think she will, it is teamwork which will see you through the worst of it. It is teamwork that will see you win the day.'

Rob Rouston, in the front rank of his section, nods his head vigorously in agreement. So does Scouse Walsh. So does Wes Khan.

'You've already served the country well,' Kyd continues. 'And I want you to know how grateful I am for all the hard work you have put into this ship since we came on board for the first time in Rosyth two years ago. Since then, we've steamed 32,000 miles, crossed the Atlantic for the first time, landed our first F-35, sailed through a hurricane, achieved the world's first SRVL and, together, we wowed New York.'

Kyd pauses once again to collect his thoughts and steady his emotions.

'Look to the future, guys, but never forget what your fore-bears have done. Don't lose sight of your heritage. It's what makes us who we are. And be very aware that we're back on the world stage, back to being able to protect our nation and our families in an increasingly turbulent world. The ship is already iconic and already has a place in the nation's heart, but we have to continue to earn that place. That means any-thing and everything you do must always be done with utter professionalism and total commitment. If there is anyone who cannot promise that commitment, raise your hand right now and walk off – no questions asked.'

There is a brief pause, but of course the only movement is that of sailors raising their heads a little higher and puffing out their chests a little further.

Kyd breathes in hard once again and then allows his earn-est expression to be replaced by the broadest of smiles.

'But, guys, being in the Navy is also about having a good time, so continue to enjoy New York. This will be the stuff of memories. And good luck with the rest of the deploy-ment and your long-term careers. If I was to give you one piece of advice it is this – *look after each other*. In peace and war your most precious resource, your most valuable piece of life-saving equipment and your most effective morale booster is the man or woman standing next to you, behind you and in front of you right now.'

Jerry Kyd takes a few seconds to survey his ship's company for the last time.

'Thank you for making this the most rewarding command of my career. Without all of you it would have meant nothing.'

Kyd descends from the dais and walks the length of the hangar to return to the bridge.

The ship's company is brought back to attention and dismissed. Everyone returns to their jobs, but very few are not talking about their departing captain and the fond memories they have of being under his friendly but effective command.

1600

Jerry Kyd has changed into civilian clothes. Blue blazer, blue shirt, striped tie and beige trousers. His uniforms and possessions have been packed and already sent ashore. He now waits in his day cabin for the new captain, Nick Cooke-Priest, to arrive for the official handover. In the far distance he can see the grey sea-boat carrying his successor across the Hudson. Given the sea state and direction of the currents, Kyd estimates it'll be at least half an hour before Cooke-Priest is on board, so now is the time for him to fulfil his final duty.

'Glen!' he calls down the passageway.

Within seconds his loyal steward is standing at the door.

'Glen. Come in,' Kyd says gently.

Peters, his face taut with emotion, takes one pace forward, across the threshold.

'Before the new captain arrives and I leave the ship, I just wanted to take this opportunity to thank you for all you've done for me over the last fourteen months.'

'It . . . It's been a pleasure, sir.'

'You've been my rock. And I can assure you I could not have done it without your support, your cheerfulness, your composure, your humour and your music.'

'That's . . . kind of you to say so, sir.' Peters' voice falters, but he does his best to summon a smile.

'Not at all, Glen. And I mean it. I just wanted to give you something as a thank you for all your hard work. Something that I hope you might find a use for.'

'Sir?'

'On the Rose Table.'

A cardboard box stands on the ship's only piece of bespoke furniture. Peters goes to pick it up, and his eyes widen in disbelief as he reads what's written on the side: *Beats Headphones, Wireless Bluetooth Over-Ear Phones with Pure Adaptive Noise Cancelling and Mic/Remote. Colour: Red.*

'Oh, sir . . .'

Peters tries to say something but fails. His eyes start to glisten. He was so determined to hide his emotions today but he had not reckoned on this.

Jerry Kyd puts his hand on Peters' shoulder.

'Glen – just enjoy these, and listen to some rocking reggae for me.'

'I . . . I will, sir. Thank you *so* much. But how did you know?'

'I am the captain, Glen. I make it my business to know everything.'

1645

Nick Cooke-Priest, the new CO, is ceremonially piped on board at the stern of the ship and greeted by Darren Houston. Together they walk the length of the QE to meet Jerry Kyd in what will soon be his day cabin. The two men greet each other warmly and sit down for a brief chat, during which Kyd entrusts his successor with sensitive or secret information concerning the ship. It's never possible to have two serving captains of the same ship so Jerry Kyd has only forty-five minutes before he must disembark. Peters brings in two coffees on his silver tray. And a plate of Hobnobs for old times' sake.

Eventually, it's time for the formal moment of handover – surprisingly perfunctory, given the enormity of what is being handed over.

'Nick,' Jerry Kyd says. 'You have the ship.'

'I have the ship,' Cooke-Priest replies. The two men shake hands once more, and Kyd leaves his day cabin for the last time. Accompanied by Darren Houston, he descends the companionway through the for'ard island to the flight deck. As he walks out into the icy New York air, he's startled to see the ship's company lined up in two rows, facing inwards.

'Oh my goodness!' he exclaims. 'I just wanted to go quietly, Darren.'

'Sir – nothing was going to stop them doing this for you.'

Kyd, clearly moved, strides towards the stern of the ship, through the tunnel of sailors standing to attention.

'Thanks, guys!' he says repeatedly.

On reaching the stern he turns to look at his ship's company for the final time. 'What a sight, Darren!'

'Yessir. It is.'

'That's what it's all about,' Kyd says. 'It's my privilege to have led these young people.'

The two officers descend to the transom, where the ship's launch is waiting. Ranged along the final passageway leading to the external doors are all of the Heads of Department, wanting to say their own goodbyes. First in line is Alastair Mansfield.

'Goodbye, Bish, and bless you for everything.'

Kyd proceeds down the line, shaking hands as he goes. 'Goodbye, Chris . . . Goodbye, Neil . . . Goodbye, Wings . . . Goodbye, Sam . . . Goodbye, Giles . . . Goodbye, Dave . . . Goodbye, Roly . . .'

Eventually he gets to Commander Logistics and the end of the line.

'Ah, Jenny!' Kyd smiles. 'The rose amongst thorns. Thanks for all you've achieved – especially that epic VertRep and your sterling efforts here in New York.'

'It's been fun, sir,' Curwood says.

Kyd looks up to address his Heads of Department.

'Thanks, everyone, for all your hard work. If you serve the new captain as well as you've served me, he'll be laughing kitbags.'

The smiling officers nod their appreciation.

'I've had a word with him, and of course told him you're all . . . very average.'

The HODs laugh and applaud.

'Guys – get that damn gas turbine sorted in Norfolk, have a great DT2 and a fantastic crossing back home in time for Christmas. I'll try to be there to see you coming in.'

With that Jerry Kyd descends the outer stairwell to the boarding platform. He steps on board the waiting launch then turns to face his erstwhile ship. Darren Houston, standing to attention, salutes as the launch pulls away and heads across the Hudson.

From the starboard bridge wing, Glen Peters watches the vessel carrying his former captain recede into the distance. Once it is out of sight, he heads down to his cabin. Having seen Jerry Kyd off the ship, his duty is done, and he now feels an urgent need to go ashore for some time on his own. He has some shopping to do – Christmas presents for the family. There is one thing, of course, he can cross off his list: *Beats Headphones, Wireless Bluetooth Over-Ear Phones with Pure Adaptive Noise Cancelling and Mic/Remote. Colour: Red.*

48. Man in a Pink Tutu

Naval Station Norfolk, 4 Berth, 30 October 2018

0800

'Take the strain, mate!' Rob Rouston yells to 'Dickie' Davies.

The two marine engineers have unbolted a section of ducting from the for'ard gas turbine compartment.

'Bloody hell, Rob,' the Brummie says. 'Hold hard there – it weighs a ton!'

HMS *Queen Elizabeth*, having transited overnight from New York, is back at Norfolk, Virginia. Nick Cooke-Priest cannot resume flight trials until he has all his engines working – and they need to know why the weld on its exhaust trunking failed in the first place. The test pilots and the two F-35s must remain at Pax River in the meantime.

The marine engineers dismantle the stainless-steel ducts and carry them to the ship's workshops two decks below. Manoeuvring them down the steep companionways is the stuff of comedy for all those watching, if not for the hapless removal men.

After much cursing and many cuts and bruises, several substantial lengths of exhaust cowling are laid out on the workshop floor.

Sweat is pouring down Rouston's face and into his black, bushy beard. 'Well, that was a work-out and a half . . .'

*

Jenny Curwood is looking with dismay at one of the advent calendars she's bought for her kids in New York. Commander Logistics has managed to consume the chocolate behind every door, from 1 December to 24 December, in three days flat.

There's a knock at her office door and she invites Glen Peters to take a seat. There's a moment's silence.

'I just wanted to make sure you're OK, Glen. I know how very sad you were to see Captain Kyd go.'

'Yes, ma'am. I served him a long time. But I'll be fine. In fact, I think I'll enjoy the change when I get used to it.'

'The wardroom know they're lucky to have you. We have a lot of baby stewards down here, and they need guidance.'

They spend some time discussing the procedural challenges before Peters rises to leave.

Commander Logistics rises too. 'I would offer you a chocolate, Glen. But I seem to have run out . . .'

A group of welders from BAE America are waiting on the jetty in overalls and hard hats for Rob Rouston. A middle-aged black man with a cheerful expression and a deep Southern drawl introduces himself and his companions. 'I'm Louis. Louis Parrot. And this is Sully and Clint.'

Ten minutes later, Louis Parrot leans in close to the split trunking with a torch and a magnifying glass, with the careful deliberation of a latter-day Sherlock Holmes. 'It's the wrong weld for the steel.' He looks up. 'It's all down to chromium content.'

One of the ducts is sent for analysis at a nearby laboratory. Two hours later, word comes back that the steel is 316 grade. Meanwhile, Rouston guides three more American technicians – Rich, Frankie and Calvin – to the gas turbine compartment, where they examine the scorched insulation around the funnel.

'We'll have it done by tomorrow,' Calvin says confidently. 'Us three've worked together for a while. Some forty years – nigh on.'

'Wow!' Rouston says. 'They've sent the A Team!'

31 October 2018

0830

'Oh my good God!' Rob Rouston shrieks.

Clint's red, white and blue wig is doing its best to escape from under his hard hat. A huge Stars and Stripes is draped over his shoulders, and a bright, salmon-pink tutu completes the ensemble.

The American punches the air. 'Halloween time, brother!'

Over the next eight hours Louis Parrot and his resplendent sidekick weld the split ducting and reinforce that which has not yet split. The only slight confusion arises over the measurements; the Royal Navy works in metric, whereas the US remains defiantly imperial. Centimetres versus inches. Conversion is comparatively straightforward, but it does spark some friendly ribbing of the Brits.

'Dude, you know what they say? There are two kinds of countries . . .' The welder adjusts his tutu. 'Those that are metric . . . and those that put a man on the moon.'

The Yorkshireman laughs. 'Fair one, shipmate. Can't argue with that!'

Eight hours later, welding and stitching complete, the engineers carry the heavy trunking back to the for'ard gas turbine compartment. Squeezing into the dark space at the junction where the mighty engine meets the funnel, the four sailors start to reassemble the system.

The next three hours are spent lining up the bolt holes and ensuring the trunking is perfectly aligned. To sustain them, they rig up an iPod with portable speakers and sing along to a range of favourites, starting with 'Ain't No Mountain High Enough' by Marvin Gaye and Tammi Terrell, and Tina Turner's 'We Don't Need Another Hero'.

'Got any Bon Jovi?' Davies asks after the first hour.

'No,' Fyans says. 'How about ABBA or Seal?'

The sound of metal scraping against metal, the occasional blow of a rubber mallet and the intermittent expletive adds extra percussion to the sailors' raucous accompaniment to 'Voulez-Vous', 'Super Trouper' and 'The Winner Takes it All'.

2000

The marine engineers exit the gas turbine compartment and lock the heavy steel door behind them.

'Right, lads,' Rob Rouston says nervously. 'Moment of truth.'

Mikey Fyans starts up the dormant Jumbo Jet engine. It responds immediately, and the internal blades start to spin. A low hum soon escalates to a thunderous roar. Will the ducting hold? Will the superhot exhaust gases be contained?

They monitor the read-outs from its many internal sensors, but mostly just listen. A sudden reduction in volume or pitch would indicate that the exhaust was still escaping and raising the ambient temperature in the engine compartment above 80 °C – the point at which it would automatically trip. They gingerly increase the revs to full power, and the turbine adopts a high-pitched scream. They wait with wide, unblinking eyes and crossed fingers.

It settles back into a satisfied purr. The welds are holding. The temperature remains well within the safety envelope.

The marine engineers save the day yet again. With a little help from a man in a pink tutu.

49. Pushing the Envelope

West Atlantic, 1 November 2018

'Three-quarter power on both levers,' Sam Stephens shouts.

'Three-quarters on both levers,' the helmsman repeats as he accelerates the ship through the water.

The Navigator raises his binoculars to view the course ahead. Visibility is good, and the sea, whilst boisterous, is clear of shipping.

'Twenty-three knots, sir. On a bearing south-south-west.'

'Very good. Go to full power on both levers.'

'Full power. Both levers, sir.'

Now with four main diesels and both gas turbines on line, HMS *Queen Elizabeth* is back on the open sea once more and well able to make the wind across the deck which the pilots need to launch with bombs for the first time.

'Wouldn't like to be on the receiving end of one of those bastards!' Scouse Walsh says.

'It would certainly spoil your day,' Emma Ranson agrees.

The two Liverpudlian aircraft handlers are watching an ITF air weapons party push trolleys laden with laser-guided precision bombs on to the flight deck. The 500 lb GBU-12 Paveway IIs will be attached to the pylons underneath each of the F-35 wings. As before, they are 'inert', the explosive payload replaced with concrete, but the pilots are interested in their impact on the aerodynamics of the aircraft rather than their capacity to blow things up.

There are eleven weapon stations on an F-35: three on each wing and five within the weapon bays. If the aircraft is flying in stealth mode to infiltrate enemy air space, it will not attach weapons externally, as that would enhance its radar signature. In stealth mode it can carry up to 5,700 lbs of internal ordnance or 'stores'. Once air dominance is secured, it will fly in 'beast' mode, with 22,000 lbs of external weaponry attached – an extraordinary payload made more so by the centrifugal forces involved. A 2,000 lb bomb on a seven-G turn will, in relative terms, increase to 14,000 lbs and exert extreme stresses on the wings.

The test pilots must now test the Lightning on short take-off launches with a range of weapon loads and weight distributions, including asymmetric loading that will unbalance the aircraft.

A fully fuelled F-35B weighs in at 47,000 lbs (with a maximum take-off weight, when laden with weapons, of 60,000 lbs). In comparison, the loaded weight of Edwin Dunning's Sopwith Pup was just over 1,000 lbs. So the potential impact and subsequent consequences of a modern fighter jet impacting on a flight deck at speed would be catastrophic in the extreme.

To launch with bombs will present the pilots with a whole new set of challenges as their loads get heavier and increasingly unbalanced in the suboptimal conditions they are looking for. Right now, the higher the winds, the lower the cloud base and the heavier the sea state, the better.

The two F-35s from Pax River have re-embarked, and all four test pilots are back on board. Gray, Wilson, Edgell and

Lippert are eager to capitalize on Hurricane Michael's boost to their testing programme. The monster storm put them way ahead of the curve, and it's an advantage they don't want to lose.

James Blackmore is particularly gratified to be back in the game, as this is his last chance to extend the test envelope. His job as Commander Air is to make sure that the ship, complete with aircraft, can be delivered for operational duties in 2021. He needs to get himself and his team back into battle rhythm and ensure that they complete the mission entrusted to them.

Famously committed and driven as both pilot and commander, Blackmore's diagnosis of testicular cancer only weeks before deployment seems to have further sharpened his resolve to succeed. Although early surgery cleared the problem, it was a wake-up call and has given him fresh vitality and verve.

Latch Lippert lines up his growling F-35 on 4 Spot. He's carrying four Paveways, two under each wing.

'Launch the jet!' The familiar order from Blackmore in Flyco.

Lippert unleashes his aircraft, and, leaping from the ski-jump, it hurls itself skyward.

Below deck, a world away from the thrills and spills of cutting-edge aviation, life is taking its habitual course. But that doesn't mean it's following the preferred script. A loud knocking has been reported from under the hull, and it's getting worse by the minute.

'What the hell's going on now?' Neil McCallum says. 'Not another bloody lobster pot . . .'

'Not a lot of those in this part of the Atlantic, sir.' The

marine engineer is checking the computer screens and sensor printouts. 'Could be a whale strike, though. There've been several pods sighted over the last few days.'

Commander Marine Engineering considers the evidence. There's unmistakable banging on the port side about a third of the way down from the stern – a violent but rhythmic sound that increases with speed, meaning there has to be something loose or something attached to the hull. Apart from the desire not to disturb those in adjacent compartments, there is always a vital strategic need to limit the carrier's sound signature. Enemy shipping and submarines will always be listening for the QE's approach. She might not be currently at war, but that's no reason not to maintain tactical silence, or at least to limit her sound output as much as possible. If she cannot do it now while working up, she might not be able to do it when fully operational.

McCallum scrutinizes a computer-generated graphic of the hull. 'The only thing out there that interrupts the main sweep of the hull is an inlet grating where we suck in sea water for the cooling system.'

'Something may have got caught in that, sir?'

'Unlikely,' McCallum says. 'It's flush with the hull, and there's nothing to hook on to.'

'Worth taking a look, sir?'

'Hmmm . . . maybe . . .' McCallum is deep in thought. The knocking sound is not slowing the ship but seems to kick in at 15 knots and then get louder with speed. They still need to make at least 25 knots for flying, so either they just live with the noise or try and do something about it. It might go of its own accord, but there's a risk that anything loose could come away and hit the propellers.

'Yes,' McCallum says decisively. 'Let's get the clearance

divers down there as soon as we can after the F-35 bombing runs are complete. We need to eyeball this ASAP.'

It is a big call for Commander Marine Engineering, because stopping the ship dead in the water for a major diving evolution means effectively taking it offline – like a Formula 1 car going into the pits for inspection mid-race. It's going to take valuable time, during which all flying will have to stop once again.

'Coming round for third circuit,' Lippert says. 'Will level off at 1,000 feet to drop stores.'

The F-35, its orange afterburner scorching the pale-blue sky, roars out of a tight turn to assume a straight path about a mile off the port beam. Everybody on the flight deck and in Flyco watches in anticipation as Lippert prepares to launch his weapons.

'Above bomb range,' Lippert confirms. 'Dropping stores in five, four, three, two, one . . .'

The Paveways leave the wings in perfect trajectories and hurtle downwards. One after another they impact the water with a sharp white explosion before sinking to the ocean floor.

'Bloody brilliant,' Scouse Walsh says. 'Now we're cooking on gas!'

Well, maybe that's the case above deck . . .

2030

Six broad-shouldered sailors are stripping off in the diving locker room. All of them are powerfully built, and most of them are liberally tattooed on backs, chests and arms. Their triceps and latissimus dorsi muscles are particularly well developed – a sure sign of strong swimmers.

As they squeeze into their wetsuits, others check their air tanks, masks and fins.

'OK, lads,' Lieutenant Commander Pete Davies says. 'It's quite blowy out there, and the sea state's increasing, so it's not going to be a walk in the park.'

The divers smile knowingly at each other.

'There's a mystery knocking somewhere in this area ...' The head of the diving unit points to a diagram of the QE's hull.

'It's your job to find out what the hell it is.'

'No clues at all, sir?' one diver asks as he zips up his wetsuit.

'No. Could be something to do with this water-inlet valve.' Davies points again to the diagram. 'It's for coolant purposes, but the grating should be solid as a rock. So no real intel on this, guys.'

'Sea monster?' Another diver grins as he picks up his tanks.

'Could be,' Davies says. 'Better take your penknife, just in case.'

'Ha! Will do, sir.'

'OK, lads. Dive at 2100, as soon as we've dropped anchor.'

2100

The team of divers heads away from the aft transom. Their RIB is buffeted by the heaving ocean as the Coxswain manoeuvres them into position.

One by one, the divers submerge. The currents are unforgiving, but the beams from their head-torches probe the darkness like lightsabres. They scour the barnacled surface slowly and meticulously, looking for signs of damage. At first all seems normal, then they locate the external grating.

405

It should be firmly fixed by dozens of securing bolts, but one tug and part of it comes away. A diver reaches inside and pulls out a large wooden wedge. Scarred, barnacled and green with algae, the initials RWS have been carefully carved into it.

2145

'What the hell is that!' Pete Davies says.

'Buggered if I know,' the first of his returning divers replies. 'Looks like a bit of oak from an old sailing ship.'

'A prop from *Pirates of the Caribbean?*' Davies suggests.

'Well, whatever it is, that's what we found on the other side of the grating. But it can't be part of the build, can it?'

'I reckon that is precisely what it was,' Neil McCallum says. 'It's a shipbuilder's wedge. To hold the grating whilst they were bolting it in. They clearly forgot to retrieve it, so it's been helping to hold the grating in place ever since.'

'Bloody hell,' Davies says. 'It must have been there for years.'

'Probably since about 2010 or '11, before the ship was floated. So, seven or eight years.'

The timber wedge, bearing a shipbuilder's initials, has steadfastly continued to serve its temporary purpose throughout power and propulsion trials in the North Sea, the transatlantic crossing, the F-35 trials, the transit through Hurricane Michael and the historic visit to New York. It is strangely appropriate that it's finally surrendered now, as the QE comes to the end of her first deployment, and is on the brink of operational readiness.

Now given a place of honour in the diving compartment, it is labelled: *Treasure from the Deep 1/11/18.*

50. The Dragon Bites Back

West Atlantic, 10 November 2018

Glen Peters is back to something like his old self. He misses being the captain's steward, but he's quickly adapted to his new role. As a team leader looking after the HODs in the wardroom there are fewer fringe benefits, but he has more responsibility and better opportunities for promotion. Right now, though, like everyone else on board, he's counting the days.

'Three weeks to go, sir!' he says cheerfully to Chris Trevethan on the stairwell.

'I can hardly believe it.' The First Lieutenant rubs his hands together. 'We seem to have been on board for ever. Who'll be there to meet you?'

'My wife, sir. And my son.'

'Excellent,' Trevethan says. 'Lots to look forward to. All routine now. Excitement over . . .'

One thousand feet above them, Nathan Gray is circling to burn off fuel before he lands. It's his fiftieth and final flight of the Developmental Testing Programme and, like his fellow pilots, he's pushed the comfort envelope ever further. Today he's been flying asymmetrically, with more weight on his starboard wing. All has gone well.

Below him, the ship rolls gently in a heavy sea, gleaming from a combination of spray and rain. The evening sun has tried its best to punch through the thickening clouds but is close to giving up the fight. The visibility might be deteriorating, but as ever the F-35 can see through the gloom with its penetrating sensors. Gray has all the information he needs on his visor display – altitude, speed, rate of descent, fuel, outside temperature and cockpit temperature. He also has his magical X-ray vision, which lets him see through the body of the aircraft.

This is by far the smartest machine he's ever flown, and he's established a close, even fond relationship with it. He was comparing the old Harrier to the F-35 with James Blackmore and the others last night at dinner. 'As we all know,' he said, 'the Harrier was a beast that wanted to kill you. The F-35 wants to wrap you up in cotton wool and sing you lullabies.'

Gray has become increasingly proud of what he and his colleagues have achieved in the last six weeks. They have executed over 200 launches, proved the concept of a Shipbourne Rolling Vertical Landing twenty times and dropped nearly 100 inert bombs. More importantly, they have established the safe operational envelope of the aircraft for the combat pilots to come. They have pushed the F-35B to its limits in varying wind conditions and states of asymmetry. In the latter stages they have moved ever closer to the cliff edges and dragons they know to be always lurking.

Today's flight, though comparatively routine, is particularly significant for Gray. It's the last of his naval career. The weight of his own contribution to the resurrection of fixed-wing flying in the Fleet Air Arm has encouraged him to call it a day. It's time to reinvent himself as a civilian test pilot. It will be a wrench to leave the Senior Service that has moulded him over the last fifteen years but he knows that if he

remained he would end up flying a desk. And real flying, specifically test flying, is all he wants to do.

He looks down through the scudding clouds at the sea far
below – a view that has become so familiar to him over the
years – and resists the urge to reminisce. He still has a job to
do, and it won't be until he's safely secured, engine powered
down, that his final flight will have been completed. There'll
be time enough to dig into the memory bank and relive former glories. And with no more flying to come on this
deployment, he'll be able to have a drink at the bar tonight.
A proper drink.

Gray focuses on his final approach. Descending slowly in a
broad sweeping curve towards the flight deck, he notices the
sea state has increased further – probably to about four or five.
The white-tops are breaking with increasing vigour, but he is
reassured to see the QE ploughing through them with her
usual composure. *Solid as a rock*, he thinks to himself.

He is at around 800 feet when the ship is momentarily hidden from view by low cloud. It's nothing to worry about, so
he prepares to activate the air-intakes in readiness for a vertical landing – today it is to be on 1 Spot, right at the bow.

Whoosh . . .

'Jesus!' Gray starts. Without warning the ambient noise in
the cockpit – normally a low hum – has increased to a deafening roar.

'What the bloody hell . . . ?'

His visor has gone blank. So too has the panel in front of
him. He has lost all cockpit electrics and all onscreen data.

'Come in, Flyco. Come in, Flyco . . .'

There's no reply from the ship.

The radio is down. He thinks fast and logically. He can't
hear them, but maybe they can still hear him.

'Cockpit electrical systems down. I have radio silence . . .
Repeat, cockpit electrical systems down . . .'

Gray stays calm. Panic will kill him. There will be a logical
explanation for what's happened, but he has to work it out
for himself.

His first thought is that a fuse has tripped. That would
account for the loss of the visor display and the dead screens.
It would also account for the sudden increase in sound level.
The Active Noise Reduction Facility would have been
knocked out.

Gray splutters as his oxygen supply seizes then kicks back
in almost immediately. The back-up system has detected a
problem and triggered the emergency supply. At least some
of the reversionary systems are operational. The F-35 is
doing its best to help him, Gray reassures himself, but there's
no doubt he's facing a real emergency. Are the dragons making one final attempt to unseat him?

The air-conditioning supply has also cut off. The cockpit
temperature has soared, and with it the humidity. Condensation is misting up the canopy. Gray holds the aircraft steady
while still approaching the ship and processing the facts and
assessing the problems as best and as fast as he can.

I haven't done anything to damage the aeroplane, he reasons. *So I
should still be on the same course, the same headings, speed and rate of
descent . . .*

*If there was a major flaw or life-threatening defect, the aircraft would
already have made the decision to auto-eject me. It has not done so,
which means the jet still has its intelligence and integrity . . .*

Once again, he feels a wave of optimism. The F-35 may
not be singing him lullabies, but the aircraft is still on his side.

With a major electrical malfunction and no communications, Gray faces the prospect of a manual landing. He must

be super-reactive to any eventuality. Locking his mind into the moment, he does his best to peer through the misted canopy but all he can see is cloud. *What the hell must they be thinking on the ship?* he wonders. *If they don't know I have a problem, they'll think I'm flying like a prat . . .*

He emerges from the cloud. 'Mum in sight . . .' He breathes a sigh of relief, although he's surprised how quickly he's coming up on her. This will need a very gentle touch, so, activating the air-intake vents, he prepares for a manual vertical landing. His mind flashes back to the old Fairey Swordfish at Yeovilton. He pictures Glenn Allison bringing the Stringbag in to land with such dexterity. Allison was at one with the airframe. Man and machine in harmony. That's what Gray has to achieve now.

The trouble is, he's not certain of his fuel state. Is he still too heavy to land safely? He's sitting in a flying bomb and knows that if he gets the next few seconds wrong he could do a great deal of damage to both aircraft and ship. He reminds himself that, if too heavy, the aircraft will work out for itself that it can't support its own weight in the hover, so would automatically fly through.

Given that he has no electrics, no navigation or night vision, he knows he would never be able to find the ship again in the dark. He'd have to fly into the night until he ran out of fuel and then ditch in the sea. Suddenly the routine outing has become a matter of life and death. His life. His death.

The important thing now is to keep level, trim and stable in the hover as he picks his landing spot. The original plan was to land on 1 Spot with the prevailing wind coming in at 20 degrees from the port side to gain another test point. Gray has abandoned that idea and now opts for 3 Spot, as near to Flyco as possible. If they can't hear him, he wants them to be able to see him and any hand signals he might make.

He manages to coax the aircraft into a stationary hover next to the ship. The air-intake behind him is screaming louder than ever, and the engine sounds like it's about to explode. But the vibrations through his body suggest it's working normally. Through the misted canopy he can see the handlers running to get clear as they realize his recovery plans have changed.

'Here goes,' he says to himself.

Then suddenly, to his astonishment, he hears the beeps and squeaks of the on-board computers as they go into reboot mode. His panel screen and visor light up like a Christmas tree as a multitude of icons start winking at him, indicating caution. The various systems come back online, and the cautionary warnings morph into confirmatory data streams. Gray scans through the reinvigorated displays to make sure there's nothing that would stop him landing safely. Everything looks good. The air-conditioning regenerates, the temperature and humidity are instantly reduced, and the canopy condensation begins to clear. After an intense thirty seconds, Gray lets out another sigh of relief. That's all it's been. Half a minute of lost cockpit electrics. But it felt like a lifetime.

He lands with a bigger jolt than normal because he decides to stay in manual mode rather than depend on the automatic functions. They'll need to be properly checked by the technicians before the jet flies again. It'll have to be quarantined until all the data is analysed.

It's only when he's safely on deck that he's able to reset his radio and talk to Flyco. 'That was one crazy ride!' he says.

'What happened, Nath?' James Blackmore asks from the Papal Throne.

'I lost electrics in the cockpit. Screen and head-up display went blank. Kaput!'

'We knew you had issues!'

'Just a bit!'

'Especially when you went to 3 Spot instead of 1 Spot.'

'Yes – I saw the lads running out of the way!'

'We were talking to you all the way in – trying to advise. You couldn't hear us?'

'Not a bloody word!'

'We didn't know that. We assumed you were just too busy to talk.'

'Yeah, wrestling a pesky dragon on my last flight!'

As Gray taxis to his parking position under the for'ard island, powers down and waits for the ITF handlers to chain the aircraft to the deck, it occurs to him that the old Harrier, the Widow Maker, would not have been as forgiving. Might even have helped the dragon bring him down.

Gray takes a deep breath, taps the side of the canopy in silent gratitude to the aircraft and climbs out. He shakes hands with his ground crew and heads across the flight deck. Before opening the steel door to re-enter the ship he turns. The F-35 is silhouetted against a bright November sun on the verge of setting but now burning successfully through the clouds after all. The golden rays refracting through the glass canopy of the cockpit flare dramatically against the ever brighter, bluer sky, lending a soft beauty to the harsh outline of the world's most lethal warplane.

Gray nods in appreciation of the moment.

'Cheers, Jak,' he murmurs under his breath.

51. Man in the Mirror

West Atlantic, 11 November 2018

1045

A thousand sailors flood out on deck and, standing four deep, form three sides of a vast square. In the middle of the fourth, a lectern has been mounted on a dais. The ship's company stand at ease whilst they await the arrival of the officers and the Chaplain.

Alastair Mansfield is down on 2 Deck with an unusually subdued Wes Khan.

'I'm sorry, Bish,' the leading chef says, 'but when I woke this morning I was certain I should not read today.'

The Chaplain puts a reassuring hand on his friend's shoulder. 'That's OK, Wes. Really. I knew you had misgivings. And the decision could only be yours.'

The two shake hands warmly and go their separate ways.

Wes Khan has been agonizing about the Remembrance Service for weeks. He liked the idea of building bridges between religions but did not wish to inadvertently insult fellow Muslims, even from afar. When he visited Ground Zero his determination to read today was reinforced, but he's also painfully aware of the sensitivities of his own family, some of whom remain troubled by his presence in the Royal Navy. It's a difficult time to be a Muslim. Especially a Muslim in the armed forces.

'I told the Bish I wasn't going to do it, Rammi,' he tells his devout Christian friend Ramesh Rai. 'The reading wasn't really a prayer, but it sounded a bit like one. I was caught between two places.'

'I know it's been a struggle for you.'

Khan nods. 'People have come to think *jihad* means war, but it really means struggle. Doing the right thing. That is the true meaning of *jihad*.'

Alastair Mansfield mounts the dais. 'Let us give thanks to those who've served in the armed forces for the Crown,' he begins. 'And in particular those who made the ultimate sacrifice on our behalf.'

With the F-35s on deck behind them, he begins by extolling the nobility, heroism and selflessness of the warrior classes.

'My friends, at the end of the First World War, exactly 100 years ago, up to 19 million had been killed on both sides, and 23 million wounded. It was the deadliest conflict in the history of mankind. And we are here, you are here, to help prevent anything like that ever happening again. But let's not kid ourselves, war is what we do. Humans are the cruellest of species, and we seem to have the seeds of our own destruction firmly planted in our DNA.'

The four-deep square of sailors listen intently as the Chaplain's voice, booming over the loudspeakers, cuts through the wind now filling the huge White Ensign on the aft flagstaff.

'Robert Burns, the great Scottish poet, talked of man's inhumanity to man,' Mansfield continues. 'The inclination for war resides in our most basic instincts. Mine too, and they call me a man of God.'

He pauses.

'I recently came close to beating someone up in a public urinal . . .'

The jaws of the assembled congregation drop in astonishment.

'I was in the restroom at the Museum of Modern Art in New York, concentrating as one does on the job in hand, and feeling secure in my own space. Until I became aware of a man to my left who'd moved closer than was comfortable. I turned my head slightly. He did too. I felt my hackles rise. My blood began to boil. There was no charity in my heart – just animus, basic aggression . . .'

A thousand pairs of eyes widen.

'Then I realized who this wretched man was.'

He pauses once more.

'I was about to thump my own reflection in the mirror beside me.'

The sailors continue to be captivated.

'Five thousand years ago, we were hunters,' Mansfield continues. 'Since 12,500 BC, there have been around thirteen years of war for every year of peace. There have been 8,000 treaties in that time, but on average they've only lasted for two years. The fact is, we are very good at war, and very bad at peace.'

Mansfield surveys his congregation.

'But there is hope. And you young people are the embodiment of that hope. Because, through your professionalism and dedication to duty you have the ability to deter hostility. That is why this great ship is here and why those aircraft are there. HMS *Queen Elizabeth* will soon be Great Britain's main conventional strategic deterrent.

'Never lose sight of that. Never lose sight of the fact that even as military people you have the ability to love as well as to hate. Therein lies our salvation. War is always painful but it is not your core business. Peace is. Consider yourself peace-mongers, not war-mongers. If fighting is inevitable, give of your best. But remain magnanimous in victory.'

The band strikes up with the naval hymn, 'Eternal Father', and everyone sings with gusto as the new captain, Nick Cooke-Priest, lays a wreath under the White Ensign.

At its conclusion, the last post is sounded, and Alastair Mansfield reads from Laurence Binyon's 'For the Fallen', written at the beginning of the First World War.

> They shall grow not old, as we that are left grow old:
> Age shall not weary them, nor the years condemn.
> At the going down of the sun and in the morning
> We will remember them.

After the service, Nathan Gray approaches Alastair Mansfield with hand outstretched.

'Great service, Bish! It made me think of my two grandads and their service in the Great War.'

'Thanks, Nathan.'

Gray turns towards the F-35s. 'I hope to God those things are never used in anger. But I think that may be a hope too far.'

'I fear you might be right, Nathan. But I pray with all my heart that you are wrong.'

52. End of an Era

0900

Latch Lippert and Wizzer Wilson are about to take the jets home to Pax River. Nathan Gray and Andy Edgell will be dropped off in Naval Station Norfolk later today. Before they leave, the four test pilots are joined by Commander Air in Flyco.

'Well done, guys!' James Blackmore says. 'It's been epic.'

'Certainly has,' Edgell replies. 'Right now, I don't want to see an F-35 ever again, but I know after two days at home I'll be itching to strap myself back into an ejection seat!'

Blackmore laughs. 'I'll give it twenty-four hours before you feel the itch!'

The pilots, physically and emotionally exhausted after four weeks of intense round-the-clock flying, are ready to go home. But, as Andy Edgell has intimated, none of them will be putting their legs up for long. All are self-confessed adrenaline junkies.

Edgell will go home to his wife Janet, and he knows the pent-up emotions will come out as tears as soon as he sees her. Janet Edgell knows full well that her husband wears his heart on his sleeve, so she'll be expecting some post-deployment blues. Edgell has cancelled his life for two years for the F-35 test programme and dedicated himself day and night to ensuring its success. That's why he knows there'll be an emotional price to pay when he wakes up tomorrow or the next day with no F-35 waiting for him to launch.

Wizzer Wilson is more phlegmatic, but he also just wants to see his family before embarking on his next flying adventure.

'I reckon I need more than a couple of days with my slippers on,' he grins. 'Maybe a couple of weeks of being pampered by the wife and kids. But then I'll need to get back on the horse for sure. That SRVL was so exciting, but I need another challenge.'

Wilson is already considering his options, but keeping them close to his chest. He may stay with BAE as a test pilot, although he is considering an offer from a company in California pioneering futuristic drone-taxis as a means of public transportation. It sounds attractive to the ex-RAF and Royal Navy pilot who still has a taste for pushing aviation boundaries.

'Well, guys,' says Lippert, the US Marine Corps pilot, 'all I know is this has been a blast and a privilege, but for me the only priority is to get home to see Amanda and little Adam. The last time I saw him was on the quarterdeck at his christening. I need to get home and reintroduce myself to the little fella.'

The insouciant Michael 'Latch' Lippert is probably the most laidback of the foursome. He is a pilot through and through, and nobody is in any doubt that he's destined for great things. Privately, he harbours ambitions to be an astronaut. He'll face opposition from the US Navy, who will want him to remain a test pilot and instructor, but for Lippert the sky is not the limit.

'Gentlemen, it's been an honour,' Nathan Gray says. 'We

came, we flew, we conquered. And we kept those dragons at bay.'

'Except that one at the end, Nath,' Lippert says. 'He came real close!'

'No way, mate. I had his measure all the way in!'

Gray, like Andy Edgell, knows that it will be difficult to go cold turkey. He's hoping his new career as a civilian test pilot will keep the adrenaline flowing. It's only when he's outside his comfort zone that he feels comfortable.

The F-35's extraordinary journey must now continue without him. There's an immense amount of work still to do before a combat squadron can fly off the ship, but he has no doubt that the magic is working. And he has a special memory that no one will ever be able to take away from him – being the first pilot to land a fixed-wing fighter jet on to the flight deck of Britain's biggest warship. It was his Neil Armstrong moment. One small step for man, but a giant step for HMS *Queen Elizabeth*. Or, to put it another way, more in keeping with his naval heritage, it was his Edwin Dunning moment.

Latch Lippert and Wizzer Wilson head out to the F-35s, say their emotional goodbyes to their flight teams and launch for the last time. They circle the ship side by side before descending for a final flypast, low and at speed, to salute those waving on deck. Then they head for the western horizon. As the roar of their engines fades, they quickly become two fast-moving specks. Then, in a blink, they've gone.

The ITF flight teams in their distinctive green T-shirts and blue helmets stand as if in a trance as they continue to watch the empty sky. The Royal Navy aircraft handlers in their yellow tunics and helmets do the same – hardly able to believe the aircraft are not coming back.

Suddenly everyone breaks into spontaneous applause and starts to shake hands and slap each other on the back. Americans and Brits have become closely bonded during the last four weeks, helping to prove the F-35B as a maritime fighter.

1400

HMS *Queen Elizabeth* heads into Naval Station Norfolk for the third and final time on this deployment. Her two attentive tugboats, the *Tracy Morgan* and the *Fort Bragg*, are as tireless as terriers, but the team on the bridge, led by Sam Stephens, want only reversionary help – a nudge here and a nudge there as they berth on Pier 11. It remains a matter of professional pride for the British navigators to bring their outsized vessel to the wall under her own steam. Dozens of American warships are moored alongside, and the punctilious Sam Stephens, under the watchful eye of Nick Cooke-Priest, has no intention of providing amusement for their local audience.

'Reverse 50 revs on port lever!' he tells the quartermaster at the wheel.

'Reverse 50, port lever, sir.'

'Steady . . . steady . . . Forward 20, both levers.'

'Forward 20, both levers.'

The QE inches in towards the quayside and comes to rest against the protecting rubber stanchions that line the wall. Perfect parking.

Half an hour later, it's time for the ITF to disembark. Robert 'Turbo' Salerno IV will miss HMS *Queen Elizabeth* and the ship's company enormously. He's developed a taste for British culture, humour and food – especially cheesy hammy eggies, toad-in-the-hole and shepherd's pie. Intimidated at first by the array of British accents on board, Turbo is now fully tuned in, though Geordie still defeats him if spoken at warp speed. He prides himself, too, that he has become almost fluent in Jackspeak.

He embraces the ebullient Scouse Walsh. 'Cheerio, shippers!'

'See ya, Turbo! Ta fer all you've done, la'. Any time you come to Liverpool . . .'

'You bet, Scouse.'

The American hoists a massive black hold-all over his shoulder and joins the queue for the gangway.

Andy Edgell and Nathan Gray's departure is as low-key as their arrival had been high. Carrying their cases to the top of the aft gangway, each pauses to salute before stepping off the ship.

Their work here is done.

53. Arctic Diversion

Mid Atlantic, 7 December 2018

1330

HMS *Queen Elizabeth* left Norfolk base a week ago. Now the canteen shutters rise to reveal 1,200 vibrantly festive dinners. Senior officers with sprigs of plastic holly pinned to their peaked caps start to load food on to plates. In keeping with naval tradition, the Heads of Department and even the captain have helped peel potatoes and parsnips, wash and pare sprouts, carrots and turnips, and now set about serving their Christmas feast to the ship's company.

1600

Everybody congregates in the hangar for the carol service led by Alastair Mansfield and the Royal Marines Band. 'Hark the Herald Angels Sing', 'O Come, All Ye Faithful' and 'Silent Night' are interspersed with Bible readings, culminating in one by the Chaplain himself.

'And in the sixth month, the Angel Gabriel was sent from God unto a city of Galilee, named Nazareth . . .'

Mansfield looks over his shoulder, as if waiting for something to happen. Nothing does. He repeats the words, only louder. From the upper balcony, Roly Brading, unable to hear his cue first time round over the roar of the air-conditioning, hurls himself into mid-air, grabs hold of a rope and slides to the ground as he would from a Merlin into a warzone. Today, however, Lieutenant Colonel Brading, though helmeted and booted, is not in full 'fighting order'. Instead, he boasts a voluminous white robe with matching fluffy wings and a silver tinsel halo. He's also attached two golden baubles to the camouflage netting on his helmet.

Brading's combat boots hit the deck with an almighty crunch. He runs centre stage, executes a perfect commando roll, and adopts the pose of an angel in prayer.

The Chaplain waits for the applause to die down before continuing.

'And the angel came in unto Mary, and said, Hail, thou that art highly favoured, the Lord is with thee: blessed art thou among women . . .'

At the conclusion of the service, Alastair introduces the ukulele band. Although nervous, after nearly five months of daily practice, they do not disappoint. A rousing rendition of 'Hotel California' is followed by 'Mister Blue Sky', 'Daydream Believer' and 'Eye of the Tiger'.

The main purpose of the deployment has been to test the F-35B, but also to forge the ship's company into an effective fighting force. In team-building terms, the formation of this band has been every bit as important as the myriad other communal activities on board. And right now they are spreading the love with some lightning-fast strumming. Everybody's up on their feet, clapping and dancing. Lead singer Matt Hicks watches his band with pride and affection. Most of them had never picked up an instrument before they'd set sail.

Roly Brading didn't need much persuading to don the Gabriel kit. Marines are up for any challenge, especially if it involves dressing up. He's now fully in the swing. So much so that the golden baubles fall from his helmet and bounce along the hangar deck, where they are deftly retrieved by Jenny Curwood.

'Do you want me to hang on to your balls whilst you dance, colonel?' she asks in all innocence.

'Goodness gracious, Commander L...' The Royal Marine's eyes widen. 'That's certainly the best offer I've had on this deployment!'

He treats her to a nifty pirouette and dances away with a chuckle. Jenny Curwood, reddening in realization of her unintended double entendre, places the baubles surreptitiously on the lectern and swiftly retreats.

As the festivities draw to a close, everybody either resumes duty or heads for their mess decks. Then the mood is shattered. Crowds gather around the main noticeboards.

Signal from the Admiralty – Immediate Diversion to the Arctic

'Oh Jesus,' Rob Rouston mutters between clenched teeth. 'Tell me it's not true.'

British aircraft carrier HMS *Queen Elizabeth* is being diverted to the Arctic with immediate effect to support a secret multinational air transport mission. Cold and foul weather rig will be issued . . .

He reads on with growing dismay until he reaches the final paragraph.

HMS *Queen Elizabeth* will be loaded with emergency provisions . . . these will include large amounts of hay, brandy and small biscuits . . . The RAF has offered to escort a bright-red aircraft to its intended destinations, though it is thought to be completely elf-sufficient . . .

'Friggin' comedians!'
A mightily relieved Rob Rouston can breathe again.

54. The Future is Not What it Used to Be

The Solent, 10 December 2018

1230

The silhouette of Spinnaker Tower beckons. The ship's company is flooding out on to the flight deck to take position for the grand return to their home port. The final Procedure Alpha of the deployment. The Royal Marines Band sets the marching beat with 'A Life on the Ocean Wave'.

'Heads up, chests out, be proud!' The drill instructors stride down the flight deck.

No one needs any urging. Not with Portsmouth dead ahead. The sight of England fills everyone's hearts. It might be a cold December day, with a bitter wind and stinging showers blowing from the east, but that's not damping anyone's spirits. In fact, the seasonal English weather adds to everybody's sense of homecoming.

Neither has the cold and the wet stopped the crowds from turning out. Thousands of people, spread along Eastney Esplanade, Southsea Common and all the way down the coast to the old harbour, have been gathering since early this morning. Their cheers, whoops and whistles are growing in volume as the nation's new flagship sails into view.

Five powerful tugs are ranged either side of the warship, making sure she maintains her line. Police boats with flashing blue lights and Fleet Protection fast boats, manned by heavily armed marines form a protective exclusion zone in case of terrorist attack.

The ship's company watches with growing excitement as they proceed down the Solent towards the clamouring crowds. The First Lieutenant urged them in this morning's Daily Orders to contemplate and savour their achievements whilst holding position on Procedure Alpha. Some may well have been doing that, but a warship's homecoming changes the emotional parameters. The emphasis is suddenly on reunion with loved ones.

Glen Peters, standing smartly at ease on the port side, can think only of seeing his wife Claudia and son Emmanuel. Scouse Walsh, further down on the same side, is already straining his eyes to see if he can spot his own family among the crowd. On the starboard beam, Frederica McCarthy, whilst thrilled to have completed her first deployment on the high seas, can't wait to see her mum, dad and boyfriend. As a sailor, Rob Rouston regards Portsmouth as his spiritual home, but he's going to leap on the first train to Ripon. He'll see his parents and brother for Christmas and catch up with his mates – after firing up his 1973 Harley-Davidson Shovelhead for a good burn-up over the North York Moors.

Wes Khan is not on the upper deck. He's preparing dinner for the duty watch (those who will have to stay on board after everyone else has gone home), but shares the excitement of homecoming. He's stirring tonight's goulash with particular vigour.

Jenny Curwood, on the upper walkway of the for'ard island, is savouring the prospect of seeing her children, but mindful of the Christmas presents she still needs to get. She's mightily relieved she managed to resist the last chocolate-filled advent calendar, so at least that can be handed over intact.

Chris Trevethan, on the leeward side of the for'ard island, has had many homecomings from foreign deployments and never fails to be moved by the experience. The gruff, wise-cracking but soft-hearted First Lieutenant goes to scratch his upper cheek – a cunning ploy to camouflage a quivering chin and the wiping away of a fledgling tear.

James Blackmore is standing on the outer balustrade of the aft island with his aviators. Commander Air is as proud as anyone on the ship after the flight testing but, like every-one else, he can only really think about seeing his family again: his wife Rachel and two daughters, Amelia and Sofia.

The Royal Marines Band, marching the length of the flight deck, are now playing a medley of Christmas carols, starting with 'O Come, All Ye Faithful'. Nathan Crossley, the giant Drum Major, is leading from the front. He maintains perfect pace and timing with his decorative mace. Frank Rochford is on the clarinet, his marching instrument, but half his mind is on the train home to Campbeltown on the Kintyre Peninsula.

Lieutenant Commander Lindsey Waudby is in the middle of the flight deck. Having left the ship in New York, she was flown back on board last night to host a gaggle of journalists and news crews who've come to cover the QE's homecom-ing. This is a wonderful, uplifting culmination for the media specialist who had to wrangle so much news interest, posi-tive and negative, throughout Westlant 18. Petty Officers Dave Jenkins and Jay Allen are beside her, wielding high-definition cameras, filming the ship's arrival as a live feed for Facebook and YouTube. Thanks to this technical wizardry, the internet community is able to witness the homecoming from anywhere in the world, and one man is doing exactly that 3,000 miles away.

It is 8 o'clock in the morning in Tampa, Florida, and Bob Hawkins is already at work in the US Central Military Command. Now promoted to acting commander, he's in the Permanent Joint Headquarters as part of a team directing forces in Iraq and Afghanistan. He's braced for another busy day, but taking time out to watch the QE live on his monitor. An American colleague is right alongside him. 'Wow, bet you wish you were there, Bob.'

'Absolutely,' Hawkins answers wistfully, picturing himself alongside his fellow officers on the for'ard island. He thinks back to the day he arrived in Rosyth to take up his job as First Lieutenant. Peering through the steamed-up window of his train as it crossed the Forth Rail Bridge, en route to a ship he'd heard about but never seen. Hawkins smiles as he remembers Dougie, the young dockyard welder. 'Dinna worry, sir. I promise you she's there . . . !' Back then he couldn't even spot her from half a mile away, but now, from a different continent, he can see the carrier as clearly as if he was standing on her. The live pictures show a line of sailors on the starboard side of the flight deck, then another on the ski-jump.

'Emma Ranson . . .' Hawkins points. 'Brilliant sailor, our Emma, a real high flyer. She did a whole deployment on USS *Harry S. Truman* before joining the QE.'

'Who's that next to her?' the American asks. 'Looks like Batman.'

'That'll be the Bish,' Hawkins laughs. 'Our Chaplain, in his trademark black cloak.'

'What's he holding?'

Hawkins leans in for a closer look.

'No idea. Looks like the branch of a tree . . . with lights on . . .'

Alastair Mansfield, having adopted his customary position at the top of the ski-jump, and braced once again against a scything headwind, holds his trident-shaped thorn branch. It's now festooned with twinkling pink and blue Christmas lights, powered by a battery strapped to the shaft.

'Oh dear Lord!' he cries as a particularly strong gust fills his cassock once again and blows him off balance.

'Steady, Bish?' Emma Ranson asks from his right.

'You OK, Bish?' Paul Ranson echoes from his left.

Mansfield stands firm, relieved he had the foresight to tie on his velvet Canterbury cap with a hefty double bow today. He is also relishing his own homecoming, seeing his wife Mary and fifteen-year-old son Aiden. The Bish tightens his grip on the thorn branch and thanks his god that everyone's returned home safely but knows that no one is the same person that departed four months ago. Everybody will have grown from the unique experiences afforded by Westlant 18. It's been a rite of passage in every sense.

HMS *Queen Elizabeth* draws near to the harbour entrance. The cheers echo across the open water, prompting the 1,000 sailors to stand an inch or two taller. The Royal Marines Band segues effortlessly from 'In the Bleak Midwinter' to 'Sailing'.

Guided by the muscular harbour tugs, Britain's biggest warship glides past the Round Tower, heaving with spectators at the entrance to the old harbour. Built during the Napoleonic Wars, the famous fortification is a prime spot from which to view warships departing and arriving. Many are brandishing Union Flags or White Ensigns. Others are raising sheets or placards with personal messages. One – *Welcome Home Daddy!* – is held as high as possible by a little girl sitting on her mother's shoulders. Further along, a man is comforting a sobbing woman beneath a huge sign emblazoned with the name 'Tommy' in bright red and yellow letters. Behind them is a gleeful young woman clutching a piece of cardboard on which she has simply scrawled *'Come and get it, Brian!'* in bright-blue acrylic. More people stand shoulder to shoulder on and around the Tower, jockeying for the best position.

At its base, a distinguished-looking man in a smart blazer and tie watches from the window of a café known as the Hot Walls, as the carrier passes no more than 50 yards away. The café is jam-packed. Everyone's chattering as they squeeze together to get the best view. Rear Admiral Jerry Kyd couldn't resist coming down to greet his old command. He didn't want to be part of the official gathering. He wishes to experience the excitement of those to whom he believes the ship really belongs.

He recalls the moment when, as captain, he looked down from the bridge to see and hear the cheering crowd bidding her farewell when she left for America. He's now happy to be sharing in its euphoria with another crowd of people, unified, whatever their differences, by pride in a very special lump of floating steel called HMS *Queen Elizabeth*. He likes to think it represents the country the way it should be: multicultural, inclusive, diverse, fully employed, productive, drug-free, all but crime-free – and completely devoid of politicians or tycoons.

He pulls on his overcoat and heads outside.

A colour party on the poop deck of Nelson's flagship comes to attention and salutes the passing carrier as a sailor 'pipes the Still' on a Bosun's whistle. HMS *Queen Elizabeth* acknowledges the salute with an answering pipe as she moves towards the naval dockyard's inner sanctum.

Within half an hour, the tugs have turned her in the basin so that her bow faces the entrance, and she is secured alongside the Princess Royal Jetty, where most of the close families of the ship's company are waiting. The gangways are lifted into place, and Chris Trevethan delivers his final pipe of Westlant 18: 'The gangway is now open.'

A stream of sailors, marines and Fleet Air Arm aviators floods on to the quayside. Glen Peters runs straight into the arms of his wife Claudia, who's holding their son Emmanuel. The three lock into a tearful but happy embrace. Chris Trevethan is hugging his wife Louise, and Alastair Mansfield his wife Mary. Emma and Paul Ranson head for home, no longer as flight-deck colleagues but husband and wife. A familiar blonde woman carrying a small child is happily greeting old friends. Kirsty Rugg has come to show off her giggling fifteen-month-old son Bobby. All around them, sailors are being reclaimed by loved ones.

There's no one to meet Wes Khan. He's still in the galley. As a Muslim who's volunteered for Christmas duty, he'll stay on board to cook for the duty watch throughout the holiday period. After Christmas, however, he'll return to Halesowen in Birmingham to be reunited with wife Shah and enjoy a long spell of leave, which will include a trip back to Kenya to see family. For now, however, the man with the most infectious laugh in NATO continues to prepare supper for the skeleton crew who must remain on the ship.

At the other end of the harbour, Jerry Kyd makes his way towards Gunwharf Quays. He stops to put a pound coin into a promenade telescope and point it west. The White Ensign is being raised on the stern of the QE, a sure sign she's secured alongside. In a year from now she will be joined by HMS *Prince of Wales*. The two will line up end to end – a powerful symbol of Britain's commitment to global policing and peacekeeping through muscular power projection. And in thirty-six short months, the QE will embark on her first operational deployment to the South China Seas – which is when she will truly come of age.

Kyd turns for home. He feels as emotional as he did in 2016 when visiting HMS *Illustrious* before her final voyage to the breaker's yard. But more poignant still are memories of his beloved *Ark Royal*'s final homecoming. The morning of 3 December 2010 had started clear and bitterly cold, but as he navigated in from the Solent, a thick, swirling fog had rolled off the Channel to enshroud the ship completely. Kyd slowed to 6 knots and only spotted the Round Tower at 3 cables' distance, less than a third of a nautical mile. The final sounding of the ship's horn was the most mournful he'd ever heard.

'We're back!' he murmurs with a final glance at the QE's two towering islands. The restoration of carrier strike capability has been a long time coming, but worth every exacting and emotionally taxing second.

Afterword

'Every battle is won before it is fought.'

Sun Tzu

I've been gripped by the story of HMS *Queen Elizabeth* since that Afghan ambush in 2007. Having subsequently gained privileged access to the supercarrier and her ship's companies across the intervening years I've done my best to translate the insights it provided into six films for the BBC – so far – and this book. I've attempted to tell it how it is, from the inside, and it will come as no surprise to you that in the process I have developed a great affection for the many remarkable individuals I've met while living and working on board. I'm proud to call them friends – even shipmates.

But HMS *Queen Elizabeth*'s story is only just beginning and there is no way of knowing how it will play out. Despite the government's determination that the new, carrier-centric Royal Navy will become the most powerful in Europe over the next decade, not everyone is yet convinced that the QE will successfully fulfil her role as our principle conventional strategic deterrent. I have no such misgivings but agree that her effectiveness will not be proven until she goes to sea in anger for the first time. In fact, I write this from my cabin on board as I have returned for the QE's first operational deployment to the South China Seas, and who knows what further insights this will afford me into the ship's unfolding destiny.

435

Whilst former First Sea Lord, Admiral Sir Philip Jones has described HMS *Queen Elizabeth* as the 'embodiment of Britain in steel and spirit', a 'triumph of national strategic ambition' and 'a post-Brexit ambassador to the globe', others have been less generous. Some have dismissed her as a totemic symbol that will be outstripped by emerging technology, a 'massive military distraction' and 'a floating white elephant'.

In June 2016 the Russian Defence Ministry mocked Britain's biggest ever warship as 'merely a large convenient naval target' and warned the Royal Navy not to show off her 'beauty' too close to Moscow's military assets. Some of our own press have been quick to dismiss her as 'beset with problems', prone to cyberattack and likely to be sunk in a heartbeat by Chinese hypersonic, sea-skimming carrier-killer missiles, and slow to applaud her manifold successes and technical innovations.

As we teeter on the brink of multiple conflicts – in an increasingly volatile environment compounded by the geopolitical and geostrategic ramifications of the coronavirus pandemic – Jerry Kyd, now eventually promoted to Fleet Commander of the Royal Navy, has no doubt that the QE and her sister ship, HMS *Prince of Wales*, will become vital components of the British arsenal.

I was present when Jonathan Beale, the seasoned BBC Defence Editor, asked Kyd whether Britain really needed not just one but two giant aircraft carriers. Beale, as ever, was playing devil's advocate, but not even he could have expected the curtness of Kyd's reply: 'So what do you expect us to do? Sail up to our enemies and throw lemons at them?'

HMS *Queen Elizabeth* is not only a warship, of course, she is sovereign territory in her own right. She has no borders and cannot be seen on any map, but her population is united in spirit and purpose, not riven by political discord, racial antipathy or self-interest. For all her sophistication and Star Wars technology, her most vital and enabling resource is exactly what Nelson valued so highly more than 200 years ago: sailors.

No one can truly know what lies ahead, but I've come to believe that the QE is already on her way to becoming an iconic symbol of nationhood, and will play a significant role in dictating whether Brexit turns out to be a disaster or a runaway, rip-roaring success. Britain is trading increasingly with more distant markets – USA, India, Japan, Australia, New Zealand and even China – and our dependence on secure sea transport for both export and import demands the strongest of navies.

When I was sheltering from enemy fire near Kajaki, Britain was engaged in what became a thirteen-year campaign in which ships had no role. For the duration of the Afghan War, the emphasis was on military land operations, and whilst the Royal Marines were actively involved, their amphibious capabilities were not called upon. Fleet Air Arm pilots such as Nathan Gray did fly combat missions over Helmand but were not required to execute their specialist maritime skills.

Political and military threats are becoming more complex by the day, but it seems clear that future conflicts will not be limited to combating counter-insurgency in landlocked segments of the Middle East or Central Asia. Whether it be defending our own territorial waters or carrying the fight further afield, HMS *Queen Elizabeth* has an active half century ahead.

Will destiny secure her a place in the great pantheon of the nation's warships? Will her name echo down the years alongside the *Mary Rose*, HMS *Endeavour*, HMS *Beagle*, HMS *Victory*, HMS *Dreadnought*, HMS *Hood* and HMS *Ark Royal*?

Time alone will tell.

Postscript

From 2017, Jerry Kyd carried two ranks, captain and com-modore, so he had two sets of uniforms. In 2019, after only a few weeks as rear admiral, Kyd was promoted to vice ad-miral and appointed Fleet Commander by the Prime Minister. A new phrase entered the naval lexicon: 'As busy as Jerry Kyd's tailor.'

He was appointed CBE in the 2019 Queen's Birthday Honours.

Glossary

ACA	Aircraft Carrier Alliance
AFFF	Aqueous film-forming foam
AWT	Above Water Tactical (radar specialist)
AWW	Above Water Warfare
BDA	Battle damage assessment
DT1	Development Testing Phase 1
DT2	Development Testing Phase 2
ETME	Electrical technician marine engineer
EWO	Executive Warrant Officer
FAC	Forward air controller
Flyco	Flying control tower
FOD	Foreign object debris
FOST	Flag Officer Sea Training
GPMG	General-purpose machine gun
HOD	Head of Department
ITF	Integrated Test Force
JPR	Joint Personnel Recovery
MES	Mass Evacuation System
OOC	Object of Concern (underwater debris)
OOW	Officer of the Watch
PTI	Physical training instructor
RAS	Replenishment at sea
RFA	Royal Fleet Auxiliary
RIB	Rigid inflatable boat
SAR	Search and Rescue

SCC   Ship's Control Centre
SOP   Standard Operating Procedure
SRVL   Shipborne Rolling Vertical Landing
STOVL   Short Take-off and Vertical Landing
TIC   Troops in contact
VAD   Vessel Acceptance Day
VertRep   Vertical replenishment via helicopter
WO   Warrant officer (the most senior of the non-commissioned officers)

Words and Phrases

Baby sailors: Fresh recruits or newly trained sailors.

Banyan rig: Usually a garish shirt – the more garish the better – worn for upper-deck barbecues or other recreational occasions.

Battle Honours: A record of combat engagements passed on from one ship to the next of the same name.

Bish: Contraction of 'Bishop', the nickname for a Naval Padre or Chaplain. Common alternatives are 'God Botherer', 'Amen Wallah', 'Sky Pilot', 'God Walloper' and 'Devil Dodger'.

Bootneck: Member of the Royal Marines. Derives from the nineteenth century when part of the marines' duty was to protect officers from mutinous or press-ganged sailors bent on retribution. To prevent their throats being slit while asleep they resorted to tying boot leather round their necks.

Bosun's whistle or call: A pipe or non-diaphragm-type whistle consisting of a narrow tube which directs air over a metal sphere with a hole on top. Historically the emanating high-pitched whistle was used to pass commands above the sounds of the wind and sea when the human voice would not carry. It is famously very difficult to 'play' and requires expert lip and lung control.

Cerberus: Codename for HMS *Queen Elizabeth* used by helicopter pilots.

Charlie Time: Time zones around the world are divided according to letters of the alphabet, so the local time to a ship will change letters as it moves across the globe. Charlie time relates to the eastern seaboard of the USA. Zulu is the time in the UK in the winter (GMT). Alpha is the time in the UK in the summer (daylight saving time)

Cheesy hammy eggies: Otherwise known as 'cheesy/hammy wam bams', are a long-standing Royal Navy favourite. They consist of a cheese and ham mixture grilled on toast which is then topped with a fried egg often accompanied by chips and a large helping of baked beans, the aptly named 'whistle berries' in sailor speak.

Clear Lower Deck: Traditional pipe ordering all personnel to cease work and muster at a specified location. It can be for work requiring many hands or to give important information.

Club Swinger or *Clubz*: Physical training instructor or PTI. Derives from the time PTIs swung heavy clubs as part of their fitness regime.

Dabber: A sailor specializing in seamanship. The name comes from their traditional preoccupation with painting the upper deck and continually dabbing their brushes into the paint. So engrossed were they that it was always said that if you stood still long enough they would paint you too.

Duff: Pudding or dessert. A double helping is called 'going double duff'.

'*D'ye hear there?*': The usual way to start an announcement or 'pipe' in the Royal Navy. The US Navy equivalent is 'Now hear this!'

Float test: To ditch something overboard. An alternative is 'Give it to the splosh-maker!'

Gash: Rubbish. A 'gash dit' is a false rumour ('dit' meaning story or anecdote).

Gen: Genuine, real, honest ('gen dit' is a true story).

Goffer: A fizzy drink, but also a wave that breaks over the bow.

Goldfish Club: A worldwide association of people who have escaped an aircraft by parachuting into water, or whose aircraft crashed in the water, and whose lives were saved by a life jacket, inflatable dinghy or similar device.

Gopping: Horrible, detestable, nauseating.

Grey Funnel Line or *Grey Funnel Cruises*: Nickname for the sea-going element of the Royal Navy.

Hoofing: Fantastic or amazing. (More of a Royal Marine word, but sailors often use it.)

Hotwet: Hot drink. A 'wet' is Navy speak for 'drink'. It follows you can have a 'coldwet' (probably alcoholic) or a 'hotwet' (beverage). A soft drink in a can, however, is called a 'goffer' (not to be confused with a wave breaking over the bow – see above). In Navy parlance a 'Julie' is a tea or coffee with milk but no sugar, i.e. 'white/none' or 'White Nun', ergo Julie Andrews in *The Sound of Music*. Conversely, a black coffee, no sugar, or 'black/none', is a 'Whoopee', from Whoopee Goldberg in *Sister Act*.

Jackspeak: The colloquial language developed within the Royal Navy over centuries (much of which has entered common usage). Jackspeak is invariably colourful, evocative and often suggestive.

'*Let go all lines*': This order is the traditional command for a warship to set sail.

Master-at-Arms: The senior Royal Navy policeman or -woman on a warship. Also known as the 'Joss'.

Matelots: The colloquial collective term for sailors. From the French *matelot* (sailor), but pronounced 'mat-low'.

Morse code: Method for transmitting information (by sound or light), using standardized sequences of short and long buzzes or flashes to represent the letters and numerals of a message.

Officer of the Watch (OOW): Officer responsible for the running of the bridge on a particular watch or 'shift'. The OOW will report to the Navigating Officer and the captain.

Oggin: The sea, although it can also refer to water generally.

Rating: A rating or rate is an enlisted member of the Navy: junior rate (able seaman) or senior rate (leading hand).

Redders: Hot, boiling, scorching (as opposed to 'icers' – cold).

Regulator: The traditional name for a Royal Navy policeman or -woman. The Regulating Branch is now called the Royal Navy Police Service.

Rig run: A run ashore in naval uniform (or rig). Not voluntary but ordered by Command on special occasions. Since 9/11 and the escalation of terrorist activity on the streets of the USA and Europe, service personnel have been either advised against wearing uniform in public or banned from doing so altogether.

Royal Fleet Auxiliary (RFA): Supply ships/tankers that service Royal Navy warships with food, ammunition and fuel. Although crewed by civilians, they are dedicated to supporting the British Fleet. They are not warships but will carry some defensive armour and weaponry.

Scran: Food. Some say it is an acronym for 'sultanas, currents, raisins and nuts' – historically a basic diet for scurvy-ridden crews – but it is more likely derived from an ancient Scottish word for leftovers.

Semaphore: Method of encoding information by the position of hand-held flags, as Nelson practised at the Battle of Trafalgar.

Shippers: Diminutive of 'shipmate'.

Sitrep: Situation report.

Spring tide: A common historical term that has nothing to do with the season of spring. Rather, the term is derived from the concept of the tide 'springing forth'.

Threaders: Tired or fed up.

Toppers: Full (either a receptacle, as in 'the gash bin is toppers', or a stomach, as in 'after double duff I'm completely toppers').

Wings: The traditional sobriquet for Commander Air. Similarly Commander Marine Engineering is called 'Engines'; the Air Weapons Engineering Officer is called 'Bombs'; the Principal Warfare Officer (Air) is 'Guns'. Commander Logistics is sometimes teasingly referred to as 'Cakes'.

Wren: The traditional name for a female sailor of the Royal Navy. It is a derivation of WRNS (Women's Royal Naval Service), disbanded in 1919, revived in 1939, and then subsumed within the Royal Navy in 1993. The term has endured as has the associated and more affectionate pet name of Jenny (as in Jenny Wren).

Writer: Secretary or logistician.

Young Officer (YO): A midshipman or sub-lieutenant serving their first sea time prior to sitting their Fleet Board examination. Traditionally YOs will experience work across all the branches of a warship as well as being 'willing' forced labour and given the 'gash' jobs nobody else wants to do.

Zulu Time: Greenwich Mean Time (see *Charlie Time*).

HMS *Queen Elizabeth*

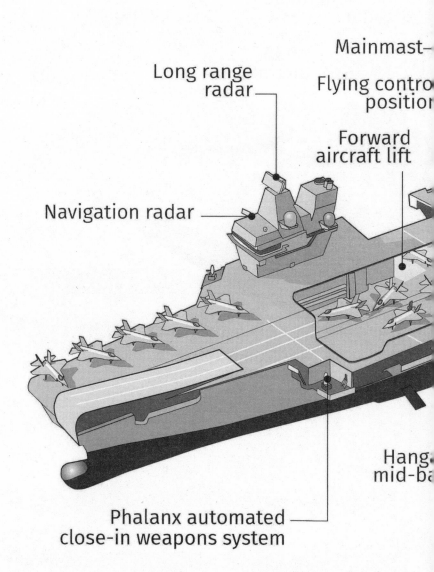

Long range radar

Mainmast—

Flying contro position

Forward aircraft lift

Navigation radar

Phalanx automated close-in weapons system

Hang mid-b

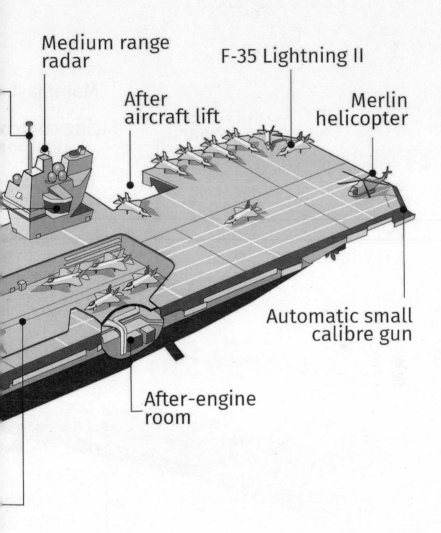

Medium range
radar

F-35 Lightning II

After
aircraft lift

Merlin
helicopter

Automatic small
calibre gun

After-engine
room

Acknowledgements

Many people encouraged me to write this book and supported me through the often challenging creative process. Mark Lucas is in the front rank for special recognition. He is my long-suffering literary agent and friend who resolutely sustained my spirit and energy from the first word I wrote to the last with his wise and unfailingly insightful counsel. He also brought to bear his famous unflappability even when I submitted grossly inflated manuscripts in such urgent need of the red pen that lesser agents would have run for the hills. Rowland White at Penguin also deserves a glorious mention in dispatches for his courageous determination not only to commission the book in the first place but also to deal with my passion for a subject that I know has not always been easy to control, coordinate and contain. This was especially the case as I was back on board the QE for her first operational deployment just as this book was being finalized and prepared for publication and communications were intermittent at best. Rowland, like Mark, was able to assert his astute, perspicacious and improving literary authority in the most gentlemanly of ways that always added positively to the book as it grew in proportion and ambition. Jo Lane, former publishing director for all James Bond publishing (so licensed with skill), lent her considerable editing experience to the job in hand. Her genuine excitement for the project continually reinforced my resolve to see it through to the end. I must also thank David Watson for his meticulous copy-editing skills and careful attention to detail when making sure every 'i' was dotted and 't' crossed.

I owe unreserved gratitude to Lieutenant Commander Lindsey Waudby – a very special and talented naval officer whom I am now proud to call a friend – who took on the enormous task of proofreading my manuscript. With a fine eye for detail, Lindsey was endlessly helpful in ensuring that I had got my facts right, my dates accurate, my naval language precise and my naval humour more or less politically correct!

The men and women of HMS *Queen Elizabeth*'s Ship's Company were tirelessly supportive of my efforts, and I am very grateful to all of them for making me feel so welcome on their ship for the best part of three years. I must make special mention of Jerry Kyd, who, as Commanding Officer, did not have to agree to me being on his ship or to afford me so much of his valuable time. But that he did, wholeheartedly and generously. Without his continued support, guidance and friendship neither the films I made for the BBC nor this book would have been possible. Lieutenant Commander (now Commander) Bob Hawkins, one of my oldest and dearest friends, helped enormously throughout – but especially in the early days when I first arrived on HMS *Queen Elizabeth*. He made me feel instantly welcome and ensured that I was absorbed into the ship's company as seamlessly and as smoothly as possible. Nathan Gray, fast jet pilot extraordinaire and now also a good friend, was forever generous in his advice and guidance, especially in relation to flying and aviation.

Kate Taylor of the Aircraft Carrier Alliance was a major supporter of the project and a prime mover in gaining me behind-the-scenes access to the ship's construction. I must also give heartfelt thanks to Steve Prest, Chris Trevethan, Alastair Mansfield, Waseel 'Wes' Mohamad Khan, Dave

Garraghty, Ricky Gleason, Jez Brettle, Neil McCullum, Jon Pearson, Scott McClarren, Pat Midgley, Derek 'Scouse' Walsh, Emma and Paul Ranson, Glenroy Peters, Kirsty Rugg, Frederica McCarthy, Rob Rouston, Roly Brading, Pete 'Wizzer' Wilson, Andy Edgell, Michael 'Latch' Lippert, Mark Dellar, James 'Blackers' Blackmore, Darren Houston, Fiona Percival, Jenny Curwood, Andy 'Sticky' Vercoe, Elise Broughton, Matt Hicks, Michelle Mattinson, 'Big' Bruce Milne, Nick Gutfreund and Arron Hoare, Kyle Heller, Dave Jenkins and Jay Allen.

Closer to home, I could not have written this book without the constant support and reassurance of my incredible team at Uppercut Films – particularly Erica Banks, Jamie Hay, Anneka Hagemann and Suzie Sharma in addition to my ever-encouraging colleague and friend Alan Clements of Two Rivers Media.

Closest of all to home and heart is my wonderful wife Christine, who, as ever, supported and endured me with forbearance and stoical fortitude as I spent every waking hour either making films about the QE or writing this book for the best part of four years. A word of advice, however: if you ever meet her, try and avoid words like 'warship' or 'aircraft carrier'.

I must also recognize the enormous contribution to my creative wellbeing afforded by Molly Malone, our impish Irish Terrier, who would often lie at my feet or at my side as I wrote or pondered into the early hours.

Finally, I reserve the most special thanks of all to my parents, both of whom served in the Navy during the Second World War. They have always been my inspiration and my strength as well as the font of my enduring passion for the Royal Navy. They were incredibly excited when I first told them that I was going to write this book – especially my father, who was himself a Fleet Air Arm pilot during the Second World War. It is a great sadness that neither of them lived long enough to see *How to Build an Aircraft Carrier* completed and published, but at the age of ninety-eight their time had come to cast off the bow lines and embark on their next adventure together. They departed for their final voyage of discovery within two weeks of each other and will be forever missed – Leading Wren Joan Shorter and Lieutenant Clive Terrill. Their influence on me, through their own love of the Senior Service and all it stands for, imbues and informs this book from beginning to end.

Chris Terrill, HMS *Queen Elizabeth*,
the South China Seas, 2021

Index

Sovereign TV 116
Stapleton, Marty 4
Stephens, Lieutenant
    Commander Sam
    F-35 launches and landings
        299, 400
    Hurricane Michael 333
    leaving Mayport 263
    in New York 360
    at Norfolk 421
    Replenishment at Sea 337–8
STOVL (Short Take-off and
    Vertical Landing) 151
Sun Tzu 435
'Sunset' 169
Supply, USNS 334, 337–40, 355–6
Sutherland, HMS 99, 101, 103
Swordfish 171–5, 411

Thales 13
Thermal Metal Spray (TMS) 28,
    286, 305
Thucydides 225
Titanic, RMS 214
Top Gun 149, 240
Tracy Morgan (tugboat) 421
Trevethan, Chris 346, 407
    Davies' Table 268–9
    F-35 landings 296
    and Kyd's departure 387
    leaving Portsmouth 181–2
    at Mayport 243–4, 254, 255
    morning rounds 185–6, 187,
        217–18, 290
    in New York 356–7
    at Norfolk 283

piping 242–3
Replenishment at Sea 334, 339
return to Portsmouth 407,
    429, 433
Tyndall Air Force Base 334
Tyne and Wear 14, 16

ukelele band 236, 346, 424
United States
    Atlantic Future Forum 376–
        83, 385–6
    see also Naval Station Mayport;
        Naval Station Norfolk; New
        York

Vanes, Chief Petty Officer
    Aircrewman Andy 173
Vercoe, Petty Officer 'Sticky' 97,
    111, 123, 223–4
VertReps (vertical replenishments
    via helicopter) 189, 339–40,
    355–6
Victory, HMS 163, 166, 169, 432

Walsh, Michael 327, 328, 329–30
Walsh, Leading Aircraft Handler
    Scouse 208–9, 210, 290
    Atlantic crossing 231
    F-35 launches and landings
        292, 306, 313
    and Fallopian tubes 326–7,
        328, 329–30
    fully laden launches 351, 400,
        404
    and Kyd's departure 389
    leaving Portsmouth 182